Globe T₁

Hope You Enjoy
Lee Morton.

Lee Morton.

Lee Morton

Globe Trekker

Matador
9 De Montfort Mews
Leicester LE1 7FW, UK
Tel: (+44) 116 255 9311 / 9312
Email: books@troubador.co.uk
Web: www.troubador.co.uk/matador

ISBN 1 905237 58 8

Cover illustration: © Photos.com

Typeset in 11pt Stempel Garamond by Troubador Publishing Ltd, Leicester, UK
Printed in the UK by The Cromwell Press Ltd, Trowbridge, Wilts, UK

Matador is an imprint of Troubador Publishing Ltd

To all the new friends I met on my travels who helped to make the experience so wonderful, Tracey and Tim for their hospitality, mom and dad for all their love and support, Julie and Chris for their assistance, Lisa, David, Chelsie, Jody, Kim, Natasha, Daz and Dave for their encouragement and support via the Internet, and Paul (Dubsey), of course.

Contents

Prologue

Distant countries, cultures and ancient civilizations, mighty mountain ranges and far away seas and oceans have long fascinated me. As a child I would sit for hours studying the pages of my atlas, following the courses of the world's great rivers and tracing the journeys of the great explorers such as Cook, Vasco de Gamma and Magellan.

My dreams seemed to be just that until one day in 2003, at the age of thirty-seven, I finally summoned the courage to follow my heart and fulfill my lifelong ambition to travel the globe. I began by putting together a list of all the countries and places that I longed to see, and researching them with the aid of travel books and the Internet. I then trimmed down my list of destinations from around thirty countries to eighteen, as it would have been impossible to fit in everywhere that I wanted to visit.

I had decided to spread my trip over a one-year period and I put together a rough itinerary based on the length of time that I planned to spend in each location. The weather patterns in certain places determined to some extent my start-date and direction of travel, having to pay particular attention to avoiding the monsoon seasons in South East Asia and South America. And so I decided to commence my journey at the start of the following year in January 2004.

After researching the various 'around the world' flight ticket options available, of which there were many, I purchased a 'One World Explorer' ticket offered by an alliance of airlines including British Airways, Qantas, Cathay Pacific & Lan. Although there were cheaper tickets on the market, they were limited in terms of the destinations they covered and they had rigid conditions attached. My ticket provided 17 flights, across four continents and eighteen countries, and cost just £1,600. In my opinion, a real bargain!

I gave a great deal of time to formulating my budget, making a conscious decision to be as thrifty as possible in respect of accommodation, which I assumed would be my greatest expense. If by staying in budget hotels and hostels I could save say £3 per day, this would equate to around £1,000 over the year, which would allow an extra ten-weeks of travel in Asia or South America. I set myself an expenditure budget of £10,000, based roughly on £100 per week for Asia and South America, and £200 per week for Australia and New Zealand, plus a 'luxuries' kitty of £3,000 for special activities such as tours and scuba diving. Added to this was the upfront sum of around £5,000 for flight tickets, insurance, a medical kit, vaccinations, toiletries, equipment, backpack, trek boots & specialist clothing.

After completing my research I announced my plans to friends, family and work colleagues. In the main the response was good and everyone was very supportive and pleased for me. My mother was delighted, my sister seemed worried, and my father thought that I had gone mad. My boss, who himself had traveled extensively, was also supportive and appreciative of the length of notice I had given him to find my replacement.

I began the process of choosing and purchasing the various items of clothing and equipment that I would need. This was a delicate operation, as unlike packing for a two-week holiday in the sun, I had to ensure that I had all of the necessary provisions for all types of weather conditions, all of which should weigh no more than 20kg and be able to fit comfortably inside a sixty-litre backpack.

One of my biggest concerns was what to do with my home. Should I let my home to a stranger who might disrespect or even vandalize it, or should I sell up and sever all financial ties? Luckily my decision was made easy by the fact that a close friend was looking for a place to rent around the same time, and so my major headache was resolved.

I signed up for a Spanish language course at the local college in preparation for South America, knowing that English is pretty much useless there.

As my departure date neared, I made several visits to my doctor for various vaccinations, around seven in total, and at great expense I purchased a supply of anti-malaria drugs. During my final couple of weeks I made the final preparations by making copies of my passport, driving license, insurance policy and other important documents which I uploaded to a secure web-site should I need them whilst away.

I enjoyed Christmas and the New Year amongst my family and friends, unsure if or when I would see them again. My office Christmas party turned out to be a joint farewell party and my colleagues presented me with a leaving gift of a mp3 player, which would come in very useful. My friends threw a farewell fancy dress party for me at a local pub, in the theme of 'people of the world'. It was a good send off, although I was a little worried that everyone appeared keen for me to leave!

PART 1

THE FAR EAST

1

The Cow is King (India)

03/01/04 to 14/01/04

"Good afternoon passengers and welcome aboard British Airways flight BA457 from Madrid to London, our flying time will be……"

I looked at the guy sitting next to me and smiled, "Hi, Lee" I said introducing myself.

"Hello, John", he replied.

"Going home for Christmas?"

"Yes, and you?"

"Yes"

"Would you like a drink sir?" the stewardess asked.

"Beer please" I replied.

"And you sir?"

"Beer please," John replied.

A smile came onto my face as I sipped my beer and contemplated my wondrous adventure circumnavigating the globe. My adventure had taken me to 18 countries covering over 100,000km, during which I had seen some of the greatest natural and man-made wonders on the planet, explored some of the worlds most ancient, sacred, mysterious and mythical locations and found myself in numerous bizarre scenarios, weird experiences, romantic encounters and dangerous, frightening and humorous situations.

Looking back, the weeks seemed to have passed so quickly; it seemed like only yesterday when my adventure had begun. As I sat back in my reclined seat, closed my eyes and fell into a deep sleep, the memories of the first day were as vivid as ever………

I held my breath; a vile smell filled my nostrils, the smell of raw sewage or of rotting vegetables, or possibly a combination of both. The narrow streets throbbed with activity, noise and confusion. The locals were actively going about their daily business. Street vendors and hawkers were selling their wares; some from makeshift wooden stalls, some out of barrows and some simply laid out on the dirty ground. Strung overhead like a huge spider web was a tangled network of electric cables and telephone wires. This was exactly as I'd been told to expect and yet it was still a real culture shock. This was Paharganj, Old Delhi's backpacker ghetto.

The entire district was grid locked with all manner of vehicles: cars and taxis, buses and trucks, bicycles and rickshaws, all jostling with each other for right of way whilst, continuously hooting their horns. Amongst the bedlam, stray dogs scavenged for scraps and sacred cows wandered aimlessly. There appeared to be no traffic laws, except of course to give way to the cow, for in India, the cow is king.

It seemed a million miles away from my home, where less than twenty four hours earlier I had waved goodbye to my family and close friends. And so here I was in Delhi, on the first day of my solo around the world adventure.

On arrival at Delhi airport I had been met by a driver sent by the hotel that I had pre-booked, to collect me and another passenger travelling on the same flight. Within a couple of minutes Darren had arrived. We introduced ourselves and then followed our driver out of the airport and to our awaiting Ambassador car, which is modelled on the 1948 'Morris Oxford' and has not been altered since it was first built in India in 1957.

As we neared the Paharganj district, the streets became too narrow for cars to pass and so we parked up and our driver escorted us through the crowded labyrinth of back streets to the 'Anoop Hotel'. Several beggars; male and female, young and old, approached us along the way. All very different yet all very similar; dirty and dishevelled, dressed in shabby and threadbare clothing and hands held out in desperation.

We checked in to the hotel and we were each shown to our respective rooms. Another shock awaited; the room was more like a prison cell than a hotel room, with tiled walls and floor and a single bed with stained linen. I opened the bathroom door and peered inside tentatively, there was a grimy washbasin, and a 'hole in the floor' squat toilet. The shower comprised of a bucket placed beneath a rusty tap. But what could you expect for 250-Rupees (£3) per night!

I met up with Darren again later and we headed out to explore our new surroundings. Darren was twenty-eight years old and from Kent. Surprisingly we had many things in common, we were both single, we were both virgin backpackers who had given up work to travel, and we were both on the first day of our respective journeys.

It was a cold day and a thick layer of smog filled the air, much to my surprise as I had believed India to be hot all year round. We wandered through the maze of back streets and alleyways in search of a bar but we were unable to find any in Paharganj. We did however manage to attract the attention of many more beggars, as well as a number of local men all keen to assist us by directing or escorting us to various establishments. All had similar advice "do not trust anyone in Delhi – except for me". One guy even claimed to be a personal friend of Mohammed El Fayed and said that his shop supplied clothes to Harrods of London.

We laughed off the various approaches and headed towards Connaught Place, laid out like a bicycle wheel and comprising of three circular concentric roads divided into blocks by several spoke like radial roads. This is the commercial hub of Delhi and home to the majority of tourist hotels, shops and restaurants. It was equally as bustling as Paharganj but much more sophisticated, the colonial style buildings here were rather grand, if a little faded.

We booked a private city tour for tomorrow from one of the many travel agents and then searched out a restaurant, where we enjoyed a good curry, washed down with a few bottles of out-of-date beer. Feeling full and exhausted, we returned to the hotel in a motorised rickshaw – a noisy, three wheeled, open sided taxi which resembled a cross between a moped and a car, which spurts the foulest smelling fumes.

My first night proved to be a restless one. I had had the foresight to bring with me a sleeping bag liner which was a blessing considering the state of the bed linen. Regrettably, I had not brought a sleeping bag and I was ill prepared for the bitterly cold night that awaited me, waking several times throughout the night shivering with cold.

Our tour driver Jay arrived early the next morning and we set off to explore the cities historical and tourist sights. We started at Rajpath, a broad avenue flanked on either side by ornamental ponds, at the east end of which stood India Gate, a forty two meter high memorial to the 85,000 Indian war dead, which resembles the Arc de Triumph, whilst at the west end stood the Presidents House, flanked by two grand symmetrical Secretariat buildings.

At Raj Ghat – the final resting place of Mahatma Ghandi, we met a party of friendly smiling school children, all dressed impeccably in blue uniform and all keen to try out their English. Unfortunately, they only knew one word – "hello", which we repeated to each of them several times.

Next stop was the Qutb Minar complex – India's first Islamic mosque built in 1193, featuring a magnificent seventy-three meter high tapering and slightly leaning carved stone minaret. We continued on to the lotus flower shaped Bahai Temple, Isa Khans Tomb and a few lesser-known monuments.

My favourite site was the domed Humayun's Tomb, which is universally regarded as the predecessor to and the inspiration for the Taj Mahal. Built in 1565 by the second Mughal emperor's widow, it holds the remains of nearly one hundred members of the Mughal clan, earning it the nickname of 'dormitory of the Mughals'.

Throughout the day we were accosted by beggars or approached by seemingly friendly locals who would chat away to us for a while before attempting one or other scam to part us from our cash. Even more annoying was being constantly hassled by strangers demanding money each time we took a photograph, irrespective of what we were actually photographing!

At the end of the day, we returned to the travel agents office to book train tickets to Jaipur in Rajasthan. The office manager made a couple of telephone calls before informing us that all trains were fully booked for the next week. He then offered to provide a car and a driver to transport us to, and guide us around our chosen destinations. I felt as though we were being stitched up, however after a short consultation, we both agreed that this would take a lot of hassle out of this leg of our journey. After a little negotiation, we agreed a price of £150 each, for a six day tour.

I had hoped that there would be a cyber-café in Paharganj, however I had been amazed to find that the district was literally throbbing with them, so after dinner, I headed to an Internet café to e-mail friends and family back home, just to let them know I'd arrived safely and all was well. Every one of the dozen or so cyber-cafés here were full to the brim with travellers, hunched over the machines vigorously typing away their travel yarns to loved ones back home, or uploading photographs from their digital cameras to their personal web-site, or researching their next destination. The information superhighway has transformed many things in life, not least backpacking, and the locals have been quick to get in on the act. This is big business, and anyone with a computer and a phone line can get a slice of the action.

The following morning Jay picked us up from our hotel and drove us to the impressive Red Fort, which dominates the Old Delhi area. Outside of the main entrance, a huge congregation of rickshaw drivers, guides, touts and vendors were vigorously accosting a large crowd of tourists. We declined the many offers of a guide, preferring to explore on our own.

We entered through Lahore gate into Chatta Chowk, a vaulted arcade of shops. The silk, jewel and gold merchants that had once traded here had now sadly been replaced with expensive and somewhat tacky tourist shops. The highlight of the fort was the magnificent sixty-pillared Hall of Public Audience, where the emperor once sat on his marble throne to receive visitors.

By mid-day we had seen all that the fort had to offer and so we returned through the crowded streets of Old Delhi to our awaiting car; on a twin-seat bicycle rickshaw with an elderly driver who struggled valiantly to carry the weight of two fat westerners.

By lunchtime we were on our way to Jaipur. The six-hour drive through Rajhastan was uninspiring. The road was uneven and dusty and the terracotta coloured landscape was flat, baron and featureless. We were forced to repeatedly listen to Jays one and only music cassette for the entire journey. Along the way we made a few stops for snacks of pakoras and bhajis and for chai, a sweet tea served in a small cup that is sold on just about every street corner in India.

We also passed several camels pulling carts laden with everything from grain to building materials, numerous goat herders, and even an elephant train. By the time we arrived in 'the Pink City', so named after the Maharaja painted the entire city pink in 1876 to welcome King Edward VII, we were all singing along to the tape, even though two of us had no idea of what exactly we were singing!

Jay was around thirty years old and of very slight build, around 5feet 4inches tall and weighing no more than eight stone, that's 1.6m and 50kg to the young. He spoke fluent English and kept us entertained with his local knowledge and endless stories of Indian customs, myths and legends. Less entertaining was his tall tales concerning his numerous 'white' girlfriends from England, Germany, Holland and Sweden, all of whom he had drove for in the past and who had apparently all found him irresistible. "They say I have great power," he stated with pride whilst clenching his fist and curling his string-like bicep. He later admitted however, that the had not so much as kissed any of these girls yet alone been intimate with them!

The following day we visited Jaipur's main tourist sites. In the heart of the old city was the beautiful Palace Of The Winds, a five storey sandstone building built to house the harem of the Maharaja, containing hundreds of lattice windows, behind which the harem could sit and watch the goings on in the street below without being seen themselves.

The highlight of Jaipur was the magnificent City Palace with its gardens and courtyards and the adjoining Jantar Mantar observatory, which at first glance appeared to be an odd collection of sculptures. Each sculpture however has a specific astronomical purpose for measuring and calculating the positions of the stars. The most unusual of the instruments is the twenty-seven meter high sundial, the worlds largest. Its shadow moves at four meters per hour and it is accurate to within two seconds; astonishing considering that the observatory was built almost three hundred years ago.

We then drove into the hills outside of the city where we visited two hill top sites, each enjoying uninterrupted panoramic views over the city and surrounding countryside: the magnificent but sadly decrepit Nahargarh (Tiger) Fort and Jaigarh Fort housing several palaces, gardens, a granary, an armoury and the worlds largest wheeled canon.

Eleven kilometres from the city we visited the majestic Amber Fort-Palace housing royal apartments, pavilions, temples, beautiful formal gardens and a palace and enjoying yet more picture-postcard views. Brightly painted elephants were available to hire, I presumed by those tourists too lazy to walk up the steep path to the fort entrance.

At Galta temple, which is dedicated to the monkey god, I had a row with a priest who demanded payment from me for taking a picture of a monkey sitting in a tree. Out of principal I refused to pay. He accused me of disrespecting his temple, but Jay said that it was he who was disrespectful. Had he simply asked for a donation I would have happily given.

Jaipur was a vibrant and colourful city. Many of the local men we saw wore brightly coloured turbans and sported wild 'handle-bar' moustaches. We saw many brightly painted elephants, camels and even a snake charmer: "The cobra is not dancing to the music, he is following the movement of the flute" Jay informed us authoritatively, as we watched from a safe distance.

We set off the following morning on a four-hour drive along a part tarmac – part dirt road winding through pleasant countryside to Sawai Madhopur, a small market town with little interest to tourists, other than its location close to Ranthambhore National Park.

En-route we saw more camel trains and goat herders, and several unusual generator powered wooden cart-like vehicles, which would not have looked out of place in a Mad Max film. We passed through several small towns and villages and for the first time in India I saw children smiling, playing and waving at the passing cars: Such a change from the sad children I had encountered in Delhi, who were too busy working or begging to laugh or play!

Ranthambore National Park sprawls over an area of 1,334 square kilometres, three times the area of the Isle of White. The dry, deciduous habitat has a rich diversity of flora and fauna, over two hundred species of birds and a wide array of mammals and reptiles. However the prime assets of the Park is its population of forty-two wild tigers, which as a result of stringent efforts in conservation, have become more and more active during the day. They are regularly seen lolling around lazily in the sun and if you are very lucky, you may even spot one hunting down deer around one of the lakes. Ancient crumbling walls, battlements, ruined pavilions and the impressive tenth century Ranthambore Fort stand witness to the park's glorious past, which was originally a hunting ground of the Maharaja of Jaipur.

In the early twentieth century there were an estimated forty thousand tigers in the Indian subcontinent. There is no accurate number as to exactly how many tigers survive today, but it is estimated to be around five to seven thousand. Fortunately, Ranthambore was declared a game sanctuary in 1955. In 1980, it became a national park and listed among the reserves protected under 'Project Tiger', a conservation effort started by the government in an attempt to save the dwindling number of tigers in India.

We managed to book ourselves on to an afternoon safari in a canter – a large open-topped truck with bench seating. Our driver sped through the park as if it were a stage of the World Rally Championship, whilst continuously spitting out of his window. Despite this, we still managed to see some wildlife: monkeys, deer, stag, bore and crocodiles. Finally, just as the safari was nearing an end, we caught a glimpse of a large tiger sitting up in long grass by the lakeside. It wasn't much of a view, but nevertheless it was enough to send us all home happy.

Our stay in Sawai was brief and early the next day we were on our way to Agra, an eight-hour drive along a dusty pot-holed road, through yet more featureless, agricultural landscape. My first impressions of Agra were less than favourable. It was an ugly, congested and polluted city and had it not been for the Taj Mahal, neither I nor I presume the millions of other annual visitors, would have come here at all.

We rose early the following morning, excited at the prospect of seeing the Taj Mahal and also in an attempt to avoid the daily tourist train from Delhi, which was due to arrive at 9.30. We were one of the first tourists to arrive and by 7.30 we had entered the grounds through an ornate entrance gateway. It was bitterly cold, the sun was just coming up and there was a heavy mist shrouding the Taj, making viewing from a distance impossible.

As the sun rose, the mist began to slowly clear to reveal the breathtaking beauty of this iconic structure, perhaps the most famous building in the world. It would be easy to spurt out all of the usual clichés, suffice to say that I was taken with the shear scale of the structure, its smooth white marble finish, its simple lines and its perfect symmetry. At each corner of its platform stand four towering minarets and on either side of the Taj stands two sandstone structures, a mosque and a royal guesthouse, each beautiful in their own rights, but somewhat overshadowed by the Taj.

We spent the entire day wandering around the lawned gardens, laid out along a central waterway with symmetrical rows of Cyprus trees. Several elderly soldiers dressed in khaki uniforms and armed with ancient rifles stood guard. What they were guarding and from whom they were guarding it, I do not know. All around the grounds, numerous workers stood chatting to each other, busily doing nothing. The only work I saw being carried out was by two oxen, plodding up and down the lawns, pulling a man seated on a wooden lawn mower type contraption.

Surprisingly, the Taj Mahal is not a palace or a temple but is in fact a mausoleum to Mughal emperor Shah Jahan's beloved second wife, who died giving birth to their fourteenth child. Construction commenced in 1631 and took an astonishing twenty-two thousand men, twenty-two years to complete.

We left the Taj around 2pm: A large throng of touts, vendors and rickshaw drivers had gathered outside and were vigorously attempting to part the now growing number of tourists from their money. Jay was waiting to drive us to the nearby town of Tundla, from where we were to catch an overnight train to Varanassi.

By 4pm we were in Tundla; we said farewell to Jay; he had been a good guide and a friendly companion over the last few days. Our train was due to depart at 9pm and so we had five hours to pass in this small town with nothing of interest to any traveller.

We managed to negotiate the hire of the only available room in the train station for £2, more to protect our luggage than for our comfort. The room was awful, containing two single beds with disgustingly dirty mattresses and a swarm of mosquitoes; the kind of room where your more like to find a cockroach on your pillow than a complimentary mint. We lit a mosquito coil, and headed into the town, much to the amusement of the locals who had obviously not come in to contact with too many westerners.

Feeling a little grubby and sporting a week's facial growth, I entered a small shed-like barbershop and requested a shave. The barber lathered my face, took out a cutthroat razor and went to work, watched by an audience of locals who had gathered in the shop doorway.

Within ten minutes my facial growth had gone. I then requested a head shave, not that there was much hair on my head to shave. The barber looked at me with fright, I don't think that he had ever shaved a head before, so it was to be a first for both of us. Halfway through his work there was a power cut. Not to be thwarted, he lit a candle and continued whilst I closed my eyes, took a deep breath and sat motionless. As I left the shop, I placed my spectacles on and was pleased to see that they stayed in position, which was a good indication that I was still the bearer of two ears!

We returned to the station to discover that our train had been cancelled. The next train wasn't due until tomorrow, but no one seemed to know at what time. In our absence the station had become overrun by hundreds of homeless people bedding down for the night in every available space. We retired to our room where we threw the dirty mattresses on to the floor and bedded down for the night as best we could on the wooden bed bases.

We spent the following morning waiting patiently for our train, which finally arrived at 2pm, fifteen hours late and twenty hours after we were dropped at the station. We settled into our compartment hoping to get some much-needed sleep, but it was not to be. The keen stewards knocked on our door regularly throughout the eleven-hour journey offering various foods, snacks and drinks for sale. I presumed they were on commission.

With over 60,000km of track running between 7,000 stations, the Indian railway system is a true beast and with 1.6million staff, it is the worlds' largest employer. We saw many of these employees, although rarely did we actually see any of them working.

Standing on the banks of the sacred River Ganges, Varanassi is said to be over two thousand years old and is one of the oldest living cities in the world. Much of it looks and feels like it hasn't changed at all over the centuries.

Located over a seven kilometre stretch of the west bank of the Ganges, are numerous ghats on which as many as sixty thousand Hindu pilgrims come each day to bathe and cleanse themselves of sin. Open-air cremations are also carried out at many of the ghats, after which the ashes of the dead are scattered on the river. Along this same stretch, thirty sewers discharge their waste into the river. Not surprisingly, the murky brown water is so heavily polluted that it is totally non-transparent. We took a boat ride down the river and witnessed a cremation at first hand. A weird, indescribable experience: Understandably, we kept our cameras in their cases!

After only eleven days I had grown tired of India. Other than Darren, I had not met any other travellers and I had found it difficult to meet or mix with the locals. Many had approached me and struck up conversation, however every meeting had ended in a similar fashion, with the seemingly friendly local attempting some kind of scam to part me from my cash.

I therefore decided that I should move on to Nepal, whilst Darren had decided to stay on in India and head south. We exchanged e-mail addresses and parted ways.

Alone for the first time on this journey, I took an overnight sleeper train to Gorakhpur. My first class compartment was basic to say the least, with two bunk style beds and a small window with bars. There was no heater and no blankets and it turned out to be another cold and sleepless night. The journey should have taken six hours but ended up taking eleven.

I wandered aimlessly around the streets of Gorakhpur looking for the bus terminal. A local man approached me and asked if I wanted a bus to Nepal. "Yes" I replied. He gestured for me to follow him and he led me not to the bus terminal, but to the office of a travel agent. Inside the office I booked a bus ticket and my first nights hotel accommodation in Kathmandu. Once more I knew that I was being ripped off, but I felt tired after my long journey and I did not have the energy or inclination to search for the bus terminal.

Within half an hour of arriving, I was on my way out of Gorakhpur: the only white face on a very old, very full and very uncomfortable local bus, heading to the border town of Sunauli: luckily it was only a three-hour journey.

I had not enjoyed my short time in India. Maybe the unexpected cold climate hadn't helped, in any event, I was delighted to be leaving. I cheered myself with the thought that things could only get better and at least I had avoided contracting the dreaded "Delhi-belly".

2

On Top of the World (Nepal)
15/01/04 to 29/01/04

A bicycle-rickshaw carried me from the Sunauli bus terminal to the border. I walked along the centre of the road and through an arch representing the official border and entered my second country, the Kingdom of Nepal.

Unfortunately, I had missed the day bus to Kathmandu and the night bus didn't depart for another five hours. With nothing here to see or do, I found a restaurant, ate lunch and drank a few beers, my first for over a week.

I purchased a ticket for the equivalent of £2, on what I was told was an air-conditioned deluxe tourist bus. However, when the bus arrived it was clearly not the same bus as that portrayed in the agents picture. If it had ever been a deluxe, air-conditioned, tourist bus, it must have been a very, very long time ago.

Once more the bus was full to the brim, there appeared to be more passengers than seats and I was the only tourist on board. The windows did not shut properly causing terrible draughts and the vinyl-covered seats were unbearably uncomfortable. The MP3 player brought for me as a leaving gift from my work colleagues helped to pass the hours.

We drove northwards along a steep and bumpy road, at times moving no faster than walking pace. My fellow passengers were much better equipped for the journey than I, and as night fell, they wrapped themselves in blankets and everyone settled down for a long, cold night, whilst I sat shivering in my jacket and found it impossible to sleep. After several hours and for no apparent reason, the bus came to a standstill. The engine was turned off and it appeared that even the driver had turned in for the night. Eventually, I too managed to fall asleep.

I was awoken by the sound of the engine starting. The sun was just coming up and our journey to Kathmandu was underway again. I learnt from a fellow passenger that our unscheduled overnight stop was the result of a general strike called by Maoist (Nepalese Communist Party) guerrillas, who were waging a campaign of violent opposition to the government that has claimed eleven thousand lives since 1996.

Nepal is a country in turmoil. In June 2001 Crown Prince Dipendra allegedly went on a shooting-spree at a dinner party, assassinating eleven members of the royal family, including King Birendra and Queen Aishwarya. He then turned the gun on himself but survived, all-be-it in a brain-dead coma. Acording to the rules of royalty, he had to be declared the new king, ruling from his hospital bed for just three days until his death.

Meanwhile, dead King Birendra's brother, Gyanendra, was on his way back from vacation. He was the only close member of the royal family who wasn't at the fateful dinner, and now he was next in line to the throne. Returning to Kathmandu, Gyanendra issued a preposterous statement that the bloodshed was the result of 'accidental fire from an automatic weapon.' Meanwhile, according to Hindu tradition – the royal bodies were quickly cremated turning any forensic evidence into ashes.

Suspicion began falling on Gyanendra, whose wife and son, Prince Paras, had miraculously survived the after-dinner shooting spree. One report questioned how Dipendra, who is right handed, could have shot himself in the left temple!

As news of the massacre spread, thousands gathered in the streets of Kathmandu demanding the truth. Few believed the story about a son gone berserk over arranged-wedding plans. Street riots followed and within a few days, five hundred and forty people were arrested and jailed. Today, Nepal is in political chaos as Gyanendra rules like a dictator, having sacked his government on Oct 4, 2002.

As we approached Kathmandu, the bus stopped at a police checkpoint. All passengers were ordered from the bus whilst armed police boarded and carried out a security check. Several of the passengers were also searched but nothing was found.

We were soon on our way again and before too long we were entering the city. I caught a taxi to my hotel in the backpacker district of Thamel, where I crashed out for a few hours of much needed sleep. In total, my journey from Varanassi had taken thirty-three hours. Every limb ached and my ass was numb from the journey; I was left walking like John Wayne and feeling as though I had been the special guest at a Michael Barrymore party!

Feeling suitably refreshed after my sleep, I set off to explore Kathmandu: a blend of old and new with wonderful open squares, ornate wooden pagodas and ageless statues. Buddhist stupas and Hindu temples stood alongside cyber cafes and discos, neon signs and satellite dishes hung on traditional wooden buildings, second hand bookshops, trekking & travel agencies, bars and roof top cafes abound.

I spent a few hours soaking up the atmosphere around Durbar Square, the tourist centre of the city, which contains various monuments, statues, temples and historical buildings including the old royal palace. To the south is the towering Kumari Chowk, home of Kathmandu's "living goddess" and Kasthamandap – the cities oldest building and one of the oldest wooden buildings in the world.

The warren of the narrow streets were bustling with activity: craftsmen and traders were busily selling various traditional handicrafts; wooden carvings, pottery, rugs, brassware, musical instruments, antiques, jewellery, woollen goods, fashion-ware, tiger balm, spices, and fake branded trekking gear.

From the vantage point of a roof top café, I watched the street life below; begging street children, barefoot and in rags, chased tourists kitted out in all the latest trekking gear. Aging hippies wrapped in woven blankets hung out in the city squares, armed police stood on guard at the numerous checkpoints and as in India, sacred cows wandered amongst the traffic. Kathmandu was a weird and wonderful place and I loved it.

I spent the following couple of days relaxing and making the most of the cafes, patisseries and bars. After checking out several trekking agencies, I booked a six-day trek in the Annapurna range and purchased a Sherpa style woollen hat and some thermal gloves to help to keep me warm.

I had expected Nepal to be a rather cold and bleak place. However I was pleasantly surprised by the mild climate. Nepal actually lies in a sub-tropical monsoon zone at a similar latitude to Mexico and Egypt. The lowlands comprise of lush tropical forests, however with eight out of ten of the worlds highest mountains, the mighty Himalayas are indeed a bleak and forbidding environment.

On my fourth day in Nepal, I awoke at 5.30am, packed my rucksack and checked out of my hotel. Lal, my trek guide was waiting for me and by 6.30am we had boarded a mini-bus bound for Pokhara. Once more the bus was full and I shared a double seat with a Nepali lady who did not want to share with me, forcing me to perch with only one cheek on the edge of the seat.

We travelled for seven hours along the spectacular 200km Prithvi highway, meandering up, over and through the heart of the western hills to Pokhara. The highway was well maintained which means that it was fast, unfortunately it also meant that it was dangerous; the evidence of which could be seen in the form of the various buses and trucks lying in the bottom of the gorge.

We followed the fast flowing emerald green Trisuli River for around 50km along the bottom of its deep valley. We were treated to intermittent views of distant snow capped peaks to whet the appetite of what lay ahead. The journey was a real pleasure and pain experience. At every bend I was thrown off the edge of my seat and across the aisle of the bus, but the magnificent scenery more than made up for it.

We stopped for lunch in the town of Mugling, after which the road crossed the Trisuli and followed the Marsyangdi River, gradually climbing up the valley. We passed by a huge hydroelectric power station, which generates around one third of all Nepal's electricity, before climbing for a few kilometres and then descending into the wide valley of the Seti River, which we followed all the way to Pokhara.

Pokhara is the gateway to the Annapurna range and is Nepal's unofficial trek capital. The city basks in a stunning position on the Phewa Tal Lake, with a glorious backdrop of snow capped mountains, located just twenty-five kilometres away to the north.

The Annapurna range contains seven of the worlds tallest twenty peaks, all over 7,000 metres high; the undoubted star of which is Machhapuchhre, nicknamed 'fish tail' on account of its twin peaked summit.

I ate dinner in a lakeside restaurant and then returned to my hotel to prepare for the trek by removing all none essential items from my backpack so as to reduce the load. My backpack still weighed around 15kg and I was concerned that I may be carrying too much weight.

Trek Day 1 – Birethanti (1,025m) to Tirkedunga (1,540m) – 6km
Over breakfast Lal warned me that for my own safety, should we come into contact with any Maoist rebels that I should not admit to being British. I decided that for the next week I would be Irish. Apparently, both the UK and US governments had supported the Nepali government in their campaign against the Maoists. (This support ended after King Gyanendra sacked his government on Oct 4, 2002).

We took a taxi to the starting point of the trek, crossed a rickety suspension bridge over the Modi Khola River and followed the trail to the village of Birethanti. By 10am we were on our way after verifying my trek permit at the police checkpoint.

We set off along the trail following the valley of the Bhurundi Khola River. The weather was quite warm at this low altitude, so after barely fifteen minutes I was forced to stop and shed some of my layers. The un-even rocky path snaked up and down the steep valley sides with many stone steps, which were tough on my knees. Lal was like the Sherpa equivalent of an Olympic sprinter; he walked at an incredible pace and I found it difficult to keep up. There was little time to sightsee or stop for photographs and it wasn't long before I began to wander just what I'd let myself in for.

As we continued, I became aware of the sound of jingling bells, slowly but surely growing louder, until finally the source of the noise became apparent. A mule train came into view comprising around a dozen beasts, all carrying heavy loads strapped onto wooden frames on their backs, and all wearing necklaces of bells. Their stick brandishing master brought up their rear, encouraging the entourage on. I stepped to one side and allowed them to pass, glad of an excuse to take a rest.

We continued along the right bank of the Bhurundi Khola River to the village of Sudame, where we stopped around noon for lunch at a 'tea-house'. I wasn't particularly hungry but was glad of the rest. Unfortunately within half an hour we were on our way again. We passed a second mule train before stopping for a further rest again around 1.30 at the village of Hille. By 3pm we had reached our destination of Tirkhedhunga; it had taken us five hours to cover just six kilometres.

Our lodge was basic and typical of the accommodation on the trail; there was no electricity, no indoor plumbing and no hot water, but it still felt like a five star hotel. I staggered into my room, kicked of my boots and collapsed exhausted on to the bed. I was the only paying guest in the lodge and so I ate dinner alone, whilst Lal ate in the kitchen with the owners. I invited him to join me but he declined. I wasn't sure if he felt uncomfortable eating with his paymaster, or whether he simply didn't like me. In any event, I decided that I needed as much rest as possible and so immediately after dinner I retired to bed.

Trek Day 2– Tirkedunga (1,540m) to Ghorepani (2,750m) 10km
I ate breakfast alone and by 8am we were back on the trail, on what I was told was to be the longest and hardest day of the trek. Once more Lal set off at a fast pace. We crossed two suspension bridges and began a horrendously steep ascent up what felt like an endless stone staircase, climbing 300m in a horizontal distance of 450m.

My backpack grew heavier and heavier with every step and within an hour I had fallen well behind and was struggling. I called ahead to Lal and demanded a rest but he ignored my pleas and pressed on regardless. Eventually, I reached the village of Ulleri to find Lal waiting for me in a teahouse. I was totally exhausted after three hours of uphill trekking with a 15kg pack on my back. Unfortunately, it wasn't long before were on the move again, passing another two mule trains during our climb up to the Village of Banthanti, where we stopped for lunch under the gaze of Machhupuchhare to the northeast.

After lunch we continued onward and upward following the

path through a rhododendron forest to the village of Nayathanti, where we made another rest stop. The weather had changed as we had climbed; there was snow on the ground and the mountains had become shrouded in mist. Yet more strength sapping stone steps followed, we made one further rest stop before finally reaching our lodge in Ghorepani at 4pm. Once more I collapsed on to my bed until I had recovered enough to stagger to the outside shower.

Again I dined alone. Afterwards I decided to try the local speciality of 'Mustang Coffee', named after the desert-like region in northern Nepal. This local, dark coloured mixture is made with coffee, sugar and oil, laced with a generous shot of local brandy and served with a layer of grease floating on the surface. The drink carried a real kick and I wondered if it was not actually named after the animal. Suffice to say, one sip was enough for me!

Before retiring to bed, I told Lal that I wanted to hire a porter as I was struggling to carry my backpack any further. He laughed and said that he would try and find a porter in the village.

Trek Day 3

Over breakfast Lal gave me some good news and some bad news. The bad news; he could not find a porter. The good news; he would carry my pack if I paid him 10US$ per day to do so. I realised that this amount must be well above the normal rate and that he probably hadn't even tried to hire a porter, however I was happy to agree to his terms if it meant that I no longer had to carry my pack.

We left our backpacks in the lodge and set of at 6am, in order to take in the sunrise from the summit of the famed vantage point of Poon Hill; one of the best spots from which to view the central Himalayan range. Three quarters of the way up the two hundred and fifty metre steep trail, Lal decided that it was too cloudy to appreciate the view and therefore we returned to our lodge to rest up for the day before trying again tomorrow. I was disappointed but grateful for the rest.

To my delight, two fellow English trekkers, Peter & Jo arrived at the lodge later on the afternoon. We sat chatting together around the log stove to keep warm and for the first time on this trek I did not eat alone. There were very few other trekkers on the trail, due in part to the current political situation and also as the peak trekking season was still a few months off.

Trek Day 4 – Ghorepani (2,750m) to Tadapani (2,590m) 10km
We rose at 5am and by torchlight we made our second attempt for the summit of Poon Hill, accompanied by Peter, Jo and their guide. Snow had fallen overnight making the going tough. We reached the summit (3,200m) around 6.30am. This was the highest point that I would reach on this trek and the highest I had ever been. The wind was howling and it was bitterly cold. On the summit stood a viewing-platform and a small expensive snack bar selling coffee and chocolate bars. Around twenty to thirty other trekkers had also made the journey; from where they had appeared from I do not know. Amongst them several Japanese people were setting up their cameras and tripods in stereotypical fashion.

In the dark we were unable to see any of the mountains but as the sun began to rise, one by one the numerous peaks appeared across the horizon. We witnessed a beautiful golden sunrise on Dhaulagiri (8,167m), the seventh highest peak in the world. Sadly however, the view of Machhupuchhare, the most beautiful of all the mountains, was disappointing as the sun rose behind it.

We stayed at the summit enjoying the scenery and taking photographs for about one hour, before making our decent back to the lodge for breakfast, after which we all set off for Tadapani together. The ground was covered in a thick layer of snow, which made the going fun but treacherous. At one point I lost my footing and slid about ten feet, almost falling over a steep ledge. Luckily, Lal caught my arm and saved me.

The trail climbed steadily up to the village of Deurali where we stopped for lunch, before descending through another rhododendron forest with magnolia and oak trees to the village of Banthanti (sharing the same name as the village yesterday) where we again rested at a teahouse. The diversity of our surroundings was amazing – rainforest with lush greenery, blooming rhododendron forests and snow-capped mountains in the distance.

We reached Tadapani around 4pm and I immediately headed for the outdoor shower. The shower room had no light and in the darkness I slipped on the tiled floor, my legs went from underneath me and my head thumped against the floor. For a few moments I lay motionless in a state of semi-unconsciousness. After what seemed like five minutes but was probably no more than a few seconds, I regained my senses. I was in real pain, I felt my head expecting to find it pouring with blood but luckily all that I found was an egg shaped lump.

Surprisingly I found myself dining alone again. I wasn't sure where Peter and Jo were and I assumed that they must have been staying in a different lodge. I had enjoyed their company, it made such a difference having someone else to walk and talk with.

The quality of the food served at the lodges on the trail was surprisingly good. Whilst not exactly gourmet, there was a reasonably diverse menu, including soups, potatoes and chicken as well as a range of hot and cold drinks. I had been pre-warned to expect a daily serving of the bland Nepalese national dish, dhal bhat (boiled rice with lentils), which indeed was offered at every lodge for those wanting to live like the locals; I did not!

Trek Day 5 – Tadapani (2,590m) to Ghandruk (1,940m) 6km
Over breakfast Lal announced that today we were to have a short, three-hour downhill trek to Ghandruk. I was concerned that Lal had miss-calculated our schedule, especially as we hadn't trekked at all on day three. I suggested that we trek for a full day in order to make up the lost time, but he was adamant that we were still on schedule and refused to discuss the matter further.

I had hoped to run into Peter and Jo again on the trail but it was not to be, infact I hardly saw any other trekkers whatsoever. We descended through more rhododendron forest and forded a couple of small streams before arriving in Ghandruk, a large Gurung village and home to the headquarters of the 'Annapurna Conservation Area Project'.

Our lodge was the best that I had stayed in on the trail and was more like a hotel, it even had electricity and an inside bathroom; however the shower was freezing cold and once again I was all alone.

This had been the most difficult day of the trek. I was tired and lonely, and I had seen the best of the scenery. Now every track, mountain, stream and forest looked the same as those I had seen on the previous days. Lal was no company at all and I was desperate for this trek to end.

Trek Day 6– Ghandruk (1,940m) to Jhinu Dhanda (1,780m) 9km
By our original schedule this was supposed to be the final day of our trek. Over breakfast I consulted with Lal again regarding our proposed route and after checking my map, I became concerned that he planned to head north, completely in the opposite direction to our original itinerary. I told Lal that I believed that we should be heading south to Pothana. Lal refused to discuss the matter with me, simply stating that he knew the best route and that it was he who made the decisions. I contemplated going it alone, but decided not to through a fear of running into Maoist rebels or of having an accident and being left stranded.

We began the day in atrocious weather; the rain poured down whilst thunder and lightening boomed and flashed across the sky. The rain soon gave way to a snow blizzard. We tried to continue on but we were eventually forced to stop and take shelter with a hospitable local family in their small, one room home.

The snow continued to fall for another three hours. We huddled around the central open log fire to keep warm and our hosts kept us refreshed with hot drinks and even made us lunch. I ventured outside and got caught up in a friendly snowball fight with the local village kids: I held my own for a while but I was eventually forced to retreat when the numbers against me grew too great.

By 1pm the snow had all but stopped and so we trudged on, but the going was very tough in the heavy snowfall. We climbed up and down several steep hills before eventually reaching our destination of Jhinu Dhanda at 5pm.

Over dinner I again raised my concerns over our schedule. Lal pretended to count on his fingers before announcing that I was indeed right after all, and that we would be unable to complete our trek on time. He then produced a calculator and began pressing the buttons and writing down figures on a piece of paper. Finally, he announced that I owed him 8,000 rupees (£60) to cover the additional food and accommodation costs incurred as a result of the extra day.

24

Suddenly everything became clear; the additional wages of 10US$ per day that I had agreed to pay him must have been a fortune to him, and therefore it appeared that he had deliberately taken me off our original route and had only trekked for half a day yesterday, in order to extend our trek and increase his earnings.

I was absolutely furious, I made my feelings known and told him that I was not prepared to pay the sum that he was asking for. Our discussion developed into an argument, and realising that we were getting nowhere, I informed Lal that I would take the matter up with his company once we returned to Pokhara. Lal's face dropped and his attitude mellowed immediately. He told me that he was sure that we could sort out the misunderstanding without involving his boss. We agreed to discuss the matter further at the end of the trek and then we each turned in for the night. I could barely believe what was happening. Sadly for Lal, I had intended to tip him well at the end of the trek, which would have been more than the amount he was trying to scam from me!

Trek Day 7– Jhinu Dhanda (1,780m) to Pothana (1,900m) 13km
We set off at 8am, once more I hardly saw any fellow trekkers and what little conversation there had ever been between Lal and I had now completely dried up. I contented myself to brief conversations with the many locals that I encountered each day, all of who would greet me with a hearty 'Namaste' (hello) as I passed them, or more usually as they passed me. I was amazed at the strength and energy levels of the local people. They would scamper up and down the trails carrying amazing loads in baskets on their backs. The children in particular were very friendly and always smiling and laughing.

Day to day life in these mountains is obviously very difficult. The steep, rocky terrain is harsh and unforgiving and the weather is punishing and often produces four seasons in one day. Yet, despite these handicaps, the people appear to be happy and content and seem to lead a rich and rewarding life.

By now the trek had lost all of its appeal to me. We trekked for eight long hours passing through the villages of Himalpani, Landruk, Tolka, Bheri Kharka and Bhickok Deuralli before finally arriving in Pothana around 4pm. Again the lodge was basic and the solar heated shower was cold, even though the sun had been shining all day long. I had blisters on both feet and every muscle ached. However, I was cheered by the thought that this was my last night in the lonely wilderness.

Trek Day 8 – Pothana (1,900m) to Pokhara (820m) 25km

Finally, and two days late, the last day of the trek had arrived. From Pothana we should have had an easy 5km, three-hour downhill trek to the village of Phedi, from where we were to catch a bus to Pokhara. My joy was short lived however. Lal informed me that overnight, the Maoists had called a general strike and there would be no buses on the road today, or for that matter any vehicles whatsoever.

I was devastated by the news and felt like throwing myself off the nearest mountain. My choice was simple, stay here for an extra night or walk all the way to Pokhara – twenty-five kilometres away. I could not stand to be here for an extra night and despite my blisters and aches, I decided to walk.

By 8am we are heading down the trail in blazing sunshine. No words were exchanged between us. By 11am we had reached the highway. I had hoped that there would be some vehicles defying the strike but there were none. I tried to hire private vehicles from farms that we passed but their owners refused my offers of cash, too frightened to defy the Maoist strike. And so in the baking sun, we marched for the remaining 20km along the tarmac road to Pokhara, like soldiers returning home from war.

We finally arrived at our hotel around 5pm. I was absolutely shattered and collapsed on to my bed for about an hour before eventually I dragged my weary body off the bed and into a lovely hot refreshing shower. Unable to walk much further through fatigue and blisters, I confined myself to the hotel for the night. I settled my debt with Lal, paying him what I considered to be the correct and fair amount of £30, exactly half of the amount that he had originally demanded.

Peter and Jo were also staying at the same hotel and we ate dinner there together, washed down with several much needed beers. I recounted my experience of the last week to them, which they found horrifying and yet highly amusing. They had started their trek the day after me and yet had arrived back in Pokhara the day before!

I had something of a lie in the following morning before wandering down to the lakeside where I again ran into Peter and Jo. We spent the afternoon together relaxing in the sunshine in the lakeside gardens.

A group young women and children sat nearby selling hand-made jewellery and handicrafts. I wandered over to them and sat chatting with them for a while. They turned out to be Tibetan refugees, who lived in a small mountain community, not far from where I had been trekking. They told me of how their families had been forced to flee their homeland, across the Himalayas into Nepal and India, following the invasion by China in 1950, or as a Beijing insists, "liberation". They recounted horrendous and emotional accounts of work camps, execution, torture, starvation and outright genocide by their occupiers, including the destruction of almost every monastery, whilst the rest of the world had sat back and simply ignored their plight. The Dalai Lama, Tibet's spiritual and political leader, resides today in Dhamsala, India, with his government-in-exile.

Although none of them had ever stepped foot in their homeland, they obviously missed it greatly. They were all very passionate about their plight and wanted the world to know about it. Saddened by their stories, I purchased a couple of items of jewellery from them as a token gesture. What else could I do?

The trek had been a real test. There were many times when I had wanted to throw in the towel, not because of the difficult terrain, or the adverse conditions, or that the eighty kilometres that we had trekked was physically difficult, although god knows all were true, but because of the loneliness and boredom that I had experienced.

Despite this however, I had actually enjoyed my short stay in Nepal and I had found the locals to be warm and friendly. I am sure that under different circumstances, had I been in a group or with a different guide, I would have had a much more rewarding and enjoyable experience.

I awoke at 5am the following morning for yet another early start, taking a taxi to the bus park, from where I boarded a bus back to Sunauli. I was pleased to find that I had a double seat to myself and I thought that my luck must be changing as I spread myself out and made myself as comfortable as one can on a Nepali bus.

However, just as the engine started up, a huge giant of a man, about six feet tall and just as wide, boarded the bus. He showed his ticket to the driver and began making his way down the aisle. I knew before he had reached the seat that he would be sitting next to me. I inched back onto my side of the seat. The giant did indeed sit next to me, taking up so much room that I became squashed against the window.

The journey however turned out to be very enjoyable. My neighbour was very pleasant and we chatted away throughout the journey and exchanged food and snacks. For the first time on this trip my transport arrived ahead of schedule, the journey taking seven hours instead of the usual nine, despite making a total of nine stops (breakfast and lunch, three toilet, three army checkpoints and one petrol).

I re-entered India and took a bicycle rickshaw to the bus park, where I searched out a bus bound for Gorakhpur. It wasn't long before I was reminded that I was back in India. "How much to Gorakhpur and when do you leave?" I asked.

"Forty-five rupees and we leave in ten minutes" the driver replied. I threw my backpack onto the roof, paid my fare and boarded the bus.

Thirty minutes later we still hadn't moved. Then, as the driver started the engine, dozens of additional passengers appeared and began clambering aboard. There were as many as four people to each twin seat, the aisle was jammed with around another twenty standing passengers and there were many more hanging off the sides and climbing on to the roof. It was utter chaos.

The driver then demanded 20-Rupees extra from me for my bag, which was by now at the bottom of a large pile of other baggage and passengers on the roof. I refused and threatened to get off. The driver shrugged his shoulders and said, "Ok, your choice". He knew I had no option and I therefore begrudgingly paid up.

With that we were on our way. Luckily the journey was short and within a couple of hours we had reached Gorakhpur.

Everyone disembarked and more chaos ensued as the passengers fought over the baggage. The cheeky driver even asked me for a tip as he threw my backpack off the roof!

I walked to the railway station, checked the departures board and found that there was a train bound for Delhi which was due to depart in six hours time at midnight. I joined one of the two long queues at the ticket office. Around thirty minutes later I had reached the counter, "A first class ticket to Delhi please" I said. The clerk shock his head and pointed to the next queue.

I joined the end of the second queue and waited patiently. Eventually my turn came around and I repeated my request. Once more the clerk shook his head and pointed to the window from where I had just come. I tried to keep calm and began to explain that I had already tried unsuccessfully to buy a ticket at the other window but it was futile, as other passengers began pushing past me to get served.

Bursting with frustration, I trudged back to the rear of the original queue. When my turn finally arrived, I had cooled down sufficiently to request a ticket in a civil manner. The same clerk that had initially turned me away, this time took my money and issued the ticket, the whole process taking almost two hours.

With around four hours to wait for my train, I found a bench on the platform and sat patiently. As the night drew in, so did the many hundreds of homeless. A small pretty girl, no more than ten years old, sat alone with just an old cardigan to keep her warm. I had saved some snacks and biscuits for the train journey, however it was obvious that she was in greater need of them than I. I took them from my backpack and held them out for her. She approached tentatively, inching nearer like an animal wanting to take the food but frightened to get too close, before snatching the food from my hand and running to a safe distance, where she sat and devoured them.

Also lying close-by was a man and six young boys, ranging in age from around four to twelve, all huddled together under one blanket. He reminded me of a Fagan type character with his band of little pickpockets, but he could just as well have been the boy's father.

It was quite a sobering experience to see at first hand so many people: adults, children and even entire families sleeping rough on the cold hard floors with nothing to keep them warm but the clothes on their backs, and if they are very lucky, maybe an old blanket.

The train finally arrived four hours late. I found my carriage and boarded my sleeper compartment to find that I was sharing with a honeymooning couple, Tracey from Edinburgh and Nathan from Pennsylvania. We chatted for a short while and then each bedded down for the night. Luckily they were just as tired as me and so we all enjoyed a good nights sleep.

I awoke around 11am the following morning to the smell of hot food being served by the porters. The remainder of the journey was fairly uneventful and I spent the hours reading and watching the scenery roll by, before the train finally pulled into Delhi station at 8.30pm. In all, I had been travelling for thirty-nine hours since leaving Pokhara, a new personal best, or worst, depending upon your outlook!

I took an auto-rickshaw straight to the 'Anoop Hotel', paid for one night and booked and paid for a taxi to take me to the airport tomorrow. The following morning, my taxi arrived only five minutes late, not too bad for India I thought. However, India wasn't about to allow me to leave without a fight. Within ten minutes of setting off the taxi broke down. "So what do I do now?" I asked, expecting the driver to call another taxi for me. "Catch the bus or stop another taxi" he replied nonchalantly. It took me about ten minutes to flag down another taxi and once more I was on my way to the airport and out of India.

3

Efficiently Weird
(Hong Kong & Japan)

30/01/04 to 06/02/04

Cathay Pacific flight CX-752 took off on time at 2.35pm from Delhi and landed on time at 10pm in Hong Kong. Immediately the difference between my new surroundings and my last were apparent.

The huge Cheek Lap Kok international airport was ultra-modern and state of art; conveyor belts transported my fellow passengers and I from the arrivals gate to the arrival hall, from where internal shuttle trains whisked us through tube like tunnels to the immigration and customs section.

Once through customs, the airport shuttle train transported me the 40km distance to Hong Kong Central Station in the city centre, from where I took my final train to Causeway Bay on Hong Kong Island. The train network was extremely efficient, the signage and directions were clear and understandable, and the trains were clean and fast; very impressive indeed.

Via the Internet I had pre-booked my accommodation at the Wang Fat Hotel and from Causeway Bay station I tried to follow the map that I had downloaded. However, once on the street, I found that the efficiency of the airport and train network gave way to chaotic mayhem. Totally lost, I wandered around the pulsating streets for about ten minutes until a pretty girl approached and kindly guided me to my hotel. Partly through gratitude, but mainly as she was very attractive, I offered to take her our out for dinner tomorrow night but sadly she declined!

It was around midnight by the time that I reached my hotel, and feeling totally exhausted after the flight, I went straight to bed. Wang Fat hotel was an odd place, approached via a small innocuous doorway between shops, which led to the entrance lobby with stairs and elevators. The hotel comprised of four apartments located on three separate floors of the tower block. Each apartment was sub-divided into individual guest bedrooms with one communal bathroom per apartment. One apartment contained the hotel reception and a communal kitchen for the guests use. During my short stay here I never met another guest.

In order to see as much of the city as possible in my short time here, I purchased a three-day tourist pass for the MTR (mass transit railway) – a bargain at just £16. This fantastic system carries over two million people every weekday along its 80km of track and through its 49 stations, making it one of the most heavily utilized mass transit systems in the world.

I spent my first day wandering around the streets of the Central district with its shimmering skyscrapers, marble shopping malls and large screen outdoor televisions, and around Causeway Bay, a shopper's dreamland with boutiques, department stores and shopping malls and yet more large screen outdoor televisions. I soaked up the atmosphere, browsed around the electronic shops marvelling at the hundreds of gadgets for sale and purchased some photographic equipment, which was much cheaper than in the U.K.

On my first night I headed to Victoria Peak, which I was told provided magnificent harbour and city views. I caught the peak tram, a funicular railway that climbs 373 metres up the mountainside to the summit, only to find that the viewing platform was shrouded in thick mist.

Disappointed, I immediately returned and headed to the trendy entertainment district of Lan Kwai Fong, a lively warren of cobble-stoned lanes containing western-style nightclubs, restaurants, delicatessens and bars. I knocked back a few rather expensive beers in a cosy bar showing live English football on television.

The next morning I took the famous Star Ferry across Victoria Harbour from Central to Tsim Sha Tsui at the tip of the Kowloon

Peninsula. The ferry has been in operation for over a century and is a fast and cheap alternative to the buses and trams, with the added benefit of stunning harbour views thrown in for free.

I ventured into Sheung Wan, the traditional "Chinatown" district that appears to have changed little in the past century. The area was teeming with activity, with all manner of traditional goods for sale: Chinese medicines, herbs and spices, dried seafood, birds' nests (for soup), as well paper cars and mobile phones (for burning at funerals to ensure a prosperous afterlife).

Later I returned to Tsim Sha Tsui, a real tourist ghetto consisting of one square km of shops, restaurants, pubs and topless bars. I explored for a while before relaxing on the promenade, a great place to sit or stroll and enjoy the wonderful views of the harbour.

I took another ferry back across the harbour to the district of Wan Chai, which contained more bars, dance halls and hostess clubs, standing alongside modern offices, shopping plazas, art galleries and international restaurants. The most prominent building is the seventy-eight storey Central Plaza, the tallest in all Hong Kong. I took the elevator to the forty-sixth floor viewing-platform, providing spectacular three hundred and sixty degree birds-eye views of the city and harbour.

That evening, I returned to the promenade at Tsim Sha Tsui to watch the nightly firework display and light-show across the harbour on Hong Kong Island. The promenade was packed ten deep with spectators. The show was good but nothing special and so I found a little bar and partook in one of my favourite pastimes, the consumption of alcohol!

On my final day in Hong Kong, I took a bus to Stanley and its famous market, selling a range of clothing and designer wear, pottery and other handicrafts, as well as the usual tourist trash. I'm not really sure why I went there, as I'm not really a market person, so after a quick look around I boarded another bus bound for Repulse Bay, with a beautiful but deserted golden beach, overlooked by some fine colonial architecture.

After lazing on the beach for a while, I took a third bus along the scenic coastal road with imposing cliff-side mansions, to the ancient fishing port of Aberdeen. I chartered a sampan for a personal tour of the harbour and a close-up view of the famous, multi-decked floating restaurants and of the brightly decorated trawlers that double as floating homes for local fisher folk.

And finally, to complete my brief tour of Hong Kong, I took a ride on a double-decker tram, which wasn't exactly the quickest way of getting around, but if you're not in a hurry, they're a cheap and fun way to get a first-class view of the city.

Before I knew it, it was time to leave Hong Kong and continue on to my next destination. I had thoroughly enjoyed my short time here; Hong Kong has succeeded in blending the best from the East and West and yet retains its Chinese culture and unique personality. I vowed to one-day return.

Not unexpectedly, my flight from Hong Kong to Tokyo departed and arrived precisely on time. I had been slightly worried about the language barrier in Japan, however I found that many of the airport staff spoke English and all the signs were written in both Japanese and English.

Narita airport is 66km from central Tokyo; I made my way to the train station directly beneath the terminal. Initially the train system seemed a little daunting and confusing, arising from the fact that Tokyo is serviced by a combination of different lines operated by different companies. This sometimes necessitates switching between not just different trains, but also different train systems. What's more, there are also twelve subway lines operated by a further two companies. The subway services are essentially the same and have good connections from one to the other, although they do operate under separate ticketing systems. Very confusing!

Fortunately however, I found the instructions on the automated ticketing machines reasonably easy to follow. I purchased a ticket to Ueno station and boarded a space-age train, which from the front looked like a bullet train and for all I know, probably was. The interior was just as impressive and more like an aeroplane than a train, with foldaway tables, reclining seats with pull out foot rests and heaps of legroom. After around fifty minutes we reached Ueno station, I followed the signs to the correct platform from where I boarded another train bound for Minnowa, not quite as state of art as the first but just as clean. I was amazed at just how easy it had all been.

I exited the subway station in Minnowa and followed my map in search of the New Koyo Hotel in the northern suburb of Minnowa, again pre-booked via the Internet. But just as in Hong Kong, it wasn't long before I was lost. Luckily, just as in Hong Kong, a friendly local came to my rescue and guided me to my hotel door. Unlike Hong Kong however, my hero was male and so I didn't ask him out to dinner!

I checked in to the hotel around 6pm, leaving my shoes in the reception as per policy. My room was traditional Japanese style, basic but clean, with a futon bed and nothing much else. Perfect for my simple needs and at around £13 per night, very cheap for Tokyo, although the most expensive of my journey so far.

I was pleased to find that there were several other western travellers staying in the hotel and I was quite looking forward to a little company over the next few days. I spent the night in the hotel chatting to my fellow guests, unfortunately however, they were all here to either work or teach and not to sight-see, and it therefore seemed that once more I would be alone.

Armed with my guidebook, I set off to explore downtown Tokyo the next morning, catching two trains from Minowa to Ueno and then onto Shinjinku. The Shinjuku district is without doubt the most vigorous part of Tokyo; two million people per day pass through Shinjuku station alone. West Shinjuku, with its forest of skyscrapers is the calm, organised, administrative and commercial hub of the city, while the east is its disjointed, chaotic, colourful, seedy and exotic counterpart, full of fast-food joints, department stores and porn shops. Surprisingly, the two sides appear to sit side-by-side in mutual harmony.

I visited the huge Metropolitan Government Office building, 243 meters high with forty-eight stories above ground and three further stories below, which is the workplace to around thirteen thousand people. I took the elevator to the free observatory deck on the forty-fifth floor and took in the fantastic city views, which spread all around for as far as the eye could see.

I spent the remainder of the day following a walking-tour suggested in my guidebook. The route took me past Hanazono-junja shrine, where I stopped briefly as it is said to bring good fortune, and God knows I needed some of that. I then passed through a maze of alleyways containing numerous small, stand-up bars until I reached the area of Kabukicho, Tokyo's most notorious 'pleasure district'.

Kabukicho is crammed with cheap restaurants, massage parlours, love-hotels, peep shows, strip joints, porn shops and 'no-pants coffee shops' where the waitresses serve 'panty-less'. For research purposes only you understand, I checked out a few of the establishments and can confirm that the coffee was very good indeed!

The following day I headed to the Ginza district – home to upmarket boutiques and department stores and to all national and international corporations. The area is ultra-modern, having been totally rebuilt following WWII carpet-bombing. I visited the Imperial Palace, home of the 125th successive emperor from the same family, dating back to the sixth century. Unfortunately however it was closed and so I only got to see the moat and outer walls. Apparently tourists are restricted to the outskirts and the gardens only. New Year's Day and the Emperor's birthday are the only exceptions to this rule.

I then headed to the Sony Building, described by the guidebooks as a must-see attraction. The building itself is a rather phlegmatic version of the sixties – a lot of function over form. Every electronic gizmo that has ever been invented can be found here, as well as many prototypes. With most of the displays being a hands-on proposition, it's an oversized kid's arcade, but I'm not a 'gaming geek' and so I found it quite boring.

The Japanese have an obsession with both karaoke and arcade games, and I was amused to see that they had successfully combined these two obsessions by creating karaoke-booths, similar to photo-booths, where would-be pop stars can sing-a-long to their favourite track from behind a draw curtain. Even more amusing are the arcade dance-machines, where ordinary folk strut their stuff in full public glare.

The strangest arcade game I saw was called 'Boong Ga Boong Ga', in which you, the player, try to cram a plastic finger up a virtual woman's ass. The harder you shove, the more reaction you get from the computerized face on the screen!

Back in my hotel later, I decided to treat myself to a Japanese style bath, of which the hotel had two (male and female). The communal sunken tub accommodates about six people and is for relaxation and therapeutic purposes only. Before entering, you are expected to cleanse yourself whilst sitting on a plastic stool under a shower. Feeling suitably revigorated by my bath, I spent the night in the hotel chatting with my fellow guests.

I was rather disappointed with Tokyo, it wasn't at all as I'd expected and I could have been in just about any other large city in the world, with a few quirky and downright weird exceptions. The first thing that I noted was the quantity of vending machines dotted all over the city, as if they are silently taking over. Japan has one of the world's highest vending machine densities, with one vending machine per an estimated twenty-three people (according to the Japan Vending Machine Manufacturers Association).

They sell the strangest variety of goods including all of the usual items such as: chocolate, sweets, cigarettes, cold drinks and even hot drinks to the downright weird including: fresh flowers, beer, fishing bait, toilet rolls, fresh eggs, rice, ice cream, pornography and believe it or not, schoolgirls used-knickers, including a photograph of the smiling girl to whom they once belonged.

The second thing I noted was the number of people reading comic books, adults as well as children, including suited businessmen. The content of these comic books is perhaps even stranger than the act of reading them. Many depict graphic scenes of blood, guts and horror as well as sexually explicit material depicting torture, gang rape and extreme violence. And then of course there are those comic books featuring sailor-suited schoolgirls.

The third thing I noted was the volume and availability of pornography, which is sold from vending machines and on just about every street corner. Disturbingly, many of these publications are devoted entirely to schoolgirl themes, their covers displaying girls posing and pouting suggestively in uniform.

But the oddest and dare I say most alarming thing was the obvious schoolgirl fetish which exists here. The schoolgirls themselves dress in a sailor-suit uniform that could only have been designed by a pervert, with white crumpled socks and very short, revealing blue, pleated skirts. Other than for a fancy dress party, I doubt very much whether you would get a British girl to dress in such a uniform, or find a parent that would allow them too for that matter. The widespread sexualisation of schoolgirls and their 'sailor suit' uniform has deep cultural roots here. At the time of writing, the age of consent is fourteen years, one of the lowest ages of consent in the world. It illustrates that the unspoken acceptance of sex with young girls is deeply embedded within this male dominated society. What would be clear-cut paedophilia in most other countries is considered the norm in Japan!

Having seen just about every tourist attraction listed in my guidebook and having been left totally unimpressed and dare I say bored, I headed to Ueno Park, which is used by fitness junkies, buskers, courting couples and the homeless. Historically, this is the Alamo of the last 'Shogunate' – the site of his futile last-ditch effort to prevent a takeover by the imperial army. It is a carefully landscaped park dotted with museums, temples and a zoo. I spent a pleasant morning strolling through the park, however it wasn't exactly stimulating or interesting, and after all, I hadn't come half way around the world to sit in a park.

Tokyo is a strange place; everything is neat and tidy, organised and efficient. Perhaps too neat and tidy, too efficient. If the train is due at 3.55 – it turns up at exactly 3.55. I found Tokyo to be characterless and lacking in soul. Maybe I hadn't given it much of a chance, I was lonely and bored and I desperately needed to be around fellow travellers, and I was eagerly looking forward to Thailand, my next destination.

And so I set off in search of the Cathay Pacific office, in order to bring my flight to Bangkok forward. I spent the entire morning pounding the streets of Ginza, I asked several people for assistance, including two policemen, but none knew where the address was.

In Tokyo, finding a place from its address can be a near impossibility. Few streets have names, addresses work by narrowing down the location of a building to a number within an area of a few blocks. So, the city would be indicated first, followed by the ku (ward), then the cho (suburb) and finally the chome, (an area of just a couple of blocks). The Cathay Pacific office address, for example is: Chuo-ku, Ginza, 2-3-6, Namikidori Building, 7/F. Very, very Confusing. Eventually, I managed to find the office and re-arranged my flight to leave tomorrow.

I spent my final afternoon wandering around the labyrinth of back streets and fashion alleyways of the Harajuku district, popular with rebellious teenagers desperate to be individual. The entire area is like a circus with performing kids, dressed to impress in gothic, vamp, S & M and punk costumes. Coloured and spiky hair, leather, studs, tartan and doctor martin boots were the favoured fashions. This was the first place that I had found in Tokyo with any life or soul and I liked it very much.

I awoke early the following morning and took two trains to the airport, arriving with less than one hour to spare before departure. I boarded the plane with minutes to spare before take-off, unfortunately however two passengers had gone missing between check-in and boarding and so we missed our take-off slot. It never ceases to amaze me how passengers can fail to arrive at the boarding gate on time – are airport shops really so amazing?

We landed in Hong Kong at 3.45pm, my connecting flight to Bangkok was scheduled to depart at 4pm and so thanks to the two forgetful idiots in Tokyo, I had missed my flight. The airline booked my on an alternative flight, due to depart at 6.30pm and gave me a 50hk\$ (£4) food voucher for my inconvenience.

4

Same, Same But Different (Thailand)

07/02/04 to 20/02/04

The plane touched down at 9pm (Saturday) in Bangkok, known to the Thais as Krung Thep (City of Angels), although its actual name is much longer: *"Krung Thep Mahanakhon Bowon Rattanakosin Mahinthrayutthaya Mahadilokphop Noppharat Ratchathani Burirom Udom Ratchaniwet Mahasathan Amon Phiman Awatan Sathit Sakkathatiya Witsanukam Prasit"*.

I caught the airport-shuttle bus to Khao San Road, the notorious backpacker ghetto in the Banglamphu district, made famous by the movie 'The Beach', in which Leonardo De Caprio and the crazed Robert Carlyle played backpackers lodging in a 100-Baht a night fleapit hotel.

I arrived around 10pm, by which time I was dripping with sweat from the intense heat and humidity. Torrential rain bounced off the road as I jumped off the bus. I ran straight into the nearest guest house – *Sawadee Khaosan* – with a large bar, open to the street, which was jam-packed with both western travellers and Thais, sitting in wicker furniture, eating, drinking and watching live English football on television.

I checked in to the only available room, which at £8 was rather expensive for Thailand, however with the rain pouring down, I couldn't be bothered to try elsewhere. The room was rather posh, at least compared to what I'd been used to so far, with a double bed, cable television, an en-suite bathroom and air conditioning – an essential requirement in Bangkok.

I headed straight for the bar, where I spent the remainder of the night watching football and drinking Chang beer. I was glad to be around other travellers and glad to be back in Thailand, on what was my fourth visit.

The following day I went in search of a cheaper hotel, eventually deciding on *Sawadee Smile Inn* – the sister hotel of Sawadee *Khaosan* – located in a quiet lane away from the noise of Khao San Road. The room had similar facilities but was cheaper at £5.

For travellers on a budget, the Khao San area is akin to heaven on earth. As well as the hundreds of fleapit backpacker hotels, with their waver thin walls, there are also lots of good value hotels and numerous budget restaurants. It is easy to while away your days and nights watching all the latest movies on pirate DVD, whilst downing bottle after bottle of good, cheap beer and devouring such heavenly delights as banana pancake.

The streets of Khao San are lined with kerbside stalls offering a variety of mainly counterfeit goods including Rolex watches, Gucci handbags & Armani jeans, as well as the usual array of tacky souvenirs, cheap jewellery and trinkets. The enterprising street vendors also offer fake I.D cards, fake university degrees (for the would-be English teachers), body piercing and street-side hair braiding for those with sufficient hair, of which I unfortunately did not. Instead, I treated myself to a tunic style top, a pair of shorts and a necklace for £3 each and a fake Northface daypack for £5.

To my surprise, I bumped into a couple of familiar faces – Peter & Jo who I'd met in Nepal. We ate dinner of noodles together, taken at one of the many street vendors and spent the night sampling the local brew.

The next morning I made enquires regarding visas for Vietnam, Cambodia and Laos with the hotel's in-house travel agent. They would cost £50 and would take four days to arrange, however I had to stipulate the dates of arrival and departure for each country and so I spent the day relaxing in a bar, planning and researching my route and schedule for the next couple of months, eventually deciding on an anti-clockwise circular route that would take me east into Cambodia, Vietnam and Laos, before re-entering Thailand in the north.

I was finding the heat and humidity strength sapping and I was feeling very lazy after all the activities and sightseeing of my first month. On my previous three visits to "the land of smiles", I had seen all of the usual tourist sights and so I spent my days here relaxing and re-charging my batteries – usually on the banks of the Chao Phraya River, in the pleasant gardens of the Phra Sumen Fortress, one of two remaining forts from the original fourteen constructed in 1783 to protect the newly built capital.

Bangkok is surprisingly a relatively new city, established in 1782 by King Rama I as the fourth capital of Siam. Over the past two centuries, Bangkok has developed into a great metropolis with a population of over eight million and it is one of the Orient's most cosmopolitan and vibrant cities, with lots of impressive skyscrapers, numerous luxurious hotels, gleaming shopping plazas and a modern international airport. Unfortunately, it also has some of the most traffic clogged and polluted streets in the world.

Bangkok has also retained its traditional charm and so the contrasts of the city are enormous – it is a mixture of East and West, rich and poor, the ancient and the modern. Shanty towns stand in the shadows of towering skyscrapers, saffron-robed, shaven-headed monks walk barefoot along the streets beneath giant television screens. Its surface has taken on the look of the present time, while underneath the old ways are very much alive and kicking.

The site of the original city was chosen for its position on the eastern side of the Chao Phraya River, giving good defence against foreign invasion. Canals were dug around the city creating a protected island, on which the king constructed fortifications, public monuments, temples and monasteries, as well as his residence and ministry offices. This palace came to be known as the Grand Palace and is today a breathtaking spectacle and Bangkok's number one tourist attraction.

After a few days of doing nothing, I decided that I should re-visit the Grand Palace, spending the entire day wandering around the grounds, along with hoards of Japanese and Korean camera-clickers. The palace occupies an area of about one square mile and consists of several buildings decorated with golden spires and ornate architectural details. There are hundreds of fanciful sculptures, mainly of mythological creatures: fierce-looking giants which stand guard at the gates, ornate dragons, bronze lions and various Chinese stone figures.

The Royal Chapel – Wat Phra Kaeo, which is in the same compound, is renowned as the most beautiful and important Buddhist temple in Thailand and houses the country's most sacred Buddha image. The Emerald Buddha, which is carved from a single block of fine jade, dates back to 1434 and has a reputation for bringing good fortune. Over the centuries the statue has travelled to different parts of the region, depending on the power centre of the time. King Rama I brought the idol back to Thailand from Laos in 1778. Today, thousands of worshippers come to pay their respects in the hope that it will bring them a little good fortune.

I also took the opportunity to visit Wat Pho, located next to the Grand Palace. Built in 1688 during the Ayutthaya period, it is Bangkok's oldest and largest temple and contains the largest number of pagodas (ninety-five) and the largest collection of Buddha images (three hundred and ninety four) in the city. It is best known for its huge Reclining Buddha, forty-six metres long and fifteen metres high. The figure is finished in gold leaf, whilst mother-of-pearl inlay ornaments the eyes and feet. A truly breath-taking sight.

Bangkok's nightlife is legendary with an abundance of inexpensive restaurants, bars, discos and clubs, not to mention it's notorious neon-lit pleasure districts of Pat Pong, Soi Cowboy and Nana Plaza. However, my evenings were usually spent in the bars and clubs of Khao San, mingling with my fellow backpackers and with the friendly Thais. However, I was finding it difficult to meet nice genuine people – most of the backpackers here were in couples or groups, whilst those alone seemed a little weird; hippies trying to get in touch with their spiritual side or seedy sex tourists who couldn't attract a girlfriend if their life depended on it.

On one particular night I ran into a couple of guys in an open-air bar, Vincent from Holland and Fin from Norway. We spent the evening consuming large amounts of Chang beer, and chatting generally about our travel itineraries, work, music and football. After mentioning my occupation and football team, Fin said "This is very strange, last year I met an Englishman on a train in China who was also a real estate agent and also supported West Bromwich Albion".

"Was his name Dubsey?" I asked, thinking that this man could be a friend of mine who was in China at that time.

Fin thought for a moment, "Yah, Dubsey, that's right."

It turned out that Fin and indeed bumped into my friend Dubsey whilst they were both travelling overland to the 2002 World Cup in Japan. What a truly small world we live in.

No visit to Bangkok would be complete without taking in Muai Thai – a style of boxing in which combatants use elbows, knees and bare feet as well as gloved fists. And so I visited the Lumphini stadium where ten bouts were scheduled between fighters from across the country. Muai Thai has a long tradition and is still surrounded by much ritual. Before each bout, the fighters carry out a ceremonial dance around the ring, kneeling at prayer in each corner whilst wearing flower wreaths.

The fights were all fierce and furious, though the best boxers displayed remarkable skills and great strength and fitness. A resident band sat in one corner and played along to each fight, speeding up as the excitement mounts as if setting the tempo. I sat in what was obviously the tourist section, divided from the locals by a mesh fence. The reaction of the spectators who yell and shout encouragement to the boxers was as entertaining as the action in the ring.

After the most pleasurable week of my trip so far, my visas were ready and it was time to say farewell to Bangkok– at least for now. I caught an early morning bus to Laem Ngop in the province of Trat, in the east of the country close to the Cambodian border. The five-hour journey on a luxurious bus was a very comfortable, in the company of several other travellers: Maarten from Holland, Kiwi Sohan, Barry and Sarah from Dublin, Martias & Mia from Germany and Swedish sisters Julia and Jenny.

We boarded a ferry at Laem Ngop for the short one-hour crossing to the paradise island of Koh Chang in the Gulf of Thailand. Once aboard the ferry, a Thai man approached us and said that our boat-ticket included free accommodation for one night at his resort on Lonely Beach at the southern end of the west coast of the island. We all thought there must be a catch, but as we all intended to stay at Lonely Beach anyway, we figured that we might as well check it out; after all we would get a free lift.

After a bumpy one-hour drive in the back of a pick up truck, we arrived at Siam Huts Resort, which looked a little run down and tatty, with rubbish scattered around. We were all disappointed with the resort and so we decided to stay for the free night and find alternative accommodation tomorrow. My stilted bamboo bungalow was basic, with a double mattress on the floor, a mosquito net, one light, one electric fan and an open-air en-suite shower room and toilet.

Swedish sisters Julia and Jenny were both very pretty and both rather shy and quiet, seeming to prefer there own company to that of the group. I spent the night chatting with them and I thought that I may be in with one of them, but I wasn't sure which one and so I didn't make a move in case I chose wrong. Our conversation turned to age; the sisters were almost young enough to be my daughters. Immediately, the atmosphere between us changed and I knew that they thought me too old.

Sadly I returned alone to my bungalow around midnight, to find the mattress crawling with ants. I spent the next half an hour squatting them before spraying around the edge of the mattress with insect repellent to keep others at bay.

I checked out early the next morning and I headed off down the beach in search of a more desirable resort. I walked for around 5km passing several small resorts, but I saw nothing that particularly took my fancy. Eventually, I turned and retraced my footsteps in order to try the resorts to the north of my original starting point.

Typical of my luck, the first resort north of Siam Huts was the perfect spot – Nature Beach Resort with simple stilted, bamboo bungalows with thatched palm tree roofs, set out in a coconut grove on a white sand beach. After a little bartering, we agreed on a price of £20 for five nights.

Lonely Beach is a one-kilometre long beautiful, palm fringed, picture postcard beach with fine white sand, situated on the northern end of Bai Lan Bay. Nowadays however, it is not so lonely with several bungalow resorts, a supermarket, a couple of Internet Cafés, a few beach bars and a diving-school.

It was easy to do nothing here and not feel guilty. Over the course of the week I spent my days and nights in the company of my new friends, lazing on the beach during the day and partying the nights away at the various beach bars, which appeared to take turns at staging parties so each night there was something going on somewhere along the beachfront.

Martias & Mia were a quiet and friendly German couple in their late twenties. They were happiest lying in a hammock smoking dope. I liked them both very much. Barry and Sarah were a friendly couple in their mid twenties and were typically Irish. Barry was opinionated, loud and assertive whilst Sarah was more reserved and appeared happy to follow Barry's lead. Kiwi Sohan was a happy go lucky lad, around twenty years old, always laughing and smiling and bursting with energy from first thing in the morning until the last thing at night. It was difficult not to like him.

I particularly spent a lot of time with Maarten as we had quite a few things in common; both in our late thirties, single, real estate agents, football nuts and shaven headed. Unlike me however, Maarten was huge – the proverbial gentle giant. And he had an unusual habit of discussing his bowel movements with anyone who would listen.

On our second night our little group went on a bar crawl along the beach, finally ending up in Bad Monkey Bar where a party was in full swing. We consumed copious amounts of alcohol, including several 'buckets' – large plastic containers filled with whiskey or vodka and Red Bull, Coke or lemonade. I spotted a beautiful girl with legs that went on for ever – Lisa from the Isle of Man. We spent the night dancing and flirting before her friend dragged her away in the early hours, which was probably a good thing as we'd both had a little too much to drink.

News of a free concert at The Doors Bar spread through the resort and so Maarten and I headed there one evening. The Doors Bar was a wooden structure open to the skies, built into the side of a rocky hill. Like most bars here, there was a 'no shoes' policy; patrons deposit their flip-flops at the entrance. We partied the night away and were joined by Sohan, Matias and Mia.

Lisa turned up later and we again spent the night dancing and flirting, whilst the band predictably played covers of seventies rock music such as Dylan, Cream, the Stones and of course The Doors. Just as we were leaving, and just as it seemed that my look with the fairer sex was about to change, a French guy arrived outside on his rented motorbike. Lisa introduced us – he was apparently renting a bungalow in the same resort as her. The frog offered Lisa a ride home. "Do you mind?" she asked. I did of course, but I replied "Your choice". Suffice to say that once again I slept alone.

At least I had been cheered on my way out of the bar by the sight of dozens of drunken backpackers trying helplessly to locate their flip-flops from the pile of literally hundreds of pairs by the entrance. A Thai barman helped out by handing oddly coloured pairs to his customers. "They don't match" one drunk said. The barman looked at them with a confused expression on his face and nodding with approval he replied, "Yes, same, same but different".

The following morning, still drunk from the previous night, my alarm woke me at 8am after barely four hours sleep. I had booked to go on a snorkelling trip at 9 with Barry and Sarah. We boarded the boat and set off. I realised that I had made a big mistake when I threw up over the side of the boat three times on way to first dive site. I felt dreadful and didn't feel like taking to the water, but I thought that maybe once I was in that I may feel better.

I donned my mask and snorkel, jumped off the boat and assumed the dead-body position with my face down in the water. After around five minutes I raised my head to see that I had drifted around 200m from the boat. I began to swim back but without fins, it was hard work and despite my best efforts, the boat seemed to get further away. Without realising, I had become caught in a strong current, which was washing me out into the open sea.

Before long I became exhausted and fearing the worst I began to panic, waving my arms furiously whilst screaming for help. To my dismay, no one on the boat noticed me. Luckily however, a German lady snorkelling close by heard my cries for help and came to my rescue. Unfortunately she couldn't actually swim, fortunately however, she was wearing a lifejacket. We bobbed up and down for a while trying to catch the attention of the boat crew, but to no avail.

After several minutes another dive-boat rounded the headland and cruised into the bay. Spotting the pair of us bobbing up and down, they reached out to us with a bamboo pole and pulled us aboard, before transferring us back to our boat. Relieved at my lucky escape, I decided to sit out the rest of the dives and catch up on some much needed sleep on the back of the boat.

To make matters worse, one of my toes had turned blue and doubled in size following an incident at The Doors Bar when, in an intoxicated state, I slipped and cracked my toe whilst walking down rocky steps to the toilet.

After my near-death experience, I decided that I would keep to tera-firma for at least the next few days. I divided my remaining time here between lazing on the beach and exploring the island, including a visit to the twenty metre high Khlong Plu Waterfall, which was well worth the 3km trek through a lush forest. I cooled off in the pool at the foot of the falls before climbing up a path to the top, where there were more refreshing pools and a beautiful view down to the sea.

Koh Chang is a tropical marine national park, boasting crystal clear warm sea with pristine coral reefs, and white sand beaches, whilst its mountainous hinterland consists of over seventy percent virgin rainforest, said to be the best preserved in all South East Asia. The island is home to a large variety of land animals, birds, reptiles and amphibians, among them Python, King Cobra, monkey, wild pig, mongoose, anteaters, bats and various lizards including the monitor.

The majority of the almost five thousand island inhabitants live off the cultivation of coconut, rubber production, fishing or off the yield of shrimp farms. However, More and more of the island inhabitants now find work in the expanding tourism industry. Sadly, development over recent years has been rapid, particularly due to the improvements of the infrastructure and the ever-increasing number of resorts.

The first Farang (foreigner) arrived on Ko Chang in 1987. Since then a new airport has been built near Trat, a new telecommunications network has been installed and a new road encircling the island is nearing completion. The tourist board expect around half a million tourists to descend on the island this year and sadly the number is rising continuously.

I caught a share-taxi – an open back truck with bench seating which cruise along the islands only road picking up and dropping off passengers all day long, to the quaint fishing village of Baan Bang Bao, built out into the bay on stilts and inhabited by fishermen, rubber and coconut-farmers. The village has become a popular tourist attraction with many restaurants offering a rich selection of freshly caught exotic seafood.

During my final couple of days I was joined in my bungalow by a gecko – a green lizard around 10cm long, which make the strangest noise, as if they are calling "Gecko" in a high-pitched tone. Geckos can climb even the smoothest of surfaces, such as mirrors or polished steel and their feet are so sticky they can hold onto a ceiling upside down. They make great housemates in the tropics, as they keep the area relatively inset free, however their conversation can become a little repetitive.

Barry, Sarah and I had arranged to move on together and we had purchased tickets for the 9am ferry to the mainland, and a subsequent mini-bus at 10.30 to the Cambodian border. We sat on our backpacks on the roadside waiting for a share-taxi for almost an hour, but the only ones that passed were heading in the opposite direction.

Finally a taxi arrived at 8.50 and we reached the ferry terminal one-hour later. We had missed our ferry but were allowed on the 10am ferry, which broke down twice on the short journey to the mainland before finally arriving at 11.15am. We presumed that our mini-bus would be long gone, but luckily it had waited for us. Inside the bus were four angry German guys who did not appear best pleased to have been kept waiting. We were soon on our way to Had Lek and the Cambodia border crossing.

My two-week visit to Thailand had cheered me greatly after the difficult start to my adventure, not least because the beaches are glorious, the weather is wonderful, the food and beer is good and cheap and the people the happiest and friendliest that you could wish to meet. But more than that, just being around other travellers had raised my spirits no end.

5

Amazing Angkor (Cambodia)

21/02/04 to 03/03/04

We reached the border town of Had Lek around 1pm and we sailed through both the Thai and Cambodian immigration and customs posts. A couple of touts were waiting on the Cambodian side; one offered to drive all seven of us to the nearby town of Koh Kong, around 10km away, for a few pennies each. We took up the offer, as it was a lot easier and just as cheap as catching the local bus.

We crossed the recently constructed 2km long bridge over the Kah Bpow River and entered Koh Kong. Our driver asked if we'd like to see his hotel, which we expected him to do. We were all pleasantly surprised by the standard of his hotel and so we agreed to stay. My room was large and clean, with fan and en-suite bathroom, and only £2 per night, which was slightly more expensive than the others but I did get satellite TV. The owner made us all very welcome, even offering us cannabis, booze and women, which although tempting, we declined.

Barry, Sarah and I ate dinner together in a small local restaurant. The only other customers inside were two fat, middle-aged, western men whom I presumed to be sex tourists. One of them disappeared through a door with a, young, pretty local girl who had been sat with them. They reappeared half an hour later looking a little flustered.

After dinner we explored the town a little, although there wasn't much to see or do. From nowhere the skies blackened, the wind picked up and the rain began to bucket down. We ran back to the hotel where Barry and the four German guys joined me in my room to watch football on TV. Our entertainment was cut short however, when the TV picture was lost as a result of the now topical storm raging outside. I was awoken several times during the night by the crashing noises and the sound of torrential rain drumming noisily on the hotel roof.

I woke at 6.30am and stepped out of the bed and straight into ankle deep water, which had flooded my ground floor room saturating my backpack, which was lying on the floor. Luckily for them, Barry and Sarah's room hadn't flooded. We were due to catch the 8am ferry to Sihanoukville, and so I didn't have time to check the extent of the damage before we checked out. We walked to the nearby ferry port and boarded the sleek ferry, which was almost empty; I lay down across a row of four seats and slept through the entire journey.

We arrived in Sihanoukville, Cambodia's premiere beach resort, around noon. We took a taxi to Serendipity Beach and checked into the first hotel that we reached – Chan Sovannkiry Guest House. I took a large, clean double room with fan, satellite TV, bathroom and balcony for a very modest £3 per night.

I immediately emptied my backpack and checked the extent of the water damage, which luckily wasn't too severe as I had stored my valuables and electrical items in sealed plastic bags. I sent my clothes to the hotel laundry and spread my remaining contents around the room to dry out with the aid of the fan.

The three of us spent the afternoon on the beach, which wasn't quite up to the standard of Thailand, but was still nice and fairly busy. There were a few tourists sunbathing and local kids played in the surf. Local women selling food strolled up and down all afternoon, some carrying their produce in baskets on their heads, and some carrying bamboo poles across their shoulders, with a bag of food on one end and a barbeque type contraption, on which they cooked the food, on the other.

We ate lunch in a beach restaurant, where we were mobbed by a group of happy, smiling, local kids selling fruit, drinks and cheap jewellery. Two girls in particular took a fancy to us. They were around ten years old, very cute and keen to practise their English. One of them said something to Barry, which he didn't fully catch. To be polite, he smiled and nodded, a fatal mistake as he'd agreed to buy a bracelet. The girls went to work beading a piece of thread, which they then tied around his wrist.

They then turned to me and offered me a necklace. They were so charming and cute that I couldn't say no. Unfortunately though, they made my necklace too short, but not to be deterred, they cut it even shorter before tying it around my ankle. The girls then announced that as we were now their friends, these items were 'free gifts'. They made it clear to us however, that we were expected to buy fruit from them tomorrow and for each day of our stay here, before making us link our little fingers with theirs to seal the agreement. They then devoured the leftovers from our lunch plates.

I set off early the next day to explore the area, hiring a moto (a motorbike-taxi) for a one-hour whistle stop tour for the sum of £4, which should have been cheaper but I made the fatal mistake of not agreeing a price in advance. There was a lot of ongoing development with a new port, railway and several large hotels under construction. No doubt the city is in for a major change over the coming years. Whilst wandering around the city, I bumped into a guy named Jason from my hometown, who recognised my Albion football shirt. We didn't know each other but it was nice all the same to speak to someone from home, however he was about to leave for the capital Phnom Penh, and so our meeting was brief.

I caught another moto back to Serendipity Beach around noon and spent the afternoon on the beach. My two little friends arrived later on the afternoon, we played a couple of games of noughts and crosses in the sand and as agreed, I brought fruit from them.

The following morning I bid farewell to Barry and Sarah and took a moto to the bus park, which was an experience considering I was carrying two backpacks weighing around 25kg. I then boarded a bus for a four hour / 230km journey north to the capital, Phnom Penh.

Once in the capital, I caught another moto to the Lakeside district on the banks of Boeung Kak Lake, an area popular with travellers, as there are a large number of budget hostels situated there. The ride was frightening to say the least, as my driver sped down pot-holed narrow dirt back streets, weaving in and out of pedestrians and traffic alike.

I booked into the strangely named Grand View Guesthouse; strange as there wasn't much of a view, but at least it was cheap and clean. By chance I bumped into Jason again who was staying in another guesthouse in the same area. We met up again later for dinner and were joined by a friendly London couple – Jim and Inga. The four of us stayed up drinking until the early hours.

I spent the following day exploring on foot. Phnom Penh retains an undeniable charm and character, more like a provisional town than a capital city, with a colonial French influence, wide, tree-lined boulevards and elegant villas and art-deco buildings, the tallest of which is under ten stories.

It is a beautiful city standing on the confluence of the Sap, Bassac and Mekong rivers, with a laid back atmosphere; saffron robed monks wander barefoot along the streets, as they have for centuries and bicycles are still the favoured mode of transport, although motorbikes are quickly taking over. The smell of fresh, baked bread from the numerous cafes and patisseries filled the air, a reminder of its French colonial past.

I strolled along the river on the paved promenade lined with fountains and formal lawned gardens. A group of young children, all completely naked, were playing with a hosepipe, spraying water over each other to keep cool in the scorching heat. I sat for a while and watched the river float by. Fishermen on small wooden boats were plying their trade in much the similar way that their fathers and their fathers before then probably had. Everyday life here appears to still centre on the river.

I passed by many interesting buildings: Wat Ounalom, the Silver Pagoda, Cambodian-Vietnamese Friendship Monument and the Independence Monument, where two newly wed couples were posing for their wedding photographs; the grooms dressed in crisp, white formal suits and their brides and bridesmaids in flowing, white silk dresses and carrying red parasols to shade them from the sun.

Later I climbed a steep stairway guarded by statues of serpents and lions to the hill temple of Wat Phnom, from which the city takes its name. The views from the summit over the city and river were worth the climb.

Many of the cities buildings are neglected and crumbling, a sad reminder of its tumultuous and violent past, as are the numerous amputee beggars, which sit on every street corner. However, the crumbling colonial architecture makes an interesting and attractive backdrop to bustling street-side cafes and the redeveloped riverfront precinct. This is a city very much on the up.

Cambodia's recent history is turbulent, bloody and sad. It was occupied by the Japanese during WWII and by the French either side of the conflict, until its independence in 1954. A peaceful period followed, which came to an abrupt end in 1969 when the USA carpet-bombed suspected communist base camps in the border regions, killing thousands of civilians and dragging the country unwillingly into the Vietnam conflict.

The following year US troops invaded the country in an attempt to eradicate North Vietnamese forces but were successful only in pushing Cambodia's leftist guerrillas, the Khmer Rouge, further into the country's interior. Savage fighting soon engulfed the entire country, with Phnom Penh falling to the Khmer Rouge in April 1975.

Over the next four years the Khmer Rouge, under Pol Pot's leadership, began a brutal campaign to turn Cambodia into a Maoist, peasant-dominated agricultural cooperative during which time they systematically tortured and killed an estimated two million men, women and even children, targeting the educated in particular. Currency was abolished, postal services were halted, the population became a work force of slave labourers and the country was almost entirely cut off from the outside world.

Vietnam invaded in 1978, responding to recurring armed incursions into their border provinces, forcing the Khmer Rouge to flee to the relative sanctuary of the jungles along the Thai border. From there, they conducted a guerrilla war against the Vietnamese-backed government throughout the late 1970s and 1980s.

In 1993, UN-administered elections led to a new constitution and the reinstatement of Norodom Sihanouk as king. The Khmer Rouge boycotted the elections, rejected peace talks and continued their guerrilla war. In the months following the election, a government-sponsored amnesty secured the first defections from Khmer ranks, with more defections following in 1994 when the

Khmer Rouge was finally outlawed by the Cambodian government.

I booked a city tour, boarding a mini-bus on which six middle-aged tourists were sat, whom I recognised as being French from their accents. "Bonjour" I said, smiling in their general direction. They nodded back but did not respond directly to my greeting; in fact they did not make any effort to speak to me what so ever throughout the entire day. They even complained that the cost of the tour did not include entrance fees, even though the tour cost only £3.

The first stop on the tour was at Toul Sleng Genocide Museum – the former Khmer Rouge S-21 prison, previously a school, the former classroom blocks were converted into cells, interrogation rooms and torture chambers. One entire block is now given to displaying pictures of all of the murdered, who were methodically numbered and photographed by the Khmer Rouge. Only seven prisoners were spared death, being sculptors who were used to turn out busts of Pol Pot. The museum was eerily quiet, some tourists whispered to each other as if in a library, but most wandered around in complete silence, shocked at the horror that they were witnessing.

Our next stop was equally as sobering – the Killing Fields, where over ten thousand bodies from S-21 were buried in 129 mass graves. All that remains today are huge holes in the ground where the bodies have been exhumed, and a glass building full to the brim with their skulls.

Amazingly, the 'top level' Khmer Rouge leaders have never brought to trial for their atrocities because, according to the UN, the independence of the tribunals is doubtful. Pol Pot died in 1998 from an apparent heart attack.

The National Museum was a more pleasurable experience; the impressive building housed a rich collection of treasures, relics and statues dating from prehistoric times to the present, including many items removed from the ancient temple sites of Angkor.

We continued on to The Royal Palace, which is similar to Bangkok's Grand Palace but surprisingly is less than 100 years old, most of the buildings having been reconstructed. The most impressive building was The Throne Hall, capped by the five-tiered, four-faced golden tower. The roof has seven-tiers tiled in orange, green and sapphire.

We completed our tour with a stop at the Russian Market, so named as most of the goods sold here had once originated in Russia. The market sold just about anything and everything, but mostly junk. I bumped into a girl from my hometown, like Jason, she approached me after recognising my Albion football shirt.

I made another early start the next day, catching the 7am ferry to Siam Reap (translated Siam defeated in reference to a 16th century victory) along the Tonle Sap River. The ferry was a cross between a speedboat and a pleasure cruiser, very long and sleek and packed to the brim with backpackers, some sitting on rows of seats below deck whilst many crammed on to the roof and sprawled out in the blazing sunshine.

I sat on roof to take in the scenery and to top up my tan. The river was teaming with activity along its entire length. We passed by dozens of small fishing boats, some operated by children, and many villages of wooden houses built on stilts over the river. Everyone we passed had a smiling face and waved at us enthusiastically.

The 200km journey should have taken four hours but ended up taking seven, as it was the dry season and in the shallow water, we ran aground three times. Each time, local fishermen came to our aid and tugged us free. Everyone on the shade-less roof, including me, was suffering from excessive over-exposure to the sun and we were all looking red-raw

The river, which is a tributary of the mighty Mekong, has a very strange characteristic; for six months of the year during the wet season, the excessive volume of water flowing down the Mekong causes the river to reverse its flow and run uphill into the lake, which as a consequence increases ten fold in area and by twelve metres in depth.

Eventually we reached the Great Lake of Tonle Sap, the largest freshwater lake in South-East Asia, containing several mobile floating villages and yet more fishing boats. Because of the low water level, the boat could not reach the dock and so small, long-tail wooden boats were sent to collect us and transport us ashore. Each boat was grossly overcrowded with around twenty people plus luggage in each. At least if we were to sink the water was too shallow to drown in I thought. My long-tail boat broke-down and so it was another half hour before I made it ashore.

Waiting at the pier was a throng of around fifty taxi drivers and hotel touts, jostling aggressively with each other for the business of the disembarking travellers. Some of the other backpackers appeared to be unnerved by this bedlam, but after my experiences in India I took it all in my stride.

"How much to Soksan Guest House" (recommended by Jason) I asked the first taxi-driver who approached me. "Two thousand Real" he replied. I smiled and nodded my agreement and followed him to his awaiting taxi, pushing my way past the other touts who were pulling at me to go with them instead. Just as I was about to climb aboard, the taxi-driver announced "I no go to 'Soksan', take you to my hotel, free money".

I didn't bother to reply, I simply turned and walked to the nearest other taxi-driver and agreed a similar fare. That done, I was led to a crowded mini-bus which drove me and around a dozen other travellers into the town centre, depositing each of us at our various hotels.

Once more the hotel was good and cheap. After a bracing cold shower, I crashed out on the bed for a couple of hours for some much-needed sleep. Later I wandered into the town centre to grab some dinner and a few beers. The town was pleasant with a small river running through the centre and plenty of small restaurants and bars. I returned to the hotel around 9pm for an early night, in preparation for a big day tomorrow; exploring the legendary lost jungle temples of Angkor, Cambodia's greatest tourist attraction and a UNESCO World Heritage Site.

Angkor was the site of a series of capital cities of the ancient Khmer empire for much of the period from the 9th century to the 15th century and was the centre of Asian art and scholarship, during which time some of the world's most magnificent architectural masterpieces were produced.

During the 15th century, nearly all of Angkor was abandoned after Siamese attacks, except Angkor Wat, which remained a shrine for Buddhist pilgrims. Cloaked by the dense jungle, the great city and temples became lost to the outside world for over four hundred years until French explorer Henri Mahout's discovery of the Angkor temples in 1860 opened up this 'lost city' to the world. Mahout wrote that, "It is greater than anything of Greece or Rome". A stream of explorers, historians and archaeologists came to Angkor and gradually the history of Angkor was slowly pieced together.

Since 1993 restoration has been jointly co-ordinated by the French, Japanese and UNESCO. Some temples were carefully taken apart stone by stone and reassembled on concrete foundations. However, because of the lack of security in Cambodia and the continuing rebel insurgency around the Angkor region, some of the temples are closed to tourists. Since the end of the civil war, international tourism to Angkor has increased, posing additional conservation problems. Visitor numbers now approach one million annually.

At 6am the next morning my moto driver arrived to transport me to the various sites, after agreeing a fee yesterday of £3 per day. We made a stop at a local store to stock up on supplies of water and baguettes, before driving along a wide, tree lined road to the entrance of the Angkor Heritage Park, where I purchased a three-day pass for 40US$/£22. By 6.30am I was standing at the West Moat of Angkor Watt witnessing the sunrise behind the famous five towers, in the company of hundreds of other tourists.

Having done my homework, I knew which of the temples I wanted to see and in which order, with the intention of avoiding the tourist buses, which according to my research follow the same route each day.

The entire area is dense jungle, dissected by numerous roads, which link the various sites. The jungle setting was the perfect backdrop providing the occasional glimpse of a monkey and the constant, repetitive sound of the jungle insects, singing from dawn till dusk, silent yet deafening. Over the course of the day, my driver transported me to each of the sites. As we rode through the jungle I would spot tantalising glimpses of stone ruins partially hidden by the thick undergrowth. At each site my driver would park his bike under the shade of a tree and nap, leaving me to explore alone. In the sweltering heat, I visited many different sites and monuments.

My homework had paid off and amazingly I was able to explore most of the ruins alone, without the hassle of hawkers or touts, and relatively free from other tourists. I felt like Indiana Jones as I explored dark, maze like galleries, crawled through gaps in the crumbling stone walls, climbed steep stone stairways, ducked through collapsed doorways, and clambered over caved-in masonry. The entire area was like a giant outdoor adult playground.

It would be impossible for me to do justice to each of the sites in just a few paragraphs, after all there are entire books dedicated to this subject alone, however I could not leave the subject without sharing my experiences of my favourite sites.

I started at the Angkor Thom, the fortified inner royal city built at the end of the 12th Century. This huge city was surrounded by a broad moat, 100 metres wide and 12km in circumference, which was reputably filled with crocodiles to deter invaders.

My first glimpse of this amazing site was the south gate of Angkor Thom. I stood at the beginning of a stone causeway, bordered on each side by railings fashioned with giant stone figures, on the left side 54 'devas' (guardian gods) pull the head of a snake while on the right side 54 'asuras' (demon gods) pull the snake's tail in the opposite direction. On the opposite side of the causeway stood a huge stone tower and the entrance to the city.

I walked slowly across the causeway, as I drew closer to the 20-metre high entrance gate, its intricate detail became apparent. The gate was shaped like an upside-down "U" and corbelled at the top so as to admit an elephant and its rider. At its base were two sets of carved elephant statues that flank the entrance on both sides. Capping the gate was three towers containing four huge carved smiling faces looking north, south, east and west.

The royal city was built as a quadrangle, nearly 3 km in each direction, surrounded by 8 metre high perimeter walls which are divided by two axes running north-south and east-west, which intersect at the centre of the city where the Bayon temple sits. A gateway lies at the end of each axis, four in total, facing the four cardinal directions. An additional gate, called the "Gate of Victory", which provided access to a terrace of the royal palace, pierces the east wall just north of the east gate along the central axis.

Within the city walls are the remains of palaces, temples and other ruins including the vestiges of the royal palace, which had been built 150 years earlier. It stood within an enclosure also containing the pyramidal religious structure known as the Phimeanakas, which is essentially a three-level temple mount with little decoration, but the views from its summit made the steep climb worthwhile.

Extending north from the eastern gate of the royal palace are two magnificent terraces; the Terrace of the Elephants and the Terrace of the Leper King. The Terrace of the Elephants served as a viewing platform for royal parties and was decorated with elaborate reliefs, depicting both elephants and mythical creatures.

At the centre of Angkor Thom stands the temple of Bayon, the centrepiece of Jayavarman VII's building program and the last state temple to be built at Angkor. It is a square enclosure formed by an elaborate system of rectangular galleries and stairways enclosing a cruciform structure, at the centre of which rises a huge tower.

Its most distinctive feature is the thirty-seven towers (originally there were 49), which rise up to its central peak. Each tower has quadruple huge, smiling faces, around 200 in total, although there can be no definitive count as some are only partially preserved. The whole temple ranks as perhaps the most remarkable of the Khmer remains and was an amazing sight.

The atmospheric combination of the jungle surroundings and the giant roots of kapok trees growing from the walls and terraces, clinging to the galleries and framing the doorways, have made Ta Prohm, built as a Buddhist monastery and university, one of Angkor's most popular and photographed temples. When the conservation of the temples began in the early 20th century, Ta Prohm was chosen to be left largely as it was found, with the jungle appearing to be strangling the life out of the temple.

Finally I headed to the principal, most beautiful and most famous monument in the city, Angkor Wat, built between 1112 and 1150 by Suryavarman II. The temple was originally devoted to the worship of the Hindu god Vishnu, but later to that of Buddha. The temple portrays the Hindu cosmology with the five central towers (which are presently shown on the Cambodian national flag) representing the five peaks of Mount Meru, the home of Gods and Centre of the Hindu Universe; the outer walls representing the mountains enclosing the world, and the moat representing the oceans beyond.

I started at the west entrance where I climbed a short flight of steps to a sandstone cross-shaped terrace with giant stone lions guarding the entrance to the two hundred and fifty metre long by twelve metre wide paved stone causeway, spanning a two-hundred metre wide moat. I stood for a short while admiring the view of the temple from a distance, which appeared to be a massive stone structure on one level, but as I was to discover later, it is actually three levels, each progressively smaller and higher than the previous.

I walked down the length of the causeway to the entry tower, positioned in the centre of the huge outer wall, which measures 1,300 x 1,500m and contains thousands of ornate columns, galleries with vaulted ceilings and decorative wall carvings and bass relief's.

From the entry tower, a 350m long by 9m wide raised stone walkway extends to the main temple complex, bordered on each side by stone balustrade carved in the shape of a snake. The land between the outer wall and the main complex would have originally contained streets of wooden dwellings for the cities inhabitants, but the land is now bare, except for two stone library buildings positioned on either side of the walkway.

I continued on to the main complex and entered the gallery of the first level, with square pillars on the outer side and a closed wall on the inner side. Both are highly decorated, on the inner side with dancing figures and on the outside with pillared windows, nymphs, and dancing male figures on prancing animals.

Off the first gallery were two cross-shaped galleries forming four, square courtyards, of which stairs lead up to the second platform. The inner walls of the second gallery contain continuous narrative relief.

The third level is reached by twelve stairways, one in the centre of each side and two at each corner, each containing forty steps. As you stand at the base of the stairs and look up to the top level, the ascent seems formidable; each stairway ascends at a steep angle of seventy degrees and the treads are so narrow that you have to climb using your hands, as if on a ladder.

At the top of the steps is a square, paved platform with two raised covered galleries that intersect at right-angles to form four, square bathing pools where worshipers would cleanse themselves. A further raised corridor runs around the edge of the platform, enclosing the entire level. Appropriately, a group of young monks were sitting peacefully on the platforms.

At each corner of the outer corridor is a tower, and in the middle is the sanctuary, a great central tower pyramidal in form, which stands at a height of sixty-five metres above the surrounding ground level, that is taller than a twenty storey building. These five towers form the famous skyline of Angkor Wat.

Not until you actually reach the summit do you appreciate the sheer size and scale of the temple. Very impressive considering that it was constructed in the middle of a dense jungle around nine hundred years ago. It is truly the most amazing manmade, or for that matter natural sight that I have ever seen. The views over the one square kilometre temple below and the surrounding jungle canopy stretching out as far as the eye could see were magnificent.

I capped a very long, exhausting and amazing twelve-hour day by watching a beautiful sunset from the sanctuary, whilst a hot-air balloon floated over the distant treetops. I then joined a slow-moving queue of people waiting to descend the sanctuary via the south stairway, the only stairway with a handrail. No one was brave enough to attempt to descend any of the other terrifyingly steep stairways.

The following day I continued my exploration of the remaining temples, all of which were amazing but could not compare to what I had witnessed previously. Later on the evening, by chance I bumped into Barry and Sarah who had just arrived; we ate dinner together, followed by a few beers.

On my final day of exploration, I arranged for my driver to take me to Banteay Srei, the remotest site some 35km away, described by my guidebook as one of the three best sights and well worth the extra time, effort and money to get to. We left at 10am and arrived around an hour later. Unfortunately though, the temple was undergoing restoration and so my journey had been in vain.

On our return, we stopped at Banteay Samre, an enchanting site with towers similar to those of Angkor Wat, where I spent a couple of hours exploring, again relatively alone. We returned to Angkor for lunch, after which I returned to Bayon, my favourite site, where I spent most of the afternoon sitting and staring up at the faces all around me, wandering just who these people might have been. I ended my exploration of Angkor by climbing the mountain temple of Phnom Bakheng, with fantastic views over the jungle canopy to the towers of Angkor Watt and beyond.

The following morning I caught the 7am bus back to Phnom Penh – an uneventful seven-hour journey, other than being stung by the largest wasp that I had ever seen.

I decided to stay in the city centre as I planned to leave tomorrow for Vietnam. I checked into the Angkor International Hotel, which sounds much nicer than it actually was. After a quick shower, I headed to the bar for a few beers and some food. The bar was full of young hostesses, a couple approached me and we chatted for a while, but they soon left me alone once they realised that I wasn't interested in paying for their company.

I popped out later and checked out the various alternative routes and modes of transport to Vietnam, deciding on the scenic riverboat route via the Mekong Delta, the ticket costing just over £2.

The following morning I departed on a one and a half hour mini-bus ride, with around a dozen other travellers, to the ferry pier, from where we boarded a boat, which would carry us down the mighty Mekong River and into Vietnam.

Karen, who I'd briefly met previously in the Russian Market and a guy named James, who lived only a couple of miles from my home, were also making the same journey. How strange that I should be so far from home, with two complete strangers who both live so close to my home.

The boat carried us at a gentle pace down the Mekong to the border, where we disembarked in order to complete passport formalities. We waited in a small restaurant whilst our boat driver took our passports to be stamped.

Inside the restaurant, a group of children appeared selling various items. They were all friendly and we all chatted and played with them; all that is except for a rude and miserable German couple who completely shunned all of the children. The guy even pushed one young boy in the chest, sending him flying across the room, much to the disgust of the rest of the group. After around an hour our passports had been returned duly stamped and we boarded another boat to continue our journey into Vietnam.

I had thoroughly enjoyed Cambodia. Like Thailand, its people are amongst the happiest and friendliest that I have ever met, I can only presume because they are just glad to be alive after what they've been through over the last forty years. Cambodia is now finally emerging from decades of war and isolation and is well and truly back on the South-East Asian travel map, and in Angkor it has one of the worlds great treasures.

6

Follow the Ho Chi Minh Trail (Vietnam)

03/03/04 to 23/03/04

We continued down the Mekong passing many floating-houses and fishing boats, on which we saw fishermen hand-casting circular nets into the river, in what I assume to be a centuries old method. After a very pleasant eight-hour journey, we finally reached our destination of Chau Doc in the Mekong Delta around 4pm.

The guide offered to take us to her office, from where we could arrange either overnight accommodation, tours of the delta or onward transport. I, along with two others, booked overnight accommodation and a bus ticket to Ho Chi Minh City (formerly Saigon) for tomorrow, whilst the remainder of the group booked boat tours of the delta.

The three of us were then transported by moto to the Mekong Guesthouse, located 6km out of town, half way up the Sam Mountain. We arrived to find that we were the only guests at the hotel, which was nice as our hosts made a bit of a fuss of us. After dinner we settled down for a quiet night in front of the TV, watching DVD movies and drinking cold beer.

By 10am the following morning, I was on a Mercedes minibus bound for Saigon, driving through The Mekong Delta, known as Vietnams rice bowl as it produces over one-third of the countries annual crop. The dusty, bumpy dirt road sliced through mile upon mile of paddy fields, sugarcane groves and fruit orchards, stretching for as far as the eye could see, in which we saw numerous conical-hat wearing farmers, labouring under the baking sun.

Eventually, after a couple of hours of bouncing up and down on the bus, we reached a surfaced road and our driver wasted no time in putting his foot down. It was a real white-knuckle ride as we sped in and out of the traffic, and on several occasions I thought we were destined for a head-on collision, but each time our driver fortunately managed to swerve at the last minute.

Eventually however, the inevitable happened; a screech of brakes followed by a loud thump. Miraculously, we avoiding hitting the vehicle in front, but in coming to such an abrupt stop, another bus had ploughed into our rear. Luckily no one was injured and the damage was surprisingly minimal. After a brief show of bravado between the two drivers, we were soon on our way again.

We reached Saigon around 5pm; I flagged down a moto to take me to the traveller's district of Pham Ngu Lao, and agreed via sign language a price of 6,000-Dong. On arrival I handed over the cash, however the driver gestured at me for more money. It soon became apparent that my driver expected 60,000-Dong and not 6,000. It was so confusing changing currencies on such a regular basis.

I wandered down the main street searching for a room. A tout approached me and showed me a leaflet for a hotel with rooms for 10US$. "Too expensive, cheaper, four-dollars" I said. He pointed me in the direction of a tailor shop. The owner showed me to a small, basic, but clean room above the shop, and after a little bargaining, we agreed on a price of 50,000-Dong (£2).

After a refreshing cold shower, I set off to explore Vietnams largest city. I was amazed at the volume of bicycles and motorbikes, some carrying three or even four people, which swarmed through the streets like a plague of insects. Theoretically the Vietnamese drive on the right, however cyclists and motorbikes take the most direct route and so use the entire road, swerving and dodging in and out of oncoming traffic and around pedestrians, using their horns liberally as if to say "watch out, here I come." There appeared to be no road rules, although right of way appeared to go according to size.

I stood on the pavement waiting for a break in the seemingly endless procession of motorbikes, but after around ten-minutes of stepping off and jumping back onto the pavement, I realised that another tactic was required. I watched the locals approach to this problem and saw that they would simply march purposefully across the road without breaking stride.

I made up my mind to adopt a similar tactic and made my move. All appeared to be going well until I made the fatal mistake of hesitating. You see, when the bikes can see which way you are going, they can simply swerve around you. But when you hesitate, they don't know which way you are going to move, and then there is a problem. Realising my mistake, I put my head down and headed for the opposite kerb, which I'm pleased to say that I made without injury.

Like Cambodia, Vietnam is an ex-French colony and just as in Phnom Penh, street-side baguette sellers are plentiful. I stopped at one stall to grab a bite to eat. Whilst waiting, I looked around and saw a wall of white approaching, as a group of literally dozens of girls cycled down the street toward me, all elegantly dressed in traditional white silk tunic and trouser outfits.

I then headed to the Saigon River, where many street children, pedalling t-shirts, cigarettes, postcards and paperback-books accosted me. I sat by the river and formulated my onward plans. Having slightly miscalculated my travel dates, I had just three weeks remaining on my visa to see this long, thin country, squeezed between the mountains in the west and the South China Sea to the east.

I visited a few travellers-cafes to check out the various transport options and I soon found that the easiest and cheapest way to achieve this was by purchasing an 'open ticket' – a jump-on, jump-off bus ticket which for £10, would carry me the entire 1,600km length of the country from Saigon in the south to the capital Hanoi in the north, and would allow me to stop off en-route at various other cities.

After dinner, I went in search of a local watering hole and found a make-shift bar set up on a street corner selling the national speciality of bia-hoi, a cheap draught beer served straight from the keg. I stopped to sample the brew and got chatting to an elderly local guy name Po. He was a veteran of the American – Vietnam

War, and he now made his living as a moto driver and guide. I arranged to meet him tomorrow for a tour of the city.

Po explained to me the changes that had occurred in South Vietnam since the American evacuation in 1975 and the subsequent North Vietnamese take over. Obviously the name of the city had been changed, although many southerners still preferred to use the original name of Saigon.

Southerners with links to the Americans were persecuted and thousands were sent to "re-education camps". Many such as Po had their papers taken from them preventing them from obtaining legal work, housing or even leave the country. These people were forced to sleep on the streets and beg, or else work illegally, often as cyclo drivers (3 wheeled bicycle taxis) of which Saigon has an estimated fifty thousand.

For ten years after re-unification, Vietnam followed a policy of relative isolation and hard-line communism, funded by the USSR. Things changed in the late 1980's following the collapse of the Soviet economy, resulting in a change in economic policy and the encouragement of foreign visitors and investment. The situation further changed in 1994 with the ending of the U.S. trade embargo. Whilst still a communist state, modern-day Vietnam now embraces the free market-economy with a vigour.

I met Po at 9am the following day for a personalised city tour on the back of his motorbike. Our first stop was the Reunification Palace, a 1960's building built by the French and later used by the U.S. as their embassy. Today it is a museum; the building and its contents have been left exactly as the Americans had abandoned it, following their helicopter evacuation in 1975. Within the building were the official staterooms and the ambassador's residence, but most interesting was the basement bunker and operational rooms, which contained original war maps and radio equipment. The original embassy cars still stood in the garage and a lone helicopter sat on the roof helipad.

We then went to the War Remnants Museum, which offered a different viewpoint on the conflict from the North Vietnamese perspective, with many references to 'American War Crimes'. It was difficult to disagree with these statements when confronted by the photographic evidence; women being beaten, the dead, disfigured and burnt civilian victims of chemical and napalm bombs, and most sickening of all, U.S. troops posing with the decapitated heads of Viet Cong (V.C.) troops, as if they were trophies.

Almost eight million tons of U.S. bombs were dropped on Vietnam, almost four times the number dropped by the U.S. during WWII. The conflict took the lives of 58,000 U.S. troops and an estimated three million Vietnamese, many of who were innocent civilians, and many thousands more were injured on both sides.

Po then took me to a temple and a Chinese market, which sold a strange array of products; perhaps the oddest was bottles of snake-wine, which actually contained small, coiled snakes. Finally, I arranged for Po to take me to a traditional massage centre, where a well-built, muscular young girl pounded my aching limbs for an hour for £6.

Afterwards I returned to Pham-Ngu-Lao district and found a bar to refresh my taste buds. Whilst there, who should walk past but Barry and Sarah. I called them in and we ate dinner together and knocked back a few beers. When I eventually returned to my room around midnight, I found that I had been locked out, and so I was forced to pound on the entrance door, waking up the entire household, much to their displeasure.

The following day I joined a tour of Cu-Chi Tunnels, a network of 248km of underground tunnels, dug by the Viet Cong during the war. The tunnels comprised up to four levels, some sections as small as 80cm square, and contained latrines, meeting rooms, kitchens, sleep dorms, school-rooms and hospitals. One section was even dug under a nearby American army base in order to protect it from aerial bombing.

Our guide was a war-veteran; although I'm not sure on which side he fought. He was very informative, telling us about the tunnel network and the people who lived and fought in them; the hardships they went through, the dreadful conditions in which they lived and the improvisation they showed to survive.

We were guided along a jungle path from which we were shown remnants of the conflict, including an abandoned tank, and various terrifying and lethal booby-traps used by the Viet Cong, designed as much to brake the Americans mentally as physically, such as camouflaged pits containing sharpened bamboo stakes.

Our group came to a standstill in a small clearing. Our guide bent down and lifted a trap door leading into one of the tunnels that was so well camouflaged that none of us had even noticed it. We were invited to climb down and into the tunnel, which although enlarged to cater for the rather larger western frame, was still too small for some of our group to fit through. I squeezed down with a couple of others and in total darkness, we made my way through the hot and stuffy, winding and very claustrophobic. ninety-metre section, until we reached the next entry point, from where we gratefully escaped back into daylight.

The tour finished with a meal of boiled tapioca and roots, washed down with a weak tea like drink. This was essentially the food on which the V.C. survived on for several years, following the destruction of the areas rice fields by the U.S., who sprayed around 75 million litres of chemical defoliants during the campaign. We all sampled the food, but no one ate more than a mouthful, as it was extremely bland tasting. How the Vietnamese survived in such conditions and on such a diet I do not know.

The following morning I began the first leg of my journey north on my "open ticket" to the beach resort of Mui-Ne, arriving around lunchtime. Myself and three other travellers disembarked, Matt from Darlington and two Donegal girls, Beth and Mary. The four of us all checked in to Bao-Tran Beach Resort, the girls taking one twin room and Matt and I another.

My first impressions were not good. The strip of beach was so narrow that when the tide was in, the beach was out, and the strong breeze whipped up the sand making it uncomfortable to be on the beach at all. The ocean did bring some welcome relief from the heat, but the waves were so huge that swimming was difficult and dangerous.

Matt and I hired a couple of bicycles and set off to explore the area in the hope of finding a better stretch of beach. Our bikes were very basic with no gears, poor brakes, poor suspension and rock hard seats. We eventually found a decent stretch of wide beach, but the windy conditions ensured that we didn't stay too long.

Matt was around twenty-two years old, and had recently completed a degree in physics, however it was a field that he had no interest in working in. Instead, he worked in a fish and chip shop and his ambition was to one day own such an establishment. If ever there was an argument against free university education, Matt was it.

The four of us spent one more day at Mu-Nei, and the following morning we left on the 7am minibus bound for Dalat in the central mountains. As we began to climb into the hills along a meandering road, the temperature cooled to a more bearable level and the scenery changed dramatically, becoming very lush and green, with scenic valleys clad in dense pine forests, which gave off a wonderful fresh aroma and which looked more like Northern Europe than South East Asia.

We arrived in Dalat around 2pm, the city where the Vietnamese come to honeymoon. The city was built around the large man-made Xuan Huong Lake, with a miniature replica Eiffel Tower standing on one bank and a golf course on another. I wandered around the cobbled, mazy streets and I was pleasantly surprised. There were numerous hotels, restaurants and bars although there was a definite slower pace, and I didn't get hassled once by touts or hawkers.

After dinner, Matt and I visited a few bars to sample the local nightlife, during which we ran into a couple of friendly, elderly local guys riding old East European motorbikes. They called themselves 'Easy-Riders' and said that they offered tourists unique personalised tours of the surrounding area. We chatted for a while and arranged for a tour tomorrow.

Our 'Easy-Riders' duly picked us up from our hotel at 8am and we spent a fantastic day driving around the local hills on the back of the slowest and noisiest motorbikes you can imagine. During the day we visited a couple of picturesque lakes and waterfalls, a couple of pagodas and to a vegetable farm where the friendly labourers, wearing the customary conical-hats, gave us wonderfully tasting, freshly picked carrots to eat.

We then went to an ethnic hill-village with an unusual five metre tall concrete statue of a chicken standing in its centre. The village comprised a mix of modern zinc sheeted homes and traditional stilted huts with bamboo walls and floors and thatched roofs. We were invited into one home in which two families appeared to live. The open room was segregated into a general living area with an open fire burning in the centre, and at the far end of the room, a sleeping area with bamboo beds raised off the dirt floor. There was no electricity and no running water, but everyone seemed happy and content.

The following morning Mary, Beth, Matt ad I departed for the beach resort of Nha-Trang. Upon arrival I immediately headed for the palm-tree lined municipal beach, stretching for 6km with glorious golden sand and inviting turquoise sea. I hired a sun-lounger and soaked up the last of the afternoon sun.

The four of us spent the evening in Jacks Bar, where we sat eating and drinking on a first floor balcony overlooking the ocean. A power-cut briefly interrupted our evening, but the staff we soon on hand with candles. I presumed that this must have been a regular occurrence.

Mary and Beth were both aged in their mid-twenties; Mary was a nurse whilst Beth was an engineer. They were both very friendly, good fun and great company, and they could both drink like the proverbial fish.

The four of us were picked up early the next morning for a boat trip to some nearby islands. The crew were keen to maximise their income by selling beer, even to the extent of keeping score between the various nationalities, so that if you fell behind they were quick to let you know that Holland, Sweden, Ireland or whoever, was one up on England. By 10am we were on our first beer.

At our first stop we all took to the ocean for a little snorkelling but there was little marine-life to see, and so it wasn't long before we were all back on board and drinking again. The westerners aboard were served a delicious seafood buffet-lunch on the top deck, whist the Vietnamese passengers ate on the lower deck. With the aid of a guitar and a small set of drums, the crew then began a karaoke session, which the Vietnamese passengers enthusiastically joined in with, whilst the westerners staged a diving competition from off the top deck. I won the award for the reddest belly!

We were then treated to the floating bar, in which one of the crew took to the ocean with a polystyrene bar, from which he served several bottles of disgustingly awful red wine. We all joined him, bobbing up and down in inflatable rubber-rings, toasting each other in turn until every last drop was gone. If we weren't drunk beforehand, we certainly were by the time we clambered back on board.

The party proceeded on the top deck whilst the boat made its return to Nah Trang. Everyone had entered into the spirit of the day and we had all got on well together. Although totally smashed, we all arranged to meet at 9pm in the "Nah Trang Sailing Club" to continue partying later.

I arrived in the Sailing Club at 9.30pm after an afternoon nap, although I still felt pretty drunk. The Sailing Club was a large enclosed beach bar with an inside disco area. Not surprisingly, none of the others from the boat trip were there except for Matt. A couple of other English guys were also inside the bar and so we spent the night chatting and drinking with them, and for the umpteenth time, I ran into Barry and Sarah again.

There weren't too many girls inside the bar and so the atmosphere was a little muted, that is until around twenty Danish students entered, everyone one of them stunning. The girls were all pretty friendly and flirtatious and they appeared to enjoy the attention they were getting.

I spent most of the night chatting about nothing in particular with one of the girls named Maria. It transpired that the girls were here on a six-week study programme. Whilst chatting, I noticed a stunningly beautiful brunette across the room. Our eyes met for what seemed like an eternity but was probably no more than a couple of seconds. Conscious that Maria may have noticed me staring at another girl, I turned back to her and continued our conversation. When I looked around again the mystery brunette had vanished.

By the end of the night it had become apparent that Maria and the rest of the Danish girls would all be returning to their hotel without any male company, and so feeling a little worse for ware and extremely frustrated, I too headed for my hotel.

As I walked up the quiet dark lane toward my hotel, two pretty Vietnamese girls approached me, "You like fuk?" The first girl asked.

"No thank you" I replied politely, as I continued to stagger toward my hotel. They jumped in front of me to stop my escape, draping their arms around me and pressing their bodies against mine.

"Just twenty dollar" the second girl said. She then took my hand and rubbed it against her inner thigh, "Mr, you not like me?" she continued.

"I have to go," I replied, as I tried to pull away.

Her hand stroked across my groin, "Ok, for you ten dollar." I shock my head and pulled away, but they were determined not to let me escape. Before I could stop her, her hand was inside my trousers.

"I think you like me," she said, and within an instant, and while I was still trying to work out what was happening, she dropped to her knees and extracted my manhood, whilst the first girl lifted her shirt, took my hand and placed it on her breast. Unable to fight it any longer, I learnt back against a wall and let nature take its course.

I then felt a hand reach into my pocket for my wallet. Although drunk, luckily I had not lost all of my senses. I pulled her hand away, fastened my trousers, handed them a ten-dollar note, and staggered the short distance back to my hotel.

After something of a lie in, the following afternoon I hired a cyclo for a tour of the cities sights. We rode out of town to Long Son Pagoda, situated at the foot of Mount Trai Thuy, on which stood a large white Buddha statue overlooking the town and the Cai River, in which a huge fleet of brightly painted fishing boats were moored. We continued to the Po Nagar Towers temple complex, which was built between the 7th and 12th centuries. Most were destroyed and only four towers are still standing, each of which is a shrine to a different deity.

That evening I went in search of Sharkys Bar, where I'd arranged to meet the English guys that I'd met the previous night. I searched without any luck for about one hour and had almost given up, when a local guy standing outside Shortys Bar called out to me, "Mr, English football here". I entered and found all of the guys inside. I'm not sure if I'd been given the wrong name or if I'd simply misheard. I left the bar around midnight after watching a couple of English football games on TV, and decided to pop into the Sailing Club before returning to my hotel.

No sooner had I entered the bar than I spotted the mysterious brunette from the previous night. She looked even more stunning than I'd remembered her, flowing hair, sparkling blue eyes and a curvaceous body. Our eyes met again and once more she ignored my smile, as if she hadn't even seen me. However, after a couple of minutes, she made her way across the room and stood just a few feet from me.

I made my move, trying to strike up a conversation about Denmark. Unfortunately as it turned out, I'd wrongly assumed that she was one of the Danish students, in actual fact she was from Minnesota, USA. Despite my cock-up, we spent the remainder of the night chatting and dancing together. The music stopped at 2am, she kissed me softly on the lips, smiled and said "thanks for a lovely night, I'm sure we'll meet again." With that Cass disappeared through the door and once more I returned to my hotel alone and frustrated.

I woke the next morning thinking about Cass and wandering whether I'd ever see her again, as I was due to leave Nah Trang on the 6pm overnight bus. I deposited my backpack at the bus company's office and headed to the beach for a lazy day.

I was engrossed in my book when I happened to look up and notice that Cass had appeared and was sitting on the beach about ten metres from where I lay. I decided to play it cool and pretend that I hadn't noticed her. After a few minutes she came over and we spent the next couple of hours chatting and getting to know each other a little better. It turned out that Cass was also about to leave Nah-Trang, having booked a flight tomorrow to Hanoi. I told her that I was leaving tonight and that I too would be in Hanoi in a couple of day's time. We exchanged e-mail addresses and agreed to meet again in the capital.

My 530km / twelve-hour overnight bus journey to Hoi-An turned out to be a nightmare. We departed an hour late, the bus was overcrowded, the air-conditioning was broken, my reclining seat didn't recline, one of the Vietnamese passengers spent almost the entire journey making very loud mobile-telephone calls, the driver continuously turned the lights on and off, seemingly on each time that I tried to settle down to sleep and off each time that I picked up my book to read. Tired and aching, we arrived in Hoi-An around 7am. I checked into the Nguyen Phuong Hotel and headed straight for the shower, followed by a couple of hours of sleep.

The city is an ancient, historical port standing on the Thu Bon River, with a long history of international maritime trade, and is a Unesco World Heritage Site. It is now very much a tourist attraction, containing numerous handicrafts, antique, art and tailor shops. However, there was still much to see here including several small museums and a Japanese Covered Bridge dating back to the sixteenth century, which has been reconstructed several times to the same original design.

The quaint centre comprises just three narrow, bustling streets running parallel to the river, all lined with wooden fronted, tiled roofed shop-houses. On the banks of the river stood a colourful market bursting to the seams with activity and all manner of fresh fish, fruit and vegetable produce. Outside on the rivers edge, fishermen were unloading their catches straight into wicker baskets, from which local women, wearing conical hats, segregated the various fish types into buckets from where they were sold.

I did a little clothes shopping, buying a couple of t-shirts for less than £1 each and a silk sleeping-bag liner for £3, which would have cost closer to £30 in the UK. I searched for a shirt in one of the numerous tailor shops but I couldn't find anything that I liked. The assistant offered to measure me up for a made to measure shirt. I explained that I didn't have time, as I was due to leave tomorrow. "No problem, only take two hour" she replied. So I picked out some cloth, chose a couple of designs and allowed her to measure me up.

As I left the shop I bumped into Mary and Beth again. They had been busy doing a little clothes shopping of their own and were now on their way to dinner. I tagged along with them and had to sit through a mini-fashion show as they showed me all the bargains they had purchased. Afterwards, on my way back to my hotel, I returned to the tailor shop and collected my two hand-made shirts, which both fitted perfectly and cost just £3 each.

Yet another early bus journey, departing Hoi-An on the 7am bus bound for Hue, the former capital from 1802 to 1945. We arrived around 1pm, which left me with around 4 hours to see the sites, as I had already decided to catch the overnight bus to Hanoi, as I was keen to meet up with Cass again as soon as possible.

I arranged a moto for a whistle-stop tour, going firstly to the seven-storey Thien Mu Pagoda, located on the bank of the Perfume River before continuing to the nineteenth century Citadel, occupying an area of 520 hectares.

The Citadel is enclosed within a 7m high and 20m thick brick and earth perimeter wall, which stretches for 10km and is encircled by a moat and canal. I entered through the main entrance below a substantial flag tower, on which flew the red national flag with five-pointed yellow star in its centre. But this was no ordinary flag; this was the largest flag that I have even seen.

There was little of interest within the outer grounds other than gardens, lakes and a couple of museums. A second moat and defensive wall within the Citadel guard the Imperial City, which once housed approximately 150 grand buildings and pavilions, of which only around 20 survive today. Within the third and final enclosure stands the Forbidden Purple City, reserved for the private life of the emperor and containing residential palaces, of which only a few remain.

After my brief visit, I caught the 5pm overnight bus to Hanoi, which once more turned out to be a horrendous journey. We made three stops in the first three hours of the journey, followed by a forth stop of around an hour to change a punctured tire. Luckily however, I did manage a few hours sleep.

The bus arrived in the capital at 8am and the western travellers aboard were transferred to a mini-bus and carried to the bus operators preferred hotel, much to the annoyance of everyone aboard, who preferred to find their own accommodation. None of us were quite sure where exactly we were and the rude and aggressive driver refused to take us to our chosen hotels. A row broke out between one totally pissed off traveller and the driver. I pulled the guy away before things got out of hand.

I headed off on foot in search of the old-quarter, where I hoped to find a decent hotel to match my budget of £3 per night, which was not easy. Eventually, tired of looking, I settled on the Green City Hotel, which matched my budget but was perhaps the worst place that I had stayed in throughout Vietnam. I headed out in search of an Internet café, hoping for word from Cass. As expected there was an e-mail from her, but the news was not good; she wanted to meet up with me at 4pm in a café by the lake, but she had booked a ticket for the overnight sleeper train to Sapa. I was gutted and set off to see the city in an attempt to take my mind off my disappointment, but I could not stop feeling miserable and it was a grey and gloomy day, which did not help.

The city was generally less frantic than Saigon, although the streets were still fairly vibrant and chaotic, and were clogged with speeding, horn tooting motorbikes. I wandered around the labyrinth of narrow streets of the bustling old-quarter, with narrow shops whose goods spilled out on to the pavements, forcing pedestrians to walk dangerously in the busy roads. This is the historic, commercial heart of the city since the fifteenth century and many of the streets here are named after the various merchants and trades that they represent – Hang Vai – Fabrics Street, Hang Da – Leather Street, Hang Bac – Silver Street, etc.

I arrived at Thuy Ta Café on the northwest corner of Hoam Kien Lake in time for a bite to eat before meeting Cass, who arrived bang on time at 4pm. We spent the afternoon together wandering around the city. I was confused by the situation that I found myself in; Cass had invited me to meet her and so I presumed that she liked me, but she had arranged to leave on the day I was due to arrive. What was I to think?

On the evening we visited The Water-Puppet Theatre to see a performance by the internationally renowned Thang Long Water-Puppet Troupe. Water-Puppetry originates from the rice fields of the Red River Delta and dates from the twelfth century. The puppeteers stand in waist deep water, hidden behind a bamboo screen, from where they manipulate wooden puppets of dragons, ducks, lions, frogs, water buffalo and people, attached to the end of long bamboo poles hidden beneath the waters surface. The puppets play, dance and fight, whilst traditional songs and music from drums, gongs and flutes play to build atmosphere and set scenes. It sounds corny but we both loved it.

We met two angry Norwegian girls inside the theatre who had booked tickets for the show from their hotel, and had paid an extra

10US$ each to be taken to the theatre door. Imagine their surprise then, when their hotel manager walked them down the street to the theatre entrance, which was located about one hundred metres from their hotel!

Afterwards we headed to a bar to spend the remainder of the evening. As we talked, I got the impression that Cass wanted me to join her, but in my confused state I did not raise the subject, just in case I was reading the signals wrong. As the time for her to depart grew nearer, she eventually said "I'm sure there will be room on the train, why don't you come to Sapa with me?" That was all I needed to hear, within five minutes we were in a taxi heading to my hotel to collect my bags and check out. We then collected Cass's bags from her hotel and drove on to the train station.

The Reunification Express was waiting as we arrived. I purchased a ticket and we boarded the train with just minutes to spare. Unfortunately we were in separate compartments, I saw Cass to hers and promised to return later once I had found mine. When I returned later, I found that Cass was sharing her compartment with a Canadian girl, her middle-aged uncle and his friend. All four were drinking beer and they invited me to join them, which I did until 2am.

I awoke the following morning to the sight of some spectacular and dramatic mountain scenery as the train snaked through the lush alpine valleys of northwest Vietnam, following the course of the Red River. We arrived at Lao Cai station near to the Chinese border at 8am and we transferred to an over-crowded mini-bus for a ninety-minute journey to the market town of Sapa.

Having done her homework, Cass wanted to stay in The Queen Hotel, which apparently had spectacular views of Mount Fan Si Pan, at 3,143m Vietnams highest peak. We soon found the hotel, Cass checked out the rooms and chose one on the second (top) floor, which should have had the best view across the valley, although we couldn't actually tell as it was so misty.

We spent our days here wandering around the laidback, virtually tourist free town, much of which had been rebuilt following the Chinese invasion of 1979 and the subsequent 17-day war. On our second day we hired motorbikes to explore a little further into the mountains, visiting the silver waterfall and Tram

Ton Pass, where we hoped for fantastic views but were once more disappointed due to the thick mist.

On our return, we stopped at a small traditional hill-village, set amongst crop fields in a landscape of terraced hillsides. The village contained around twenty wooden huts and was home to the Hmong hill-tribe people. Pot-bellied pigs and chickens ran freely through the village scavenging for scraps, whilst children played happily in the dirt. From the moment that we arrived, the womenfolk hounded us to buy clothing and jewellery from them. Although I didn't actually want or need anything that they had to sell, I felt that it was rude to visit their village and not do so, and so I brought an embroidered tunic and matching hat. As we left the village, we passed a young boy on the roadside riding bareback on a huge water buffalo.

Vietnam has over fifty ethnic groups totalling around seven million people, of which the Hmong are the largest. This group are scattered throughout all of South East Asia, without a country to call their own. They are easily recognisable by their indigo coloured, embroidered clothing. The men wear hats, tunics, baggy trousers and baggy shirts. The women, many of whom carry babies on their backs in sling-like woven blankets, wear hats, tunics, ankle length skirts, aprons, and lots of chunky silver jewellery. They seem generally friendly and have quickly learnt how to pedal their goods for the tourist dollar.

On our second night in Sapa, Cass announced that she wanted some 'own-time' and so I left her alone in the room whilst I spent the night in a bar. I couldn't understand this girl, one moment she talked of us travelling together, and the next moment she wanted to be alone. I felt too old for such games, and so I decided that tomorrow I would return to Hanoi, with or without Cass.

The next morning I woke to find that all power was down in Sapa and that a dense fog had cut visibility down to just a few metres. I took a stroll whilst Cass slept, and I discovered to my horror that the quaint town had been transformed overnight into a tacky "tourist attraction", with taxi-drivers, hawkers, and Hmong and Red Dao ethnic hill-tribes people, all vying for the tourist dollar from the foreigners who had arrived for the weekend on the train and buses from Hanoi.

Around 6pm a mini-bus arrived to pick me up and transport me to the train station. Already on board were a group of teachers who had been working in Hanoi teaching English; Emma and Chris from England and Sue from Canada. We boarded the train and discovered that we were sharing a compartment. Chris and Sue immediately claimed the bunks on one side of the compartment. Referring to the sleeping arrangements, Emma asked, "Do you prefer to be on top?"

"Lets have a few drinks and get to know each first" I replied.

She turned bright red whilst the others laughed out loud, but it helped to break the ice. We spent the remainder of the night sat on our bunks chatting and drinking beer.

My visa was due to expire in three days time and I did not want to leave Vietnam without seeing the Halong Bay, an area of outstanding natural beauty and yet another Unesco World Heritage Site. And so I booked a two-day boat trip of this region, and a bus ticket to Laos for £9 each. I had arranged to meet Emma, Chris and Sue for dinner in a bar in the French quarter, but they didn't show and so I ate dinner alone followed by a few beers.

I was picked up by a mini-bus the following morning and driven to a bus-park, from where I should have boarded a tour bus to Halong Bay. Unfortunately, the bus had been overbooked and was already full. I was put in a taxi with a Swedish couple and we were driven to another bus-park, where we were put onto not a tourist bus with reclining seats and air-conditioning as we had been promised, but on an old and dirty local bus, which was noisy, uncomfortable and over-crowded.

We drove for around four hours before eventually stopping in Haiphong City, where we were then put in a taxi and driven to yet another bus-park, where we boarded a second bus, which was even worse than the first. We drove for another one and a half hours until we eventually reached the dock where several boats were moored. Our fellow travellers who had been fortunate enough to get a seat on the tour tourist bus, were sitting outside a restaurant after finishing the complimentary lunch.

The numerous boats were ready to depart and so there was no time for us three stragglers to eat. We were all pissed off at our treatment, however I was determined to make the most of the rest of the tour. Once aboard our vessel, we set off across emerald waters toward Halong Bay whilst the crew prepared a special meal of noodle-soup for me.

Once more it was a grey, misty and miserable day, which somewhat spoiled the spectacle. We passed numerous vegetation-covered islands and limestone outcrops, of which the bay is home to an estimated 3,000, the remains of a giant prehistoric reef, which stretched from Guilin in China to Thailand's Phang Nga Bay (more of this later). We stopped at one island and we were transferred to small boats, which carried us ashore to explore an impressive cave system, containing large grotto-like vaults.

The day ended at Cat-Ba Island around 5pm. Some of the group had elected to spend the night onboard the boat whilst the majority, including myself, had opted to spend the night at a Hotel ashore. At dinner, our group split into the usual three sub-groups; the drinkers – which generally comprised of the Brits, Irish, Scandinavians, Aussies, Kiwis, Canadians and Americans; the locals; and finally those that didn't fit into either of the others – usually the French, Israelis and the over forties. Suffice to say that I was in the drinking group with Rory from Dublin, Rich from England and his Swiss girlfriend Isabelle, Canadian Nancy and John and Steve from Australia. After dinner we all headed out of the hotel to The Flightless Bird bar where we spent the night partying. It transpired through the evening that everyone aboard had paid different amounts for same trip, ranging from £8 to £20; suffice to say that some of the group were not pleased.

After breakfast our merry little band was once more herded onto the boat for the four hour return journey across the bay. On route local hawkers, some of who were young children, selling fruit and drinks from small wooden rowing boats and coracles, intercepted us. Where they had come from in the middle of the sea I do not know.

I was lucky enough to get a seat on the tourist bus for the return journey to Hanoi, which was a much more comfortable and swift journey than that which I experienced on the outward journey. We arrived around 4pm and with just three hours to kill before catching the overnight bus to the Laos capital, Vientiane, I headed to a bar for a few beers and a bite to eat.

I returned to the hotel at 6.30pm to collect my backpack and laundry, which I had deposited before departing to Halong Bay. I checked my laundry and found that my favourite t-shirt had developed a large iron-burn hole. I complained to the hotel manager but he refused to accept responsibility, saying that the t-shirt must have been already damaged.

When the bus arrived I found Rory onboard, having decided to join me. The bus was surprisingly spacious and comfortable, and I was lucky enough to catch some sleep, until around 2am that is, when we were awoken by cries of "Vientiane". In a semi-conscious state, I grabbed my belongings and staggered off the bus, only to find that we were being transferred to another bus for the remainder of our journey.

Our new bus was typical Vietnamese; old, dirty, over-crowded and to makes matters worse, fully laden with a cargo including numerous bags of rice and various boxes of produce, electrical goods, stacked glass sheets and smelly buckets of live crabs, all stacked in the central-aisle or jammed in the foot-wells of each seat, so that all passengers were forced to sit uncomfortably with their knees around their ears. One poor Japanese guy had to lie in the central-aisle on top of the cargo, as there were no available seats. At least there were no chickens I thought, as all had been destroyed following the recent outbreak of bird-flu in South-East Asia.

The journey was murderous as we snaked along often un-surfaced roads over the mountains, to the incessant noise of crying children and the bus radio, which blared away continuously. I hardly managed any sleep and by the time that we reached the town of Cae-Treo on the Laos border around 9am, I was totally shattered.

I was not sorry to be leaving Vietnam, although I did have some happy memories and had generally enjoyed my time there. Many people predict that Vietnam is set for a tourist boom, but I cannot see it. The beaches, nightlife and food can not compare to Thailand, the temples and historic sites are dwarfed by Angkor in Cambodia, and the scenery is no better than Laos and Northern Thailand, as I was about to find out. More importantly however, I had found the people to be less than friendly, especially in comparison to their Thai and Cambodian neighbours.

The Vietnamese generally appear to dislike western tourists, and they make no attempt to hide the fact, but they are more than happy to put up with them in exchange for the mighty dollar. They are yet to learn the golden rule of capitalism; that the customer is king.

7

Chilling on the Mekong (Laos)

24/03/04 to 04/04/04

After successfully negotiating customs and immigration, we all re-boarded the bus to continue our journey through Laos to Vientiane, crossing the Annamite Mountains via the Kaew Nua Pass. We stopped around 11am for lunch at a small restaurant in the town of Lak Xao. There were no menus available at the restaurant and no one spoke English, so the six western travellers aboard went hungry, whilst the bus driver and the local passengers tucked into their meals.

Afterwards, the driver slumped into a chair in front of the TV, put his feet up on a table and settled in to watch what I could presume was his favourite show. We waited patiently but when after an hour he still hadn't moved, we all became a little restless and we began demanding that our ride recommence. The driver raised three fingers, which we took to either mean three hours or 3pm, either way we were not happy at having to stay any longer than was absolutely necessary in this backwater town. Eventually at 1pm, realising that there was a mutiny at foot, the driver stirred himself and we were on our way again.

Feeling hungry, dirty and totally exhausted, we eventually arrived in the capital at 7pm after twenty-four hours on the road. We searched for a decent room, but the majority of available accommodation was either poor quality or overpriced. We eventually settled for the Sihom Guesthouse, which was located about 2km out of city centre, but for £6 per night was very pleasant, with private gardens and air-conditioned rooms with satellite TV and private bathroom. After a much-needed shower, we searched out a restaurant and feasted on a meal of chicken, chips and vegetables, washed down with four beers. Delicious and we had change out of £3.

Like Vietnam, Laos too is a communist state, which only opened its borders to foreign investors and tourists in 1991, following the collapse of the USSR. It is the poorest and least developed nation in South East Asia and its landscape and people have changed little since the first French explorers arrived over a century ago. Even today, a good proportion of Laos's six million population are ethnic hill-tribes people such as the Hmong.

Modest and simple, Vientiane is more like a provincial town than a capital city. It stands on a broad bend in the mighty Mekong River, which is the lifeline of this landlocked country, running its entire length. There was a definite laidback feel here, very unlike anywhere else in South East Asia. I saw so many saffron robed monks walking around the streets that I presumed that there was a Buddhist convention in town. There wasn't too much traffic and what there was didn't continuously hoot their horns, you could browse around the markets and shops and look at the goods without being hassled to buy, the people were very friendly, and the food and beer was cheap and surprisingly good. I immediately liked Laos.

The weather was very humid and hot, around 35-degrees, which made me feel very lazy, especially after the epic bus journey. I spent much of my time here in Nam Phou Place, the centre of the city, or to be more precise, in the Scandinavian Bakery located there, which sold freshly brewed coffee and a delicious assortment of sandwiches and patisseries.

After a couple of days of relative inactivity, Rory and I decided to move on, taking a 160km 3 hour bus journey north to the town of Vang Viang, passing through beautiful lush green hills and dense forests on route. Occasionally we would see an ugly scar in a hillside, or smoke rising from the forest, which indicated the beginnings of the slash and burn technique of clearing, which will no doubt radically alter this beautiful landscape for the worse over the coming years.

On the bus was a Kiwi couple, Ian and Monica, who we'd met

previously on the nightmare bus journey from Hanoi to Vientiane. It was nice to continually bump into familiar faces as I made my way around the well trodden "gringo-trail" of South East Asia, especially after my lonely experiences at the start of my trip. It meant that I was never really on my own, even if I wanted to be.

Scenic Vang Viang is built on the east bank of the Nam Xong River, encircled by rolling hills to the east and jagged limestone escarpments to the west, jutting into the sky like spikes on a dragons back. The small town has just two streets, with an open market in its centre. However there was a busy backpacker scene here with a generous number of bars and restaurants, it was a perfect spot to relax and re-charge the batteries. It was not so much sleepy as downright comatose.

The following morning Ian, Monica, Rory and I met for breakfast in a cosy little restaurant, where Rich and Isabelle, who Rory and I had met on the Halong Bay tour, were already sat. The six of us decided to spend the afternoon partaking in Vang Viang's number one activity of "tubing", which is basically floating down the river in tractor inner tubes.

Although it was the dry season, there was just about enough water in the river to carry us downstream. We spent a wonderful six hours floating leisurely down the river, basking in the sunshine and taking in the wonderful scenery. The enterprising locals had set up makeshift bars at roughly one kilometre intervals along the river, from where they would hold out long bamboo poles to pull you in for regular pit stops of alcoholic refreshment. Throughout the day, we saw lots of happy, smiling kids playing and swimming in the river like water rats, some so small that I would imagine that they could probably swim better than they could walk.

Our little group met up again later for dinner, after which we retired to a typical Laos backpacker bar, with low-level tables and scatter cushions in-lieu of chairs, where we watched a DVD movie. Afterwards, Rory and I moved on to another bar to watch Arsenal take on Manchester United live on TV, whilst the rest of the group retired to bed.

Mary and Beth, who I had last seen in Hoi-An, were sat in the bar, and we joined them to watch the game, after which Rory went to bed whilst I stayed with the girls drinking until 4am, when the bar closed. I staggered back to my hotel to find that I had been locked out, and so I returned to the bar where the obliging owner allowed me to spend the night amongst a bed of scatter cushions.

I was awoken around 7am the following morning by the bar cleaner, who was trying to rearrange the scatter cushions amongst which I slept. I'm not sure exactly who got the biggest fright. I returned to my hotel which fortunately now was open, and I spent the rest of the day in bed feeling both tired and ill, possibly as a result of the twenty-six mosquito bites that I acquired, but more likely due to the excessive amounts of beer that I had consumed.

I forced myself up and out later to eat, even though I did not feel hungry. Afterwards I felt much worse, so I returned to my room and spent the rest of the night running back and forth to the toilet with diarrhoea, the first sickness of my trip.

The following day continued in much the same vain until there was simply nothing left in me to pass. I ventured out and walked down to the river, where I ran into Rory who was leaving town tonight. We agreed to stay in touch and meet up again in Thailand.

Come evening I was feeling much better and I ventured out to an internet café to check my e-mails, receiving message from Cass that she was in Vientiane and would be here tomorrow. I met with Rich and Isabelle for dinner, it transpired that both Rich and Monica had also been ill with diarrhoea, and so the cause must have been something that we had all eaten.

Having fully recovered, I rented a mountain-bike the following day, and set off to explore the surrounding countryside with a hand-drawn map that I had purchased. Unfortunately, the map bore no resemblance to the local area, and so after riding up and down numerous hilly, dead-end tracks in the sweltering heat, I gave up and headed to the river to cool-off. Abandoning my bike and clothes, I spent the rest of the afternoon chilling on the riverbank and taking the occasional dip into the refreshingly cold water.

When I returned to town later, I found Cass sat in a restaurant opposite to my hotel. She seemed as pleased to see me as I was to see her, saying that she had cut short her time in Vientiane in order to catch me up. We ate dinner together and then spent the night in a bar, carrying on from where we had left off, as if we had never been apart. We spent the following day at the river relaxing, chatting, reading, and playing with a group of local kids. That night a tropical storm brought torrential rain and a spectacular thunder and lightening show, which we watched from the safety of an open-fronted bar.

The following morning, after a fantastic week in Vang Viang, we caught the 9am bus to the former capital, Louang Prabang. The five-hour journey along the Old Royal Road was very pleasant, as we drove through meandering mountain roads with dramatic scenery, and for a change, there was ample room on the bus to stretch out.

Tiny, regal Louang Prabang was designated a World Heritage Site in 1995 and reminded me of Hoi-An in Vietnam. It stands on confluence of Mekong and Nam Khan Rivers in a dramatic valley ringed by steep mountains. Its quaint centre has an abundance of temples and watts, and traditional timber fronted shop-houses accommodating art and antique shops, restaurants and bakeries.

After dinner, Cass went for a massage and I headed to the bars, where I bumped into a few familiar faces, Rich and Isabelle in the first, and Ian and Monica and Barry and Sarah in the second. On my way back to the hotel, another storm erupted and in my rush to get back, I tried to take a shortcut down a side street and ended up getting lost. By the time that I had found my way back to my hotel, I was soaked through from head to toe.

The next day we climbed the three hundred and twenty steps to the summit of Phou Xi (sacred hill) temple overlooking the town and providing a stunning panorama of the Mekong and Nam Khan Rivers, the surrounding countryside and the distant mountains. Over the course of the day and evening we ran into Rich and Isabelle and Barry and Sarah, and we all arranged to meet up tomorrow and visit a spectacular waterfall of which we'd heard.

Over dinner I announced to Cass that I had decided to fly to Thailand in a couple of days time. She asked me to stay with her and go trekking in the north. I enjoyed her company very much and part of me wanted to stay with her, but I knew deep down that it was time to move on alone.

The following morning our little group met for breakfast, after which we negotiated with a tuk-tuk driver to carry us to Kouang Xi Waterfall, 35km away. We drove along a series of dirt roads, passing through several small hill-tribe villages, during which kids armed with water pistols and buckets of water continually soaked us. The excited kids were preparing for the forthcoming Songkran festival, which celebrates the Buddhist New Year. It seemed that the main purpose of the festival was to throw copious amounts of water over anyone and everyone. It was great fun and actually quite nice, as it helped to keep us cool in the scorching heat.

Our driver dropped us at the start of a track which we followed for around 15-minutes past several small falls and emerald green plunge pools, until we reached the base of the main waterfall, which consisted of four separate cascades tumbling over sixty metres.

We discovered a narrow steep path which we followed past the 'danger keep out signs' to the top of the falls, where we were rewarded with fantastic views over the surrounding countryside. From our vantage point, we were able to see the full splendour of the falls, which actually comprised of two separate falls, each of approximate equal height. The top falls discharged into an intermediate pool, which was hidden from the base, and which in turn tumbled into the lower pool. We climbed and scrambled down a steep, treacherous path to the pools edge, from where we all stripped of and dived in to the crystal clear, freezing cold water.

After breakfast the following day, I kissed Cass goodbye and headed to the smallest airport that I had ever been to, which comprised of just two rooms; the arrival and departure hall which contained just one check-in desk, and the departure lounge which was a small room with around twenty seats, which overlooked the solitary runway. We boarded a small propeller-driven aeroplane bound for Chiang Mai in Northern Thailand, which hardly surprisingly departed on time, as I think that this was the only flight of the day. The one-hour long flight was a real bargain at £40 when compared to the overland alternative, which would have saved me £15, but would have involved a two-day boat journey down the Mekong, followed by two long buses journeys.

I had thoroughly enjoyed my brief stay in Laos, so much so that I made a promise to myself that I would one-day return to explore the rest of this beautiful country, and give it the due amount of time that it surely deserves.

8

Ladyboys and Leaches (Thailand Revisited)

05/04/04 to 09/06/04

Within an hour of takeoff we were touching down in Chiang Mai in northern Thailand. I took a taxi to The Royal Guest House and checked into a basic but clean room. The price of the rooms at The Royal varies depending upon the floor you stay on, becoming cheaper as you go higher as there is no lift. My sixth floor room was just £3 per night, but the best thing about The Royal was that it was located in the thick of the action, close to the city moat and night bazaar, and that it had a swimming pool.

Chiang Mai has a striking mountain backdrop, over 300 temples and a quaint historical aura. The city was founded in 1296 and you can still see the moat that encircled the original city. It's also Thailand's second largest city with much to offer the visitor; food, accommodation and shopping are all top quality and cheap, and unlike Bangkok the nights are pleasantly cool.

For the first time in a couple of months I found myself alone, having left all my friends behind. I lazily spent my days relaxing by the hotel pool in the company of a book, unlike most travellers who come to Chiang Mai for adventure; trekking in the mountains, bamboo rafting, and visiting the local hill tribes, which I too had done on my first visit here a few years back. My nights were spent in the local restaurants and bars, or at the lively night bazaar, which sprawls along several blocks between the eastern moat and the river.

I could not miss the opportunity however to visit the mountain of Doi Suthep, standing 1,676 metres above sea level. A taxi carried me the sixteen kilometres distance up a winding road to the mountain, dropping me at the base of a three hundred and nine step stone staircase leading to the summit, which was guarded on either side by stone balustrades ornately carved in the form of giant serpents. Standing on the summit is Wat Phra, one of Thailand's most sacred wats and a major Buddhist pilgrimage site, consisting of shimmering golden stupas, buddah statues, and a bell house. Inside the temple is an exquisite, copper-plated chedi (a bell shaped tower) topped by a five-tiered gold umbrella. The aerial views of the city and surrounding countryside weren't bad either.

Its importance, as well as its location, owes much to the legend of its founding; a Buddha relic, which some say glowed, magically replicated just before it was about to be enshrined in the big chedi. A monk placed the relic on the back of a sacred white elephant, and it was decided that a temple would be built on the exact spot where the elephant stopped. The elephant eventually climbed to the top of Suthep Mountain, trumpeted three times, turned around three times, knelt down and died. And so King Ku Na built the original chedi here in 1388.

On my fourth day in Chiang Mai Cass arrived, but it turned out to be an unhappy reunion, as we ended the night rowing about religion of all things. I wasn't in the mood to argue over a subject that I had no interest in, and so I hailed a tuk-tuk, put Cass in it, and kissed her goodnight. The following morning I was awoken early by loud banging on my room door. I opened it to find Cass outside with her backpack. I allowed her in and we crashed out on the bed for another couple of hours and made up.

Afterwards I informed Cass that I had pre-arranged to meet two friends from home in Bangkok at Easter, and so would be leaving this evening. I invited her to join me but she declined, as she wanted to trek in the area. She then tried to talk me out of going, but I explained that my friends were travelling a long way to see me, and so I could not let them down. She accepted my decision, but for the rest of the day she kept reminding me that this would be the fourth time that I had left her. I promised that we would see each other again.

I arrived in the capital at 5am after an uneventful overnight bus journey. It was the eve of the Songkran Festival and so rooms in the Khao San area were in short supply, and those that were available were either very expensive or fleapits. Eventually though I managed to find a half-decent room for £4 per night.

I had a few errands to run and things to organise: I brought a wedding present for my friends John and Sarah, and I had 13 rolls of photographic film developed, both of which I hoped my friends would take home for me. From one of the areas many dive shops, I then booked a scuba-diving course on the island of Koh Tao.

Later on the afternoon I ran into Rory again, and we spent the rest of the day and evening in the local bars. We ended the night in Gulliver's Travellers Bar, which was packed to the brim with locals and travellers, some dancing, some playing pool, some watching football on TV, and some just drinking. We did a little of the first three and a lot of the fourth.

The next day Rory and I each checked out of our respective hotels and caught a taxi to the upmarket Sukhumvit area on the opposite side of the city, where my friends Toney and Coley were due to stay. Sukhumvit has many international hotels, restaurants and shops catering to foreign tourists, but no backpacker hotels. Eventually we found a cheapish room in the Ra-Jah Hotel.

I popped to the Nana Hotel later and by chance bumped into my friend Tony on the hotel car park. We shared a couple of beers and arranged to meet later for dinner, along with Tony's Thai girlfriend. We duly met up later and the three of us ate dinner together, followed by a few beers. Strangely Rory didn't show up, although I had invited him to join us. Tony would be heading north to meet his girlfriends parents tomorrow and so our reunion was brief, however my other friend Coley was due to arrive tomorrow, and so I looked forward to seeing him.

Returning to my hotel around midnight, I found the room empty. Rory returned about half hour later and we headed out together to sample the notorious nightlife and bars of Nana-Plaza. The majority of bars tend to have a friendly, laid-back atmosphere and they play a mixture of Thai and western music, often at high volume. The girls who work in these bars are generally uneducated and come from poor rural areas. They are usually aged 18 to 25, dressed modestly in jeans and T-shirt, and are very pretty. Many of them work to support their families, often eventually returning to their villages with a nest egg. Within minutes of sitting down, you can be assured that a girl will sit beside you, look into your eyes, smile and say "alo, wat yur name? wher yu from?"

The Go-Go Bars are a different kettle of fish however. They are generally unfriendly, less laid-back, dark and seedy, and contain a stage on which the girls' dance in skimpy clothes, swim suits, or their underwear, sometimes with numbers attached to them as if for sale. These bars are the human equivalent of a cattle market.

The patrons of these Go-Go bars are a varied and strange bunch; they could be old, fat, hunch-backed, and have a face like a robber's dog, but from the moment they sit down in one of Nana-Plaza's bars, a bevy of the most beautiful girls will descend on them like flies around a dogs arse.

Thailand's sex industry however is greatly over-exaggerated by the western media. According to international human development reports, around 200,000 Thais offer sex services, that is around 3% of the population, which ranks well below India, Taiwan and many western countries. The difference in Thailand is that prostitution, although illegal since the 1950's, is very much considered part of everyday life, whilst in the west it takes place firmly behind closed doors. Thailand has a long-standing concubinary tradition and until the mid 20th century, most men of wealth had at least one mistress, and often several. Indeed the traditional Thai system mia yai (major wife, minor wife) made it sociably acceptable for a man to have many mistresses. You may recall King Rama IV, from the film 'The King and I' who had many concubines.

Sukhumvit was much too expensive for Rory, and so he returned the next day to Khao San. I headed to the Nana Hotel in search of Coley, who by chance had just arrived. We headed straight to a local bar to catch up and within minutes we were both soaked through and our faces had been painted with a water and dough mixture. It was the first day proper of the Songkran festival and the streets were lined with revellers, armed as in Laos with buckets of water and water pistols.

We partied until the early hours, before returning to Coleys twin-bed room, which he had kindly invited me to share. We checked out of the Nana Hotel the next day and tried to catch a taxi to Khao San. However the first two drivers we approached refused to go near to Khao San as they said that the streets there were bedlam and impassable. Luckily though the third driver agreed to take us.

We arrived to find that the taxi-drivers were right; the party here was in full-swing and the entire district of several streets was crammed with thousands of Thais and westerners, merrily dancing, drinking and of course, throwing water. In order to drop off our bags, we attempted to make our way to the dive-shop from where I had booked my dive-course, and from where I was due to catch my overnight bus this evening to Koh Tao. However the crowds were so great that we were carried along with them, often in the opposite direction to that which we wanted to go.

Eventually we reached the shop and dropped our bags off, before returning to the party. At 4pm Coley departed on a bus to the beach resort of Pattaya; It had been good to see my old friends after so long away from home, all be it briefly. I partied on until around 8pm, when I too departed to catch my bus.

Although the bus was quite luxurious, the journey was very uncomfortable on account of my wet clothes. We reached the port town of Chumphon at 5am and after a short wait, we boarded the ferry for the three-hour crossing to Koh Tao.

Koh Tao (Turtle Island), along with Koh Samui and Koh Pha-Ngan, is part of an archipelago of eighty islands located in the southern Gulf of Thailand, of which only six are inhabited. Due to the abundance of marine life and coral, it is Thailand's diving Mecca, and its surrounding waters have a good visibility of between ten and thirty meters and have a constant, pleasantly warm temperature of around 30-degrees Celsius.

The ferry docked at the pier at the islands main town of Ban Mae Hat, where a guy from the dive school was waiting to pick me up and drive me to Buddah View Resort at Chalok Baan Kao beach. The resort was located right on the beachfront and boasted several chalet style rooms, a dive shop, a classroom block, a small swimming pool, and a bar and restaurant which overlooked the sea, whilst just outside the resort was a mini-supermarket, an internet café, and a pharmacy.

The horseshoe shaped bay was straight out of a postcard, with giant spherical shaped rocks standing at either end which looked like natural sculptures, sandwiched between which was a fine white sand beach with swaying coconut palms and azure coloured sea shimmering in the sunlight.

Later on the afternoon I was introduced to the head dive-instructor, Jack from England, and my three fellow students, Marleen and Amarilla from Sweden and Kelly from California. I must admit that I felt rather lucky to be in this group as they were all young, beautiful, fit and female. Life doesn't get much better than this I thought.

We completed a questionnaire and watched a video presentation of the Padi (Professional Association of Dive Instructors) Open-Water Dive Course, which we would all be taking over the coming four days. The following morning I found myself in the classroom for the first time in many years, learning the principals of buoyancy and water pressure, and the basic scuba techniques. We then sat two simple multiple-choice tests, which we all passed without any difficulty.

We broke for lunch before meeting again on the afternoon at the pool, where our instructor Alex from Germany, and his assistant Trent from Australia, kitted us out with, and taught us how to set up, all the necessary equipment. Once in the pool, we practised a number of under-water techniques over and over again until we had all mastered them, including various hand signals, removing and de-misting our masks, clearing and removing our regulator hose through which you breath, reading our pressure gauges which indicates the amount of air we have left in our tanks, and just in case we should run out of air, we were taught how to share an air-supply with a dive-buddy.

The next day a truck drove us to pier from where we boarded a dive-boat, which carried us to Ao Leuk (Deep Bay) for our first sea dive. We practised the same under-water techniques again, sometimes kneeling on the seabed in just 4 or 5 feet of water, after which Alex led us on an underwater swim around the bay, going down to a depth of 5 metres. There wasn't much marine-life to see, but it was a good experience all the same.

We spent the following morning again in the classroom

studying more diving theory, followed by two more multiple-choice tests and a final examination, which was more difficult than the tests. After lunch, we were driven to the pier for our first two proper sea dives. As the boat headed out, I mentioned to Alex that I felt a little queasy. Alex immediately told me that if I was even the slightest unwell, then I could not dive. I was gutted as I knew that I was well enough to dive, but I understood that Alex could not take any chances.

As Alex, Trent and the girls submerged, I sat quietly on the boat, realising that I would now be one day behind my group and therefore I would have to join another group. The girls completed both dives, and on our return to the pier they chatted excitedly about their experience and the fish that they had seen. I was pleased for them but at the same time I felt very envious.

There was a friendly atmosphere and a good international mix at Buddah View, amongst both the dive students and the instructors, who were generally European, with a couple of Japanese and Australian thrown in for good measure. There were also a large number of trainee instructors here such as Trent, many of who had stayed on at the resort after themselves passing their Open Water Course here.

My evenings were generally spent in the company of my group and a couple of the trainee instructors including Tom from Weymouth and his German girlfriend Sabine, Peter from Poland, Harriet from England and Robin from Manchester, who I spent the most time with as we were of a similar age and outlook. Robin had quit his job, sold his house and left home to travel the world, however after three months he was still in his first destination of Thailand.

We usually hung out in the resorts beachside bar and restaurant, or in one of the several nearby resorts, which all had similar facilities. On a couple of occasions we travelled by share-taxi to the islands main town of Ban Mae Hat, or to the more developed Sairee Beach, which both had a wider choice of restaurants and bars and was generally livelier. My favourite haunt was AC Bar, which had a large dance floor and a private beach, lit at night by fire torches and candles floating in the sea. We would usually sit on bamboo mats on the beach, drink, chat, and watch the spectacular nightly fire shows, in which dancers performed whilst twirling flaming battens.

The next afternoon I met my new dive instructor, Phil from Scotland, his English assistant Chantel, and my new group of three English friends who were here on a two-week holiday. We boarded the dive-boat and headed to the first dive site called White Rock, which comprised of a wide band of coral reef with an impressive diversity of hard and soft corals. We dived to a depth of 12metres and we saw numerous species of exotic looking fish including: wrasse, butterfly, angel, morays, clown and trigger.

I struggled initially with my buoyancy and even crashed into rocks and corals on a couple of occasions, cutting my fingers in the process. Mid-way through the dive however, everything I'd been taught clicked into place, and I was suddenly able to glide through the water, like a bird floating on the thermals, able to control my body position through my breathing pattern, rising as I inhaled and falling as I exhaled. It was the most amazing feeling of freedom and weightlessness. We surfaced after 38 minutes and clambered back on board the boat, where the crew had prepared some light refreshments. I felt ecstatic.

One hour later we had arrived at the second dive-site called Japanese Garden, with hundreds of hard and soft coral formations creating the impression of an oriental garden. Whilst kneeling in a circle on the seabed practising a few skills, a large Napoleon Wrasse, about one and a half metres in length, approached and swam amongst us. This fish was so tame that it allowed Phil to stroke it, and it followed us for the remainder of our dive, which again lasted 38 minutes. With good visibility of 15metres, we again saw an abundance of small multi-coloured coral fish.

There was an air of expectation and excitement on the boat the following day as we headed to a site called Chumphon Pinnacle, comprising four granite pinnacles carpeted with anemones, which is considered to be the best dive site in the area, as well as being home to reef sharks. The girls from my old group were also on board, on the first day of their advanced course, having completed their Open Water course yesterday. Phil had taken ill and so I had my third instructor in as many days, Julie from England supported by Chantel again.

We entered the sea using the 'James Bond forward roll' method and as we had now all mastered all of the necessary skills, we spent the entire 40-minute dive exploring this wonderful underwater world, diving to a depth of 18metres and with 25metre visibility, we saw stingray, giant grouper, tuna and large shoals of barracuda and batfish, as well as the usual assortment of small reef fish. Unfortunately we saw no sharks, but I did see my old group at one point, such a strange experience bumping into familiar faces at the bottom of the sea.

We practised underwater navigation techniques using wrist compasses at our second and final dive site called Twins, so named because it is formed of two groups of granite rocks, which are covered in corals and sponges, divided by sandy patches and a colourful coral garden. Again we saw more of the usual marine-life plus blue spotted rays, scorpion fish and pink anemones.

Back at the resort-bar later, having satisfactorily completed four dives and having passed all of the theory tests, we were confirmed as qualified open-water divers and awarded with our certificates, logbooks and PADI membership cards. I spent the evening again in the company of my old-group, visiting a restaurant in the town of Mae Haad, during which I developed a severe earache and became unable to equalise the pressure in my ears. I returned to the resort and sought help from the nurse at the pharmacy. After a brief inspection, I was told that I had developed an ear infection. I was given some eardrops and antibiotics, and told not to dive for a few days until it had cleared.

I decided to stay on at Buddha View for a few more days as I hoped to complete my advanced dive course once the infection had cleared. However, as I was unable to swim or drink alcohol whilst on medication, I was finding it difficult to be in the company of Robin and Trent. So I spent the next few days relaxing on the beach during the day, and watching the nightly movies at the resort bar.

Although my tan was coming on very nicely, I was becoming bored and frustrated, especially when everyone else seemed to be having such a great time. I was also off my food and I was having problems sleeping, whilst my ear showed no signs of recovery. After a few days I decided to visit another clinic in Ban Mae Hat and seek a second opinion. The nurse took one look at my ear and said, "Your ear full wax, drops no work". She cleaned my ears and gave me a different course of antibiotics.

After a couple of more days of inactivity, and with my ears still no better, I decided to put the advanced dive course on hold and move on. I took a one and a half hour ferry crossing to the nearby island of Koh Pha-Ngan, a tranquil island retreat popular amongst backpackers, with pristine beaches and secluded coves, however it is more famous for its legendary full moon parties, which attract thousands of revellers each month.

At the pier were several pick-up trucks, each displaying signs for the various resorts around the island. I climbed into the back of a truck displaying the name Thong Nai Pan Yai, a beautiful remote bay located on the north-east coast. This area is relatively undeveloped and is still pretty wild, and accessible by only one road, which initially was good, but before long the tarmac ended and we were driving along a steep and rutted dirt road, over hills and through dense jungle-like vegetation.

The softly curved white sand bay surrounded by mountains covered in rich tropical rainforest was indeed the image of paradise. I selected a simple wooden beach bungalow which had a veranda, 24hour electricity, fan and a bathroom, for just £3 per night. The bungalow style resorts here were well spaced out giving a feeling of tranquillity, and for the next few days I relaxed, read and generally lazed on the beach or in my newly purchased hammock that I had strung up on my veranda.

Because of the medication, I still couldn't go into the sea or drink alcohol, and consequently within a few days I was again feeling bored and lonely. I was finding it difficult to meet people, maybe I just wasn't making enough effort, or perhaps I was feeling sorry for myself. The bars here seemed a little too bohemian for my liking, with resident guitar strumming hippies in most, and 24hour Bob Marley in the rest.

I was at a low-point at this time, but thanks to the power of the Internet and 'instant messaging,' I was able to keep in regular contact with several of my close friends back home, which helped to keep my spirits up.

My earache had gone but I was still unable to equalise, so I took a taxi to the islands one and only hospital in the main town of Thong Sala, which was really just a clinic. A doctor carried out a brief examination of my ear and confirmed that the infection had healed, but my right ear canal was excessively red and swollen. She prescribed a different type of antibiotic and advised me that if the problem was no better in three days time, to visit a specialist at the International Hospital on the nearby island of Koh Samui.

After less than one week on Koh Pha-Ngan I decided to move on, catching the ferry to Koh Samui, the regions major tourist destination, nicknamed the coconut island as it produces more than one million coconuts for export each month.

Knowing that there would be much there to keep me occupied, I headed to the islands main resort of Chaweng Beach, which is a true international resort with accommodation to suit every budget and hundreds of shops stocking an array of local and international goods. Chaweng is also the nightlife capital of Samui with numerous bars, pubs, nightclubs, cafes, and wonderful restaurants serving food from all over the world, as well as all of the major multinational chains including: McDonalds, KFC, Pizza Hut and Starbucks, and an assortment of English, Irish, German and Scandinavian bars and restaurants. Although I hadn't travelled half way around the world to frequent such establishments, it was a nice change whilst I was feeling unwell.

Chaweng was unfortunately very expensive, and so my choice of accommodation was a little limited. I eventually found a reasonable room, for a reasonable price, in a reasonably central location. The only drawback was that the room was located in the same building as Chaweng's premiere 'lady-boy' cabaret theatre, which performed nightly Vegas style shows. The performers were all male, or more correctly were all once male, most of who have either had or were having sex-change treatment. They were all extremely convincing with their big hair, high heels and elaborate sequined dresses, and I don't mind admitting that I have been with much uglier girls!

The seven kilometre long beach at Chaweng was beautiful, with soft, white sand and lined with coconut palms, which provided a nice shade from the scorching sun. Once you've settled in your spot, there is no need to move again, as there are plenty of vendors pounding the beach selling fruit, fried chicken, ice cream, drinks, sarongs, t-shirts and an assortment of souvenirs.

Although busier than any of the other beaches that I'd been on, it was still relatively quiet and was a great place to people watch. On one occasion I watched a group of around twenty Israelis attempting a world record for cramming the highest number of people onto one beach towel. Why they were so tightly congregated when there was plenty of space on the beach I have no idea.

Another of my favourite people-watching venues was Soi Green Mango, a street of lively outdoor bars, restaurants, and food stalls, at the end of which is the popular Green Mango nightclub. As the night progresses, the entire street becomes one enormous outdoor party, with each bar playing its own brand of music at maximum volume. The street attracted a mix of male and female, and Thai and westerner punters, many of whom seem to come here just to party, while others seemed to be here to meet members of the opposite sex.

Still unable to equalise my hearing, I visited the Koh Samui International Hospital, for a prearranged appointment to see an ear specialist, who was unavailable as he was in a meeting. So I was taken by ambulance to a private clinic, where a specialist tested my earring with a tuning fork, and checked the passageways in my ears, nose and throat for blockages. She confirmed that the infection had indeed now cleared, but that I had suffered a ruptured eardrum. Fortunately, she reassured me that the damage was not permanent and the swelling should subside in a few days time. I was very relieved indeed.

After a pleasant week on Samui, I decided to head to Khao Sok National Park, where I had arranged to meet up with Cass again. Before departing, realising that there would be limited provisions at Khao Sok, I brought a book, photo film, insect repellent and tobacco, which the doctor had advised me to take to rub into my skin, as it apparently repelled leeches, which are aplenty in Khao Sok.

From Na Thom pier on Samui, I took another ferry to Don Sak on the mainland, passing through Ang Thong Marine National Park, which contains 42 limestone islands of weird and wonderful shapes formed by erosion. Some have caves and secluded beaches surrounded by coral reefs, while others have sheer rock-faces, rising hundreds of metres vertically out of the sea. This is part of the same prehistoric reef system that I had seen at Halong Bay in Vietnam, and which I would see more off at Khao Sok and on Thailand's Andaman Coast later.

Don Sak was not so much a town as a ferry pier, being the closest point on the mainland to Samui. Its coastline was stunningly beautiful, with more limestone monoliths and mountains rising vertically out of the blue ocean, and lush, dense green woodland sandwiched between which was a glorious palm tree lined white sand beach.

A mini-bus carried me to a travel-agents office in the city of Surat Thani, from where I was put into a tuk-tuk with a middle-aged German couple. Whilst waiting for the driver, the husband said, "My ticket says 11.20 and it is now 11.24, this is not good enough."

I presumed that they had just arrived and probably weren't too familiar with Asian ways, so with a smile I said, "This is Asia not Europe, time as little meaning here".

With a confused expression on his face, he repeated, "But my ticket says 11.20."

The tuk-tuk driver soon arrived and conveyed us to the bus-park, from where I boarded the next bus bound for Khao Sok. The three-hour journey carried us through a dramatic, prehistoric looking landscape of dense jungle and huge limestone monoliths shrouded in mist.

Covering an area of 739 square km, Khao Sok National Park is one of Thailand's best-kept secrets, encompassing the oldest evergreen rainforest in the world, said to be 160-million years old. Straddling the central mountain range of the Thai-Malay peninsula, Khao Sok owes its stunning beauty and rich biodiversity to rainfall and geography. Monsoon rains sweeping in from both the Andaman Sea and the Gulf of Thailand are trapped by the densely forested mountains, bringing a deluge of 3,500mm of annual rain, making it the wettest place in all of Thailand.

Lush tropical evergreen forests, deep valleys, rivers, lakes, caves, and towering limestone crags, shrouded in veils of cloud and morning mist, lend a haunting beauty to this landscape. It isn't the dramatic beauty however, but rather the extraordinary diversity of flora and fauna that elevates Khao Sok from the merely scenic to the unbelievable.

The richness of the tropical forest flora, the abundance of fresh water and the shelter of the mountains combine to provide one of Asia's last viable habitats for large mammals needing extensive ranges for their survival. Residing here are 48 mammal spices including: elephant, tiger, leopard, tapir, Malay sun bear, Asiatic black bear, otter, gibbon and several monkey species; over 180 bird spices including several kinds of eagle and hornbill; several snake and reptile species including cobra and python; hundreds of insect and arachnids including scorpion, tarantula and golden orb web spider; and an amazing 38 spices of bat.

Tall emergent trees and a tangle of figs and woody climbers dominate the dense forest, whilst evergreens such as bamboo, rattan, ferns and palms all fight for light beneath the canopy. It is also home to many varieties of orchid and three species of plants that are not found anywhere else in the world including the very rare parasitic Rafflesis Kerri Meijer, which is the World's largest flower with a diameter of 80cm.

I disembarked the bus at the edge of the park where around a dozen brochure brandishing resort owners and touts were waiting. I had pre-arranged to meet Cass at Arts Resort, but no one from that resort had turned out to meet the bus. Luckily a friendly lady name Toi, who owned one of the other resorts, offered to drive me there. In a new four-wheel drive truck, we drove into the forest following several narrow dirt tracks to Arts Resort, but unfortunately Cass wasn't there. Toi offered to take me to her resort, which she said was the nicest in all of Khao Sok, and as she had been kind enough to assist me, I accepted her invitation.

We drove on for another half hour, further into the forest along bumpy and part flooded dirt roads until we reached Toi's resort called Far Out, which certainly lived up to its name. It was the remotest of the parks resorts, set deep in the forest on the banks of a small river, and in the shadow of a towering limestone mountain. It contained six wooden guest bungalows and Toi's family home, which also doubled as the resort restaurant. Each bungalow was constructed above the forest floor on stilts with a flight of steps leading up to an open verandah, and they were well spread out, giving a feeling of isolation. It was a beautiful, secluded location, and ideal for anyone looking for a real jungle experience, and I was the only guest.

"How much you like to pay" Toi asked.

"As little as possible" I replied.

"Ok for you 100 baht, now rainy season, this ok for you?" Toi responded.

100-Baht was equivalent to £1.50 and so I didn't hesitate. After settling in to my bungalow, I returned to the restaurant where Toi informed me that she had made some enquiries and had tracked down Cass to another resort. She took me there on her motorbike, but unfortunately the single female who had checked in earlier was not Cass.

We returned to Far Out where I ate dinner with Toi's family. Toi told me that she, like most of the other resort owners, was born and bred in this area and that the entire community were like one big family, all looking out for one another. It was a nice concept. After dinner I returned to my bungalow where I sat in total darkness on my verandah, listening to the wonderfully deafening sound of the jungle all around me.

I was rudely awoken early the next morning by thudding noises on my bungalow roof, followed by high-pitched screams and screeches, and the sounds of branches snapping. I lay silently for a few seconds, my eyes darting between the door and the shuttered window wandering what was outside. The sounds grew more distant and so I climbed from the safety of my bed and mosquito net, pulled on a pair of shorts, and headed to the restaurant. Toi's family were going about their daily business and seemed unconcerned by the commotion. I pointed towards the source of the noise, which by now was some distance away. "Monkeys" said Toi's sister Yah, in a matter of fact way.

I ordered breakfast and sat watching the monkeys playing in the treetops about 50metres from the restaurant. Toi pulled up in her truck with Cass sat alongside her, who she had picked up off the morning bus. I carried her backpack to the bungalow and we returned to the restaurant for breakfast.

Immediately afterwards, feeling brave we set off to explore the jungle, following an overgrown track that looked as though it had seen very little use recently. I walked into a thick cobweb, which wrapped itself around me. Seeing a huge spider fall to the floor, Cass screamed and ran ahead, leaving me to untangle myself. The track ended at the rivers edge and continued again on the opposite bank. We presumed that it must have been fairly shallow so we waded across, only to find that it was actually waist high. We continued along the trail for another half hour, but after being stung by numerous insects, pricked by various sharp plants, sinking into gooey mud, and with dark clouds drawing in, we decided to return to the resort. April was the beginning of the monsoon season here, which brings heavy rain on most afternoons or evenings, combined with sweltering temperatures and high humidity.

Over dinner two new guests who had arrived earlier in the day, Scott from Aberdeen and Miranda from Wales joined us. We were all keen to see more of the jungle and Toi suggested a two-day trip to the Khlong Pha Saeng Lake in the center of the jungle, which she could arrange for £30 each. It sounded like a perfect trip and so we arranged to go in the morning.

The four of us met for breakfast, before setting off to the lake 60km away in the back of a pick-up truck with our guide Nok. Once there we boarded a long-tail boat with an outboard motor, and we set off across the stunning manmade lake, 165km at its longest point, constructed around twenty years ago after the valley was flooded. Rising vertically out of the vast body of water, and out of the surrounding dense jungle, were more mysterious looking limestone mountains and monoliths providing an eerie feel to the beautiful surroundings.

After a pleasant two-hour journey across the lake, we reached a small wooden restaurant with a jetty, attached to which were several floating, raft bungalows constructed of bamboo. These basic floating huts would be our overnight accommodation.

After lunch, I rubbed my tobacco over my feet and ankles and Nok guided us on a jungle trek, during which we saw lots of wildlife: long-tail macaques sitting high in the trees, lizards and various other reptiles and amphibians, scorpions and spiders, dozens of bird species including eagles and the great horn bill, which are easily identifiable before they come into sight by the deep whooshing sound its large wings make when they fly.

Every ten minutes or so we would stop and check our feet and ankles for leeches, removing them by forcing them off with twigs. It was important to check regularly as the leaches grow dramatically in size and become harder to remove, the longer they have been feeding on your blood.

After a couple of hours we reached Nam Talu Cave, with beautiful stalactite & stalagmite formations, and a river running through it. We entered and in torchlight we followed the river through the one kilometre long cave, wading through the shallow sections, swimming through the deep sections, and sliding down ledges and waterfalls where necessary. The one-hour adventure was an exhilarating experience and well worth the collection of leeches and insect bites that we suffered.

We returned to our floating bungalows and with no showers, we swam in the lake to freshen up before dinner, after which we sat in candlelight chatting and listening to the sounds of the jungle. The girls went to bed around 11pm, while Scott and I stayed up until midnight, during which I had my first beer and Sang Tip (Thai whisky) for over two weeks.

The following day we trekked, scrambled and climbed for two hours up to a 300m high viewpoint, enjoying stunning uninterrupted views across the lake and jungle canopy, which spread to the horizon like a huge green blanket. Afterwards we returned to our boat and continued our exploration of the lake, motoring towards small bays before cutting the engine and allowing our momentum to carry us silently towards the bank so as not to disturb the wildlife.

We stopped for lunch at another floating restaurant, during which a spectacular storm blew in, its fierce winds and torrential rain whipped up huge waves on the previously placid lake causing the floating restaurant to bob violently up and down. Within an hour the storm had passed over, and we were able to continue back across the lake to the pier, where Toi was waiting to drive us back to her resort.

That evening I sat up with Toi and her family chatting, whilst the others retired to bed early after dinner. Suddenly the restaurant was swamped by a plague of moths, obviously attracted by the light. Toi's family became very excited, running around squatting the creatures with anything they could get their hands on, and collecting them in a large plastic drum.

The next day we set off on a ten-kilometre trek to a waterfall, accompanied by Toi's family, who each carried with them a paper bag containing snacks of the local delicacy, fried moth. Throughout the day, Cass hardly left Nok's side, leaving me to walk with Scott and Miranda. However, I was enjoying the company of my fellow Brits more than that of Cass, and so I didn't mind. On a couple of occasions, Cass would ask me what was wrong, obviously wanting me to be jealous of the attention she was paying to Nok and wanting a reaction. But the truth was that I had now lost all interest in her and I was fed up with her adolescent games, and so when I told her there was nothing wrong, I really wasn't lying.

The leaches absolutely loved the taste of my tobacco soaked blood, so much so that by the time we reached the waterfall, I had removed a total of twelve from my feet and ankles. We swam in the refreshing waters of the pool beneath the falls, and sat for a while to rest. On the long trek back, I made the fatal mistake of not stopping to remove leeches, so that by the time that we had reached the resort, four huge leeches, swollen to many times their original size, had clamped themselves to my feet. After a struggle, I managed to remove them all, but I was left with blood pouring from my wounds, which I could not stop as leech bites contain an anti-coagulant. My wounds looked far worse than they were however, and there was actually little pain.

That evening, Cass and I each packed our rucksacks ready to move on to Malaysia in the morning, however with our relationship in tatters, I had decided to go it alone. Instead of heading to the Perhentian Islands as we'd previously planned, I decided to head to Kuala Lumpur in order to get as far away from Cass as I could.

The following morning I woke early and left while Cass was still asleep. She had no idea that I was leaving without her and after her behaviour, I felt as though I owed her no explanation. Toi gave me a lift to main road where I intended to catch the first local bus of the day at 7.30am. Unfortunately though I missed the bus by a couple of minutes and the next one wasn't due for another hour. I knew that if I waited Cass would soon be along, and I did not want to argue with her anymore, so I made some enquiries and discovered that there was a mini-bus departing to the city of Krabi at 8.30am.

Once aboard the mini-bus, I realised that I'd left my rather expensive Gortex jacket with Cass, so I asked the bus driver to stop at the public bus stop where I expected Cass to now be waiting. I got off the bus and walked across the road to where Cass was indeed waiting. "Do you have my jacket?" I asked. She opened her backpack, pulled out my jacket and handed it to me without saying a word. I returned to the mini-bus and we were headed off. That was the last I saw of Cass.

The bus arrived a few hours later in Krabi, another spectacular region with towering cliffs and yet more dramatic limestone features, similar to those on the gulf coast. I decided to spend a couple of days here and visit the strange and beautiful Phang-Nga Bay, which contains hundreds of tiny, vegetation covered, limestone islands. In days gone-by, Phang Nga was a favourite haunt of pirates, as its islands contain many hidden caves and tunnels, some of which lead to interior lagoons, known locally as hongs.

In order to get a close-up view of the bay, I booked a boat and kayaking trip, which although a little touristy, was an excellent way of exploring the area and provided the opportunity to discover some of the islands, caves and beaches.

We paddled in sturdy inflatable canoes to one island and entered a small cave, which we followed in torchlight. At the end of the cave we were able to see sunlight through a small opening, however the gap between the ocean surface and the rocks above was too low to pass through. We sat patiently for about ten minutes waiting for the tide to lower sufficiently to allow us to pass. The tide did lower slightly, but there was still insufficient room, so our guides jumped overboard to provide us with enough room to lie flat in the canoe. They then deflated some of the air out to reduce the height of the canoe in the water, and with just inches between the top of the canoes and the bottom of the rocks, our guides then pushed us through the opening.

We emerged suddenly into bright sunlight and the unique, hidden realms of the mystical hong, a collapsed cave system open to the sky and surrounded by towering limestone walls, surprisingly rich in unspoiled vegetation and wildlife, including hundreds of monkeys and birds.

Later we visited Koh Ping-Gan, famous for its huge pillar like rock which rises out of the ocean, which was immortalised in the Bond movie 'The Man With The Golden Gun'. The entire area surrounding this island is indeed spectacular, but the beauty was somewhat ruined by the number of tourists here and the tacky market selling souvenirs, which had sadly been erected on the nearby beach.

I had hoped to re-visit the beautiful Andaman Islands of Phuket and Phi-Phi, two of my favourite places in Thailand. Unfortunately though, my visa had already expired and so I decided to skip them. Little did I know at the time, but these islands and there friendly inhabitants would be devastated in a few months time by the 2004 Boxing-Day Tsunami.

After five weeks in Thailand, it was finally time to depart and so I took a bus from Krabi to Hat Yai in the deep south of Thailand, which had been marred by recent violence following Islamic uprisings. Luckily I saw no trouble and I was soon on another bus bound for Penang in Malaysia. At the border I was fined £15 as my visa had expired, and after paying with the last of my Thai baht, I re-boarded the bus and entered Malaysia.

9

A Little Piece of England
(Malaysia and Singapore)
10/05/04 to 15/05/04

The bus drove onto the vehicle ferry for the short 20-minute ride across The Straits of Malaka to George Town, the capital city of the island of Penang, where we arrived around 8pm. Named after Britain's King George III, George Town was founded in 1786 by the British East India Company as a base for the company in the Malay States and it is the oldest British settlement in Malaysia.

My onward bus to Kuala Lumpur was due to depart at 11.30pm and so I set off to make the most of my 3hours here. Although modern skyscrapers rise out of city, its streets still retain a distinct Chinese flavour and are alive with antiquity and tradition, wet markets and bazaars, traditional trades and retail shops, trishaw peddlers and hawkers. It is a living historic city and an architectural gem with one of the largest collections of 19th and early 20th century buildings in Southeast Asia.

My third bus of the day duly departed on time, crossing the Penang Bridge to the mainland, one of the longest bridges in the world, and before long I was asleep again. I was not too pleased when we arrived in the Kuala Lumpur at 3.30am the next morning, as the travel agent had advised me that the bus would arrive at 6am, thus saving me the cost of a night's accommodation. As it was I would now have to find and pay for a room for the remainder of the night, which would be difficult at such an early hour. I boarded a taxi and asked the driver to take me to a cheap hotel. He took me to Attapsana Homestay located in the heart of the city in an area known as the Golden Triangle. Unfortunately the hotel was closed and so I rang the doorbell waking the entire household. An elderly lady opened the door and welcomed me inside her home, where I took a small room for £5 per night; not exactly what I was looking for, but I couldn't say no after waking all of her family.

The next morning I woke early and set off to explore the Golden Triangle; a small city in itself, dominated by the world famous Petronas Twin Towers, standing 452metres high, which have become one of the city's main symbols and were the tallest building in the world until less than one year ago, when the Taipei 101 Financial Centre was completed at 508metres.

Set in an enormous tropical garden, the Twin Towers are a striking glass-and-steel combination consisting of two similarly shaped towers joined by a 58metres long double-decker sky-bridge at the 41st and 42nd floors, 175metres above street level. At ground level is the KLL Centre, a 6-storey retail podium housing a discovery centre, an 864-seat concert hall, an art gallery, a food court and a luxurious shopping gallery containing the most exclusive collection of stores that I had ever seen under one roof. Alas I could not afford to shop in any of the outlets on my meagre budget.

Unfortunately, this being a Monday the sky-bridge viewing platform was closed, so I headed to the Menara Telecommunication Tower, at 421metres high it is Asia's tallest and the fourth tallest tower in the world. Luckily it was open and I took the elevator, which transported me 276metres in under 1minute to the tower head, which holds a revolving restaurant and the public observation platform, with stuning panoramic views of the city.

I spent the afternoon and evening exploring the remainder of Golden Triangle, surrounded on all sides by ultra-modern shopping, commerce and entertainment outlets including cinemas, bowling alleys, pubs, clubs and live music venues. This area also contained all of the expensive hotels and restaurants, including many western fast food outlets and a few that I had never seen before, such as "Kenny Rogers Roasters" chicken restaurant.

The following day I put on the same smelly clothes as yesterday as all my other clothes were being laundered following my week in the jungle. I was joined at breakfast by a friendly English couple on the first leg of their travels, three Irish girls, and a Belgian girl who had been travelling for only 8 weeks but was a real know-it-all and already an expert on Asia, advising the others on the region. Her geography wasn't too good and so I corrected her a couple of times. She didn't reply but instead gave me a dirty look.

The Irish girls were on a three-week holiday visiting Singapore for one week, Malaysia for a second before returning to Singapore for the third. "I love Asia, especially Singapore", one of the girls said.

"Me too, but Thailand is my favourite" I replied.

"I have no interest in visiting Thailand" she replied, in a matter of fact way.

"How many times have you visited Asia?" I asked.

"This is my first time".

"It's my fifth visit and I also love Singapore, but in my opinion it is the least Asian city here" I retorted.

She didn't reply, and realising that I was making enemies quickly, I made a hasty exit and headed off to explore further.

I walked to the nearest monorail station and asked if there was a tourist all-day ticket available.

"Where do you want to go?" the attendant asked.

"Everywhere, I'm a tourist" I replied.

"But where do you want to go?"

"Everywhere, I want to see the entire city, I'm a tourist".

"Yes, but where exactly do you want to go?" she asked again

"Oh forget it, I'll walk" I responded, before heading off on foot.

I returned to the twin towers in the hope of visiting the free viewing platform, which was open, however first I had to obtain a timed ticket and so I patiently queued. I requested a ticket for the latest available time and was allocated a 4.45pm slot, after which I took a subway train to Chinatown.

Colourful Chinatown is a congested blend of shops and markets, activity and noise, where generations of Chinese immigrants have lived in the narrow streets and traded their goods from ground floor shophouses while living upstairs. The opium dens, gambling houses and brothels of the old red light district now frantically trade as shops selling everything imaginable. The central section, Jalan Petaling, is a frantically busy market that is closed to traffic and alive with music and giddy aromas from local food stalls. As I walked north, I came into a strangely familiar looking area with elegant colonial buildings and a cricket pitch. Merdeka Square was once a focal point for the British colonial presence in Malaysia, and the area where they replicated a little piece of Victorian England, with benches set amongst flower gardens, gently cascading fountains and the gothic style Cathedral of St. Mary the Virgin, built in 1895.

The buildings surrounding the square blend an intriguing mix of Moorish and Victorian detail. Situated on one corner of the square is the mock-Tudor Selangor Club, built in 1884, which continues to welcome the elite of society, much as it did during the height of the British empire.

Dominating several blocks opposite is the Sultan Abdul Samad building, constructed by the British in 1897 as the seat of the colonial government, but which now houses the Supreme and High Courts. It is a grand, beautiful and powerful looking building with Moorish-inspired arches, and a 40-metre clock tower affectionately dubbed "Big Ben", topped with a golden dome and flanked on both sides by two majestic domed towers.

The graceful KL Railway Station was built in 1910 and features more Moorish-style horseshoe shaped arches. Renovated in 1988, the station now provides air-conditioned comfort and modern facilities for rail passengers bound for Thailand, Singapore and within Malaysia. Across the street is the Malayan Railway Administration Building, another Moorish extravagance from the British colonial period.

Built in 1907, Masjid Jamek is the oldest mosque in KL. This striking redbrick and marble building is inspired by the mogul architecture of northern India and was designed by a British engineer who had served in the Raj. It has three domes; the biggest dome at the centre was rebuilt after collapsing in the 1990s. At the corners are two red and white striped minarets.

After a wonderful day exploring, I returned to the Petronas Towers for a third time and was finally able to visit the sky-bridge, all be it for only 10-minutes, however the views were a little disappointing and less impressive than those from the Menara Tower, as sky-bridge is less than half way up the building.

Afterwards I took another subway train to Little India where narrow, hectic streets are lined with small, busy shops stocked with exquisite saris, gold, jewellery, brasses, silverware, textiles and carpets, and the smell of mysterious perfumed oils and jasmine hang in the air. As darkness fell, I returned to Chinatown and was amazed at the difference that night brought; peddlers and hawkers had taken over, and the combination of street stalls, food, haggling and bright lights dazzled the senses, while coloured lights illuminated the aging facades above the shophouses.

Malaysia's love of Western culture and capitalism is abundantly clear in Kuala Lumpur. In just 130 years, it has grown from a tiny muddy village to Malaysia's dynamic capital, a bustling city of two million people. However, although KL appears to be leaping forward with its glittering skyscrapers and futuristic appearance, scratch beneath the surface and you will discover that it still retains an alluring charm.

I was pleasantly surprised by Malaysia, having been a little apprehensive before my arrival. Geographically speaking it is one of the most easterly Islamic countries, however it is perhaps one of the most western in its attitude. The people I encountered were all very friendly, polite and helpful, while the streets were both safe and clean. This was the first Islamic country that I had visited and it was not at all as I'd imagined. Only a small minority of women and hardly any of the men I saw wore traditional clothing, in fact many of the younger women wore clothes as revealing as anywhere in the west, except perhaps for Newcastle!

The following morning I telephoned Qantas Airlines and rescheduled my flight from Singapore to Australia, bringing it forward by one week. I checked out around noon and caught a taxi to the bus station, from where I caught the 1pm bus to Singapore. The bus was the most luxurious that I had ever travelled on, a double-decker with air-conditioning and huge armchair like seats with pull out leg-rests, which fully reclined into a near horizontal bed-like position. As we pulled away, a voice over the intercom welcomed us aboard and ran through our route, journey time and safety procedure. We were then served drinks followed by a hot lunch, after which, feeling very contented, I reclined my seat and fell to sleep. I was awoken at 5pm by the steward's voice over the intercom announcing that we were approaching the border, and by 6pm we were crossing the causeway linking the Malay Peninsula to Singapore.

The bus journey ended at the Orchid Copthorn Hotel on the outskirts of the city. As I didn't recognise any of the surrounding buildings, I wasn't quite sure where I was and so I tried for about an hour to flag down a taxi, however the traffic was moving far too quickly and so my attempts were unsuccessful. Eventually I was fortunate to be in the right place at the right time, as a taxi stopped close by to drop off a passenger.

I asked the driver if he could recommend a good, cheap hotel close to the city centre, and he obliged by taking me to The Tropical Hotel in Chinatown, where I checked into a small single room, which was the most expensive accommodation of my trip so far at £20 per night.

I spent the evening wandering around the crowded, bustling streets of Chinatown, Singapore's cultural heart which still provides glimpses of its past with its numerous temples, decorated terraces and its frantic conglomeration of merchants, shops and activity, and where fortune-tellers and calligraphers are still very much part of every day life. By chance I discovered a traditional open-air food court comprising a collection of individual stalls serving a staggering variety of cheap Asian cuisine: Chinese, Malaysian, Thai, Indonesian and Indian. I appeared to be the only tourist amongst the numerous locals, but no one seemed to mind my presence.

At first glance, Singapore appears shockingly modern and anonymous, but it is an undeniably Asian city with Chinese, Malay and Indian traditions, which contrast to bring the city to life. Super-safe and mega-clean it may be, but its sensual pulse beats relentlessly beneath its disciplined surface.

I set off the next morning to carry out two tasks. Firstly I had to find a Pentax service centre in order to get my camera repaired. And secondly I had to visit the main post office to collect a package of guidebooks and other goodies sent from home in preparation for my next destination, Australia.

Task one proved to be very difficult; there were two Pentax service centres listed in Singapore, one of which was 25km outside the city, so I obviously made my way to the other by a combination of bus and taxi. Unfortunately when I arrived at the address I found that the centre had closed down. I then made my way by train and taxi across the city to the second address, which fortunately was still open. I explained the problem to an engineer, who repaired the fault within a few minutes.

I then caught a local bus and a train back across the city to the main post office, a journey of over an hour. Once inside the vast modern post office, it took around ten minutes to find the 'poste resante' office, from where I duly collected my parcel. Poste Resante is a wonderful and free mail holding service offered by post offices around the world. As long as you know approximately when you will be in a certain city, you can have mail forwarded to the head post office of the city, care of "Poste Resante", and upon proof of identity your mail will be handed over. I then returned by train to my hotel where I crashed out exhausted, my two simple tasks had taken the best part of 8-hours.

I spent the evening on the banks of the Singapore River, which is a great place for waterfront drinking and alfresco dining. Once Singapore's busiest port, Boat Quay has been transformed into a popular hangout for locals, expats and tourists, with chic cafes, high-end restaurants, yuppie pubs and designer galleries. The food was a little too rich for my budget so I contented myself to a couple of beers, with picturesque views of the river thrown in for free. I ate dinner and sank a few more beers at an outdoor hawker food stall at nearby Clarke Quay, where 19th century shophouses have been converted into trendy restaurants and bars.

The following day I headed to Little India, the focal point of Singapore's large Indian community. The first Indian settlers arrived in Singapore with Sir Stamford Raffles as assistants and soldiers back in 1819, followed by many more looking for work in the late 19th century. In this modest but colourful area of wall-to-wall streets, the senses are assaulted by pungent aromas and Hindi film music. Here you can buy a made to measure suit, colourful silk saris, ethnic jewellery, silverware and brassware, wood carvings, jasmine garlands, freshly ground spices or a picture of your favourite Hindu god or Bollywood star.

That evening I stumbled on a little bar just around the corner from my hotel called Cloud Nine. I ordered a Tiger beer and the barmaid poured me a 4-pint jug. I sat at the bar and got stuck into the jug, whilst the locals took turns singing their favourite karaoke tunes. A couple of local guys joined me at the bar and we spent a pleasant hour chatting about English football, of which they were very knowledgeable. I offered my acquaintances a beer, which they duly accepted, after which they departed. No sooner had a finished the last drop off my jug, than a fresh one appeared on the bar. I pulled out some money to pay and was pleasantly surprised when the barmaid said, "Your friends already pay."

I was close to finishing the second jug when a girl approached and asked if she could join me. She spoke impeccable English and we chatted for a while about nothing in particular. She then asked if I'd like to play cards with her, and I of course accepted. After a couple of hands, she asked if I'd like to make the game more interesting, I thought that perhaps she was a card shark, never the less I agreed. She then ordered and paid for a jug of vodka and orange and announced that the looser of each hand was to take a drink from the jug. I eventually stumbled out of the bar around 2am after a fantastic night. My only regret was that the following morning I could not remember the names of any of my new friends.

On my final day in Asia, I headed to downtown Singapore for a little sightseeing. Sir Stamford Raffles created the framework that remained the blueprint for central Singapore through generations of colonial rule and the republican years of independence, by moving the business district south of the river and making the northern area the administrative centre.

Places of interest include the imposing Victorian Empress Place Building built in 1865 that now houses a museum, art and antique galleries; the Padang, where cricketers once played; Raffles Hotel, a Singaporean institution which has become a byword for oriental luxury; and several imposing churches, such as St Andrew's Cathedral and the Cathedral of the Good Shepherd.

Built in 1887 the iconic, grandiose Raffles Hotel is one of the world's last great 19th century hotels, and still exudes its unique charm and splendour. I entered the Long Bar, decorated with natural wooden finishes in a plantation style theme, and with rows of connected palm blade ceiling fans swaying rhythmically from side to side to cool the air in much the same fashion as they have for over a century, however the cord pulling servants have now been replaced by electricity. I ordered a Singapore Sling in the very place where it was created, and then almost fell off my stool when I received the bill.

After recovering from the shock of the price of a Raffles Singapore Sling, I headed to the shopping Mecca that is Orchard Road, where I brought some clothes in readiness for Australia. Being at the epicentre of Singapore's shopping and entertainment industries means Orchard Road never sleeps. Dominated by high-class hotels, this is the playground of Singapore's elite, who are lured by the exclusive shopping centres, nightspots, restaurants, bars and lounges.

Feeling a little run down after a long and tiring day, I popped into a massage booth within one of the shopping centres, knowing that this would be the last chance for a long time to get a good authentic rub down. The pretty masseuse instructed me to strip off my clothes, wrap a towel around my waist and lie face down on the couch. She left the room and returned moments later with various oils, which she rubbed into my shoulders, back, arms and legs whilst straddling me. She then ordered me to turn over, which I did only to be greeted by the sight of her white uniform dress hitched around her waist and unbuttoned to her naval revealing the majority of her naked body beneath. Without saying a word, she continued the massage, whilst I, like any normal red-blooded male, grew very aroused. She smiled and pointed at my erection, "Yu like mi massage too?"

I nodded my agreement.

"10dollar extra, ok?"

I nodded again, and like the true professional she was, she completed her work, and left her customer feeling very satisfied!

I returned to my hotel, checked out, and caught the train to the airport. Qantas flight QF82 to Darwin, Australia took off on time at 10:5pm, and for the first time in my life I crossed the equator as I departed Asia after very happy and a memorable five months.

PART 2

AUSTRALIA &
NEW ZEALAND

10

Stars and Swag Bags (Northern Territory)

16/05/04 to 29/05/04

The plane touched down at 4am in Darwin, capital of the Northern Territory, in an area affectionately known Down-Under as The Top End, for obvious reasons. A huge queue formed at immigration, as every last passenger was required to complete a lengthy questionnaire relating to the purpose of their visit, before being interrogated by three uniformed officers.

Eventually I reached the front of the queue and a stone-faced officer took my questionnaire and passport, flicked through the pages, and without looking up asked, "How long are you planning to stay in Australia?"

"Three months," I replied.

"Where are you planning to visit?"

"The Northern Territory, Western Australia, Adelaide, Melbourne, and the east coast from Cairns to Sydney."

He looked up and stared coldly into my eyes, "In three months?" he said, as if disbelieving my reply.

"Yeah, three months."

"And just how are you planning to travel around?"

"Flights, buses and tours."

"Have you pre-booked any of these flights, buses or tours?" he asked, again in a way that suggested he did not believe me.

I handed him my flight tickets, "These are booked but I haven't arranged any buses or tours yet."

He studies my tickets thoroughly "Do you know anyone

residing in Australia?"

"No" I lied, although I'm not sure why I did.

"Ok, and do you have anywhere to stay in Darwin?"

"Thanks for asking, but I've pre-booked a hostel" I sarcastically replied.

He stared at me again for a couple of seconds, before handing my passport back, and with a nod of his head, he signalled that I should move on.

I took the airport shuttle bus, which for just over £2 dropped me outside the door of Frogshollow Backpackers Hostel. This would be my first experience of hostel life and I was a little apprehensive. It was now 5.30am and the reception was closed, however a sign on the counter read, "If you arrive before we open at 6am, please take a seat in the common room, turn on the TV and help yourself to tea or coffee." My kind of place I thought.

Some of the hostel guests were sitting outside by the pool, not so much early risers as night owls, still out from the previous night. At 6am the manager arrived, checked me in, and provided me with a large bag containing a bed sheet, pillowcase, plate, bowl, cup and cutlery, before giving me a quick guided tour of the establishment, finishing at my dormitory.

I tiptoed quietly into my dorm, not wanting to disturb any of the other sleeping guests. In the dark, I wasn't sure exactly which of the eight bunks were free and which were taken, but I could just about make out that one of the upper bunks was definitely empty, so I clambered on for a couple of hours sleep. I awoke around 9am, ate the complimentary self-service breakfast of cereals and coffee in the dining room, and I spent the morning lazing by the swimming pool, getting to know a few of my fellow guests.

Although cheap compared to home, Australia was expensive in comparison to Asia, and so I would need to be a little more fugal here; staying in hostel dormitories as opposed to private hotel rooms, and cooking my own food instead of eating out everyday. My first task was to visit local supermarket to stock up on my food & drink supplies, which I labelled and placed in the communal kitchen in the customary backpacker fashion.

Along with a few of the other hostel guests, I spent my first evening at the weekly Mindil Beach Night Market, which sold various typical Australian and aboriginal items such as didgeridoos, boomerangs and wide brim hats, as well as a great selection of mostly Asian hot snacks and food. An aboriginal band provided music in an unusual style, a cross between rock and Rolf Harris.

Afterwards we headed to Mitchell Street, the cities main entertainment area, where we spent the evening sitting outside one of the pubs until 2am. I ordered my first Aussie beer. "We don't sell warm beer like you 'pohms' like it mate, do ya fancy a cold one instead?" the barman asked. I didn't have a clue what he was talking about, but I was to hear this type of comment over and over again from Aussies. On the barman's recommendation, I ordered a Victoria-Bitter, which was actually a larger, and not at all bad.

I never quite understood the phrase "pohms" that Aussie's use to refer to we English. The term refers to 'Prisoner of Her Majesty', which the vast majority of early settlers here were. So it is actually the Aussies who are the pohms, not the English. I tried explaining this on numerous occasions during my time here, but I could never find an Aussie intelligent enough to understand.

As I was still in the tropics, the climate was similar to that which I'd left behind in South East Asia, hot and sticky. Darwin is actually closer to Singapore than it is to Melbourne. This close proximity with Australia's northern neighbours is reflected in the town's multicultural and cosmopolitan atmosphere.

The next day I walked into the compact city centre and explored a little. Most of what you'll want in central Darwin is within two or three blocks of the main shopping centre, Smith Street Mall. It is a pleasant yet strange place, surprisingly more sophisticated than I'd expected, yet it still had a distinct frontier town feel; and everyone appears to drive a Ute (utility vehicle), which is an open backed station wagon.

Until World Way II, Darwin was just a sleepy, dusty outpost without any direct link to the rest of Australia. During the war the town became an important base for Allied action against the Japanese in the Pacific, during which time the road south to the railhead at Alice Springs was surfaced, finally putting the city in direct contact with the rest of the country. Attacked sixty-four times, Darwin was the only place in Australia to suffer prolonged attack during the war, with the loss of two hundred and forty-three lives. A railway link to Alice Springs was finally completed in 2003. Equivalent in size to France, Italy and Spain combined, the Northern Territory is a vast, empty land covering 1.3million square kilometres, and with a population of just 200,000, each resident has effectively over six square kilometres to themselves. The major tourist centres are linked by sealed or gravel roads, otherwise dirt roads and tracks are accessible only by four-wheel drive.

Transportation around Australia is a problem for travellers as distances here are vast, and unlike Asia or Europe, there is generally little public transport out of the major population centres. The options are therefore either to rent or buy a vehicle and self-drive, or take guided tours, which can be expensive. I decided that my best option would be to take tours, and back at the hostel later I arranged two; the first a three-day jeep and camping trip to Kakadu National Park, departing tomorrow at 7am; the second a six day camping tour through the heart of the Red Centre, taking in Uluru (Ayers Rock) and finishing in Alice Springs. That evening I packed my daypack with the items that I would need for the tour and locked everything else in my main backpack, which I stowed in the hostel luggage storeroom.

At 7am the following morning a jeep collected me from the hostel and drove me to the 'Kakadu Dreams' tour company office, where I met the other eight people who would be accompanying me; Caterina and Kamila from England, Avi and Corina, a young Israeli/German couple, Elanor from Melbourne, Filly from Taiwan and Ralph and Sheree, a middle aged couple from Victoria, who were travelling around Australia by motorbike on their first ever holiday.

Our guide Justin was the stereo-typical Aussie male, with wide brim leather Stetson type hat, sleeveless shirt, tight cut-off shorts, and flip-flops, or thongs as they are known Down Under. We loaded our bags into a trailer, which was already full of equipment and food, and we climbed aboard the jeep. With one person sitting up front with Justin, and the rest of us sitting in two rows of four in the rear, on benches facing one another, we set off toward the park. I had chosen Kakadu Dreams as they sold their tour as a 'nature based, culturally active tour aimed at the adventure traveller looking for an experience rather than just another sightseeing tour'. I wasn't quite sure what that meant, but I thought it sounded good.

As we drove out of Darwin along the Arnhem Highway, Justin informed us that over the next three days we could expect much driving along dirt tracks and lots of bush-walking, and he gave us an introduction into the beliefs and customs of the Aborigines, the keepers of this land. Aborigines believe the world was created during the 'Dream Time', a mythological period when the acts and deeds of powerful ancestral beings such as the rainbow serpent, shaped the land and populated it with humans, animals and plants. Aborigines believe some of the ancestors metamorphosed into nature (rock formations or rivers), where they remain spiritually alive. These spirit ancestors are credited with giving the Aboriginal people their laws and customs. Many of the stories passed down from generation to generation are akin to our fairy-tales, and many contain cautionary tales.

Our first stop was at The Adelaide River, which is actually nowhere near to the city of the same name. We boarded a small boat and set off in search of crocodiles, and it wasn't long before we had our first sighting. In fact I'm not too sure whether we spotted him or he spotted us, in any case, the huge reptile swam across the surface of the river toward us, his powerful tail slithering from side to side propelling him forward.

This huge five-metres long estuarine (salt water) crocodile, was so well known by the boat skipper that he had a name, Hannibal, on account of the fact that he apparently had a tendency to eat other crocs which strayed into his territory. One of the crew tied a piece of meat to a line and dangled it over the side of the boat from a fishing rod. He lunged out of the river and took the bait in mid air, to our gasps of astonishment.

We continued our voyage down the river whilst the skipper gave us a commentary on crocodiles, dispelling some of the urban myths and providing gruesome details of their ability to kill. In total we saw eight crocs, including one three-metre long female that was able to leap her entire body length out of the water in pursuit of a free meal.

We returned to the jeep and continued along the Arnhem highway to Kakadu National Park, located 133km from Darwin and covering 20,000 square km. Kakadu was the setting for the Crocodile Dundee movies and is a World Heritage listed park, characterised by exceptional galleries of Aboriginal art and diverse wildlife. Like over fifty percent of the land in the Northern Territory, Kakadu is actually owned by the aboriginal tribespeople, who lease the land back to the government. Many of the aboriginals still live within the park grounds and many are employed as rangers.

Although located in a tropical zone, Kakadu is not blessed with exotic rainforests and is not an area of great beauty; like much of northern Australia, it is an area of flat tropical savannah woodland with a kind of grey, rather unattractive, monotony produced by low scrubby vegetation. The park also contains 250-metre high sandstone escarpments, floodplains, billabongs, and numerous lakes and rivers. The reality is that Kakadu's World Heritage status is based on its aboriginal heritage and its importance as a wetlands area, not on its physical beauty. The park contains over 1,000 plant species, a quarter of all the freshwater fish species found in Australia, and over one-third of all the bird species.

We stopped for a picnic lunch at the East Alligator River, named by Phillip Parker King in 1820, mistaking the crocodiles in the area for alligators. After lunch we continued to Ubirr, which contains some of the best displays of Aboriginal rock paintings in the Northern Territory. We followed a track around to a lookout, high on the rocky escarpment, from where the views over the wetlands were spectacular, if not exactly beautiful. Scientific investigation of this region has yielded the oldest evidence for man's presence in Northern Australia, dating back around 23,000 years.

On route to our overnight campsite at Yellow Water, we drove into a torrential storm; raindrops the size of gob-stoppers bounced off the road and drummed on the windscreen and roof. With no sign of an end to the storm, Justin decided to head to the companies permanent 'wet-season' campsite at Cooinda. The campsite comprised of a large marquee type tent, inside of which were erected several dome tents, a large dining table and a food preparation area with a sink and a gas barbeque.

All of the meals on the tour are supplied and cooked outdoors; picnic type lunches, and dinners cooked in the true outback style on the campfire. In torchlight, we all helped prepare our chicken and vegetable stew dinner. A few of us had brought some beer along, which we duly cracked open. I had purchased a twelve pack of beer, considerably more than anyone else, and so it was no surprise that I was last to bed around midnight.

Justin woke us around 6am, having already prepared our breakfast. We ate, cleaned up, packed, re-loaded the jeep and set off. Fortunately the rain had ceased and so we returned to Yellow Waters to take photographs, before heading to the town of Jabiru, which has grown around the development of uranium mining at the Ranger Mine, and more recently through park tourism. The piece-de-resistance of the town is the tacky-looking Four Seasons Cooinda Hotel, constructed in the shape of a giant crocodile.

As you would expect, Justin was somewhat of an expert of the local flora and fauna, sharing his knowledge on the various local animals and plants, explaining their various uses, such as the plant which produces soap when you remove the leaves, add a little water and rub it between your hands, and the ant which produces a bubble of lime from its behind, which you can lick for refreshment. Throughout the tour we saw loads of wildlife; snakes, lizards, huge spiders, wallabies, and hundreds of birds and insects.

Perhaps the oddest creature we saw though was the frill-neck lizard, an amazing creature about 80cm long. As its name suggests, it has a frill around its neck, like an Elizabethan collar, which normally lies in folds around the shoulders. As we happened across it, it stood on is haunches and opened its mouth wide, and like an umbrella, its frill folded out, displaying a broad, rounded expanse of bright orange and red scales. It then hissed at us in an aggressive manner, causing us all to retreat swiftly, after which it scampered away and disappeared up a tree. This frill is opened by the lizard when frightened to make it appear larger, and is one of its defensive strategies against predators. It was certainly effective, for such a small creature it really did look quite ferocious and rather frightening.

We ate another picnic style lunch at a billabong, after which we walked to the nearby Anbangbang Gallery, with more aboriginal rock art, and a number of nearby walks, including one to a 600metre high lookout, and another to some cool forest pools, where we freshened up and swam. We then drove to our overnight campsite near to the Mary River, stopping to collect firewood along the way.

We paired up and erected our tents. Kat asked if she could share with me, and I of course agreed, well, it would have been rude not to. Justin cooked a delicious kangaroo and vegetable stir-fry dinner over the campfire, which I washed down with the remainder of my beer. We sat around the campfire chatting after dinner; Justin produced his didgeridoo, and we all took turns at trying to play, which was a lot harder than it looked; most of us, including me, couldn't even produce a note. One by one, everyone slowly turned in for the night, and once more I was the last to retire. No sooner had I entered the tent than Kat farted, so loudly that everyone heard, and assumed that it was me. Kat fell into fits of laughter, which brought on more farting. The smell was so bad that I was forced to leave the tent until the stench had cleared.

Justin woke us again around 6am. The sun was just rising, the campfire was alight again, breakfast was set out on a fold-up table, and fruit bats were fluttering overhead between the surrounding treetops. Within half an hour we were on the road again heading to Yirmikmik waterfall. We then drove the short distance to the spectacular Gunlom falls, made famous in the movie *Crocodile Dundee* as Echo Pool. We climbed up the escarpment to the top of the falls, explored and swan in the refreshing rock pools and small cascades there. After lunch we walked to the base of the main falls where we took another dip in the beautiful emerald green plunge pool.

Around 3pm we finally departed and headed back to Darwin, stopping on route to look at some amazing cathedral termite mounds, reputedly eighty years old, standing around 5metres tall and resembling natural phallic symbols. We arrived in Darwin at 7pm, and I returned to Frogshollow Hostel, where I took a much-needed shower, followed by dinner, and then feeling totally exhausted, I retired to bed for an early night.

Knowing that I would be booking on more camping tours, and now realising that my kit was not up to the harshness of this country, the following day I headed into town to purchase some supplies, picking up a sleeping bag, inflatable pillow, wide brim hat, batteries and most importantly insect repellent.

The people that I'd met at the hostel previously had all moved on, so I spent the evening alone, people watching in the lively bars on Mitchell Street. The locals are a blend of rednecks and hippies. The preferred dress of the local guys is rugby shirts with turned-up collar, shorts and knee-length socks, they drink to excess and never dance. The women dress more conventionally in jeans and a t-shirt, they too drink excessively, and they dance, although not that well. The music played in the bars was also a little odd; Michael Jackson's Thriller album was the music of choice, although the Proclaimers and Dexy's Midnight Runners are also very popular. Darwin appeared stuck in an eighties time warp.

The next day I brought an all-day bus ticket and set off to explore the city. I headed firstly to The Sailing Club, where I hoped that I would find a kind-hearted member who would take me out for a few hours. Sadly there were very few members around on account of a car-rally taking place nearby in the outback; apparently most locals had gone along to watch.

I then walked along the coast path to the Northern Territory Museum and Art Gallery, which although was small and contained few exhibits, was surprisingly very good. As you would expect there was a collection of Aboriginal art, and of artefacts from the Pacific and South-East Asia. There was also an enormous stuffed salt-water croc named 'Sweetheart', which gained notoriety in the 1970's for attacking several aluminium dinghies at a popular fishing spot.

However, my favourite exhibit was that of Cyclone Tracy, the greatest natural disaster in Australia's history which devastated Darwin on the night of Christmas Eve 1974. By dawn on Christmas morning most of the population of 48,000 were made homeless by the highest winds ever recorded on the Australian mainland. The exhibition features documentary footage, before and after photographs, interviews which locals who witnessed the disaster, and a room in which eerie sound recordings of the fateful night were played in total darkness, giving you the sensation of being there.

I left the museum and waited at the bus stop outside. I was soon joined by a chatty Aussie girl, who said she remembered seeing me at Kakadu; apparently she had also been there with another tour group. "Where are you going?" she asked.

"To the marina and then Cullen Bay" I replied.

"Great, I think I'll join you". I wasn't keen on having a companion, and I hoped that she would stay on the bus, but unfortunately she followed me off and proceeded to accompany me around the marina, talking constantly about everything and nothing. At one point I unfolded my street map in order to find the quickest route to the harbour, and to my utter astonishment she took the map from my hands and tried to tell me where "we" should visit. I retrieved my map, and told her that "I was going to the harbour, and perhaps she should go where she wanted to, alone". I then walked to another bus stop, and completely oblivious to my comment, she followed.

"Why don't we walk there?" she asked.

"Because I have a bus ticket." I replied.

"It's not so far, lets walk"

"I'm catching the bus, but you can walk and I'll see you there" I replied.

Unfortunately she did not take the hint, following me onto the bus. There wasn't much to see at the harbour so after a quick look around, I announced that I was heading back to my hostel. She looked at me as if I had betrayed her, we said goodbye and headed off in separate directions. I'm not sure why, but afterwards I felt guilty for some reason.

Once more I spent the night on Mitchell Street, where I bumped into Kat and Camilla. We ate dinner together and then headed to Shenanigans Irish Pub, where a live band played cover versions of 70's and 80's hits until the early hours. On my way home later, I stopped at a public telephone box to call my friends back home, knowing that they would all be together watching the F.A. Cup Final, as we do every year. I managed to chat briefly with a few of them, however I didn't get much sense from them as they all sounded totally pissed.

The next morning I woke at 5am and by 6 I was sitting on an 'Adventure Tours' bus about to commence a six-day tour through the heart of the outback to Alice Springs, 1,500kms away. One person had failed to show up, so we spent an hour driving around all of the various local hostels looking for him. Eventually we located Geordie Terry, who had overslept. He boarded the bus with his guitar slung over his shoulder, and sat down without even an apology, much to the annoyance of the rest of us.

With only twenty-four passengers aboard the fifty-seat bus, we all had a double seat on which to spread out and relax. Our first day commenced with a 315km drive to Katherine, along the Stuart Highway, which runs from Darwin in the north to Adelaide in the south, slicing the continent in half. As we drove, our guide and driver Dan, and his assistant Rachel, gave us a running commentary.

I soon made friends with a number of the group; Rich from Bristol, Andreas from Austria, Liam and Lucy from Leeds and Essex respectively, Tracey from South Africa, Lars from Berlin and Nick from London. The remainder of the passengers, especially 3 miserable German guys, made no effort to mix and generally kept themselves to themselves.

We reached Katherine for lunch, after which we entered Nitmiluk National Park, better known as Katherine Gorge, owned by aborigines since 1989 and leased back to the N.T. Government on a ninety-nine year lease. We were offered a choice of activities; canoe down the Katherine River, take a boat ride down the same, or simply relax and do nothing. A group of twelve of us chose to canoe, we paired up, I with Rich, and set off in Canadian canoes paddling leisurely upstream through the first of a series of thirteen gorges, chiselled from the sandstone plateau.

It took around two hours to reach the rapids linking the first and second gorges. Three of the groups carried their canoes around the rapids rather than try to paddle through, whilst the remaining three of us decided to go for it. The first two attempts ended in failure and ultimately a dip in the river. Rich and I made the third and final attempt, paddling furiously against the force of the fast current, manoeuvring around the rocks. We were almost through when the current turned us side on and pushed us into the rocks, and ultimately capsized us. We surfaced to find our canoe, paddles and all of our belongings floating away downstream, but luckily the rest of our group were on hand to retrieve our belongings. We swam ashore and rested up in the sunshine for a while, before walking along the bank to take a look at the second gorge, with stunning 100-metre high red cliff faces rising vertically from the waters edge.

All six canoes made the return journey downstream together, during which things got a little boisterous and out of hand, with lots of splashing and overturning of each others canoes. Rich and I took two more dips before we eventually reached the safety of the pontoon. We later found out that there were freshwater crocs in the river, but Dan assured us they wouldn't attack unless provoked!

On our way back to the campsite, we made a beer stop in Katherine; a group of seven of us contributed around £5 each to buy two slabs of beers (forty eight bottles). Back at the campsite, Dan and Rachel prepared and cooked dinner, whilst we settled into our tents and generally got to know one another better. Afterwards, we sat around the campfire chatting and drinking, and later on Terry produced his guitar and we had a little sing-a-long until around 1am.

We were woken at 5am the next morning, and by six we were on the road again, with 670kms of road in front of us. We made our first stop of the day at Mataranka, where we swam and generally lazed in the open-air thermal pools, which were a lovely 30-degrees Celsius. However, the area had a terrible smell, caused by droppings from the thousands of fruit bats, which were hanging upside down in the surrounding palm trees.

We made a second brief stop at Daly Waters, with a population of just twenty-three, and home to one of Australia's first international airports; before the advent of the jet engine, Daly Waters was the furthest point that a plane could fly on its journey from Sydney to Europe or Asia, before needing to refuel. Local legend as it that this is the place where the Queensland and Northern Territory Air Services (Qantas) were formed, however it appears that this is nothing more than a local myth, probably thought up for the tourist trade. Today it is a little used airstrip and is also home to the outback's oldest pub, which we visited for lunch and a pint. Hanging from every conceivable place was the bras and knickers belonging to various female travellers who had stopped off here over the years.

The journey south was monotonous and boring, the road was long and straight, the landscape flat, dusty and desolate, with only a scattering of trees and bushes, becoming more barren and the earth more red as we went. We passed a few huge road trains; multi-part trucks up to fifty metres long that threw up dust clouds in their wake. We saw a little wildlife, mostly cattle, a few camels, a couple of dingo's and my first kangaroo, lying dead by the side of road. The boredom would be occasionally broken by the sight of a roadhouse or occasionally a vehicle driving in the opposite direction; the occupants of both vehicles waving at each other as if long lost friends!

We eventually reached the backwater town of Tennant Creek, which developed during the gold rush of the 1930s. We stocked up on beer again, before continuing onto our campsite, where we spent a similar evening to the previous. I had never witnessed a night sky like this before, a blanket of thousands of twinkling stars; we could clearly see the Southern Cross constellation, which is depicted on the Australian flag, and the beautiful Milky Way. Most of the group slept in tents, whilst Terry, Rich and I slept outside in swag bags, a type of canvas outdoor sleeping bag with a thin mattress inside. We eventually fell to asleep around 1.30am.

The Australian outback is one of the worlds deadliest environments, and is home to about one hundred and forty species of snake, of which around one hundred and twenty are venomous, although only twelve are likely to inflict a wound that could kill you. And Australia has two spiders whose bites can cause death – the red-back and the funnel-web. A variety of other venomous spiders, such as the mouse spider and the wolf spider are not deadly but their bite can be painful. Luckily we survived the night and the following morning we were treated to a lie-in, being woken at 6am as we only had 515km to cover.

Our first stop of the day was at Battery Hill Gold Mine, where we went underground and were given a one-hour tour of the now redundant mine. We continued on to the Devils Marbles, where we spent an hour wandering around and climbing on the mysterious, huge seven metre spherical granite boulders. Geologists credit their formation on water erosion, whilst aborigines credit the rainbow serpent.

We continued south, during which we drove along a 48km stretch of road without a single bend, before stopping for lunch at Ti Tree. The afternoon continued in much the same fashion. We stopped briefly on the Tropic of Capricorn, where a signpost had been erected, I presume for tourists to photograph. Finally at around 6pm, we reached our final destination of Alice Springs, in the heart of the Red Centre.

Founded as an overland telegraph station in the 1870's, Alice had a rough-and-ready, frontier town feel. We checked into Melankas Hostel where I shared a dorm with Terry, Rich and Lars. We spent the night in the bar next to the hostel, where we sank a few beers and generally celebrated with an end of tour party. The night ended on a sour night however, following an altercation between Terry and a group of local rednecks, over space on the dance floor!

After only three hours sleep, I woke at 5am for the next leg of the tour, which would take us around the Red Centre. Adventure tours had three identical tours all departing from the hostel at the same time, and so there were chaotic scenes in the reception as backpackers tried to locate their correct group. I eventually found my group, and discovered that the only others from my previous group were the three miserable German guys.

Our guide Sally introduced herself, and after checking our names against her register, she discovered that we were one person short. The culprit this time was Nick, who didn't normally drink but had had two beers the previous night. We finally departed at 7am and in heavy rain we drove west towards our first destination of Watarrka National Park (Kings Canyon) 325km away. We reached Kings Canyon Station around lunchtime, to find that the surrounding creeks and rivers were rising quickly and were dangerously high, making the only road to the canyon impassable. With no option, we were forced to turn back and return to the main highway, from where we headed south toward Uluru, or to give it its English name Ayers Rock. The rain continued to pour, and the bus became damp, cold and miserable. Spirits were lifted briefly when we thought that we had our first sighting of Uluru on the horizon, but the enormous monolith turned out to be the lesser-known, flat-topped Mount Conner, towering 300metres above ground level.

We eventually reached our campsite at 6.30pm after a very long and miserable day. Everyone was expected to contribute to the workload, preparing or cooking the food, or building the campfire, and everyone except for the German guys chipped in and did their bit. We were all feeling down, as we would not get chance to see Kings Canyon again due to our tight schedule. Sally apologised, not that she was responsible for the weather, however some of the group were less than understanding.

We were woken at 5am in order to catch the sunrise behind Uluru. Fortunately the rain had stopped and immediately after breakfast we hit the road for a short journey to a viewpoint on the west side of the rock. We were all to be disappointed however, as there was a lot of cloud cover which ruined the spectacle. After half an hour we returned to the bus and set off to Kata Tjuta National Park (The Olgas) around 30km west of Uluru.

Kata Tjuta has been a sacred dream site of the native aborigines for over 20,000 years. The name translates to 'many heads' and refers to the thirty-six huge domed rocks that make up the site, the highest Mount Olga standing 546-meters above sea level, that is 200-metres higher than Uluru. We spent a very pleasant four hours leisurely trekking along the 8km 'Valley Of The Winds' trail, passing through the valleys between the mysterious and magical rocks. It really did feel as though we were in a very special place; beautiful, enchanting and captivating.

We returned to our campsite for lunch, and once more the German guys disappeared to their tent to avoid any work. We were all totally pissed off with them, and so we made our lunches and left their food unprepared. Whilst sitting around the campsite eating, the German guys appeared from their tent and walked to the food table, where of course there was nothing for them. They looked bemused and called to Sally, asking where their food was. Sally explained that neither she, nor the rest of the group, had come here to mother them, and so they must help with the food preparation and cleaning up, just like everyone else. They made themselves sandwiches, after which they cleaned up for everyone.

We spent the afternoon at the Aboriginal Cultural Centre, which contained displays relating the Aboriginal stories of Uluru's and Kata Tjuta's origin. On our return to the campsite, we stopped at Uluru for sunset, and we were treated to a spectacular natural light show as the rock appeared to change colour as the sun faded, turning from a bright glowing orange to scarlet, to deep maroon and finally brown. It really was an amazing experience to watch this happening in front of our eyes. The sandstone rock is actually grey, but is covered with a distinctive red iron oxide coating, making it appear to glow in sunlight. The rock and surrounding ground gets its rust color from oxidation, hence the slang name for the area, 'The Red Centre'.

Once more we woke early and fortunately on this occasion we were able to witness a beautiful sunrise over Uluru, with more brooding colour changes. Towering over the surrounding flat scrubland, Uluru stands 348-metres high, 3.1-km long, 1.9-km wide and is 9-km in circumference. However, the visible part of the rock is actually just the tip of an enormous monolith estimated to be 6-km below ground. Uluru holds deep significance to the local Aboriginal Anangu people. On 26 October 1985, the Australian Government returned ownership of Uluru to them, who then leased it back to the Government for 99 years as a National Park.

I was very confused at whether or not to climb Uluru. I certainly wanted to, but many articles and books that I had read suggested that it was wrong, as the Anangu people feel that it is disrespectful of the sacred status of Uluru. Having chatted to a few of the Anangu people in the cultural centre, none of them had actually told me not to climb, they had simply said that they felt sadness when people climbed for the wrong reasons, or disrespected their site. Also, the aboriginals traditionally have a duty to safeguard visitors to their land. They feel great sadness when a person dies or is hurt, and each year several people do indeed die whilst attempting the climb.

Knowing that I would not disrespect the rock, I decided that I would climb. Unfortunately when we arrived at the base of the rock, the climb was closed due to dangerous high winds, although at ground level it was very calm. A notice posted at the gate said that a park ranger would return at 9am to re-evaluate the situation. Rather than do nothing, I joined the others in a walk around the base, which was surprisingly wonderful in itself; when viewed from a distance and when seen in photographs, Uluru looks just like a large red tin-loaf shaped rock. However close up it is far more interesting than I'd imagined, with numerous gorges, caves, crevices and valleys. There are also many Aboriginal paintings, along with descriptive boards explaining their meanings. After a couple of kilometres, I decided to return to the climb in the hope that it would now be open, but it was not. I sat and waited for the ranger, realising that we were due back on the bus at 10.30am, and so if it did open soon I would be late. However I was determined not to miss the opportunity to climb if it arose.

Eventually my patience paid off when at 10am the ranger opened the climb. I was second through the gate, followed by Steve and Claire from my group. The climb was steep and hard going, a chain had been fixed on the steepest section, which I used to pull myself up, although it stopped nearly half way to the top. Clare became frightened and didn't want to continue, and so I left them both behind and continued alone, taking regular rest breaks to regain my breath.

Eventually I reached the summit where the winds were so strong that they felt as though they could blow me straight off the top. From the summit, the true vastness of this barren, flat land could be appreciated, and the views of the Olgas to the west and Mount Conner to the east were breathtaking. But the most amazing aspect of Uluru was the rock itself, containing pools, waterfalls, craters and knolls, all hidden from sight from the base. It was a truly amazing sight and a wonderful experience that I will never forget.

I didn't linger for as long as I would have liked at the summit, knowing that the rest of the group would be waiting for me on the bus. I made a slow descent, stopping occasionally as I went take photographs. I passed Claire and Steve who were continuing up after regaining their nerve, and by now there were many more people also making the ascent. I realised why the Anangu people do not like people to climb; many were ill prepared, some were either too old or too young, others looked in no physical shape for such a challenge, many wore inappropriate footwear such as flip-flops, and one stupid guy was even carrying his young son on his shoulders. Several would-be climbers thankfully realised they were not up to the task, and gave up partway, but many more pressed on regardless. The current estimate is that on average, one person per month dies either directly or indirectly as a result of climbing the rock, mainly due to heart attacks, although quite a number wander too far and fall off the edges.

Claire and Steve caught me up at the base and by the time we reached the waiting bus we were almost an hour late. Sally had realised that we had made the climb and she was happy for us, although the rest of the group seemed a little putout that we had kept them waiting.

Uluru made international headlines for all of the wrong reasons when two-month-old baby Azaria Chamberlain disappeared on the night of 17 August 1980 on a camping trip with her family. Her parents reported that she was taken from their tent by a dingo, but they were arrested, tried and convicted of her murder in 1982. The Chamberlains made several unsuccessful appeals, but not until the chance discovery of a piece of Azaria's clothing in an area full of dingo lairs were they successful. Both were subsequently released, and although the case is officially unsolved, their tale of a dingo attack is now generally accepted.

We returned to our campsite for lunch, after which we were due to commence the long drive back to Alice Springs. Whilst tucking into our grub, a jeep arrived carrying an Adventure Tours representative, who announced that there were eight spare places up for grabs with another tour-group heading to Kings Canyon tomorrow. Despite everyone complaining a couple of days ago at missing out on seeing Kings Canyon, only two of us took up the opportunity, myself and a French girl named Morgan.

We were dropped off at a service station where our new tour group were waiting for us. On board were a couple of guys that I had met at the summit of Uluru, and Terry from the earlier tour. We immediately set off for a long drive to Kings Canyon, arriving at our campsite in time to witness the sunset over the George Gill

Ranges. Our guide, Banjo prepared dinner whilst we lit the campfire and cracked open the stubbies (beer bottles).

This was a much friendlier and livelier group than my previous one and I soon made friends. Everyone contributed to the cooking and cleaning, and after dinner we stayed up until the early hours playing party games and drinking, before bedding down in swag-bags. Amongst the group were three mates from Blackburn, all kitted out in khaki, multi-pocketed combat type trousers and matching shorts, shirts, waist-coats and wide-brim hats, as if they were on Operation Desert Storm!

We arrived at 8am the next morning at Watarrka National Park, a scenic landscape of rugged ranges, rock-holes and 100metre deep gorges, sculptured by the elements, which act as a refuge for many plants and animals. We trekked for 3hours around the 6km-looped Canyon Walk, which began with a steep climb to the top of the Canyon, then followed the rim; the views were spectacular. Approximately half way along the walk, the trail descended back into the canyon to the 'Garden of Eden', a delightful area of plunge pools and waterfalls, and lush vegetation. We then climbed the opposite canyon wall and continued along its rim back to our starting point.

Back at the campsite later, we cooked the remainder of our food for lunch, and then commenced the long 500km drive back to Alice Springs. We again spent the evening in Melankas club, where we had another lively end of tour party. I spent most of the evening chatting up a Norwegian girl named Liz, but as the night progressed, the conversation slowly fizzled out and I found myself talking more and more to Morgan. Terry was not best pleased, as apparently he liked Morgan, and he became a little aggressive toward me. I told him to grow up. He then headed to the dance floor and got himself into another fight with a different group of locals. The end result was that everyone ended up alone!

The next morning I woke at 9am, packed my bags and headed to reception to checkout. Liam and Lucy who I had met on the first leg of the tour were also checking out, and we shared a taxi to the airport, from where they were due to fly to Melbourne and I to Broome in Western Australia. In total I had covered about 3,000km over the last week, and not until now did I finally appreciate the sheer vastness of this country.

11

The Long & Lonely Road
(Western Australia)

30/05/04 to 18/06/04

The small half full Qantas plane touched down in Broome after a pleasant two and a half hour flight and with no immigration or customs to worry about, I was soon on the airport shuttle bus heading for Cable Beach Backpackers Hostel. I checked into a mixed dorm to find that I was sharing with an English couple and a single English girl. The rain appeared to have followed me, pouring down all day long, so I lazed around the hostel, taking the opportunity to rest up after my previous hectic fortnight.

Broome is situated on the North West coast of Western Australia, and is marketed as 'where the outback meets the Indian Ocean'. The small town, with a population of less than 14,000, grew out of the discovery of the world's largest pearl shell. Like many towns in Western Australia and the Northern Territory, it has a frontier town feel and a laid-back aura, and until the mid 1980's was only accessible by a dirt road.

The following day I took the hostel shuttle bus into town and brought a new pair of jeans, a sarong, and a travel adapter, to replace items stolen; my trousers and sarong from the Darwin hostel washing line and from the poolside respectively, and my travel adapter from the hostel in Alice. It seemed strange that I had managed to complete five months of travel through Asia without one single theft, yet within two weeks of being Down-Under, I'd had three things stolen.

I posted a parcel containing items that I needed for New

Zealand to myself, care of Poste Resante, Sydney, for collection when I arrived there in a couple of months time. I then headed to the Chinatown area, where many of the original Chinese settlers had lived, but it turned out to be no different to the rest of the town and rather a disappointment. I then visited the Sun Cinema, which first opened its doors in 1916 and is said to be the oldest open-air cinema in the world. However the cinema turned out to be only part open-air and a little disappointing, it is in fact housed in a corrugated factory type building with one wall missing allowing the free flow of air.

On my third day in Broome, the sun eventually made an appearance and I walked to Cable Beach, said to be one of the six best beaches in the world. At twenty-two kilometres long, it is certainly big, but size isn't everything and although it was nice, I was not overly impressed. To make matters worse, throughout the afternoon noisy jeeps drove back and forth. The beach was long and straight, there were no picturesque bays or coves. Not only was the beach long, it was also wide, so wide in fact that it took a full 5minutes to walk from the back of the beach to the sea. I took my first dip in the Indian Ocean, which was also a little disappointing as the water was colder than I'd expected and was cloudy, possible due to the recent rain.

Beyond the beach was the beginning of the flat and barren Great Sandy Desert; there were no lush green hills or picturesque mountain backdrop, no cliffs, no giant boulders. A few palm trees had been planted to create the impression of a tropical paradise, however it had failed. In my opinion Cable Beach wouldn't have made the top six beaches in Thailand, let alone the world. I read for a while before falling to sleep. When I awoke around 5pm, I found that the beach had begin to fill with sunset viewers, some carrying bottles of champagne and glasses, as if this were the first, or possibly last ever sunset.

After a relaxing few days in Broome, I departed on the 'Easyrider Backpacker Bus', which for £200 provides a 'jump on – jump off' service along the 3,000km long west coast from Broome in the north to Perth in the south. Three buses a week ply the route, providing travellers with the opportunity to stop off and spend a couple of days or more in any of the towns along the way.

The bus arrived at 7am and I boarded along with an English guy name Matt. We were the only two passengers aboard as most backpackers were migrating in the opposite direction toward the sun, being wintertime in Australia. Beneath clear blue skies, we drove along the Great Northern Highway on a 610km journey through a flat, featureless landscape of desert and scrub, broken occasionally by the sighting of an odd tree. Every 200km or so we would pass a roadhouse containing a petrol station, post office, pub, shop, hotel and campsite, often the only such facilities for hundreds of kilometres.

We stopped for photographs at Eighty Mile Beach, before continuing on to our final destination of Port Headland, where we arrived at 4pm after a long, boring day. Arguably the largest state in the world, Western Australia covers one-third of the Australian continent. Places that look relatively close on the map are actually hundreds or even thousands of miles apart.

On the way into town, we passed the longest train that I have ever seen, stretching endlessly into the distance on the purpose-built track to carry iron-ore from Newman, said to be one of the world's biggest mining operations. Since the 1960s, Port Headland has been the centre of a thriving iron-ore industry, exporting to Europe and the Far-East, and its natural harbour handles the largest tonnage of any Port in Australia.

We checked into the only hostel in town, converted from an old motel, and whist there, another Easyriders Bus arrived, full to the brim as it was heading north. We dined that evening with several passengers from the other bus, which pleased me as I was already growing tired of Matt, who was only twenty-two, very immature, nerdish and quite boring. He carried his camera everywhere and took pictures of anything and everything, insisting on showing every person he met his snaps on the cameras digital screen. He also bragged constantly of the number of girls he had bedded, including 20 on a backpacker tour bus in New Zealand. But his most annoying trait was that he always had to have the last word, and would often make sarcastic comments; one time I said that I was hot. "That's because your standing in the sun" he replied. I didn't even waist my breath with a reply.

There was little to see or do in Port Headland, and so at 7.30am the next morning, we were on the road again travelling inland en-route to Karijini National Park in the Hamersley Ranges, which stretch for more than 400km. We arrived around noon and immediately set off to trek through the stunning 100-metres deep Dales Gorge, chiselled by the waters of the Fortescue River, their strata in horizontal stripes of blue, mauve, red and brown.

These cool gorges have created an oasis of lush green vegetation, sheltered from the brilliant sunshine, which provides a habitat to many different types of birds, reptiles and animals including: rock wallabies, dingoes, red kangaroos, geckos, goannas, and a variety of snakes. We made our way down the side of the gorge to the crystal-clear Circular Pool, and followed a track at the base of the gorge to Fortescue Falls and Fern Pool, but unfortunately, we did not have time to take a dip.

"Karijini is the largest canyon system in the world," the guide declared.

"What about the Grand Canyon?" I asked.

"Oh yeah, Karijini is the second biggest."

"What about the Colca Canyon?"

"Never heard of it."

"It's the worlds deepest canyon."

"Oh, well Karijini is definitely the biggest in the southern hemisphere."

"The Colca Canyon is in the southern hemisphere."

"Oh, well its bloody big anyways, that's all I know."

The Aussies are very nationalistic and extremely biased towards all things Australian, and quite ignorant of the rest of the world. You soon realize once you arrive Down-Under that everything here is the portrayed as the biggest, best, longest, largest, oldest, or deadliest in the world; and they truly believe it. Why Australians have to over-hype everything is a mystery to me. Karijini was indeed very beautiful, and it would have been sufficient to simply describe in that way.

We departed after a few hours and drove to the nearby township of Tom Price, purpose-built by Hamersley Iron Mining Company in 1965 after rich deposits of iron-ore were discovered in the nearby Hamersley Ranges, to accommodate those working the mine. Our accommodation was a portacabin containing bunk beds, a sink and a fridge, located on a campsite with all of the usual facilities. We cooked dinner in the campsite communal kitchen, during which a kangaroo bounced in, took a look around, and bounced back out again. I ran back to my room to grab my camera, but it was not in my bag; I could only assume that I had dropped it at Karijini earlier.

I was awoke at 6.30am the next morning by strange squawking sounds, and looking out of the window the campsite was covered with a flock of pink coloured parrots. By 7.15 we were on the road again, for another long day of monotonous driving. We stopped for lunch at Nanutarra Roadhouse with a population of just twenty. I telephoned the Karijini visitors centre to see if my camera had been found, but unfortunately it had not. I also tried to call the police at Tom Price to report the loss and get a reference number for my insurance claim, but they were closed for the weekend!

Our driver Josh was a strange character with an awful taste in music. Throughout the journey he bounced up and down in his seat to the beat of the music, regularly punching his hand in the air with his thumb and small finger pointing outward in some kind of weird salute. Although in his mid thirties, I'm sure that he thought that he was still a teenager.

We eventually arrived in Exmouth at 4pm, and headed straight to Bundegi Beach, 12km out of town, where we swam and snorkelled for an hour. We checked into Pete's Backpackers, which was part of a camping and caravan park, and we were given the keys to another portacabin type room. We opened the door to find that it was already occupied by what seemed like a small army, judging by the amount of luggage scattered over the floor. To ensure maximum occupancy, the small room had two sets of triple height bunks, each with little headroom. This must be akin to sleeping in a submarine I thought. Unhappy with the room, we returned to reception and were given the keys to an empty room.

Dutch ships first visited Exmouth as early as 1618, but it wasn't until some 350 years later in 1967 that a town was settled and Exmouth was established as a support town for the joint Australian-United States Naval Communications Station, some fifteen kilometres north along the peninsula. Much of the navy activity has been mothballed, but some of the buildings are still in use. At the tip of the peninsula, near Bundegi, thirteen naval communication transmitter towers dominate the skyline, the highest soaring 388-metres into the sky.

Exmouth also happens to be situated alongside many spectacular beaches, coral lagoons and one of the worlds' most pristine and accessible reefs. Ningaloo Reef is Australia's largest fringing coral reef and runs 260km along the length of the North West Cape. Many different varieties of soft and hard coral can be found here, as can a wide array of marine wildlife including the largest fish in the ocean, the whale shark.

We spent the evening in Graces Tavern chatting with a group of other travellers, including a couple of attractive girls. Lady-killer Matt came over all shy, "I need a rest from women" he said. I didn't even notice later that he had returned early to the room, and by the time I returned around midnight, he was tucked up and fast asleep.

The next morning I was woken at 6am by the sound of Matt packing up to leave. I had decided to stay in Exmouth and catch the next bus in a couple of day's time. When I eventually stirred from my bed, I found the campsite full of cockatoos, and several emus were wandering around in search of food scraps.

I spent the morning wandering around the small town, returning to the campsite around mid-afternoon, just as a northbound, jam-packed Easyrider bus arrived. I introduced myself to the new arrivals and whilst chatting, I learnt that they were going snorkelling at Turquoise Bay about 60-km away. Cheekily I approached their driver and asked if I could join them. Before he could answer I said, "Thanks very much", and duly climbed aboard.

The pristine Turquoise bay was beautiful and certainly lived up to its name, but its best feature was its location on the world famous Ningaloo Reef, which begins just 100-metres from the shore. Running parallel to the beach was a riptide, which we used to our advantage by walking about 300metres up the beach before entering the sea and swimming out to the reef, allowing the rip to carry us effortlessly over the reef back to our starting point. We were warmed to be wary of strong currents at the southern end of the beach due to a break in the reef further out, and so it was important to swim ashore before reaching this point or the currents could carry you out to the open ocean. About a dozen of us spent a wonderful couple of hours floating down the reef over and over again, during which I saw some wonderful coral formations and a multitude of marine life, including my first wild turtle, and happily, no one got washed out to sea.

Around 5pm we re-boarded the bus and drove to the Vlaming Head Lighthouse, built in 1912 and now fully restored. The site provided magnificent views of the North West Cape and the reef. The bus driver handed out plastic cups and topped them up with cheap sparkling wine, which we drank whilst watching the sunset over the Indian Ocean. On our return to the campsite, we saw dozens of kangaroos bouncing along the roadside, apparently they are more active around dusk.

The next morning I was picked up at 6am by 'King Divers' and driven to Tantabiddi boat ramp, along with fourteen other day-trippers all exited at the prospect of swimming with whale sharks. We were transferred by inflatable dinghy to the Darling Isabelle, a gold coloured motor-yacht, which was just four-months old and was kitted out with a plush white leather interior.

The Ningaloo Reef is the closest part of Australia to the continental shelf where whale sharks are believed to live. Dubbed the gentle giants of the sea, whale sharks are the largest fish in our oceans and they can grow up to eighteen metres in length and have a mouth more than one metre wide, but are harmless plankton eating filter feeders. They visit the waters off Ningaloo Reef annually between the months of March and June to feed.

Whale sharks are protected in Australia by the Wildlife Conservation Act, which limits the number of operators who are allowed licenses to provide swimming tours with these majestic creatures. The operators are extremely professional and governed by numerous regulations; only one vessel at a time may enter a 'contact zone' around the shark and for a maximum time of ninety minutes; The first vessel to arrive is deemed to have contact, the second vessel must keep 250-metres away, and any subsequent vessels 400-metres away; The contact vessel must not approach closer than 30-metres and should approach from ahead of the sharks direction of travel; There should be no more than ten swimmers in the water at any one time and they must not approach closer than three metres or attempt to touch or restrict the normal movement of the shark; Motorised propulsion, flash photography and scuba diving in the close proximity to the shark is prohibited.

Around half a dozen boat operators share the services of a small aeroplane, whose job is to circle the ocean spotting the sharks and report their position and direction of travel to the boat operators.

We cruised firstly to the inner reef for a spot of snorkelling. Around 10am the skipper received the first radio call from the spotter plane, and we were summoned back to the boat. As we set off in pursuit, we were split into two groups of seven people, each group with a spotter whose job was to locate the shark in the water and swim alongside it with one arm raised in the air so that we swimmers could easily identify the location and path of the shark. We cruised to a position ahead of the shark's path and excitedly I leapt off the stern of the boat with the first group. Unfortunately though the shark dived and we lost contact, and so we all clambered back aboard, somewhat disappointed at the anti-climax.

We didn't have long to wait however for the second sighting and we were soon speeding off again. Once again we were the first vessel on the scene. The next group took to the water about 50-metres ahead of the shark. The boat then cruised around 100-metres further on and I took to the water again with my group. I lay on the surface face down peering hopelessly through my mask into the vast blue, not really sure where the shark was, just hoping to get a glimpse. Suddenly out of the murk, the huge beast appeared, mouth gaping wide. I was unable to move or get out of the way, but the shark gracefully manoeuvred itself around me and continued on its path. I tried to swim alongside it but it was much too quick, and within a couple of seconds it had gone.

Over the course of the day, we swam with three other sharks, the largest of which the crew estimated to be around eight metres in length. We were able to follow two of them for a considerable time allowing each of us to swim several times in their company and see them close up. At one point I managed to get to close to the shark and his tail brushed against my head as he breezed by. On another occasion I was able to swim alongside a shark for what seemed like ten minutes, but was probably no more than one or two, nevertheless, it was exhilarating.

The perfect day was capped when we sighted pods of minky and humpback whales on our return to port. This had been one of the best days of my life, however there was a slightly sour end to the day when my video camera got splashed by salt water and consequently stopped working.

At 6.45 the next morning the 'Easyrider' bus set off on the next leg carrying just two passengers, myself and a French girl, who disembarked at the first stop of Coral Bay 150-km along the coast. Three new passengers boarded; two young girls, Aussie Carla and Hilda from Norway, and forty-seven year old Sam from Yorkshire, who had a series body odour problem. We continued south for another 220km to the town of Carnarvon, where we stopped for lunch. I visited the local police station and finally managed to report my camera as lost, and so obtain the necessary insurance reference number.

Carnarvon is an old sheep town, first settled after original settlers drove 4,000 sheep from York (east of Perth) seeking warmer agricultural land. By 1883, Carnarvon had enough settlers for it to be gazetted as a town. Today the area has some of Australia's largest sheep stations, many the size of small European countries. The main street is forty metres wide, a legacy of bygone days when long 'camel trains' transported supplies and stock; apparently camel trains require a large amount of room to turn and change direction whilst carrying a full load.

After lunch we pressed onto Shark Bay, a series of gulfs, inlets, islands and bays, containing an abundance of unique flora and fauna. It is home to a 14,000 strong breeding group of rare dugong's, around a tenth of the world's population. These dugong's feed on the Wooramel Bank, which is said to be the world's largest seagrass meadow, covering 1,030 square kilometre, and stretching for 129km along the coast. It has twelve varieties of seagrass and has taken over 5,000 years to reach its present size.

We stopped at Hamelin Beach to see it's colony of stromatolites, which are said to be the earliest known life form on earth. The low tidal flow in Shark Bay has resulted in a level of salt twice that of normal seawater. In these salty pools, stromatolites grow at a rate of less than 1mm per year. The discovery of these 'living fossils' was akin to finding a live dinosaur. A boardwalk has been erected to view these unusual life forms, which are about 60cm tall and resemble mushroom-shaped rocks; interesting but not exactly exciting.

Billions of tiny white 'coquina bivalve' sea shells form a 60km long beach aptly named Shell Beach, where we stopped briefly on the next leg of the journey. The deposits are some seven to ten metres deep and stretch into the calm bay. This strange phenomenon occurs, as this shellfish has no natural predator, enabling it to exist in huge numbers for thousands of years. Once they die naturally, they are washed ashore where they have formed this strange beach. The effect is brilliant; a long, snow-white beach bordered by aqua blue ocean waters.

After another long and tiring day, we eventually reached our overnight destination of Denham, Australia's most westerly town and the first place that Europeans visited on the mainland. The Dutch were the first to arrive here in 1616, followed by the English explorer William Dampier on his second voyage to Australia in 1699, naming the area after the abundance of sharks he saw. However due to the lack of water, the area was not settled until English Captain H.M. Denham arrived in 1858. Denham town is compact with a population of around 1,500 people. The town still contains a few original buildings, including the Old Pearlers Restaurant on the waterfront and St Andrews Church, both constructed of blocks made from compacted coquina bivalve shells.

We spent the evening in the local pub, together with three Celt guys that I'd met in Exmouth; Andy from Scotland and Austin and Mick from Ireland. In fact they were the occupants of the untidy room that I'd refused to stay in. I ordered a beer and the barmaids eyes widened.

"Were am yo from?" she asked.

"The same place as you I presume" I replied, and of course I was right, she was indeed from my hometown, although we didn't actually know each other. She was backpacking around Australia and had stayed on here to earn a little money.

Our little group spent the evening drinking, playing pool, and generally flirting with one another, during which the previously shy and retiring Helga became more and more outgoing, before suddenly breaking down and sobbing uncontrollably. Apparently she was upset that Carla was receiving more attention than she. Strange girl I thought.

When I originally commenced my tour of Western Australia, my intention was to take my time and stop off for a few days at a time at various places en-route. However, I had greatly underestimated the sheer emptiness of this state and the lack of facilities in the various towns, many of which were little more than roadhouses. Consequently I had become quite bored, especially with the tiring, monotonous bus journeys. I had therefore decided to continue to Perth with as little delay as possible.

After only four hours sleep, the three Celts and I woke early for a visit to nearby Monkey Mia, the world famous beach where friendly bottlenose dolphins swim to shore to interact with eager humans. Sam had also intended to come but unfortunately we couldn't wake him. This small group of dolphins have been visiting the beach at Monkey Mia daily since the 1960's of their own free will, and are part of a much larger pod that live further out in the bay. They arrive most mornings and visitors can walk amongst the dolphins in the shallows. During our brief visit, eight dolphins turned up including three generations spanning twenty-eight years; grandmother, mother and her four-week old calf. They appeared almost tame, and very relaxed around people; I wandered just who was observing who?

Afterwards we returned to Denham to wake and collect Sam, who was still a little drunk from the previous night. We set off along the spectacular coast road, stopping at Eagle Bluff, where on a clear day whales, dolphins and other wildlife abundant in this area are often seen splashing on the surface. Unfortunately we didn't see any wildlife, however we weren't too disappointed as this stretch of coast affords breathtaking views, with gorges and rugged coastal scenery, where the precipitous sea cliffs in impressive red-and-white-banded layers of sandstone loom over the crashing white foam from the Indian Ocean.

We continued into Kalbarri National Park and stopped at a lookout with a superb panorama; the lower reaches of the Murchison River winding its way through dramatic red gorges with 150-metre high cliffs on either side. By early afternoon we had reached Kalbarri town, a delightful fishing town with a population of just 1,800 people, sitting on the estuary of the Murchison River.

After almost one week of none stop travel, the final 600km of road lay between us and Perth. Once more we made an early start and set off along the Batavia Coast, named after the Dutch East India Company flagship Batavia. The Batavia was wrecked in the Houtman Abrolhos Islands in 1629, almost 150 years before Captain James Cook's 'discovery' of the eastern coast of Australia. Many Dutch merchant ships were wrecked between 1629 and 1727 on the treacherous reefs along this coast, but what made this shipwreck special was the extraordinary drama that followed.

In 1628 the Batavia sailed from the Netherlands on her maiden journey to Batavia in the Dutch Colonies in Indonesia. The journey to disaster was to take eight months, during which bad weather and disagreements between the commander and the skipper divided the crew, to such an extent that mutiny was suggested. Before the mutiny could take place however, the Batavia ran aground on the Houtman Abrolhos, some 60km of the coast.

The Commodore knew they were in dire straights and so he set sail in search of drinking water, together with some thirty other crew members and most of the food and water supplies. They left behind two hundred and sixty-eight people, who felt so betrayed by this desertion they named the island 'Traitor's Island', a name it still bears to this day. Those left behind were in a dreadful situation and some died of thirst in the first week, before rain helped replenish supplies of water. The unfortunate survivors were then to play a part in one of the most horrible tales of mutiny and murder ever told.

Jeronimus Cornelius, the most senior company man amongst the survivors, turned out to be a psychotic killer with an uncanny ability to control others. He ordered one group of soldiers to a distant island in search of water and abandoned them, hoping they would die. He then split the remaining survivors amongst some of the closer islands, none of which had any water. With a loyal band of murderous young men, Cornelius then began to systematically hunt down and kill anyone he believed would represent a burden on the limited resources, or a threat to his reign of terror.

Cornelius had intended to send the soldiers to their deaths, but instead he had sent the only group of men that could threaten his regime to the best island in the Abrolhos, containing a natural store of water and food in the form of numerous wallabies, birds and eggs. Over the following weeks, Cornelius first tried to tempt the soldiers to join the mutiny, before resorting to attacking them, but the soldiers were able to fend the mutineers off.

Meanwhile, the commanders' group had aborted their search for water on the mainland, and had made their way to Batavia, the journey taking thirty-three days. After their arrival in Batavia, the commander returned to rescue the stranded survivors. On September 17, 1629 the commanders' rescue ship appeared on the horizon and in short time the mutineers were all rounded up. Some were tortured to confess, some like Cornelius were hung on one of the islands, two were marooned on the coast of W.A., and the rest were taken back to Batavia, where most of them were executed. In total, the mutineers had murdered one hundred and twenty-five men, women and children.

We left Kalbarri the next morning and continued south with nine passengers; the three Celts, Sam, and four new passengers now aboard the bus, including an English guy named Ron who I immediately hit it off with. After six long hours, we arrived at the stark desert terrain of Namburg National Park, better known as The Pinnacles Desert. We strolled along a path through this strange and mysterious landscape containing thousands of limestone pillars, sporadically scattered and protruding from the vast yellow, rippled sand dunes. These limestone formations vary in size and shape; some are just a few centimetres whilst others stand up to four metres tall. It is an eerie, haunting landscape which resembles a natural graveyard.

Exhausted, I slept for the remaining 260km drive, waking just as we entered the state capital Perth around 4pm, after ten hours on the road. Our little group had bonded well over the last couple of days, and so we all checked into The Witches Hat Hostel together, which came highly recommended by several travellers heading north. We spent our first night in Perth in the hostel drinking until

2am, before the staff ordered us to quieten down and go to bed.

I awoke blurry eyed the next morning after a sleepless night, in which it seemed that several of my all male dormitory roommates were having a snoring competition. I walked into the city centre and dropped my video camera off at a repair centre, and spent the remainder of the morning shopping for a new still camera, this being the first town of any size that I had been to since the loss.

Perth is a cosmopolitan city and lies on the banks of the Swan River 19km from the coast. It covers an area of around nine square kilometres, and is home to a melting pot of nationalities, which belies its status as the most isolated city in the world. It contains many modern, multi-story buildings, busy streets, shops, restaurants and nightclubs, just like any other modern city, but on a relaxed, smaller scale. The central shopping area comprised of just two parallel streets approximately five hundred metres long, with various small streets, malls and arcades linking them. It was smaller than I'd expected, and certainly much smaller than one would expect a city with a population of over one million people to be.

That evening our little group from the Easyrider Bus headed to the Chinese food court for an 'eat as much as you can' buffet dinner, after which we headed to the bars of Northbridge, a district one block back from the city. After dark, Northbridge springs to life, it is Perth's cultural and entertainment area, and is home to a number of pubs, nightclubs, bars, cafes, shops, galleries and a large concentration of restaurants. On our return to the hostel we again sat up chatting in the kitchen, until once again we were told off like naughty children.

The hostel turned out to be a nightmare; the long-term hostel guests were a close knitt group and very different to us. They didn't seem to do much other than watch TV and only went out once a week on a Saturday night. The manager was like a strict headmistress who gave you a stern bollocking in front of everyone if you broke any of the house rules; no eating or drinking in the TV room, no loud talking after 10pm, no loitering in the kitchen, and no running in the corridors, not really, made that one up – but you get the idea. I personally received a couple of stern lectures; which were so severe that I thought the headmistress was going to make me stand in the corner with my hands on my head!

The next day we headed to the Subiaco Oval Stadium, home of the West Coast Eagles who were due to play Adelaide in the AFL (Aussie Rules Football). We found a pub near to the stadium and settled down to watch England rugby union team take on the All Blacks. England were soundly thrashed, much to the pleasure of the locals, who despite disliking their Antipodean neighbours, they appear to positively hate the English. Like the Scots, Welsh and Irish, the Aussies support two countries, their own, and anyone playing against England!

Afterwards we left the pub and walked to the stadium in readiness for the game, only to find that it was a sell out, and as we didn't have tickets, we returned to the hostel disappointed.

Being a Saturday, we were invited to join the hostel crowd on the weekly visit to Black Betty's Bar. We each put $10 into a drinks kitty, and the bar would double the total amount collected, however the money could only be used to purchase $8 jugs of beer; so effectively for our $10 outlay, we would each receive two and a half jugs of beer.

The night started well, the bar was lively, the music was thumping and the beer flowed. Our organiser proudly told us that they had never managed to drink the full tab, however within two-hours we had polished off every jug. The regular hostel crowd were not happy and accused us of drinking too fast. For the remainder of the evening there was a definite tension in the air, and our two groups grew even further apart.

Unhappy with the rules and now bad atmosphere at the Witches Hat, Ron and I checked out the next morning and checked into the nearby Ozi Inn Hostel, a much more acceptable establishment where excessive drinking and partying was vigorously encouraged. The facilities and cleanliness could not compare to the Witches Hat, but there it was much friendlier and I liked it very much; and there was cable TV showing all of the Euro 2004 Football Championship games.

We watched England's opening game against France in the hostel TV room, which was packed with about thirty travellers, although only around half a dozen were actually interested in watching the game. Some of the girls just wanted to be around the guys, some of the guys just wanted to be there as if its cool to watch and talk football, irrespective of whether you actually liked it. A couple of Aussies joined us too, although they had no interest at all in football; they cheered for France throughout the game, not that they wanted them to win, they just preferred to see England loose. One cockney guy in particular really annoyed me, continually referring to every England player in his 'barrow-boy' accent as 'legend'. A couple sitting behind me talked all through the first half about anything and everything except for football, luckily though he fell asleep at half time and didn't wake again until after the final whistle. A couple lay on the floor in front of the screen kissing and cuddling throughout the game, and another girl kept asking why the game was being played at such a ridiculously early hour (the game kicked off at 2.45am local time), obviously unaware of time zones. Despite all of the distractions, I still managed to watch and enjoy the game, that is until the final minute when France scored twice to snatch a victory from England's grasp. Shell shocked, I headed to bed at 5am.

Over the course of the week, I generally hung out in the city centre, visited some of Perth's sights and suburbs, or relaxed on the banks of the Swan River or in Kings Park. Kings Park is said to be one of the biggest city parks in the world containing 400-hectares of virgin bush land plus beautifully manicured gardens. It is located on a hill in the west of the city, and offers fantastic panoramas of the city skyline, the Swan River and the rolling Darling Ranges to the east.

Perths most recognisable landmark and perhapes its most unusual was the Swan Bells, siting on the edge of the river; a modern glass spire bell tower and a copper structure representing the sails of a ship, it houses twelve bells, originally cast in 14th century England, a bicentenial gift from the UK to Australia.

The state museum contained a few interesting galleries and exhibits including a meteorite collection, and rocks from Mars and the Moon; a large collection of minerals, diamonds and other precious stones; various stuffed native Australian animals displayed in Victorian style glass cases; and a collection of local marine life including an enormous twenty-five metre long blue whale skeleton. My favourite exhibit however was the four-metre long megamouth shark; an extremely rare and unusual species set in its own is preservative bath, sunk in the ground in the courtyard. The species is distinctive for its large head and is unlike any other type of shark. The species was first discovered in 1976, since when thirty-two other specimens have been found, the majority in the Pacific Ocean. I had never heard of it before and I had never seen anything quite like it

I spent one day in the nearby suburb of Freemantle, a delightful fishing town full of culture and history, at least by Australian standards that is. It boasts some of Australia's best examples of Victorian and Edwardian architecture, containing galleries, shops, pubs, and nightclubs scattered throughout its quaint streets. Many artists, professionals and others seeking a life outside Perth come to live and work in 'Freo', giving it a somewhat bohemian atmosphere. I ate fish and chips for lunch on the harbour-side, wrapped in paper like back home, but they didn't taste anywhere near as good.

I was not enjoying hostel life; sharing dorms with strangers, being woken early in the morning or late at night by people checking in or out. Once woken, I found it difficult to return to sleep, and the inconsiderate nature of others amazed me; I always made a point of packing the evening before checking out, and would tiptoe into the dorm late at night, so as not to disturb anyone. However few others seemed to be so considerate; it was not unusual to be woken early in the morning by the sound of rustling plastic bags and zips being opened and closed, or by someone returning to the dorm late at night and turning on the lights, or by chattering drunks who thought nothing of holding a conversation at some ungodly hour. The worst though was trying to sleep whilst an amorous couple were shagging in the same room!

The social side of hostel life however was good, and I was meeting a lot of likeminded people from many different countries and cultures, although mainly British, so at least I was never short of drinking partners. My nights were often spent in the pubs, bars and restaurants of Northbridge with Ron, and Adam, Rich, and Craig, our Welsh dorm-mates.

On one evening, a small group of us headed to a bar in the

Northbridge area to watch England beat Switzerland 3-0. After the game, we were standing outside the pub chatting to a group of other travellers when Rich and Adam ran past, being pursued by a group of aborigines; Adam had blood pouring from his head. It transpired that he had been smashed over the head with a bottle by a group of drunken aborigines in an unprovoked attack. The hostel manager took him to the hospital where he received seven stitches. Luckily he was otherwise ok.

After nine days, the longest period I had spent in any one place since Koh Tao, it was eventually time to move on. Perth was a lovely city, but four or five days here would probably have been sufficient, and I had begun to get bored of my surroundings. And so with anticipation it was off to Adelaide on the next leg of my Down Under tour.

12

Southern Comfort
(South Australia & Victoria)
19/06/04 to 03/07/04

The plane touched down in Adelaide just after 3pm; outside a mini-bus sent by Backpacker Oz Hostel was waiting to pick me up and drive me to their establishment in the heart of the city. The hostel was very clean and agreeable; on the ground floor there was a small reception and tour desk, a well equipped communal kitchen, a bar with a free pool table, and a large open plan lounge and TV room.

I spent the afternoon and evening in the hostel getting to know my fellow guests. Around midnight, Dutch friends Fok and Bastian, Richard from England, and Hazel from Ireland, announced that they were going out for the night, "If anyone wants to join us they have ten minutes to get ready", they shouted. Always up for a night out, especially on a Saturday, I quickly spruced myself up and joined them. We visited several bars and pubs, including one seedy basement bar in the red light district, containing a number of unsavoury looking characters. I felt more uncomfortable here than at any other time of my journey so far, and after just one drink we left. We ended up in a trendy cocktail bar, where we partied until closing time at 4am. We staggered back to the hostel, where I discovered that Richard, Hazel and Fok were my dorm mates.

The next day I awoke around lunchtime and set off to explore Adelaide on foot. The city was well laid out on a grid pattern by the early colonists, and built out of stone, giving it a solid, dignified look. I strolled the short distance to Victoria Square, a large pedestrian square which marks the city centre, and then continued down King William Road passing several distinctive period stone buildings, the most impressive of which were: the Renaissance-style Town Hall built in the 1860s with its distinctive arches, the Treasury Buildings, which have been renovated and converted into a plush hotel, and the G.P.O. with its grand Victorian clock-tower. There are also a number of statues depicting British historical figures such as King George V, Queen Victoria and Robert Burns.

Rundle Mall, the main shopping area in the heart of the City, was fairly small and a little disappointing. There were however some interesting and unusual statues, including two polished stainless steel spheres, around two-metres in diameter, and four bronze pigs depicted in lively poses as if they were out walking the streets in search of a bargain.

North Terrace, opposite the Torrens River, is Adelaide's cultural boulevard containing many excellent examples of early South Australian architecture including the Art Gallery of South Australia, the Migration Museum, the restored Victorian Mortlock Library, the grey marble Parliament House and the Museum of South Australia. From here I crossed the Torrens River over the King William Road Bridge, close to the Adelaide Oval cricket ground, and spent an hour watching the river drift by, before retracing my steps back to the hostel.

I spent the evening in the hostel watching movie videos and eating pizza. That night I was woken by the sound of Richard and Fok chatting.

"What time is it?" I asked.

"Four O'clock" answered Fok.

"I'm so thirsty" I said.

"Would you like some juice, no bits, just juice?" asked Richard.

I took a drink, and then returned to sleep; however I was left with a strange feeling of deja vu.

The next day I caught an original vintage 1929 tram to the seaside town of Glenelg, which turned out to be a little disappointing as there was little of interest to see, despite the fact that it was advertised as 'historic Glenelg'. In all fairness though, this wasn't exactly the tourist season, in fact it was actually the middle of winter here and the weather in South Australia and Victoria is colder and wetter than anywhere else Down-Under at this time of year. Everyone here complains of the cold, but it is nowhere near as cold as a British winter, more like an autumn day, or even a bad summers day.

I spent the afternoon and early evening in a bar with Richard, Hazel and Fok, returning around 10pm to get some sleep in order to watch the next England football game against Croatia, which kicked off around 4am local time. For some strange reason I woke in the middle of the night, to find the light on and Richard standing motionless in the centre of the room, fully clothed and holding a plastic shopping bag. After a few minutes he turned off the light, got undressed and climbed into bed.

Despite setting my watch alarm for 3am, I unfortunately failed to wake for the game. Over breakfast I told Hazel of the nights events. "He's weird,' she said, 'On Saturday night he woke me and asked me if I wanted some juice, no bits, just juice".

"He did the same to me a couple of nights ago" I replied.

I later saw Richard in the hostel lounge, "Do you sleep walk?" I asked

"No, why do you ask?"

"Well I saw you last night standing in the middle of the room holding a shopping bag."

"Oh that, I was going to check out"

"But it was the middle of the night Richard"

"I know, that's why I didn't check out". There was nothing more I could say. Richard was indeed a strange character and I never felt comfortable sleeping in the same dorm as he.

Fortunately, I had received a kind invitation to stay with some old friends who had emigrated to Adelaide a couple of years previously, Tracey and her boyfriend Tim, and so I jumped at the opportunity. Tracey arrived to pick me up one afternoon, and drive me to her home in the Port Adelaide district. On route we picked up Tim and stopped off to catch up over a coffee at a café overlooking the marina. This was the first time I had seen them in seven years, the last time being my thirtieth birthday party. We spent the evening in their home chatting and drinking wine. That night was the best sleep that I had had for longer than I cared to remember. It was so good to be in a comfy bed again, without the disturbances of a hostel dorm.

The next day, whilst Tracey and Tim were at work, I explored the streets of Port Adelaide, and its harbour and docks. Sadly the docks are mostly redundant now, many of the once grand Victorian buildings here are falling into disrepair and the area is generally run down. It reminded me of my childhood, growing up in the industrial West Midlands during the recession of the 1980's. I ate lunch in a harbour-side pub and returned to the house to await my hosts.

In the years after WWII, Australian's became increasingly aware of their vulnerability and isolation, and grew ever more fearful of Japan, who had bombed the northern cities of Darwin and Broome. To combat this threat, and in order to increase its population, so strengthening its economy and its ability to defend itself, the government introduced a program of 'assisted passage' to British and Eastern European migrants. Between 1947 and 1968, over 1million migrants emigrated to Australia, including my aunt Kath and uncle Joe, who left England in 1955 on the £10 assisted passage programme.

Whilst in Adelaide, I met my aunt and uncle for the first time; they were now in their twilight years. They too lived in Port Adelaide and I spent a full day at their home, chatting about their emigration, the similarities and differences between England and Australia, sport and football, and of course our family. It was a strange feeling being in the company of family that I didn't really know. We ate lunch and dinner together, my first roast dinner since leaving home seven months ago, followed by apple pie and ice cream; just like home, well almost.

Tim and Tracey were wonderful hosts, they looked after me and made me feel very much at home during my short stay. On my penultimate day Tim drove me into the Adelaide hills and to Mount Lofty, a lookout with panoramic views over the city and surrounding countryside. Unfortunately though the rain was bucketing down so we couldn't see a thing. We stopped in Hahndarf, settled in 1839 it is the oldest surviving German settlement in Australia, and is now a major tourist attraction.

There are many old German-style buildings here, including the German Arms Hotel where we stopped off to sample the beer. We returned to the city around 4pm, picked up Tracey from work and continued to the huge Central Market, which dates back to 1869 when the site was established as a venue for growers and wholesalers to sell directly to the public. The market was buzzing with sounds, colours and wonderous aromas. Friday night must be a real social occasion at the market, as it was full of couples and families out for the night. There was a massive range and diversity of produce; fresh fruit and vegetables, meat and fish including varieties that I'd never heard of before, several coffee stores selling literally hundreds of varieties of coffee beans, cake stalls selling delicious looking home-made treats, hundreds of varieties of cheeses, and several stalls selling speciality gourmet products introduced by the immigrants from around the globe. We treated ourselves to a coffee and brought some cakes to take home, and then visited the Asian food court where we ate dinner.

The following morning Tracey and Tim dropped me off in the city centre as I continued my journey. We said our farewells and I departed Adelaide on another tour bus, which was to take us through the South Australian hills and the Grampian Ranges, and finally along the Great Ocean Road to Melbourne, in the adjoining state of Victoria. At 7.30am, the 'Groovy Grape' tour bus departed with just ten passengers aboard, so there was plenty of room to stretch out.

The group was the oddest I've travelled with so far on this trip, consisting of a mixture of nationalities including a non-drinking German engineering student name Stefan, who bored everyone to death with his constant talk of German technology and inventions, a uncharacteristically quiet American guy name Josh, who became my drinking partner, two Swiss sisters who didn't join in with anything, two crazy Japanese girls name Chika and Aiko, and three Korean girls who sat on the back seat and would instantly fall asleep within moments of the bus setting off. Our driver and guide Scorch was the most enthusiastic guide. He'd been doing this job for eight years and so had done this trip hundreds of times, and yet you would have thought that it was his first trip; he seemed genuinely as exited to see some of the sights as we were.

The Japanese and Korean girls, like many foreign students, had come to Australia to learn English. I didn't really understand the sense in this, as most Australian's can't actually speak the language themselves. The Aussie language is a bastardised version of English with many words derived from slang. In addition, most Aussies appear to have difficulty with words over two syllables, and so shorten most beyond recognition, then add a vowel to the end. To pass as an Aussie is easy, just talk through your nose, shorten your words, and add an I or E to the end!

We travelled along the Dukes Highway and made our first stop in the small farming town of Keith, where we had a pie for breakfast from a lovely little bakery. Continuing on we passed through the aptly named Bordertown and crossed the state line into Victoria. We turned off the main highway and stopped briefly in the township of Frances, with a population of just twenty-two people. I had a pint in the only pub for miles, but none of the group joined me!

We continued on to Mount Arapiles, Australia's main rock climbing venue, where we stopped for a picnic lunch. Stefan decided to go for a walk and didn't return, so for the next half hour we drove around the surrounding dirt roads looking for him. Eventually we tracked him down, sitting on a rock by the side of a road looking lost and confused.

By mid afternoon we were in the fabulous Grampian Ranges, where we trekked to Mackenzie and Broken Falls, which were both pumping with water following the recent rains. We saw mobs of wild kangaroos and dozens of emus. As night drew in, we drove to our overnight accommodation in the town of Halls Gap, stopping on route to buy supplies of food and alcohol; Josh and I brought a case of beer between us and Chika and Aiko brought some wine. The rest of the group were apparently teetotal.

We arrived at Brambuk Backpackers, which was unlike any hostel that I had stayed in previously and was more like a mountain lodge, with a large communal lounge with a central open fireplace, wooden floors, communal kitchen, and annex dorms with private bathrooms. I was sharing a dorm with the other two guys, and after dropping my backpack on my bunk, I headed to the lounge.

As I entered I literally bumped into an unexpected familiar face, Jo who I'd first met in a mountain lodge in Nepal back in January, and then again in Bangkok in February. Back then she had been travelling with a guy name Peter, but it transpired that they had had a falling out and had gone their separate ways. Neither of us could quite believe it, and we spent the evening chatting about our respective journeys. What a small world it really is.

Afterwards, Chika and Aiko returned to our room with Josh and I, where we played cards and drank until the early hours, whilst Stefan sat on his bed watching. The girls finally staggered to their dorm around 2am, both pissed as farts.

By 7.30am the next morning we were heading back into the Grampian's where once again we trekked through a landscape of stunning rock formations up to two lookouts called The Pinnacle and The Balconies, with breathtaking panoramic views across the valleys below. After another picnic lunch, we departed the Grampian's and headed south, arriving at the town of Warrnambool around 3pm, from where we commenced our journey along The Great Ocean Road.

This rugged stretch of coast is one of the worlds great coast drives, where the huge waves of the ferocious Southern Ocean have battered the cliffs to form some wonderful rock formations. We stopped off at several scenic viewpoints taking in the Bay of Islands, Bay of Martyrs, The Grotto, London Bridge, The Arch, Sentential Rock and The Twelve Apostles.

These rock formations are formed by the gradual erosion of softer limestone areas, creating caves in the cliffs. These caves eventually wore away through wave and wind erosion to become arches and when they collapsed, rock islands were left detached. These giant rock stacks soar from the swirling waters of the Southern Ocean and are a central feature of the spectacular Port Campbell National Park. The dramatic and imposing limestone cliffs that are the backdrop to The Twelve Apostles tower up to seventy metres, while the tallest of the rock stacks is around forty-five metres high.

The formations were all equally beautiful, however one of my favourites was the Grotto; a semi-circular shaped natural amphitheatre, linked to the ocean by an arch. Whilst we were standing inside watching the ocean beyond, a huge wave crashed through the arch and for a second I thought we were going to be washed away, and so did Chika and Aiko, who screamed hysterically and ran for there lives, much to my amusement!

Along with hundreds of other tourists, we watched a spectacular sunset over The Twelve Apostles; the sky turning bright pink and then deep purple. Immediately after sunset all of the other tourists departed on their buses, but we stayed on and were treated to the sight of penguins swimming ashore and scampering up the beach.

We spent the night at The Ocean House Backpackers Hostel, positioned right on the beach at Port Campbell. It was even better than the previous hostel, and comprised a beach house with four dorm rooms, four bathrooms, a lounge with an open-fire, a kitchen and a veranda overlooking the ocean. After dinner, Scorch produced his didgeridoo and entertained us with a short story, using different notes and sounds to represent characters and animals. We then all took turns, and on this occasion I successfully produced a note, helped by a few beers of course.

Scorch woke us at 6am the next morning, the low humming sound of his didgeridoo acting as an alarm call, and by 7 we were on the road. We returned to London Bridge and The Twelve Apostles for sunrise, which was equally as stunning as yesterday's sunset. We then headed to Loch Ard Gorge, named after HMS Loch Ard, which sank here in 1878. The few bodies recovered from the shipwreck are buried in the cliff-top cemetery. We descended the wooden steps to the beach where the disaster unfolded, engulfed by the towering cliffs, with a narrow opening out to sea through which the wind howled.

The Loch Ard was an iron clipper, which sailed from England in 1878 with fifty-four passengers and crew, and a cargo valued at more than $100,000. Three months after leaving, the ship was mercilessly crushed against the rocks one foggy morning, and within fifteen minutes the Loch Ard sank. Only two people survived the wreck: crewmember Tom Pearce and passenger Eva Carmichael, who was travelling to Australia with her family. Tom clung to a lifeboat and was washed into the deep gorge that now bears the ships name. Eva, who could not swim, clung to a chicken coop to keep afloat. Hearing her cries for help, Tom swam to her aid and dragged her to safety. There was to be no fairy-tale end to the story though, after their recuperation, Eva returned home to England and they never saw each other again.

We continued our journey along the 'Ship Wreck' coast; the ferocious Southern Ocean continued to batter the coastline throughout the journey with its huge swell and high waves. We made a brief visit to Cape Otway National Park, a cool temperate rainforest where we stopped at Maits Rest and trekked along a raised boardwalk, which stretched into the heart of the lush forest of towering trees and ferns. Scorch later drove up a narrow dirt track lined with eucalyptus trees, in which we saw several wild koalas; a couple were even clinging to branches whilst asleep.

We returned to the coast road and stopped for lunch of fish and chips at Apollo Bay, before continuing on along the surfer's coast, passing through the pretty towns of Lorne and Anglesea. We made a brief stop at the famous Belles Beach to watch dozens of surfers, known locally as 'shark bait', trying to ride the most enormous waves, and then we made a final stop for an hour in the town of Torquay, the self-proclaimed surf capital of Australia.

We finally arrived in Melbourne at 7pm after a fantastic three-day trip. The Great Ocean Road had truly lived up to its name, which can't be said about all things Down Under, and fortunately the weather throughout the trip was dry and sunny, which produced the most amazing pink and purple sunrise and sunset skies.

Scorch had recommended and booked me into The Victoria Hotel. I checked in and discovered that the hotel was actually an Irish pub with dorm rooms above; not exactly what I was hoping for, but at least it was cheap at less than £30 for a week. My dorm was like a pigsty with clothes and rubbish scattered all over the floor. I made space for my backpack in one corner of the room, showered, changed and headed for the bar.

I seemed to be the only non-Irishman staying there, and subsequently I suspected that I may be in for an awkward week, but my fears were misplaced and it wasn't long before a friendly group of lads and girls invited me to join them. By the end of the night, everyone seemed to know my name, which probably wasn't too difficult for them to remember, as everyone else appeared to be named either Patrick, Dermot, Mick or Shamus.

Over the course of the week I made a few friends in The Vic and had many a good night in the bar, although the choice of music from the jukebox was a little repetitive and annoying; Kenny Rogers' song 'The Gambler' was the favourite, and was played on average around a dozen times a night.

The strangest thing about The Vic was that everyone staying there seemed to have been there for all their time in Aus, most hadn't travelled anywhere else, and several rarely ventured outside the pub at all, either working during the day and drinking through the night, or sleeping until lunch time and then drinking for the rest of the day and night. Very strange and very sad!

Not wanting to waist all my time in Melbourne in a drunken stupor, I chose to spend my days exploring the city, which Victorians regard as the cultural and fashion capital of Australia, and with a population of more than three million it is Australia's second largest city. It is the first city that I had visited in Australia, which actually felt like a city and not just a big town. The centre consists of a seven square kilometre rectangular grid of streets bordered by the Yarra River to the south. The buildings are large and grand, the streets are busy, and there is a multitude of shopping malls, skyscrapers, cathedrals and churches. Countless restaurants, bars and boutiques line the alleys and arcades off the main streets, and a fantastic transport system with a mix of new and old trams grace a network of tracks that run throughout the city.

Within a couple of hours of arriving I knew that I loved it. I spent my entire first day exploring the city, a blend of old and new. The cultural heart of the city is the ultra-modern Federation Square, a vast public meeting place with irregular shaped structures, a large screen TV and a stage. Opened in 2002, it is definitely a 'Marmite' building, inspiring instant love or hate from most. Standing opposite is the splendid Flinders Street Station. Apart from being the hub of Melbourne's transport system, it is one of the city's great landmarks and icons. Opened in 1884, the Victorian station dominates the intersection of Flinders and

Swanston Streets, together with the grand Gothic St Paul's Cathedral, which stands diagonally opposite.

More grand buildings lie to the north; the recently renovated domed and pillared sandstone State Library, built in the 1850's with its classical Italianate façade, has been a Melbourne landmark for almost 150 years; the flamboyant City Baths, built in 1860 to stop the people bathing in the river, and the Town Hall. The most impressive public building is the three-storey stone Parliament House, built in 1856 with sweeping steps, elegant lamps, grand colonnade, suggesting solidity and strength.

I strolled along the Yarra River, from where you can see the MCG (Melbourne Cricket Ground), one of the most famous sporting stadiums in the world. The river separates the city from the parklands that surround the Royal Botanic Gardens, and the Southbank development, once an old and neglected industrial area, which has been rejuvenated with shops and restaurants, trendy cafes, food courts and a five-star hotel.

I thought it would be nice to take a tram ride, and so I decided to head to Melbourne's beach resort of St Kilda for the day, or should I say that I tried to. The Melbourne trams are fitted with P.A. systems enabling the drivers to communicate and interact with the passengers, informing them of buildings of interest along the route, etc. This driver was like no other, shortly after boarding he announced, "This tram is currently running late. It will therefore be necessary to speed up, which may result in a crash. Our final destination is therefore unknown at this time." Half of the passengers looked terrified by this statement, whilst the others appeared amused. The wacky and amusing comments continued throughout the journey.

"The tram will shortly be stopping at the hospital for the driver to collect his weekly medication".

"No passengers, this is not a normal driver".

It was fun to watch the horrified looks on the faces of new passengers. After around twenty-minutes, the driver announced, "As we are behind schedule, this tram will no longer be going to St Kilda. All passengers wishing to go to St Kilda should therefore get off the tram and catch another one". No one was quite sure whether this was a joke or a serious statement. Everyone was looking around at each other and there was much muttering and shrugging of shoulders. Half of the passengers disembarked, whilst those that remained sat looking confused. I approached the driver, "is the tram going to St Kilda or not?" I asked.

"Haven't you been listening to the announcements?" he asked sarcastically.

"Yeah, but like everyone else, I don't know which are genuine and which are jokes".

"Well the last one was genuine, we are definitely not going to St Kilda," he said with a smug look on his face.

Fortunately the next tram wasn't too far behind and within fifteen-minutes I was in St Kilda, a bay side suburb once the haunt of prostitutes and drug addicts, which has seen a remarkable resurgence over the past twenty years and is now one of Melbourne's most fashionable areas to live and visit. It is known as the bohemian party suburb, although on the day I visited it appeared very quiet. I could only presume that today the 'bohemian residents' were off on a day trip.

In the centre of the town stood a permanent 1950's style funfair called Lunar Park, with merry-go rounds with horses, a helter-skelter, roller coasters, a ghost train, and the usual assortment of booths and stalls. The entrance was through the gaping mouth of a frightening looking moon-face, which resembled The Joker in the Batman movies.

There was a promenade running along a narrow strip of beach containing the usual tourist style shops, cafes and restaurants, and not too much else. It was very quiet and the few people that were out and about were wrapped up as if it were Moscow in December. I walked up the pier to the marina, from where there was a beautiful view back across the bay to the city skyline. I found a little beach side café and had a coffee and potato cake (scallop), before catching the tram back to the city, which luckily had a sane driver.

Melbourne is the undisputed sporting capital of Australia; it staged the 1956 Olympic Games and will stage the 2006 Commonwealth Games. The Australian Grand Prix, the Melbourne Cup (horse racing), the Australian Open tennis tournament, and the AFL Grand Final are all staged in Melbourne, which is in fact the birthplace of the AFL; the city has six teams in the league.

One evening I headed to the futuristic Telstra Dome with half a dozen of my Irish friends to watch a local derby between Essendon and the Kangaroos, my first Aussie Rules Football Game. Our £6 tickets gave us entry to all areas of the stadium, but did not guarantee a seat; unlike football back home, there was no segregation. Constructed in 2000, the oval shaped stadium was wonderful; three-tiers of seating beneath a retractable roof, sixty-six corporate boxes, two large internal video screens positioned at either end of the stadium, and a superb sound system. Within the stadium are numerous small TV screens showing images of the game, refreshment areas with seating, plentiful supply of toilets, and dozens of ATM's and public telephones. Capacity for football games is just under 54,000, although the seating plan can be altered to accommodate up to 74,000 for other sporting events and concerts

We made our way up to the third and top tier where we watched the first half of the game from a balcony, which provided a birds eye view of the action. Two old guys of Greek extraction stood next to us, vocally supporting the Roo's and getting very carried away; so much so that I would not have been surprised if either of them had suffered a heart attack. They helped me out with the basic rules, and before long I had got the jist of the game, which is a mix of rugby, Gaelic football and stupidity, and lasts for four thirty-minute quarters. The players are allowed to kick, punch, throw or run with the ball, so long as they bounce it every ten steps. It is extremely physical and it appeared that just about anything goes, other than pushing in the back. The posts are similar to rugby, but with a net below the crossbar to form a goal. Six points are awarded for a score in the goal, and 1 point for a score between the posts.

I wore my blue and white-stripped Albion football shirt, and supported the Roo's who played in a similar kit. By half time Essenden had built up a healthy twenty point lead. There was a good atmosphere, with lots of banter between the opposing fans, but no chanting or singing as in British football. Essenden maintained their lead until mid-way through the third quarter when the Roo's began a remarkable come back, eventually running out winners by 100 – 79. The good natured banter between the fans continued outside the stadium as we made our way back to The Vic, where we continued to drink until the early hours, whilst singing along to Kenny Rogers.

The next evening I travelled to the Crown Casino to meet up with Liam and Lucy, who I'd met on the first leg of the Red Centre tour around a month earlier. I waited outside the main entrance for around half an hour but they didn't show up. I entered the casino and spent an hour or so loosing a few of my Australian dollars. The casino was vast, spread over three floors, its main gaming floor stretching for more than half a kilometre and includes a series of smaller themed rooms. It contains hundreds of gaming tables and pokies (slot machines) and is open twenty-four hours a day, although on my budget an hour was all it look to realise that I would be better off in the bar of The Vic. I later discovered that Crown is so vast that it doesn't have one main entrance, it has several, and Liam and Lucy had been waiting at another. We never did meet up again.

Located on the southern bank of the Yarra River, Crown is Melbourne's premier entertainment venue offering an assortment of leisure venues in a luxurious environment. It is home to two world-class hotels, conference facilities, twenty-six restaurants, more than thirty bars and three nightclubs, a ten-pin bowling alley, cinemas and Australia's largest indoor theme park. It is also a live entertainment venue and claims to be 'the place to see the biggest names in local and international entertainment'. It proudly boasts, "Well known artists such as Suzi Quatro and Village People have performed to sold out crowds here". But whilst the entertainment might not be premier league, it's shopping is truly second to none, boasting a collection of the world's leading designer names all under the one roof.

I had thoroughly enjoyed Melbourne and was sad to be leaving, but at the same time I was looking forward to a new adventure and a warmer climate, and I desperately needed to top up my tan, which was fading fast.

13

Probably the Best in the World (Queensland)

04/07/04 to 04/08/04

The flight to Cairns was delayed due to the late arrival of an interconnecting flight. Eventually the delayed passengers boarded; around 50 American school kids, taking up several rows of seats in front of me. Consequently the flight was a nightmare; the seat directly in front of me was reclined up and down continually, and the kids generally argued, fought and teased one another throughout the three-hour flight.

We landed in Cairns just in time; another ten minutes and I could have been on a murder charge. I telephoned the Bohemia Resort, who sent a car to pick me up. The resort was modern, clean and plush, with an outdoor spa bath and a beautiful pool with sail-like sunshades over, an open-air bar containing a pool table, and an outdoor dining area with a large screen TV. The dorms were clean and spacious and contained just 4 single beds. I spent my first afternoon relaxing by the pool in the sun, and the evening in the resort bar making new friends.

The next day I went to the post office and collected my video camera, which had been posted here after being repaired in Perth. I spent the rest of the day wandering around the city, which was pleasant enough, containing the usual assortment of tourist related shops, cafes and bars. It is a modern city with a relaxed atmosphere and is the primary gateway to the Great Barrier Reef and the

Tropical North Queensland region. According to the tourist board, it is the safest tropical city in the world; there they go again giving themselves a 'best in the world' title.

However, for a holiday town I was surprised and disappointed to find that Cairns did not actually have a beach. To compensate, a 4,800 square metre artificial saltwater swimming lagoon had been built off the promenade, complete with white sand beach. The nearest swimming beach to Cairns is ten minutes away by car, with many other beaches within twenty-five minutes of the city, however for much of the year the sea is out of bounds for swimmers due to the presence of stingers (box jellyfish) and sharks, and so the lagoon offers visitors an all year safe swimming environment.

There were pleasant grassed areas to lie around and catch a few rays, or relax in the shade of a palm tree alongside the interesting and unusual galvanised steel fish sculptures that line the promenade. Running along the coast is a beautiful esplanade; beautiful that is when the tide is in. When the tide goes out, unless you're a keen birdwatcher, the view across the mud is not so pleasant. Shady trees, landscaped gardens and open spaces all contribute to the leisurely atmosphere on the Esplanade, along which are dotted picnic areas and public barbeques. I spent a pleasant afternoon leisurely walking along the wide, meandering wooden boardwalk, arcing around the seawall of the lagoon, sweeping past the boats in the marina, and around to the pier and Trinity Inlet, from where boats to the reef depart.

I popped to the tourist information centre for advice on buses to the northern beaches, however this information was harder to come by than I expected. Australian tourist information centres are actually commercial operations, geared to selling tours, not providing free information as they do in the UK. However after a little perseverance, I managed to obtain the required information.

Whilst in Melbourne, I had booked a tour package including: a 'jump on-jump, jump off' bus ticket from Cairns to Sydney, a three-day trip to Cape Tribulation, a diving trip to the Great Barrier Reef, a three-day jeep safari on Fraser Island, a three-day sailing trip around the Whitsunday Islands, and ten nights accommodation at various destinations, all for the bargain sum of £315. Booked separately, this package would have cost close to £500.

I spent the next day relaxing by the hostel pool, soaking up the sun. The hostel had fantastic facilities, however the staff were generally miserable, unfriendly and most unhelpful, and consequently I was not happy there. However my accommodation here was pre-paid for within my package, and so I stuck it out. Amazingly I had met a total of twelve people at Bohemia who were from the Birmingham area, and so it was home from home; several were fellow Albion fans and one evening we all wore our shirts in the bar. Very sad I know.

In preparation for a dive-trip on the Great Barrier Reef, I visited Reef Teach, for a very entertaining, informative, passionate and enthusiastic talk about the reef environment, conducted by a mad Irishman name Paddy; a marine-biologist and scuba dive instructor, who had been giving this lecture every evening for twelve-years. It was well worth the few dollars and was a great way to learn about what you will be seeing while at the reef.

I woke bright and early at 6am the next morning and caught the hostel shuttle bus to the reef terminal, from where all the boat tours to the barrier reef depart. Inside the terminal were the desks of around twenty boat tour companies, and hundreds of people, either rushing around in a state of confusion or queuing at the various desks. I took my place in the queue for Down Under Dive Company, and once checked in, I made my way along the jetty to Osprey V, the largest motor yacht at the jetty.

Once aboard, I was directed to an upstairs lounge, which was set aside for the sole use of the scuba diving passengers, of which there were six of us. The boat soon filled with around two hundred sightseers and snorkellers, who were packed into the large, crowded main lounge. We set off for the outer Great Barrier Reef, and en-route we were asked to complete a form exonerating the firm from any liability should we die or be left on the reef. The dive master then gave us a safety briefing, after which we were free to stroll around the boat.

I relaxed on the sundeck in glorious sunshine, and a couple of hours later we had reached the first dive site called Saxon Reef. We six scuba divers were the first of the ships passengers allowed into the water. The ships dive instructor guided us around the reef, during which we saw lots of marine life, similar to that at Thailand. When we surfaced about forty-minutes later, the sea around the boat was choc-a-block with snorkellers splashing around on the surface.

The Great Barrier Reef is undisputedly the world's greatest reef system, stretching more than 2,000km along Queensland's northeast coast, and has been described as one of the seven natural wonders of the world. It is a World Heritage Listed area, and is home to more species of plants and animals than any other area of this size in the world. It consists of 3,000 individual coral reefs with 400 types of coral, 618 tropical islands and 300 coral cays.

On route to the second dive site called Hastings Reef, we stretched out on the sundeck and were served a hot barbeque style lunch. Once there, the snorkellers were allowed into the ocean first; there were so many of them all clustered in the same small area that I was surprised that they hadn't frightened off all of the fish. Again we were guided around the reef, which was similar to the first site. I was a little disappointed, it might be the biggest reef in the world, but the coral and marine life that I'd seen was no better than that in Thailand. In fact, some sections appeared dead, and in my humble opinion, I thought this section of the reef was over commercialised.

The next day I checked out of the hostel, excited at the prospect of a three-day tour to Cape Tribulation in tropical northern Queensland, where the lush rainforest meets the reef, the sea is always blue, the beaches are golden, and the sun always shines; at least that's what it says in the brochure. The Tropics Explorer tour bus arrived to pick me up at 7.30am. I was quite pleased to find that I was the only male aboard, other than the driver who was a dead ringer for Ricky Jervais.

Our journey north was quite uninspiring as we drove through mile upon mile of sugarcane plantations. We eventually reached The Daintree Rainforest, where we were led on a guided walk. At the Daintree River we were treated to a wildlife river cruise, although there was little wildlife to see other than a baby croc, one kingfisher and a small tree snake. I attempted to use my video camera for the first time since it was repaired, only to find that it was still broken.

As we approached Cape Tribulation we saw a number of road signs warning of emu type birds crossing. Our guide informed us that these were the cassowary; a solitary, flightless pre-historic looking bird with an elongated casque (bone helmet) on top of its head, a glossy black plumage, a vivid blue neck and two red wattles. This rare and endangered bird is native to the tropical rainforests of far north Queensland. As many of their forest homes have been lost to clearing and development, cassowary numbers have fallen and they face real threats to survival; it is estimated that approximately only nine hundred remain in the wild.

Our guide went to great lengths to warn us of how dangerous these birds are; they grow as tall as a man, weigh up to 85kg and can run up to fifty kilometres per hour. They fight by leaping in the air and kicking forward, sometimes with both of their three-toed feet, the middle one of which is a formidable dagger-like claw up to 8cm long. They are also intensely curious, but sadly not very bright, which can lead to some rather unfortunate incidents. Should we come face-to-face with one, we were advised not to run but to back off slowly, as these birds like nothing more than a chase, make ourselves look as big as possible as they are less likely to attack something which looks bigger than itself; and to keep something solid between us and them, such as a tree!

We eventually reached Cape Tribulation around lunch time, which like many geographical features along the east coast of Australia, was named by Captain James Cook, after the trials, and of course tribulations, of becoming grounded here on his first voyage of discovery in 1770. We were each dropped at our chosen accommodation, I along with the majority, at The Cape Trib Beach House. My dorm consisted off a wooden forest hut with two pairs of bunks and a bathroom.

I immediately headed to the beach; the sand looked grey not golden, the sea was brown not blue, the sky was overcast with a blanket of thick, grey cloud and the sun was no where to be seen. I couldn't help but feel a little disappointed. I strolled down the beach and along a forested path to a lookout point, continually looking over my shoulder as I went for the fearsome cassowary. Perhaps I was being a little hard on Cape Tribulation, after all it wasn't the best of days to judge it on. Surveying the bay from the lookout, it was indeed pretty, with forested hills providing a nice backdrop to the beach. Looking further out across the bay, the sea was a turquoise colour, and I could only presume that the brown colour close to the shore was caused by mud and silt being washed into the sea from the forest and streams.

I returned to the resort and telephoned the camera repair centre in Perth, informing them that the repair had not been successful, but they refused to accept my word and said that I should return the camera to them at my own expense, and pay for any further work. After a short, heated argument, I advised them that I was not prepared to do this and so I would instruct my credit card company to seek a full refund. Seething with frustration, I headed to the bar for the night.

The weather was still no better the next day. I again walked for a few kilometres down the beach, reaching another resort around lunchtime. There seemed a much friendlier atmosphere and ambiance there than at my resort, and so I ate lunch there followed by a couple of beers, after which I returned to the beach where I spent a relaxing couple of hours reading under a palm tree.

On returning to my room, I found that I had two new female roommates; a tall, thin, red haired cockney girl who looked like Bianca from Eastenders, and a nursery school teacher from San Francisco. The three of us headed to the bar together for happy hour; it transpired that there was a band playing at one of the other resorts, and a free mini-bus had been laid on to take people there at 8pm. Not being one to miss out on a party, my two roommates and I joined around a dozen others on the bus.

The bar was packed to the rafters with a mixed crowd of backpackers and redneck locals. The band was ok and the night quite enjoyable. I spent the evening flirting with my two roommates and three other English girls. Unable to stick to just one girl, I ended up alone again!

The rain poured down the following day. I checked out and spent the morning in the bar reading. The Tropics Explorer Tour Bus arrived around 1pm and we set off on the return journey to Cairns, crossing the Daintree River on a vehicle ferry en-route. Luckily the rain stopped briefly to allow us a half hour walk around Mossman Gorge, where the Mossman River tumbles its way over and around huge granite boulders, creating cool, clear freshwater pools. We stopped for an hour in the upmarket town of Port Douglas, which was nowhere near enough as much time as I would have liked there.

We finally arrived back in Cairns at 6pm, and I checked into a new hostel called The Asylum, which could not compare with Bohemia Resort for facilities or cleanliness, but was much more friendly and lived up to its name. My dorm bed cost just £6 per night and included free coffee and tea, free Internet use, and a free dinner voucher for The Woolshed Pub in town; I couldn't afford not to stay here. I walked to the Woolshed later for my free dinner, paying an extra £2 to upgrade to T-bone steak and chips, which I washed down with a few beers.

The following morning, with the rain pouring down, I rested in the hostel and drank gallons of free coffee. I telephoned a local video camera repair centre, and once the rain stopped, I caught two buses into the suburbs to their premises. I explained the problem, the assistant took my camera, turned it on, pressed a couple of buttons, and then said, "I don't think we can help you."

"Why not?" I asked.

"Because it's broken."

"Yes, but you're a video camera repair centre."

"Yes, but we can't repair this."

"Well what kind of repairs do you do?"

"Sorry"

Annoyed and frustrated, I left the shop muttering obscenities along the lines of, "Useless, backward Aussies", and returned to the hostel where I spent the remainder of the day reducing my stress levels by the pool.

Each Monday evening, The Asylum holds a pub-crawl for it's guests, and this being a Monday was no exception. We met in reception at 6pm, paid over the sum of £4, for which we received a T-shirt, and vouchers entitling us to a free meal and several free drinks. The hostel mini-bus then ferried us into town. We started in the Woolshed, where we had free dinner, before continuing on to several other bars.

As the night progressed, everyone became more and more pissed and uninhibited. I got chatting to a girl from

Wolverhampton, whose accent was so broad that she sounded like a female Noddy Holder. The more she drank, the more outrageous she became. Suddenly without warning, she changed from being a fun, happy go lucky type to a complete psychopath, telling me how she had stabbed numerous men for not treating her well. I could not rid myself of this girl, until eventually she went to the toilet, and I took the chance to make a sharp escape, catching a taxi back to the safety of the hostel.

The sun had finally made an appearance on my final day in Cairns, and so I decided to visit the northern beaches, buying an all-day bus pass. I stopped firstly at the picturesque Trinity Beach, with a curved, palm lined beach and a pleasant town with a couple of shops and cafes. I spent a pleasant hour on the beach, before climbing the steep steps to a viewpoint high on the cliffs, with splendid views over the bay. I then caught another bus to Palm Cove, the most northerly of Cairns beaches, which again was very beautiful and where I lazed on its virtually empty beach.

The time to depart Cairns and commence my journey south had finally arrived and the next day I took the Premier Bus on the first leg of my journey down the east coast of Australia. My first destination was the nearby town of Mission beach, where we arrived two-hours after departure. There were a couple of hostel mini-buses waiting at the bus-park to pick up passengers. One of the drivers was from Birmingham, and so I went with him to The Mission Beach Shack, located right opposite the glorious 14km long, white sand beach.

I spent my first day here relaxing on the beach, soaking up the sun. The compact town contained a few shops and a small mini-supermarket. It is possibly the best place to see the Cassowary as the local community and government have set up a sanctuary here to protect the endangered bird. However the outlook for the Cassowary is pretty grim: approximately only forty adults, and thirty-one chicks are roaming the forests of Mission Beach, of which only seventeen are breeding females. It would seem as though it is just a matter of time before this creature becomes extinct.

I soon made friends with the other travellers at the hostel. With little to do in the way of nightlife in Mission Beach, I spent my first evening in the games room with three lads from Jersey and English girls Emma and Joanne, drinking and playing pool until around 3am.

At 7am the following morning we were rudely awoken by the sound of blaring music. The door to my dorm then burst open and a voice yelled, "Could the person who has left dirty dishes in the sink please get up and wash them". I put the pillow over my head and tried to sleep, but with the music still blaring, I couldn't. Pissed off at the childish behaviour of the manager, who had felt it necessary to wake the entire hostel over something so petty, I got up and walked to the beach with Emma and Joanne, where we caught up on our sleep under the shade of a palm tree.

A few of the guys from the hostel arrived later and we played five-a-side beach football, which began quite friendly but soon became very competitive, as these ladish games always do. All of the hostel guests congregated in the games room that evening for a pool competition. Once more the three Jersey lads and I chipped in together to buy a case of beer. I was aching all over from the football game earlier, and so I retired to bed early around midnight.

The following morning I caught the 9.30am Premier Bus to Townsville, and I found myself sat next to Mike from Middlesborough, who I'd met briefly on the previous bus from Cairns. The journey through rich cane fields and banana plantations was uneventful, and we arrived at the Townsville bus terminus around 1pm. Mike and I were both heading to Magnetic Island, located just eight kilometres off Townsville. Inside the bus terminus were various agents offering accommodation on the island. We each booked a package to include return ferry transport and two-nights accommodation. The ferry departed at 4pm across the Cleveland Bay and within half an hour we were docking on the island. We caught a local bus to Horseshoe Bay and checked into Geoff's Place, a campsite and resort of "A-frame" log cabins, which reminded me of the beach huts in Thailand.

Magnetic Island was named by Captain James Cook because of the apparent 'magnetic' effect it had on the ship's compass as he passed by in 1770. Cook's concerns seem to have been unjustified, as subsequent tests have shown no magnetising qualities in the island's predominantly granite boulders.

We spent our first evening in the open-air resort bar. The campsite was full of the strangest looking ground dwelling birds called curlew; their legs are long and thin, and their haunting wails sound like a crying baby. When approached by humans, they either scamper away or freeze, as if trying to blend into nature. There were also a lot of mischievous and foraging possums, which look like giant squirrels.

The next morning Mike and I set off to explore the island on foot. We commenced our exploration at the aptly named Horseshoe Bay, with a pristine beach, a few shops and cafes, and one pub. At the Eastern end of the beach we walked along the trail through a steep gully of dense forest to an open ridge, winding down to the secluded Balding Bay, which was even more beautiful than Horseshoe; a circular bay with large granite boulders at either end, which reminded me of Koh Pha-Ngan in Thailand.

We spent the day trekking along steep rough tracks to several other bays; Radical, Florence and Arthur, which were all very beautiful, unspoilt and relatively deserted, probably due to the lack of facilities and the difficulty in getting to them due to the limited road access. From Arthur Bay the track turned inland and rose through lush forest up to a lookout point called 'The Forts', a series of concrete gun emplacements and observation posts which were built during WWII to protect Townsville in the event of a Japanese invasion. The uninterupted views across the entire island from here were breathtaking.

By now we had been walking for six-hours in burning sunshine and we had used up all of our water supplies. We followed a track from The Forts down to a car park, where luckily a German couple in a campervan kindly topped up our water bottles. We returned to The Forts to take in a beautiful sunset over Horseshoe Bay to the west, after which we walked back to our resort, eventually arriving at 7pm. We showered, ate dinner at the resort barbeque, sank a couple of beers, and by 10pm we were in bed after a long and exhausting, but very satisfying day. Magnetic Island was the most beautiful and unspoilt part of Australia that I had seen so far, and yet relatively few backpackers or tourists visit it. Perhaps that was the reason that I liked it so much.

Mike left early the night morning on the first ferry to

Townsville, and after a little lie-in, I followed a few hours later. I caught up with him in town, storing my backpack in his room whilst we wandered around the town. Mike had decided to spend a couple days in Townsville whist I was catching the afternoon southbound bus. We walked the length of the attractive esplanade, called The Strand, which was lined with palm trees and neat lawns, with lots of public facilities including: children's play areas, a cycle and jogging track and permanent keep-fit equipment. The pier even had stainless steel sinks and preparation tables for use by the fishermen.

Being a Sunday, there were lots of locals out; walking, fishing or just lazing on the lawns, some eating picnics, others cooking on the public barbeques. The glorious beach at Townsville was voted Queensland's beach of the year for the last two years, and in the sea just off it many people were enjoying the various water-sport options; kayaks, small sail boats and rowing boats. Townsville seemed the perfect family town and it was very agreeable indeed.

I duly caught the 1.30 bus and arrived around three-hours later at Airlie Beach, gateway to the Whitsunday Islands. From the bus-park I walked into the town and soon located my accommodation, The Seaview Apartments. I walked past a group of drunks sitting on the patio, and entered reception, which was empty. One of the drunks followed me in, and asked if they could help me. It turned out that they were the staff.

Despite pre-booking a bed a few weeks earlier, and phoning to confirm two-days prior to arriving, there was no record of my booking on the computer system. After much pressing of computer keys, they managed to find an available bed in apartment seven, and with key in hand I headed off. Unfortunately all the beds in apartment seven were already taken, so I returned to reception, and was given a key to apartment three. Again there were no spare beds in apartment three, and I returned to reception again, by now feeling very pissed. Two girls were in the process of checking out of a double bed room in apartment seven when I returned to reception, and so I was given the keys to this room. No sooner had I sat on the bed than the receptionist arrived to inform me that the manager would not allow me to stay in a double room on my own, and so I must move to a single bed, which they had now located. By now I was furious, however I controlled my temper and moved to the apartment.

Inside the apartment, several people were sat in the lounge, glued to the TV watching Australian Big Brother. I greeted them with a friendly "hello" as I entered, but they were all either too engrossed, or just too ignorant to reply. The available bed turned out to be a bunk in the corner of the apartment lounge. Amazingly, ten beds had been squeezed into the tiny apartment, which was originally designed as a self-contained unit for three people, comprising of a lounge, kitchen, bathroom, one single bedroom and one double bedroom. The larger bedroom now housed two sets of bunk beds, the smaller bedroom one double bed, and the lounge a further two sets of bunks. I'm sure they would have put a bed in the kitchen if they could have made room.

This blatant overcrowding would certainly not be allowed in the UK, on health and safety, public hygiene, and fire safety grounds; I dread to think would be the outcome if a blaze was to start in one of these apartments. Australian hostels have been marred over the years by a catalogues of disasters, and its safety record is both appalling and frightening. In September 1989, six travellers from Austria, Sweden, Denmark and the UK were killed when fire swept through a hostel in Sydney's Kings Cross. In March 1993, about one hundred and thirty backpackers were evacuated from a hostel in Fremantle following an arson attack. In 1995, Governor-General Bill Hayden calls for better fire control systems in backpacker hostels. In August 1996, ten backpackers were evacuated from a hostel in Rockhampton, Queensland, which was gutted by fire in an arson attack. In January 1997, two hundred travellers fled a fire in a Melbourne hostel. In June 1997, one English backpacker was killed in a house-fire at Woolloomooloo, four other backpackers escaped.

And in the worst incident of all, on 23 June 2000, a blaze swept through the wooden Palace Backpackers Hotel in the town of Childers, about 300km north of Brisbane. About seventy people, including twenty Brits, were rescued, however the fire claimed the lives of fifteen young backpackers; seven were from the UK, three from Holland, three from Australia and one each from Korea and Japan. For me, this was yet another example of why Australia is a second world country.

I didn't feel like hanging around the apartment, so I showered and headed straight out to find a pub. My first impressions of the town was not good; it was very touristy with lots of overpriced souvenir shops, and numerous theme pubs and bars. The streets were full of pissed-up kids; lads in football shirts, girls in next to nothing, staggering from bar to bar, swaying arm in arm, shouting and singing. I could have easily been in Blackpool or Benidorm I thought. I returned to the apartment around midnight to find everyone fast asleep, much to my delight.

The next morning I set off to explore Airlie and give it another chance, after all I had not been in the best of moods yesterday. By day Airlie was much more agreeable, the shops appeared less touristy and there were some pleasant cafes and restaurants, which I hadn't noticed last night. The thing that stood out though was the quantity of sailboat tour operators, which seemed to be every third or fourth shop. The small beach was nothing special, but there was an artificial beach and swimming lagoon, similar to those at Cairns and Townsville.

I was booked onto a sailboat departing tomorrow on a three-day cruise around the Whitsunday Islands, and so I phoned the tour operator to confirm the departure details. It was fortunate that I did as the boat I was due to sail on was out of the water being repaired, so I walked to the tour operators office to see what other boats were available. After being shown leaflets of several other boats, I plumped for The Banjora, which would cost me a little extra but included a free scuba dive and was for three nights not two. Better still, it sailed at 7pm this evening, so I wouldn't have to spend another night in the atrocious apartment.

Back at the apartment later, I packed my small rucksack with the essential items that I would need for the cruise, and put everything else in my main backpack which I deposited in the resort storeroom. I cooked the remainder of my food for dinner, and then at 6pm I walked to the Abel Point Marina, where the Banjora, a 60foot, 52 tonne, steel ketch was moored.

When I arrived at the marina, nine other guests were already waiting; Aussie couple Andy and Nicky, Phil from Ireland, English couple Neal and Alex, Canadian mates Dan and Ryan, and Irish sisters Margaret and Clare. We were welcomed aboard by our aboriginal skipper, Skip, his assistant Chris, female dive instructor Ainsley, and Ted, the eccentric English deckhand and cook. Before setting sail, Ted took our booze orders and headed to the bottle shop to collect them, whilst we each claimed a bunk and settled in. Around 8pm we pulled out of the marina under motor and cruised out into the open sea; we cracked open the beers in the saloon and got to know each other. By 11pm we were in Hook Passage, between the Hook and Whitsunday Islands, where we dropped anchor for the night.

The Whitsunday Islands are a group of seventy-four mostly uninhabited islands; many are lush forested national parks, which lie in the sheltered waters within the Great Barrier Reef, providing perfect sailing conditions. The islands were named by Captain Cook, who sailed by them on Whit Sunday 1770, or so he thought. However he had failed to adjust his calendar when crossing the 180th parallel (international date line), and so the islands should really have been called the Whit-Mondays.

I was awoken at 6.30am by the sound of the ships engine starting. We ate breakfast in the galley as we motored to Tongue Bay on Whitsunday Island, where we dropped anchor and went ashore on the inflatable tender. Ainsley led us on a walk along a forest track, climbing to Hill Inlet lookout at the far north end of the beach. The view of the inlet and Whitehaven beach was the most stunning I had ever seen, like a watercolour landscape of swirling white sand and endless shades of blue, green and turquoise sea, beyond which stood a backdrop of lush green forest.

We spent half an hour snapping away at this most spectacular photo opportunity, before making our way down to the beach, which was every bit as good as it looked. Stretching for 6km and facing the morning sunshine, it consisted of a very fine dazzling white sand, so pure that it felt like flour between the toes. We spent a fabulous couple of hours relaxing, playing and swimming in the crystal clear, brilliant azure water, which was warm yet refreshing. And what's more, having sailed here last night, we had the beach all to ourselves. Whitehaven beach is possibly the world's perfect beach, and that is as much my opinion as the biased Aussies'.

Several other boats began to arrive around noon and so we returned to the Banjora and cruised to the nearby Hook Island, where we anchored for lunch at the aptly named Luncheon Bay. After lunch Ainsley escorted four of us on a scuba dive, which was excellent, especially the coral formations. We ended the dive by walking out of the sea onto the beach, where Chris was waiting with the tender to transport us back to The Banjora. It transpired that my three fellow divers had, like me, all recently passed their PADI Open Water Certificates on Koh Tao; even more amazingly, Alex and Neal had learnt at the same dive school. We anchored that night at Stone Haven Bay on Hook Island, and Ted cooked up a fabulous barbeque dinner of chicken, steak, sausages, potatoes and salad, washed down with lashings of beer.

The winds were blowing the next morning and so for the first time we were able to hoist the sails and put the Banjora through its paces. There was a three-metre swell and we got thrown around a little, which was great fun, although the Irish girls didn't think so; they were both seasick. We lunched at Maureen Bay, again on Hook Island, followed by an hour of snorkelling and some time on the beach. Afterwards we sailed to Hayman Island and anchored for the evening at Blue Pearl Bay, where we spent the evening chatting and drinking in the saloon, and Ted once more prepared a wonderful feast, which we quickly devoured.

The next morning six of us took the plunge for a second scuba-dive. Ainsley asked us to submerge to the seabed and sit on our knees in a circle, promising us a surprise. We did as requested and within seconds a giant Napoleon Wrasse, similar to the one at Koh Tao, joined us. The curious fish swam between each of us as if welcoming us to is home. He was so friendly that he even allowed us to stroke his smooth scales, which had a leathery texture, not at all as I'd expected.

After taking photographs of each of us with the fish, Ainsley then led us around the reef; she accompanied Ryan and Dan who were not certified, whilst I paired with Chris and Alex with Neal. Initially the dive was nothing special, until we reached 'the maze', which consisted of gorge like corridors in the reef and was teaming with fish and wonderfully coloured coral. Chris and I, and Alex and Neal got a little carried away exploring and we managed to loose contact with Ainsley. As per procedure in such cases, we searched unsuccessfully for them for about one minute, and then slowly ascended. Once on the surface, we regrouped and submerged again to continue the dive, which was by far and away the best of my short diving career; both the coral formations and marine life here was much better than that at the barrier reef off Cairns.

Back aboard the Banjora, we ate lunch before setting sail for port. On route we spotted a pod of humpback whales, including a mother and calf that swam alongside our boat for about ten minutes. After passing around Hayman Island, the wind picked up to speeds of forty-knots, stirring the ocean and producing huge waves, which tossed us around, and once more the Irish girls were violently sick.

Back on terra-firma, I had around five-hours to kill in Airlie before catching another bus on the next leg of my breakneck tour of Australia; just enough time to pick up my backpack from Seaview Apartments, shower and change clothes, eat dinner and check my e-mails. After successfully completing all of my tasks, I boarded the Premier bus at 8pm, for a ten-hour overnight ride to the little-known town of Agnes Waters.

We arrived at 6am the following morning, the sun was not yet up, I had no accommodation booked, and I had no idea where I was going. Whilst travelling down the east coast, I had met many backpackers who had raved about this tiny laid-back town, and in particular a hostel by the name of Cool Bananas. And as luck would have it, the bus dropped me around one hundred metres from that very hostel. I hadn't expected anyone to be up at this hour, but as I walked up the path to what looked like a large bungalow, the door opened and a cheerful looking guy smiled and said, "G'day mate, looking for a bed?"

"Morning, yeah" I replied.

"Come in, reception opens at seven, make yourself at home, there's tea and coffee in the kitchen, and if you need a shower they're out back." Now that's what I call a welcome.

The original bungalow acted as the hostel reception and lounge. Patio doors led to the pleasant rear garden with a spacious patio area with a barbeque, benches and tables, informal lawns, and hammocks strung between palm trees. Off the garden were a two-storey accommodation block, and spotlessly clean kitchen and sanitary facilities. The place had a casual, laid-back atmosphere and certainly lived up to its name. I liked it very much and I spent the next couple of days relaxing and lazing on the pristine, deserted beaches, and the evening at the hostel drinking and chatting to my fellow guests.

There were a couple of familiar faces staying at the hostel; Lee from Cardiff who I shared a dorm with in Cairns, Jan and Sue who I'd met at Airlie Beach, and Kerry and Siobhan from Ireland who I'd met at Cape Tribulation. Around lunchtime, a local tour company arrived at the hostel offering free rides over the sand dunes to the nearby, oddly named town of '1770', in the hope of drumming up some future business. Around a dozen people in total took up the offer, and we were treated to an adrenalin-pumping ride along dirt tracks, over dunes, and along a stretch of beach to the town.

1770 was so named because, yes you've guessed it, Captain Cook landed here in that year. It was a small pleasant town with a population of just eighty-two, a small harbour, a pleasant beach, and one pub. After a brief look around, we took a leisurely walk back to the hostel along the beach. Amongst the little group was an Irish lady named Bev, around fifty years old, who seemed very familiar to me, yet I couldn't quite work out why as we'd obviously never met before. Once back at the hostel, I was relaxing in the garden when suddenly out of the blue something came to me.

"Bev, do you have a daughter?" I asked.

"Yes, and a son" she replied.

"Has your daughter been travelling?"

"Yes, she's in Perth with her boyfriend at the moment, why?"

"Is she named Sarah?"

"How do you know her name?" she asked, seeming a little unnerved.

"Is her boyfriend name Barry?"

"Yes, yes, how do you know?"

"I think I travelled with them in Asia"

"But how did you know she was my daughter?"

I explained that there was something about her that I'd recognised, and I'd only just realised that it was her voice; she spoke exactly like Sarah.

Opposite the hostel was a motorbike hire shop, which offered a guided motor-scooter tour of the local area. I joined a group of about twenty people from the hostel on the tour, most of who were motorbike virgins like myself. We were given brief instructions on how to operate the 'rev and go' machines, and then we set off in convoy, with one guide up front and a second at the rear. Initially we moved quite slowly, but as we got used to the bikes, so the confidence grew and the speed picked up. The convoy soon split into two groups, with the more confident riders up front and the more cautious at the rear, riding at their own steady pace. We rode along practically deserted roads, through small wooded areas and open countryside, stopping on a couple of occasions to watch wild kangaroos grazing. We stopped off at the pub in 1770 for a quick beer before returning to the hostel as night drew in.

And so on to the next leg of my journey, catching the 6am bus to Rainbow Beach. We arrived at noon and I checked into Dingos Backpackers Hostel. Rainbow Beach was a small, pleasant town, with a few shops, a couple of bars, and a nice beach with multi-coloured strata cliffs. However visitors do not stop here for the beach or to see the cliffs, they stop here as it is one of the gateways to nearby Fraser Island.

Fraser Island, at 124km long and covering an area of 163,000 hectares, is the world's largest sand island, and is World Heritage listed. Amazingly there is no soil on Fraser, just huge expanses of sand on which ancient rainforests grow along the banks of crystal-clear creeks. It is also a place of exceptional beauty, with long uninterrupted clean white beaches facing the Pacific Ocean surf, flanked by strikingly coloured sand cliffs.

Dingo's Hostel organise jeep safaris to Fraser, and tomorrow I would be going on such a safari. On the afternoon I attended a pre-tour meeting, along with forty-three other hostel guests, during which we were divided into four groups of eleven people. We watched a video of the island, and were briefed on what to expect, and the dos and don'ts. The meeting put a lot of emphasis on safety, including what to do in the event of an attack by wild dingoes, which is basically to cross your arms on your chest in an unassertive stance; and if that failed, we were advised to fight them off aggressively!

My all English group spent the evening in the hostel bar getting to know one another over dinner and a few beers; Dave and Neal from Essex, Leanne and Jen from Manchester, Chris and Kate from Liverpool, and a group of four friends studying at Warwick Uni; Dan, Trini, Ellie and Alexis. Everyone seemed very nice and friendly and we all instantly bonded.

The entire hostel rose early in preparation for the safari. We were shown to our jeep and told to check the equipment against the inventory; two tents, map, gas bottle and stove, folding table, large water container, axe for cutting firewood, eleven sets of plates, bowls, cups and cutlery, and two eskys (cool boxes), one containing food and the other alcohol, which we had ordered the previous evening. The designated drivers, of which I was one, were briefed on how and when to operate the four-wheel drive system, after which we loaded all of the equipment and our baggage onto the jeep roof, and at 9am all four jeeps set off for in procession to the nearby ferry jetty.

Once on the island the four jeeps each headed off in separate directions. Dave had been to Fraser a few years earlier and so he was able to recommend places to visit, or not to, as the case maybe. We drove for around an hour along the main beach, which stretched as far as the eye could see in both directions. With no sealed roads on the island, the beach doubles as the main highway and the aeroplane take off and landing strip. Inland, scenic tracks and walking paths have been cut out of the forest to provide access to some of the largest lakes.

We turned inland and drove down a bumpy track running through the surprisingly lush, dense forest, towards Lake McKenzie. We parked the jeep and walked along a forest track, emerging from the undergrowth to the site of a stunning blue lake, fringed by white beaches, and dense forests. It was an amazing sight, beautiful crystal clear water, sky blue colour around the perimeter and cobalt in the centre, and we had it all to ourselves. We all stripped off and ran in; the water was freezing cold but so pure, like mineral water. We spent a couple of hours sunbathing, swimming, and generally fooling around, before walking back to the jeep where we made sandwiches for lunch.

There are more than forty freshwater lakes on the island, each with special appeal and all ringed by white sandy beaches. Some are pristine clear 'window' lakes like McKenzie, formed when a depression exposes part of the regional water table, but the majority are called 'perched' lakes because they are perched high up in the dunes, and are effectively giant rainwater puddles held in dune hollows by a layer of sand rendered impermeable by reed humus rotting into it over centuries.

We returned along the forest track to the main beach, and continued north, enjoying the scenery and looking for a suitable campsite as we went. We finally set up camp in a spot just off the beach, sheltered from the ocean by sand dunes. Just as we had begun to erect the tents, jeeps from two of the other groups arrived and began setting up camp either side of us. That evening we had a joint first night party. The guys made one huge campfire, whilst the girls prepared dinner for their respective groups. By 5.30 it was pitch black and we sat around the fire drinking and chatting. A wild dingo appeared sniffing around, we all kept our distance and realising there was no scraps of food to be had, he soon left. The party continued into the early hours, the booze flowed liberally and the small Irish contingent led the singsong.

I awoke around six the next morning with a splitting hangover. Dying for the toilet, I picked up the shovel and wandered off to find a secluded spot behind a bush. I dug a hole, pulled down my trousers and squatted. A wild dingo appeared out of the forest and sat a couple of metres away, staring at me. I swung the shovel in his direction hoping to scare him away, but to no avail, and so I pulled up my trousers and returned to the safety of the tent.

With no shower facilities here, after breakfast we headed to Lake Wabby to bath in its clear waters. Wabby is the islands deepest lake at over eleven metres, and was formed when moving sand dunes blocked a watercourse. Running along its entire north bank is a steep sided dune, which we hurtled down before diving into the freezing water. Still feeling the effects of excessive amounts of alcohol, I took the opportunity to catch some more sleep in the shade of a tree for an hour.

Leaving the lake, we walked up and over the dunes. From the summit, the full beauty of the island could be surveyed, a lunar type landscape of endless sand dunes stretching in every direction, the highest reaching up to 240-metres above sea level. We plodded through the deep sand along a valley, our footprints the only ones in this constantly moving landscape of swirling clouds of sand.

We spent the rest of the morning putting the jeep through its paces on the tight forest tracks, before returning to the beach where we sped along at speeds of 90km per/hr. We stopped at Eli Creek, the largest creek on the eastern side of the island with a flow of eighty million litres of water a day, where we stopped for lunch. Afterwards we continued north along the beach, stopping briefly at the remains of the wrecked Maheno, a former trans-Tasman luxury liner and a WWI hospital ship, which now lies rusting on the beach. Whilst there we saw two whales swimming parallel to the shore about one hundred metres out to sea.

The tide was coming in fast and although we had intended to travel further north, we thought it unwise too, worried that we could be stranded by the incoming tide, so instead we searched out a suitable campsite, eventually finding another sheltered spot in the dunes.

The lads set up the tents and made the campfire, whilst the girls prepared dinner, which we ate sat around the fire as the day slowly turned to night. We finished off what was left of our alcohol supplies, after which we all retired to bed early, everyone having peaked the previous night.

Not surprisingly, having retired at such an early hour, we all woke early the next morning. It was bitterly cold, and so we sat in our sleeping bags on the beach, watching the orange sunrise over the Pacific Ocean. After breakfast we drove further north along the beach to Indian Head, an elevated headland. We parked up at the base and walked up to the cliff top lookout, positioned on a narrow ridge with uninterrupted views of long, white sand beaches stretching in either direction.

As beautiful as the coast is, swimming in the sea is a definite no-no as the waters which fringe the island are home to a deadly array of predators. The water was so clear that from our vantage point we were able to see several rays, a few sharks, and a couple of dolphins. From our lofty position, we were also fortunate to witness the amazing sight of a shark, which I would guess was around four-metres long, stork and attack a lone dolphin, our birds-eye view was perfect to watch the amazing battle of wits, which the dolphin won. He was simply much too quick and agile for the shark and so escaped unharmed.

The waters off Australia are frustratingly out of bounds for swimmers due to the deadly dangers that await. There are one hundred and twenty-five species of shark, rays, and skates in the waters of the Great Barrier Reef alone, and sharks have killed more people in Australian waters than anywhere else in the world. However there are many other deadly creatures present in Australian waters including: around thirty-two species of sea snakes, the Portuguese man-o-war, and even salt water crocodiles are regularly found in the seas. The saliva of the blue-ringed octopus contains a poison so potent that it causes immediate respiratory paralysis and death can occur within two-hours; each of the twenty-six spines of the stone fish carries enough venom to kill a man; nicknamed the stinger, the box jellyfish is arguably the most poisonous of all animals. It has claimed the lives of many swimmers and children have been known to die within minutes of being stung. Even some species of the cone shell are highly dangerous, possessing enough venom to kill a man. Whilst on the island, we decided against swimming in the sea and contented ourselves with the islands beautiful lakes!

We returned to the campsite and cooked the remainder of our food for brunch, and with only a few hours left on the island, we returned to our favourite spot, Lake Mackenzie, where we spent a lazy couple of hours. Too soon, it was time to leave this beautiful, wild and unique wilderness. On our return drive along the beach to the ferry jetty, we had the shock of our lives when a light aeroplane landed just in front of us.

Once back in Rainbow Beach, we were instructed to drive the jeep to a local garage, where a mechanic inspected it for any damage caused by our negligence. Once given the all clear, we returned to the hostel where the equipment was checked back in by the staff, after which I headed for a much-needed hot shower. The whole Fraser experience had been wonderful, and I had been lucky to be part of a great group.

The next leg of my journey was to carry me down the coast to Noosa. Dave and Neal from my Fraser group, and a German girl named Saskia were also heading in the same direction on the same bus, and so we made the three-hour journey together, arriving around 3pm. Neal had earlier managed to book a private house for us to jointly rent. Our host was waiting at the bus stop to pick us up and drive us to the house, located a couple of miles south of the town centre in the Sunrise Beach district. The house was basic but clean, Saskia took the main bedroom, Dave and Neal took the second room with bunk beds, and I took the small third single bedroom.

Noosa marks the northern point of the Sunshine Coast, and comprised of four distinct suburbs; the fashionable upmarket tourist resort of Noosa Heads, containing luxury hotels, fine restaurants, designer boutiques, and trendy bars; the residential district of Noosaville; the shopping zone of Noosa Junction; and the beautiful, pristine beach areas to the south of the town including Sunshine, Marcus, Peregian and Sunrise, where we were staying.

Over the next couple of days I made the most of the house and my single room. This was the first time that I had slept alone in a room since Adelaide over a month earlier, and it was blissful. We generally spent the next couple of days on the beach, and the nights in the house, eating home cooked food, watching TV, playing cards and drinking cheap wine.

On our second night we cooked a barbeque in the garden. Renting the house next door were a group of American students on a university exchange programme. We chatted to them for a while, or should I say we tried chatting to them; they were friendly enough but very immature, shaking beer cans and spraying each other, and generally spilling more than they were drinking, as if it was their first ever drink, which it probably was.

Dave and Neal were very tight-fisted; they would eat any food going on the hostel 'free shelf' (food left by departing guests), would only buy food that was reduced in price, even if it were passed its sell by date, would drink the cheapest box-wine before going out so as to save money in the bar, would only use the internet at public libraries which was free, and would walk five kilometres to save a 1$ bus fare. Despite this however, they were both friendly and good company.

Feeling energetic after a couple of days of inactivity, I walked up to Laguna lookout, with panoramic views across the coast, the Noosa River, and the small forested national park, nestled between the town and the coastal headland. I spent the rest of the day walking along the coastal path of the national park, which was pleasant enough but hardly warranted the national park title. After three pleasant days in Noosa, it was time to move on and part company with my housemates.

After a three-hour bus journey I arrived at the huge Roma Street transit centre in Brisbane, the state capital and the third largest city in Australia. I headed for the northern suburb of Fortitude Valley and checked into The Tourist Guesthouse, which was aimed at local travellers and businessmen more than backpackers. My small dorm contained just four beds, a kitchen area, a TV and a small private garden.

After checking in, I immediately headed to the city centre for a quick look around. Brisbane reminded me very much of Perth, a relatively small city standing on the banks of a river of the same name, comprising a blend of grand period looking buildings and modern skyscrapers.

I returned to the guesthouse to find that I had two new roommates; Ben from Yorkshire and Noel from Dublin. We headed into the city centre together that night, and en-route we ran into three other English lads also seeking the cities nightlife. We ended up in The Down Under, a backpacker's bar serving cheap beer and playing thumping tunes. Three of us entered a speed drinking competition, however we were embarrassingly knocked out in the first round by a team of Yanks, including one girl. Our blushes were spared a little as our victors went on to win the competition. We partied the night away until the early hours, before staggering back to the guest house.

Ben, Noel and I spent the following day on the south bank of the river, redeveloped as part of the Expo 88 Exhibition, with numerous bars, cafes and shops, gardens and a forest walk, an open-air arena with a giant TV screen showing live pictures of a tennis tournament, and an artificial beach and swimming lagoon similar to that at Cairns. We then caught a bus to Mount Coot-Tha Reserve, a hill eight kilometres from the city centre, with a restaurant and viewing gallery on its summit, where we spent an hour enjoying the three hundred and sixty degree views over the city and distant bay.

We spent the evening in the guesthouse bar; the two main stories on the TV news that evening were of bushfires burning out of control at Sunrise Beach, and of a shark attack off Noosa. My decision to leave Noosa couldn't have been timed any better!

Ben and Noel moved on the following day and I again spent the day in the city centre, checking out the sights that I had missed previously. After three-days in Brisbane, my time in Queensland had drawn to an end and I took a bus along the Coast Highway toward New South Wales. We passed by the Gold Coast as we went, Australia's most commercialised area with a thirty-five kilometre strip of beach and one continuous high-rise, modern development, culminating in the resort of Surfers Paradise. I had no interest in spending any time in such an ugly and crass location, and was happy just to view it from the bus window.

I had thoroughly enjoyed my month in Queensland; the weather, the beaches, the scenery, and the nightlife were all fantastic, and the memories of scuba diving on the barrier reef, sailing at the Whitsunday Islands, feeling the sand of Whitehaven Beach between my toes, and camping in the wilderness of Fraser Island would stay with me forever.

14

Following in Cook's Footsteps (New South Wales)

06/08/04 to 13/08/04

The bus arrived in Byron Bay at 4.30pm after an enjoyable 8-hour journey along the coast. I checked into Byron Bunkhouse Backpackers Hostel, which had a nice laid back atmosphere, with a large open plan lounge, and a first floor balcony running around the perimeter of the building with chairs, tables and hammocks.

I took a walk around the small, relaxed town with its umpteen bead shops, tattoo and piercing parlours, and surf outlets. It had a village-like atmosphere and a bohemian reputation that attracts a colourful mix of alternative types; surfers, dread-locked backpackers, ageing hippies, artists, poets, musicians, performers and healers. The Age of Aquarius had arrived in Byron!

In Byron commercialised karma rules and just about every business offers services to either cleanse and restore your body, mind or spirit, or products that will help you towards vibrant health and well being. Pilgrims flock here in their thousands for beauty, health and healing, spiritualism and therapy, yoga and pilates, meditation and relaxation, massage, aromatherapy, acupuncture, Shiatsu, and intuitive bodywork. You can even see into the future by having an astrology, tarot or psychic reading, or sit with an enlightened guru, or reflect and review your life with an experienced Leadership and Vision Coach, whatever that may be. It's all available in the Byron Experience!

Along with a Dutch guy from the hostel name Rudy, I went out that evening to a backpacker party bar called Cheeky Monkeys. Inside, taking up several bench style tables at the front of the room, were a large, boisterous group from one of the 18-30 type tour buses; downing copious amounts of alcohol and being encouraged to partake in risqué party games on the stage, which generally involved removing items of clothing, or performing sexual acts. We sat at a quiet table at the back of the room with a jug of beer. Two Canadian girls later joined us, Naomi who was very fit and good looking, and Dawn who was the complete opposite. Naomi sat next to Rudy and before too long their faces were locked together, whilst Dawn and I spent the remainder of the night drinking jugs of beer and chatting about nothing much. I returned to the hostel around 2am with a headache, whilst Rudy returned the next day with a smile.

I was due to depart Byron on the overnight bus and so I decided to make the most of my short time here and see as much of the place as I could. I spent the morning walking along the coastal path, winding across the cliffs to Cape Byron lighthouse, the most easterly point in Australia. On route I thought that I had spotted a couple of whales in the ocean, so I clambered across the rocks to get a better view. But my sighting turned out to be not whales, but a pod of about a dozen dolphins, which initially I thought were just playing, but as I watched them I realised that they appeared to be herding a shoal of fish towards the rocks, the fish so tightly packed together below the surface that they looked like a large black ball. It was an amazing sight to witness at first hand, the type of thing you would normally only see in a wildlife documentary.

I spent the afternoon at the pristine beach, surrounded by lush rainforests. It was a beautiful setting, yet there was something very weird about the place; tanned surfers shared the beach with the joint smoking sixties children dressed in sailor pants, sandals and cheesecloth tunics. Most sat cross-legged in little clusters, and had one or more members with a musical instrument of some description; guitars, bongo drums and didgeridoos the most common. I found a quiet spot to myself, stretched out, closed my eyes and spent a couple of hours cleansing and restoring my body, mind and spirit in the glorious sunshine!

I wished that I'd have had more time to spend in Byron, but my time in Australia was running out and I wanted to spend my final full week in Sydney. And so at 7pm I commenced my final bus ride, a thirteen hour overnight journey to Sydney. I climbed into my sleeping bag, spread myself out across a double seat as best I could, and slipped into a deep sleep.

I woke just as we were entering the city suburbs, and as we approached downtown I caught my first, fleeting glimpse of the iconic harbour bridge and opera house. We arrived at the main bus and train terminal at 6.30am on Saturday morning. I immediately purchased a weekly travel pass, which allowed twenty-four hour use of the public trains, buses and ferries for the bargain price of just £16.

I took the subway train to the Kings Cross Station, and spent a couple of hours checking out numerous hostels, until I eventually found one that met my requirements and budget, Kanga House Hostel. It seemed perfect, not only was it cheap at just over £50 for a weeks accommodation, it was spotlessly clean and located in the quiet tree-lined Victoria Street. And from the window of my second floor room there were great views over the city and harbour to the Opera House.

After a quick shower and change of clothes, I excitedly set off to explore the city, catching the train from Kings Cross to Central Station. I walked the short distance to the harbour, which was even more magnificent than I'd imagined. I stood at Circular Quay, the harbours main ferry terminal, which was busy with numerous yellow and green ferries pulling in and out every couple of minutes, picking up and dropping off hoards of tourists and commuters.

I sat on the harbour wall and surveyed the scene around me. To my right stood the glimmering, sail like roofs of the Sydney Opera House, and to my left spanning the harbour, was the magnificent bridge; both instantly recognisable symbols of both Sydney and Australia. I followed the path along the harbour wall to the world-famous Opera House, taking in the views from all sides and from various angles.

Inspired by the sails of the yachts on Sydney's scenic harbour, the Opera House is in my opinion one of the most beautiful buildings in the world. It occupies a magnificent position at Bennelong Point on the south side of the harbour, conveniently situated with Circular Quay and Harbour Bridge on one side and the Royal Botanic Gardens and Lady MacQuaries Chair on the other. It is an enormous complex and consists of five different performing venues and includes the Opera Theatre, a concert hall, cinema, bars and restaurants. Queen Elizabeth II formally opened the Opera House in 1973, which was designed by Danish architect Joern Utzon in an international competition. Throughout the construction numerous problems were encountered, and as a result, Utzon eventually resigned. To this day he has never returned to see his masterpiece.

I returned to Circular Quay and caught a ferry to Darling Harbour, just so I could pass under the famous harbour bridge en-route, and it was so good that I caught the next ferry back and did it again. I then walked from Circular Quay to The Rocks. Circular Quay and The Rocks form the heart of the city and was the location of the first English settlement in Sydney. The settlers constructed their first wooden shacks along the natural rock ledges near the water's edge, thus the area became known as The Rocks and Sydney's first named street was here – George Street, in honour of the British monarch of the time, King George III.

The area was once the centre of the colony's maritime and business enterprises, with large warehouses and factories, which has been completely restored and renovated. The cobbled, twisting alleyways, old courtyards, colonial buildings, and converted warehouses have a charming old-world character which have transformed The Rocks into a thriving harbour-side tourist area, full of souvenir shops and cafés, galleries and museums.

I spent my first evening in Kings Cross, which is both the main backpacker area and also the red light district, probably due on both counts to the quantity of budget accommodation, bars and cheap eateries here. It was a great area to be based, just a five-minute train ride or fifteen-minute walk from downtown. It was a bizarre place where budget cafes stand next to posh restaurants, strip joints next to swanky nightclubs and massage parlours next to beauty parlours. I ate dinner in a little Indian restaurant and then watched a rugby game in a sports bar on the notorious

Darlinghurst Road. When I eventually left the bar, the road and surrounding area was alive with all sorts of weird and wonderful people; locals, backpackers, prostitutes, drunks, night-clubbers, drug dealers and drug addicts, however I didn't see any trouble whatsoever.

Over the course of my week in Sydney, I used my travel pass to the full, visiting many of the suburbs and travelling extensively around the harbour on the superb ferries. The ferries provide a wonderful moving vista of this enormous, beautiful natural harbour, which contains hundreds of small beaches, coves, bays and mini-harbours. Its waters are busy all day long with ferries, yachts, pleasure boats, kayaks and water-taxis. The harbour is breathtakingly beautiful and provides a fantastic backdrop to the city skyline.

The best and most scenic ferry ride is the half hour journey to Manley, located on a narrow peninsula with vast cliffs on the North Head of the harbour entrance. It is a popular and fashionable suburb, famous for its vast pedestrian mall called Causo, and its beaches, positioned on either side of the town, one on the Pacific Ocean, and the other on the sheltered harbour side.

On the opposite harbour entrance is Watsons Bay, which occupied an equally stunning position as Manley, but had a feeling of remoteness. On the harbour side of the headland was a small beach and a ferry jetty, and on the ocean side were steps and a coastal path running along the steep cliffs. The views from here back across the harbour to the city were wonderful, especially at sunset.

Sydney's other famous landmark is the Harbour Bridge, affectionately referred to by the locals as 'The Old Coat Hanger'. From The Rocks I climbed the stairs up to The Harbour Bridge, comprising eight vehicle lanes travelling in both directions, two railway tracks, a cycling path on the north side and a pedestrian walkway on the south side, which I strolled along admiring the harbour views as I went. In the centre of the bridge I came to a brick tower, where I climbed the two hundred or so steps up the Pylon Lookout, which provides a stunning view back across the harbour to the city. Inside the Pylon Lookout there is a museum with displays detailing the construction of the bridge, which took nine years to build and was opened in 1932. It is 502-metres long and 48.8-metres wide and the top is 134-metres above sea level. Before its construction, the only way to cross the harbour was by ferry, or to take a twenty kilometre road journey around. Once across the bridge, I spent a couple of hours on the northern banks exploring the quieter, residential suburbs. Few tourists visit the north-side as there are few attractions here, however the views back across the harbour to the city are splendid. Located at Milsons Point close to where the harbour bridge reaches the north shore is Luna Park, a historical amusement park, first opened in 1935. The entrance features a giant face of the moon, similar to that at St Kilda.

A mono-rail links Downtown to Darling Harbour and Chinatown, previously thriving dockland areas with factories, warehouses and shipyards. Darling Harbour was reinvented in 1998 as part of the Australia Bicentennial celebrations. It now has a very appealing appearance and offers a number of attractions; restaurants, bars and shopping. The aquarium, convention centre and National Maritime Museum are also located here; in the harbour when I visited were a naval warship and a beautiful tall ship.

At the Chinatown end of Darling Harbour is the Chinese Garden, a peaceful haven in the centre of the city. Asthetically, Chinatown is little different to anywhere else in Sydney. Other than the volume of Asian people, the quantity of Asian restaurants and shops, and the Chinese arch at the end of Dixon Street, you wouldn't actually know where Chinatown starts or ends.

Each day I walked through The Royal Botanical Gardens on route to the Central Business District and the harbour. It is a great spot for relaxing, strolling, and soaking up the sun, with splendid harbour views thrown in for free. For horticulturists, the gardens contain an Oriental garden, a large cactus garden, the contemporary Pyramid shaped Glasshouse, and the Sydney Tropical Centre.

From the gardens it is just a short walk around the headland to Mrs Macquaries Point, from where a flight of steps leads up to Mrs Macquaries Chair. The best views of the Opera House and Harbour Bridge are from here, especially for sunset and at night, when the iconic structures are floodlight. Subsequently, each time I visited the area it was choc-a-bloc with camera clicking tourists, just like me.

A pleasant spot to escape busy city life is Hyde Park, which like its much larger namesake in London, is an oasis in the heart of the city, with lawn gardens and lovely mature trees. It appeared especially popular amongst the city workers. This area was declared a park as early as 1792 and Australia's first recorded cricket match was played here in 1804. At its northern end is the impressive art-deco fountain, with ancient Greek mythological statues.

No trip to Sydney would be complete without a visit to the beach, and the nearest ocean beach to the city centre, only 8km away, is Bondi, Australia's most famous beach. Bondi was a pleasant horseshoe shaped beach, with an esplanade running along its entire length, however it was much smaller than I'd expected and didn't live up to its massive reputation. The sand was clean and golden, but Bondi is a surfers not a swimmers beach, several of whom were riding the huge waves when I visited. There was little else to see or do at Bondi, perhaps it would have looked more appeasing in the summer.

I was thoroughly enjoying Sydney, but just when everything seemed to be going swell, Australia once more succeeded in derailing my plans. When I first arrived Down Under three-months ago, I posted from Broome to Sydney a parcel to myself, care of poste resante. I visited the main post office to collect the parcel; the old man behind the counter typed my details into his computer. "I can see that we've received it, but its no longer here," he said.

"Then where is it?" I asked.

"Someone has probably assumed that you weren't coming to collect it, we usually only keep mail for one month".

"One month, every other post office in the world keeps mail for three months".

"Sorry"

"So where exactly is my parcel now?"

"Its been forwarded to the Dead Letter Department".

"And where is the Dead Letter Department?"

"Were not allowed to say".

"You've got my parcel but your not allowed to say where?"

"Sorry, I can give you our customer services telephone number".

"Can't you phone them for me?"

"No sorry, would you like the number?"

I took the telephone number, left the post office, found a public telephone and called the customer services department, explaining the situation and assuming that it would be relatively easy to resolve the problem and re-unite me with my parcel. The customer services department had no customer service skills whatsoever and they were generally unhelpful, refusing to put me in touch with the apparently secretive Dead Letter Department.

Frustrated, I returned to the post office in the hope of finding a kind soul with just a little customer care skill. I explained my problem to a cheerful looking young guy. "Oh, the Dead Letter Department" he said as if he understood what I was going through. He disappeared into a rear office and emerged shortly afterwards with a piece of paper. He handed it to me, winked his eye and said, "Don't tell anyone where you got this number". I thanked him, returned to the public telephone and dialled the number.

"Dead Letter Department" the voice at the other end answered.

"Hello, I understand that your holding a parcel that belongs to me".

"Who's calling?"

"My name is Lee Morton".

"Where did you get this number?"

"Your customer services department gave it to me".

"Oh, right, what's the name again?"

"Morton, Lee Morton".

I heard the sound of computer keys being pressed. "We don't seem to have any mail in the name of Morton".

There was a brief silence. "Was it expensive?"

"That's hardly relevant, are you telling me it's lost?"

"Someone has probably assumed that you weren't coming to collect it".

"So what is the normal procedure when you assume that a customer is not coming to collect a parcel?"

"We only normally keep mail for one month you know".

"Evidently, and I presume that it's normal practise to help yourselves to any unclaimed parcels once you've decided that a customer is not coming to collect?"

"Do you want the telephone number of the customer services department?"

"I already have it thank you" I replied, before slamming down the phone.

I then telephoned the customer services department again, who offered no assistance or even an apology. Instead I got the standard reply, "We can send you a claim form, which you should complete and return. We will then investigate".

"But I'm due to leave the country in a few days time".

"If compensation is offered, payment can only be made to you in person by cheque, as you will be required to sign" she continued.

"So let me get this straight, if you decide to compensate me for throwing away my parcel, I will need to return to Australia to collect the cheque?"

"That is correct sir. Would you like me to send you a claim form?"

"I'm not interested in compensation, I thought that you may be concerned to discover that your staff steel customers mail, but obviously I was wrong. A simple apology and a little understanding was all I was looking for".

"Would you like me to send you a claim form?"

"There doesn't appear to be much point. It is because of things like this that Australia is, and always will be, a second world country" I ranted, before hanging up. Inside the parcel were a couple of shirts, a New Zealand travel-guide, a couple of novels, and most importantly some anti-malaria medication required for my impending visit to South America.

Needing to escape the city, I booked a day trip to the nearby Blue Mountains. A tour bus picked me up at 7am, and we then spent the next hour driving around the city picking up other passengers. Eventually we headed out of the city, stopping en-route at the Olympic Park, purpose built to stage the 2000 games. All of the Olympic facilities have been successfully recycled; the tennis arena is now the National Tennis Academy, the aquatic centre is now a public swimming facility, the basketball arena is now used as a concert hall, the main stadium, described by our guide as 'the worlds biggest Olympic stadium', now hosts rugby and AFL games and the occasional music concert, and most impressive of all, the athletes village has been sold off as individual private homes, creating a new city suburb.

At 11am we reached the Blue Mountains, which are neither blue nor mountains, but are beautiful all the same. We walked through an area of parkland in which a large number of wild kangaroos were grazing. They were obviously very used to people as they didn't bounce off as we approached. Our group comprised of mostly tourists not backpackers, and this was probably the closest that any of them would get to the outback. Consequently, my fellow passengers were all rather more excited than I to see kangaroos.

We stopped for lunch in a small mountain town, after which we drove to a scenic lookout with views across a picture postcard valley with sandstone ridges on either side, which the guide called 'The Australian Grand Canyon'. The star attraction was the Three Sisters rock formation, and Wentworth Waterfall, which unfortunately contained little water. We walked down a track to the lush fern filled forest floor, and caught a funicular railway back to the summit, described by the guide 'as the worlds steepest railway'. The Aussies really do love to give their sights and attractions a world title!

With just a couple of days left in Australia, I headed downtown to shop for a few items in preparation for New Zealand, and confirm my forthcoming flight from New Zealand to Chile; I had been on a waiting list for three months. I had visited Qantas offices in every city I had been to in Australia, and on each occasion I was advised not to worry as the seats would be allocated closer to the departure date. When I visited Qantas in Sydney their representative told me that this particular flight was fully booked for eight months in advance, and although I was on the waiting list, there was no guarantee that I would actually get a seat.

I was devastated and confused by this news and it didn't seem as if there was any thing I could do about it. That night I typed e-mails to the head offices of Qantas and British Airways, explaining the situation and asking how they could sell 'around the world' tickets when they can not guarantee to actually get you around the world. I went to bed that night feeling worried and depressed, believing that the remainder of my journey was about to be ruined.

The following morning I returned to the Qantas office determined to thrash out the problem with a senior staff member, and hopefully get the problem resolved. The receptionist typed my details into her computer system and announced that my seat reservation had been confirmed that morning. I don't know whether it was just coincidence or whether someone had acted on my e-mails; either way, I was delighted and relieved.

In celebration, I popped to a downtown pub and treated myself to a beer and a juicy steak for lunch. Buying a beer in Australia is not as straightforward as you might think. In the UK we have a pint or half, in Aus, depending on which state you are in, you may get a glass, a pot, a schooner, a handle, a middle, or a pint, which to confuse matters further, isn't actually a pint in volume. Each state has its own favourite brand of beer, usually the brand brewed within the particular state; ask a Victorian and they will tell you VB or Carlton is the best, Western Australians prefer Swan or Emu, South Australians go for Coopers, Queenslanders drink of choice is Castlemain, and here in New South Wales, Tooheys is the amber nectar. They even have a beer called Piss; imagine the reaction if you were to walk into a pub in Dudley and ask, "A pint of your finest piss please."

Each day along the harbour, I saw several aborigine buskers, the majority playing the traditional didge, some dancing, and one even playing Caribbean steel drums. These individuals seemed intent on making the most of their lot, but the majority of aboriginal people that I'd encountered over the last three months seemed like strangers in their own land. Aborigines are considered very much like second-class citizens in Australia, in fact they were not formally recognised as citizens at all until 1967. Many live in appalling conditions and alcohol and substance abuse is rife, especially amongst young men.

After WWII, integration of 'the blacks' into white society became the aim of the government. The main objective was to 'assimilate' Aboriginal children into European society over one or two generations by denying and destroying their Aboriginality. Between 1910 and 1970 up to 100,000 Aboriginal children were taken forcibly or under duress from their families by police or welfare officers, in the hope that they would adapt to European culture. Most were under five-years old. Speaking their languages and practising their ceremonies was forbidden. Parents were not told where their children were and could not trace them. Children were often told that they were orphans, family visits were discouraged or forbidden, and letters were destroyed. Most were raised in Church or state institutions, the rest were fostered or adopted by white parents. Many suffered physical and sexual abuse. Food and living conditions were poor, they received little education, and were expected to go into low grade domestic and farming work. These people became known as the 'stolen generation'.

The physical and emotional damage to those taken away was profound and lasting; most grew up in a hostile environment without family ties or cultural identity; as adults, many suffered insecurity, lack of self esteem, feelings of worthlessness, depression, suicide, violence, delinquency, abuse of alcohol and drugs and inability to trust, and lacking a parental model, many had difficulty bringing up their own children.

The policy was a complete failure and in 1972 it was abandoned. A National Inquiry was set up in 1995. Its 1997 report 'Bringing Them Home' contained harrowing evidence. It found that forcible removal of indigenous children was a gross violation of human rights, which continued well after Australia had undertaken international human rights commitments, and it was racially discriminatory, because it only applied to Aboriginal children on that scale.

The Government has refused to apologise or offer compensation, and some people of the stolen generation have commenced legal action for compensation against the Government. The cases have been hard fought, as Government lawyers are arguing that removal of children was done for their own good!

On my final day in Australia, I spent part of the morning reorganising my overweight backpack, disregarding many items that I no longer wanted or never really needed. Once the cull was complete and my backpack was back down to a manageable weight, I then visited the post office and sent a parcel home containing items no longer needed, such as my scuba-mask; and this time I took out insurance!

I couldn't leave Australia without seeing Botany Bay, the place where it all began way back in 1770; the spot where Captain James Cook first stepped foot on Australian soil and claimed it in the name of England. And so after seeing to my chores, I headed to the suburb twelve kilometres south of the city centre. Today the area is still the first place that many foreign visitors arrive on these shores, as Sydney (Kingsford Smith) International Airport is located here. Botany Bay is now a major industrial site and a container ship terminal, and there is little of a tourist nature to see.

On Friday, April 20 1770, Captain James Cooks expedition became the first recorded Europeans to have sighted Australia's eastern coastline. The landmark of this sighting is generally reckoned to be a point lying on the southeastern coast of the state of Victoria, which Cook named Point Hicks after the Lieutenant who was the first to spot this Land. The ship's log recorded the historic sighting as being Thursday April 19, however, Cook had not made the necessary adjustments when they had earlier crossed the 180th meridian of Longitude, so the actual date was April 20.

In 1766, the Royal Society hired James Cook, then a Lieutenant in the Royal Navy, to sail to the Pacific Ocean to observe and record a transit of Venus across the Sun, in order to obtain measurements which could be used to more accurately calculate the distance of Venus from the Sun. If this could be achieved, then the distances of the other known planets could be worked out based on their relative orbits.

In command of HM Bark Endeavour, he sailed from England in 1768, rounded Cape Horn and continued westward across the Pacific to arrive at Tahiti on April 13, 1769, where the observations were duly made. Once the observations were completed, Cook then departed in order to execute the secondary purpose of his voyage: namely, to search the south Pacific for signs of the postulated southern continent of Terra Australis.

The Royal Society believed that it must exist, however Cook had his own personal doubts on the subject. With the help of a

Tahitian, who had extensive knowledge of Pacific, Cook managed to reach New Zealand, becoming only the second European in history to do so (behind Abel Tasman over a century earlier). Cook mapped the complete New Zealand coastline.

Cook then set course westwards, and sailed until land was sighted on the southeastern coast of the Australian continent. The Endeavour continued northwards along the coastline, keeping the land in sight, Cook charting and naming landmarks as he went. A little over a week later, they came across an extensive but shallow inlet, and upon entering it moored off a low headland fronted by sand dunes. It was here, on April 29 that Cook and crew made their first landfall on the continent, at a place now known as Kurnell. At first Cook named the inlet Stingaree (Stingray) Bay after the many such creatures there; this was later changed to Botanist Bay and finally Botany Bay, after the unique specimens retrieved by the expeditions botanists.

Cook continued northwards, charting the coastline of what is today New South Wales and Queensland. A mishap occurred on June 11 when the Endeavour ran aground on a shoal of the Great Barrier Reef. The ship was seriously damaged and his voyage was delayed almost seven weeks while repairs were carried out on the beach that he named Cape Tribulation. Until this point, Cook was unaware of the existance of The Great Barrier Reef, however he was aware that there was something lying offshore to the east which was responsible for the calm seas.

While there, the expedition's scientific members commenced the first major collections and documentation of Australian fauna and flora, and contact was made with the local Aborigine inhabitants, which were mainly peaceable. From the aboriginees encountered here the name "kangaroo" was to be entered into the English language, coming from the local name for a Grey Kangaroo, which was gangaroo.

Once repairs were complete the voyage continued, eventually passing by the northern-most point of Cape York Peninsula and then sailing through Torres Strait between Australia and New Guinea, before rounding the north west Australian mainland en-route to Batavia, to put in for repairs. After three-years at sea, the Endeavour finally sailed up the Channel and anchored off the

English Downs in 1771, and the rest as they say, is history.

Today Australia is without doubt the undisputed backpacker capital of the world. In 2004 almost half a million backpackers visited Australia, staying an average of sixty-nine days, which accounted for over a quarter of the total international visitor nights. Over a quarter of those backpackers were from the UK, staying on average almost three-months, and spending some £981million, that's an average of more than £2,300 each. In addition, many backpackers come to Australia on 'working visas' and so contribute enormously to the economy of this nation.

I had thoroughly enjoyed my week in Sydney. Before leaving I made one last visit to the harbour to see the Opera House and Harbour Bridge. These icons are the undisputed main attractions of Sydney, dominating every harbour view they seem to draw you to them. But the real ace card is the harbour itself; without it, I believe Sydney would be no better and no worse than any other city that I'd visited, but because of it, Sydney is probably the most beautiful city that I have ever visited.

My time to leave Australia had finally arrived. In my three months here I had travelled over 17,000km and covered the entire length and breadth of the country, and I'd seen every city and state (with the exception of Tasmania). In hindsight though, I think that I may have tried to cram too much in to my relatively short time here, which had resulted in me rushing from place to place a little too much.

Despite the numerous little setbacks here, and in spite and despite of the people, who are perhaps the most conceited, arrogant and self-opinionated that I have ever met, I had actually enjoyed Australia a lot. I'd seen some amazing sights and done some amazing things, and the memories of climbing Uluru, sleeping under the outback stars, swimming with whale sharks, driving along the Great Ocean Road, diving on the Great Barrier Reef, sailing in the Whitsunday Islands, exploring Fraser Island, and of course Sydney, would all stay with me forever.

However, I can't help feeling somewhat disappointed that Australia didn't quite live up to the utopia that it portrays. Whilst the cities of Melbourne and Sydney are indeed fine, the east coast is both beautiful and exciting, and the wilderness is strange and unique, the reality is that the majority of this vast continent is a barren wasteland of desert and shrub, and outside of the main population centres, facilities are either very basic or simply non-existent, with little to see or do.

My alarm woke me at 5am the next morning. The pre-booked airport shuttle bus arrived on time at 5:30 and by 6 I was at the airport and on my way to a new adventure in New Zealand.

15

Snow and Sheep
(New Zealand, South Island)
14/08/04 to 02/09/04

The flight from Sydney to Christchurch was uneventful until we crossed the snow-capped peaks of New Zealand's Southern Alps, which looked close enough to touch. Once over them we hit some turbulence causing the plane to shake vigorously and on several occasions we suffered a sudden loss of altitude. The feeling of fear amongst the passengers was so evident that you could have heard the proverbial pin drop, and the feeling of relief was obvious once we landed safely.

I was expecting New Zealand to be cold, being the middle of winter here and all, so I was pleasantly surprised to find clear blue skies and the sun shining brightly upon my arrival. I caught a bus from the airport to the city centre, and was further surprised to see just how English this land looked; traffic islands, green lawns and brick and stone buildings with tiled roofs.

From the city centre I walked to Occidental Backpackers Hostel in Latimer Square. It was 3.30pm when I checked in, and I immediately set off to explore the city before nightfall. Although Christchurch is the South Island's largest city, it is quite compact and somewhat smaller than I'd imagined. The centre was very clean and orderly, with tree-lined avenues and grey-stone nineteenth century buildings which gave it an elegant, English town feel. Many of the shops had wooden frontages and reminded me of my childhood growing up in the 1970's.

Cathedral Square is the epicentre of the city, the Gothic

Cathedral the most dominant structure. I climbed up its spire for a bird's-eye view of the small city, which fortified my original opinion that Christchurch is a city in name only. Standing in the square was an unusual, modern, metal sculpture called The Chalice, which looked rather like a giant steel vase. On the opposite side of the square two men were playing chess on a large outdoor board with giant pieces, and running along the square and around the city centre on a looped track was a vintage tram. It was very civilized indeed.

On my return to the hostel I headed to the bar for my first taste of Kiwi beer, and I spent the evening in the company of an English girl named Tara and an Irish girl named Gear (pronounced bear). We ate dinner together in the hostel, followed by a few more beers. Three English lads joined us later; Rob, Jim and Phil.

Around 9pm we decided to venture out and experience Christchurch nightlife, which turned out to be pretty good and a little more sophisticated than I'd expected. The locals were dressed to impress, however we were all dressed casually; I wore jeans, a fleece top and boots, the same clothes as I had had on all day. I felt a little scruffy but no one seemed to mind, and a good time was had by all. We returned to the hostel around 2am to find the bar still open and showing live TV pictures of The All Blacks rugby game in South Africa. I stayed up and watched until around 4am, when finally my speech failed me.

Hardly surprisingly I woke with a stinking headache the next morning. I headed out for a walk to clear my head. The weather was very different to that on my arrival; it was bitterly cold and there was snow in the air. I strolled along the Avon River, which looked like a Christmas card scene; its narrow willow lined banks covered in a layer of snow that had fallen overnight. I ate breakfast at McDonalds before returning to the hostel for a lazy day in front of the fire, relaxing and reading tour brochures. I again spent the evening in the company of Tara and Gear, but unlike the previous night, by 9pm we had all retired to our respective beds.

Suffering from the cold climate, I headed into town the next morning to purchase some winter clothing; gloves, a thick top, and a woolly hat. I then took my still broken video camera to a repair centre, leaving the camera with them to fix whilst I continued my journey.

In order to travel around the country and see all of the sights, I had decided to book a seat on a backpacker tour bus, of which there were three to choose from; The Kiwi Experience primarily catered for the eighteen to thirty crowd and was nicknamed 'The Fuck Truck'. Newman's Coaches provide scheduled services linking New Zealand's main commercial and tourist centres, but seemed to cater more to the Saga crowd. The Magic Bus seemed to cater to a mixed crowd of travellers and came highly recommended, and so I booked a nationwide travel pass with them.

And so the next morning I woke early at 6am in preparation for the first day of my tour, which was to commence with the 224km Tranz-Alpine scenic train journey to Greymouth, crossing the Southern Alps from one coast of New Zealand to the other. At 7.45 I was picked up by a shuttle bus and driven to the railway station, which was oddly located on an industrial estate. The Tranz-Alpine Train was waiting at the platform. I boarded and settled into my seat, next to a Korean girl who couldn't speak English and opposite a middle-aged, miserable-looking local woman who made no effort to speak, or even smile, throughout the entire journey.

The train pulled out at 8.15 and passed through industrial suburbs until we finally reached the fertile patchwork farmlands of the Canterbury Plains. We climbed steadily through spectacular gorges and the valleys of the Waimakariri River, passing over numerous viaducts and through umpteen tunnels, and before long we were in a rugged, alpine landscape encircled by towering, snow-capped peaks. At the centre of the train was an open-sided viewing carriage; I made my way there and attempted to photograph the scenery, but it was bitterly cold in the open air, and each time that I attempted to take a picture, we either passed a tree or entered a tunnel. Eventually I gave up and returned to the warmth and comfort of my seat, from where I sat back and enjoyed the splendid views. We stopped briefly at the town of Arthurs Pass, 920-metres above sea level, before descending through lush beech forest to the West Coast town of Greymouth, arriving around 1pm.

A car from Neptune Backpackers Hostel was waiting at the

station to pick me up and drive me to their establishment. The hostel was great; the lounge had a large screen TV and a free pool table, there was an outdoor spa-bath in the garden, and the dorms were small and contained beds not bunks; however I was the only guest.

As per my usual routine, I immediately headed out to see the town, which was the most drab, uninspiring town that I had seen on my travels so far; the River Grey certainly lived up to its name. But at least the weather here was better than that which I had left behind; the skies were clear and the sun was shining, although it was still very cold. I returned to the hostel to find that a group of five travellers had checked in, but they seemed content in their little group and made little effort to include me in their conversation.

With nothing to do here, I decided to make the most of the hostels facilities; I put on my shorts and climbed into the garden spa-bath and dosed in the bubbling, soothing hot water. When I later opened my eyes, around a dozen faces were staring at me over the garden fence from the windows of the Magic Tour Bus now parked outside. No doubt these were the people I would be travelling with tomorrow.

When I returned to my room I found that I had four new roommates; Russell from Scotland, Emma from England, Becky from Ireland and Adrienne from France, all of whom were travelling on the Magic Bus. We introduced ourselves and they invited me to join them for dinner and a few beers.

We spent the evening in The Railway Inn, joined by Steve and Benny, two English guys also travelling on the bus but staying at a different hostel. Dinner consisted of an 'eat as much as you can' barbeque for just £1.50, which we washed down with numerous three-pint jugs of beer costing just £2. Not surprisingly, before long we were all a little pissed.

Three local fishermen joined us; they were seeking deck hands for their boat on its next sailing in two days time. The wages of $2,000 were tempting, and I'm sure the experience would have been good, but I didn't like the idea of being stuck on a smelly fishing boat in the open sea for two weeks.

The bar closed just after midnight and the fishermen invited us back to their boat to continue the party, although I think that they were only really interested in partying with the girls. We kindly declined their offer, except for Steve that is, who left with them.

By 8am the next morning we were on the Magic Bus. We called at two other hostels to pick up passengers, including Steve, much to everyone's surprise. In total there were about twenty-five passengers aboard aged roughly between twenty and forty, the majority of whom were British. We drove south along the west coast towards the town of Hokitika where we stopped for breakfast. Steve was the butt of the morning jokes, most of which included the words 'sailor and sea-men', but he took it all on the chin, although I hope not literally off course!

We made a second brief stop at the historic gold rush town of Ross, which was now really just a tourist attraction and outdoor museum. We continued on past more stunning scenery of snow-capped mountains, before reaching our destination at 1.30; the picturesque town of Franz Josef, standing at the base of the glacier from which it takes its name.

During the journey a brochure and booking form had been passed around the bus containing various optional activities, all offered at discount prices. I had booked a 'Heli-Hike' of the glacier for tomorrow, and a kayaking trip for this afternoon. I checked into Montrose Backpackers Hostel along with Russ, Steve, Benny, Emma, Adrian and Becky, and then we all immediately headed out for an afternoon of kayaking on Lake Mapourika.

We were joined on the lake by a Brazilian couple and two English girls named Kate and Deb, who were travelling on 'the fuck truck'. Our guide Wayne gave us a quick demonstration of how to manoeuvre the kayaks, which were steered by a rear rudder operated by foot-pedals located inside the kayak. The lake was magnificent, the surface like a natural mirror perfectly reflecting the snow-covered peaks of Mount Cook and Mount Tasman. We spent a wonderfully tranquil three-hours leisurely paddling around the lake, admiring the beauty and serenity of the location. To cap a wonderful day, Wayne produced a CD for each of us containing photos taken throughout the day, which were excellent, although there did seem to be a lot more snaps of the girls than the guys.

We spent the night in the Blue Ice Café Bar, joined by Wayne,

Kate and Deb. I'd got on well with both girls earlier and so I thought I was in with a chance, however as the night progressed, the girls became very intimate with one another and ended up in a passionate clinch; just my luck, I'd spent the entire night trying to chat up a pair of lesbian's, much to the amusement of the rest of the group!

When I woke the next morning the dorm was empty, Steve, Russell and Benny having already left to go on a glacier trek, whilst I was booked on a 'Heli-Hike'. At the company office I was provided with an ice pick, a pair of boots and a set of ice-cramps, which fit to the sole of the boot to provide grip on the ice. A group of nine of us then boarded a helicopter, which transported to the top of the glacier.

It was my first time in a helicopter, and I found the feeling of hovering quite strange yet exhilarating, as if you weren't moving particularly quickly until you bank, and then you get the feeling that you are moving to fast. The birds-eye views of the glacier were indescribable. We landed on its surface where our guide was waiting for us; carefully and slowly, prodding the ice to check for unsafe areas as we went, he guided us across the magical icy wilderness of caves, ravines, crevasses and ice walls. We leapt across the ravines and crevasses, slid on our backsides down steep banks, and with his pick our guide cut steps into walls of vertical ice allowing us to scale them. Amazingly, close up the glacier actually appears to be blue in colour, the illusion created by the refraction of light through ice.

After around four-hours on the glacier in bright sunshine, the helicopter returned to pick us up and return us to town, during which we were treated to a scenic flight over the glacier. From above, the full glory of the twelve kilometres long glacier could be seen; it is essentially a constantly moving ice river, formed when snow accumulates over time, turns to ice, and begins to flow outwards and downwards under the pressure of its own weight and the forces of gravity. Emerging from its base is the Waiho River, which flows on for a further nineteen kilometres to the Tasman Sea. Far below, I could see a group of people on the lower section of the glacier, like ants on a white bed-sheet; no doubt they were my roommates on their trek.

After a pleasant couple of days spent enjoying the countryside around Franz Josef, and our nights either drinking in the bars or playing cards and watching movie videos in the hostel, it was soon time to continue our journey. The Magic Bus transported us south passing Fox Glacier before stopping off at Lake Matheson, often called 'the Mirror Lake' due to it's clear reflection of the Southern Alps which dominate the skyline. We stopped for lunch at the town of Haast, before turning inland and crossing Haast Pass into Mount Aspiring National Park. We made a third and final stop at Thunder Creek Waterfall, where some of the passengers disembarked in order to travel by jet-boat to our final destination of Wanaka. The scenery throughout the day had been wonderful, beautiful lakes, lush forests, plunging waterfalls and snow-capped mountains in every direction. Such a marked contrast to the barren lands of Australia.

All accommodation in Wanaka was pretty much fully booked and all of the other passengers except for me had pre-booked their accommodation, so I ended up staying alone in the only available accommodation I could find. My cabin at the Wanaka Caravan Park was basic, containing four bunks, a table and chairs and an electric heater, with communal toilet, shower and kitchen facilities nearby. The cabin was also a little more expensive than a dorm bed at around £10 per night, but at least I had the room to myself, which would be a nice change from shared dorm accommodation.

Wanaka is a year round resort town; water-sports in the summer, snow-sports in the winter, however it is very much unspoilt and occupies a picturesque location on the beautiful lake of the same name, under the gaze of the snow-capped peaks of Mount Aspiring National Park. It was very agreeable indeed, the perfect place to recharge the batteries.

Over the next couple of days I generally relaxed and hung out with the Magic Bus crowd, however our group had reduced in number as one by one everyone moved on, leaving just Myself, Steve, Russ and Emma. We spent our evenings either in one or other hostel drinking cheap wine and playing cards and board games. The bars in town were primarily frequented by posing ski and snowboard types, with designer clothes, tanned skin and bleached blonde hair. I didn't like them very much.

The next leg of our journey took us to Queenstown, New Zealand's premier resort town. On route we stopped off at the delightful Arrowtown, another historic gold-miners settlement with century old sycamore trees and beautifully preserved original character buildings. We made a second stop at Kawerau Gorge to see the world's first commercial bungee site, arriving just in time to see an adrenalin junky throw himself off a bridge toward the river forty-three metres below. Not for me thank you!

We four checked into the Alpen Lodge Hostel, where we were given a four-bedroom annex dorm, with its own kitchen, bathroom and lounge with pool table and TV. Very nice indeed.

I wandered into town alone that night, in search of a bar showing English football, as my team West Brom were playing local rivals Aston Villa. Luckily I found a bar showing the game, and I sat with a jug of beer and watched a 1-1 draw, in the company of just two other customers. Obviously West Brom and Villa are not a big draw in New Zealand. After the game, the bar filled up quickly as Arsenal's game was being shown next; I stayed on and watched that game also, joined by Steve and Russ.

Nestled on the shores of Lake Wakatipu, and surrounded by the majestic peaks of the Remarkable Ranges, Queenstown was named because 'it was fit for Queen Victoria'. It is New Zealand's premier visitor destination and as the reputation as the adventure capital. It would have been easy to blow my entire budget here, as whatever the weather; the activity options are almost endless. You can throw yourself, quite literally, into many of the activities such as bungee jumping, paragliding and skydiving, not to mention white water rafting, jet boating, or mountain climbing.

Seemingly every other shop in town is involved in the ski industry; selling or hiring clothes or equipment. There are two major ski-fields nearby; Coronet Peak 15km away is the more established, and the Remarkables are one of the few commercial ski areas in New Zealand offering cross country and Nordic skiing. I had never skied before and quite fancied taking some lessons, however I didn't have time to get on to the slopes, which was probably a good thing, as knowing my luck I would have probably broken a leg.

For those without a death wish, other activities include horse riding, kayaking, fishing, trekking, or take a lake cruise on the steamship TSS Earnslaw. And if action isn't your thing, then you can shop and enjoy the constant day and all-night entertainment provided by the restaurants, pubs and nightclubs; or simply find a quiet spot to take in the beautiful surroundings.

The next day was bitterly cold and so I purchased some more winter clothing – another fleece top, some thermal long johns and a thermal t-shirt. The four of us then caught the Skyline Gondola, which rises 446-metres up the steep slopes of Bob's Peak to a restaurant near the summit. Also located here, positioned on an overhang over the mountain was a 'bungee-swing'. The views over the town and across the lake to the surrounding mountains from here were magnificent. High above the lake, three paragliders were drifting effortlessly on the thermals.

A short walk from the restaurant we came across a 'downhill luge,' which is basically a mountain go-cart run over a meandering track with banked sides, hairpin bends and chicanes. We had a couple of runs, which were great fun and just about the cheapest thing to do here. On the afternoon we walked part way around the lake, covering about fifteen kilometres in a steady four-hours.

That evening we hit the town to celebrate Emma's thirty-second birthday, armed with numerous two-for-one and half-price drinks vouchers. Over the course of the night we visited half a dozen bars, all of which were packed and positively thumping with a real party atmosphere. Emma, Steve and Russ left around 1am, all totally smashed. I stayed out for another hour with an American girl named Melissa. When I entered our dorm later, all three of my roommates were fast asleep; Steve on the floor, Russ wrapped up in his sleeping bag with a woolly hat on, and Emma talking gibberish in her sleep. It had obviously been a good night.

Russ moved on the next day whilst myself, Steve and Emma hired a car for three days to travel to Milford Sound, in the remote area known as Fiordland. We were given a quick demonstration on how to fit and remove snow chains, should we need them, and by 11am we were on our way. Emma was hung over from the previous night and I had a headache, so Steve volunteered to drive.

The road to Milford Sound is one of the worlds finest alpine drives. From Queenstown the road winds around the bluffs above the lake before entering farmland en-route to Te Anau, nestled on the tranquil shores of Lake Te Anau, where we stopped briefly in the town to fill up on petrol and food. Leaving Te Anau the road turned north and ran parallel to the lake, before entering a beech forest of the Eglinton and Hollyford Valleys. As we continued, the mountains closed in, the scenery became more dramatic and hostile, and the temperature dropped still further; it was so cold that stalactites hung from the trees and bushes along the roadside. A blanket of snow covered the ground, and we passed numerous avalanche-warning signs as we drove through the rugged landscape. We made a couple of stops to take photographs and each time we were greeted by kea birds, strange looking little fat mountain parrots that would waddle up to our car hoping to be fed.

We crossed 'The Divide' (between the eastern and western sides of the Southern Alps) and steadily climbed to the Homer Tunnel, a straight road tunnel with unlined granite walls, which was first opened to private traffic in 1954. From mouth to mouth it measures 1,270 metres long and has a steep 1:10 gradient. On emerging from the tunnel, the road zigzagged down to be met by Mitre Peak towering from the glassy waters of Milford Sound. We had seen only a handful of vehicles all day until just outside of Milford, when a convoy of tourist buses drove past in the opposite direction, commencing their return journey back to Queenstown.

We arrived at the Milford Lodge Hostel around 4pm and we checked into a cabin-style room. The hostel facilities were fairly basic and so we spent the evening huddled around the fireplace in the communal lounge until around 11pm. The night was one of the coldest I have ever known. I slept in several layers of clothes inside my sleeping bag beneath layers of blankets.

We woke around 8 the following morning; a skin of ice had formed on the inside of the window pane. We each made our own breakfast and packed lunches for later, before driving the short distance to the Milford Sound Visitors Centre where we parked the car. The entire area was completely deserted; we entered the boat terminal and checked out the various boat-cruises on offer, eventually deciding to join the first cruise of the day. At around 10am we were escorted to our boat along with six other tourists.

The boat was the smallest at the jetty but it looked brand new and was luxuriously fitted.

Milford Sound was incorrectly named by Captain James Cook, as it is in actual fact a fjord, that is a glacially overdeepened valley, usually narrow and steep-sided, extending below sea level and backfilled with salt water following the downward slide of the glacier into the ocean.

Our cruise took us on a looped circuit around the fjord, which is famed for the almost vertical mountains rising from its waters, the undisputed king of which is Mitre Peak at 1,683metres. Several waterfalls plunge from the mountain walls into the ocean. We were accompanied for a short while by a pair of bottlenose dolphins, and we saw a number of fur seals basking on the rocks. We briefly left the fjord and entered the lively Tasman Sea, before circling and returning to the calmer waters of the fjord, following the opposite bank back to the jetty. Milford is renowned for its rainfall, averaging six-metres a year, however throughout the morning the sun had fortunately shone brightly in a cloudless blue sky.

Once back on dry land, we returned to the car and headed back toward Te Anau. Just as we were departing the convoy of daily buses from Queenstown arrived carrying hundreds of day-trippers. How fortunate we had been to miss the crowds. We stopped at 'The Divide' where we walked part of the famous 'Routeburn Track', twisting through a mossy forest of fuchsia, ferns and beech, and passing some steep falls before reaching Key Summit at 918-metres. The two-hour walk was worth the effort for the views, especially to the west of snow-covered, glacier-carved mountains just a few kilometres away.

Some of the most wild and dramatic scenery in New Zealand can be found in Fjordland, a World Heritage area featuring lonely fjords, endless stretches of shimmering lakes, granite peaks, and waterfalls tumbling hundreds of metres into virgin forested valleys. It is a truly breathtaking area of unspoilt natural beauty.

We arrived back in Te Anau around 4pm, and we checked into Te Anau Backpackers Hostel, where we spent the night soothing away our aches and pains in the hostels large spa-bath. The following day followed much the same pattern; we drove back toward Queenstown and stopped en-route at Rainbow Reach. We parked here and crossed the Waiau River via a suspension bridge, following the Kepler Track on a fifteen kilometre, five-hour return trek to Lake Manapouri, passing through a dense beech forest with a thick moss carpet, and over a kettle bog with a wetland viewing-platform. Once at Lake Manapouri, we sat on tree logs on the beach, and ate our pre-packed lunch of sandwiches, whilst looking out across the clear blue lake to the exposed mountaintops.

We arrived back in Queenstown to find accommodation hard to come by, and consequently we all ended up in separate hostels. Steve had decided to stay on for an extra day in Queenstown, whilst Emma and I caught the Magic Bus the following morning to Dunedin, the main business centre for the region of Otago. In 1848, Scottish migrants established a town here, giving it the ancient Gaelic name of Edinburgh. Thirteen years later gold was discovered about 120km inland in Central Otago, and the small settlement of Dunedin became the commercial centre of the nation.

Dunedin is billed as 'a thriving city of Scottish heritage, possessing a combination of cultural riches, fine architecture and natural wonders'. However, I found the town disappointing, there was little to see or do and the architecture, whilst grand for a small town in New Zealand, was nothing to write home about. We visited the art gallery and left within 20minutes; it contained the type of art that only pretentious pratts could enjoy; a video of a flag flying in the wind, metal shapes hung haphazardly on a wall, and wine glasses randomly arranged on a table. We spent the evening in the hostel lounge watching movie videos with around a dozen other travellers; that is until a South African girl insisted on watching 'Four Weddings And A Funeral', which caused the room to empty within minutes.

After a hectic first fortnight in New Zealand, I spent the following day resting up in the warmth of the hostel and seeing to a few chores, such as my growing laundry. Steve arrived the next day on the Magic Bus, and the three of us visited the local Speights Brewery for their tour, which was extremely boring. However the end of tour sampling session was reward for our patience; we managed to sample the entire range of Speights six beers in half an hour.

The following day I left Dunedin, and for the first time in New

Zealand I found myself alone as I headed north along the east coast. We stopped for lunch at a beachside restaurant near to the Moeraki Boulders, large spherical rocks. We then drove through lush green farmland of the Canterbury Plains, framed by the highest peaks in the Southern Alps, to Christchurch, thus completing a complete loop of the South Island.

I tried to check into Base Backpackers Hostel, but for reasons beyond my comprehension, the jobs-worth of a receptionist would not allow me to check in without seeing my passport, which was located in the bottom of my rucksack, and so I took my business to the nearby Warners Hostel.

I immediately visited the Video Camera repair shop and collected my camera, finally repaired around three-months after damaging it in Australia. I spent the evening in the hostel chatting to two girls from Leeds, who were travelling around the world in the opposite direction to me, and so we shared information on destinations and accommodation in the places we had been to.

The next leg of my journey took me from Christchurch through Canterbury, travelling north along the coastline to Kaikoura, a relatively short three-hour drive. I checked into Dusky Lodge Hostel, which had a cosy atmosphere, with log fires in both lounges, and a swimming pool, sauna and spa-bath. Kaikoura is the whale-watching capital of New Zealand, and I had intended to take a boat trip whilst here, however the weather had been unkind to us and all trips for the day were cancelled. I therefore spent the day relaxing and making the most of the hostel facilities, and the evening chatting with a gorgeous girl named Fiona from Manchester.

The final leg of my South Island tour finished with a journey from Kaikoura to Blenheim, driving north along the beautiful stretch of coast. We continued through the lush vineyards and hilly pastures of Marlborough to Picton, a small town on the edge of the beautiful Marlborough Sounds. I checked my bags into the airline style arrivals counter at the ferry terminal and boarded the Inter-Island ferry, which would take me across the Cook Strait to the North Island.

I had thoroughly enjoyed my time in New Zealand's South Island, which is a nature lovers paradise with everything from dense forests to crystal clear lakes, and golden beaches to snow capped mountains, not to mention the odd sheep or two. It is a really beautiful land, but after a while you start to take for granted the spectacular scenery, for around every corner is another breathtaking view.

16

Hot Rocks
(North Island, New Zealand)
02/09/04 to 17/09/04

The Inter-Island ferry pulled out of harbour on time at 12.30 on the short voyage across the Cook Strait to the North Island. I found a seat by one of the numerous TV's and settled down to watch an English football game being screened. Before I knew it, we were entering Wellington harbour. I disembarked and collected my backpack from the airport style baggage carousel in the terminal building. Hundreds of passengers were stood outside the terminal, there were no buses and only a couple of taxis, which were quickly snapped up. With seemingly no other option, I walked into the city looking for a hostel.

After around half an hour I came across the City YHA which occupied a good location in downtown, and not wanting to walk any further, I checked in. I immediately set off to explore the world's most southern capital, known to kiwis as "Windy Wellington" because of its location in the roaring forties latitudes, and its exposure to omnipresent winds coming through Cook Strait. I wandered around the streets of downtown, the heart and soul of the city, divided into the quarters of Cuba, Willis, Lambton and Courtenay, where my hostel was located. There was little difference between any of the quarters; I think that they were probably devised by a marketing man to give the city a more cosmopolitan feel.

Wellington is more densely populated than most other towns in New Zealand, due to the small amount of building space available between the picturesque harbour and forested green hills. However with a population of just under 165,000, it is a relatively small and friendly city, and being only two kilometres wide it was easy to explore on foot. It is not only small but also low, with very few high-rise buildings. The most striking feature of the cities architecture is the collection of historical timber houses perched in the green hills surrounding the harbour.

The hostel was converted from a hotel and had great communal facilities on the ground and first floors including two kitchens, two dining rooms, two TV lounges, a reading room, a travel desk and a laundry. The spacious and clean dorm rooms were located on the five upper floors. But the hostel was too large and impersonal, and had an institutional feel, and during my stay here I didn't make any friends.

Over the next couple of days I leisurely explored the capital. I set out early one morning to walk to the lofty viewpoint of Mount Victoria. However I soon wandered what I'd let myself in for; the muddy track was unkempt and overgrown and it soon became obvious that this route was rarely used nowadays. I was forced to trudge through thick mud and scramble up and down steep banks. When I eventually emerged from the forest at the summit, I was covered in mud and must have looked like a tramp to the sightseers there. The views looking out over the city and bay were ok but nothing special, and so after taking the customary panoramic snapshots, I returned to the city via the conventional public bus.

I spent another morning exploring Wellington's waterfront, starting at Queens Wharf I followed the harbour around past The National Museum "Te Papa" and Chaffers Marina to Oriental Bay, where several cafes overlook a stretch of golden sand. The waterfront has been regenerated and a number of key historic buildings had been sympathetically restored and converted to restaurants, bars and apartments, including the old Bond Store, which now houses The Museum of Wellington City and Sea. Open spaces and pedestrian walkways have been landscaped to allow people to walk at the water's edge and enjoy the harbour views.

An interesting and unusual pedestrian footbridge featuring indigenous artwork, which looks as though it has been built from old wooden-pallets, links the waterfront to the cities Civic Square;

a large block paved open space with unusual modern architectural features including palm tree shaped steel lamp-posts, a metal globe suspended in mid air and a large vase shaped sculpture.

From the city centre I caught the 'Wellington Cable Car', which is actually a funicular railway, to the Botanical Gardens located on the hill to the west of the city centre, opposite to Mount Victoria. At the summit is a small museum dedicated to the 100-year history of the cable car, which was first opened 1902. I spent a little time wandering around the Botanic Gardens; 25-hectares of unique landscape, protected native forest, conifers, specialised plant collections and colourful floral displays, and with wonderful views over the city and across the harbour.

I also spent a pleasurable few hours at the wonderful, recently built National Museum Te Papa, which was one of the best museums I had ever visited. My favourite exhibit was called 'Awesome Forces', which explains through models, diagrams, and interactives how plate tectonics, earthquakes, volcanic eruptions, and erosion have changed the surface of the globe and shaped New Zealand, whose position astride two mighty tectonic plates is graphically outlined. New Zealand's seismic activity and volcanic eruptions, and their effects on people and the land, come to life through large screen projections, animation, and a shaking 'earthquake house'.

'Signs of a Nation' is an exhibit on the Treaty of Waitangi, standing in an imposing wedge-shaped space, underneath a high cathedral-like ceiling. The treaty was essentially a bargain that was struck between Maori and the British Crown. The Treaty document itself – both as a giant replica and with the words of its two versions set large on the walls – has a strong presence in the exhibition. As you walk through a thicket of pole clusters, voices can be heard presenting the different views of New Zealanders on the Treaty, from the time of signing through to current opinions. It tells the story of the breakdown of the treaty relationship, when it came to be ignored by successive settler-dominated governments in the nineteenth century, through to its renewed recognition in recent times. Personal stories of people whose lives have been affected by the Treaty are displayed on the walls. One sign read "The missionaries came to our land and brought the message of their god. And whilst we knelt and bowed to their god, they stole our land".

After a pleasant few days in the capital, I continued my Magic Bus tour to Napier. Our driver was a huge Maori, built like the proverbial outhouse. There were only seven passengers aboard, all very friendly; a German couple, a Japanese girl, a German girl, and two guys that I palled up with, Andy from Sheffield and a Swiss guy named Ollie. The first stop of the morning was at Mount Bruce Wildlife Centre to view the Kiwi-bird and visit the Tuatara breeding programme. The Tuatara is one of New Zealand's rarest creatures.

We arrived in Napier around 1.30 after an uneventful four-hour journey. Napier is said to be the finest art-deco city in the world. The city was completely razed in 1931 by an earthquake and ensuing fires, which killed two hundred and fifty eight people. The city centre was subsequently rebuilt in the popular 'art deco' style of the day, and the centre is now recognized as architecturally unique. The whole place has a 1930's English seaside town feel, there are even old classic cars driving around. It was a beautiful city but very quiet, almost deserted.

I checked into Archies Bunker Hostel with Andy. We popped out that evening for a beer and ended up in an Irish bar, although the only thing Irish about it was the name and the green wallpaper. We were joined at our table by an elderly woman named Val, who turned out to be not only the local drunk but also the local nut case. We brought her a couple of beers and listened to her stories and jokes. "You don't want to stay in a hostel,' she said, 'I make a lovely breakfast!"

Andy was a good-looking lad with shoulder length blonde hair. Whilst he was in the toilet, I said to Val "Have you ever met royalty before?"

"Who's royalty?" she asked.

"Andrew is the Prince of Denmark"

"Really?"

"Yes, but keep it to yourself, he doesn't like anyone to know".

For the remainder of the evening, Val did her best to sit as close as possible to Andy and every time he spoke, she answered, "Yes prince", much to his bemusement. We finally left the bar around

11pm in an attempt to find somewhere livelier, but every other bar in town was closed. Napier was like one of those weird towns in 'Tales Of The Unexpected'.

We continued on our journey the next day to the town of Taupo, which occupies a stunning position on the shore of the lake with which it shares its name, beneath a backdrop of snow capped volcanic mountains. At 616 square kilometres, crystal clear Lake Taupo is the largest fresh water lake in Australasia and is fed by forty-seven rivers and streams, although it has just one outlet – the Waikato River, New Zealand's longest. The lake was created by the largest known volcanic eruption of the past 5,000 years, and the entire area is quite literally a hotbed of geothermal activity.

Andy and I checked into Sunset Backpackers Hostel, which was a little out of town but was quite homely and pleasant. Inside the hostel, I looked through tour brochures of flights over the snow-covered volcanic peaks of the world heritage listed Tongario National Park. Of the four alternatives, one stood out in particular, a floatplane, which takes off and lands on the lake. Without hesitation, we booked an afternoon flight.

The friendly hostel owner drove us to the lakeside and dropped us at the small cabin office of Taupo Float Plane. The office was locked so we sat outside and waited patiently. After a few minutes we heard the hum of an aeroplane engine, and a couple of minutes later the high wing Cessna Floatplane appeared over the mountains, swept down, landed on the lake, and taxied to the wooden jetty in front of us.

Tongario World Heritage National Park contains three magnificent volcanoes; Mount Ruapehu, Mount Tongario and Mount Ngauruhoe, better known as the scary 'Mount Doom' in the movie 'Lord of the Rings'. Mount Ruapehu is the highest point in the North Island and has a number of peaks, the highest of which is Tahurangi at 2,797m. It also contains eight named glaciers, the only glaciers in the North Island. The hot acidic crater-lake near to its summit has had over sixty recorded eruptions since 1945, the last in 1995 when the crater-lake disappeared completely, however it is now slowly reforming.

We boarded the small plane, I sat in the front, Andy sat in the back together with an English girl who worked in the local tourist office, who was getting a free ride so she could sell flights to tourists. We sped across the surface of the lake and slowly climbed into the sky, tracking south above the lake to over-fly Turangi, Mount Pihanga, Lake Rotoaira, Blue and Emerald Lakes and the Tama Lakes to the summit of Mt Ruapehu, which we circled allowing us a view of its crater-lake. A thick blanket of snow covered the volcanoes and craters. We saw smoke emitting from one of the craters through the snow and way below we could make out the ski fields and ant like skiers on its slopes.

Starting our journey north again we travelled onto Mount Ngauruhoe to view the centre of this classic volcano, then over the flat topped Mount Tongario viewing the Red Crater, turquoise coloured lake and old lava flows, before we began our descent over Lake Taupo, which from above was a greenish blue colour, and we could make out the lava reefs below the surface. We made a very smooth landing on the lake and taxied toward a cliff face, which contained Maori carvings and artwork. The pilot turned off the engine and we all got out of the plane and stood on the float; the pilot unclipped an oar from the side of the plane, which he used to paddle us to the cliff for a close up view. We then took off again and flew over the remainder of the lake before making a second equally smooth landing at the jetty. Our hour and half trip had been wonderful; the scenery was as spectacular as anything I had ever seen and the sensation of taking off from and landing on the water is one I will never forget.

The next day Andy set off early on a guided trek of The Tongario Crossing, a walk over the volcanoes, which we had flew over yesterday. Meanwhile, I walked out of town to the Waikato River Trail. At the start of the trail was a warm geothermal spring entering the river. I stripped off, climbed into the water and relaxed in the natural hot bath for about half an hour.

I continued along the trail for about an hour until I reached a footbridge at Huka Falls, New Zealand's most visited natural attraction. At this section of the river, the water is forced into a narrow channel around fifteen metres wide and ten metres deep, from the previous one hundred metres wide and four metres deep. The force of the water is frightening has it thunders through the long channel, before crashing into the river ten metres below. More than 220,000 litres of water tumbles over this cliff face every second.

I sat at a bench and watched the river roar by as I ate some sandwiches, which I had prepared earlier. I then continued to the nearby geo-thermal area called 'Craters Of The Moon', which was almost deserted of people. The entire area was one large smouldering site of craters and bubbling mud pools, and of steam hissing and smoke bellowing from the earth. I walked around the circular trail, which linked several wooden viewing platforms overlooking the main craters and mud pools. It was an eerie, almost mystical, alien like setting, quite unlike anything I had experienced before.

Suddenly the silence was broken when a party of school children arrived, running around the trail, shouting, screaming, and throwing rocks into the craters and pools, whilst their supervisors left them to their own devices. I continued around the trail trying to avoid these kids but they were everywhere, and so after barely an hour here, I reluctantly left, catching a bus from outside the park entrance back to town.

When I arrived back at the hostel Andy was fast asleep on his bed, and feeling pretty worn out myself, I did the same for a couple of hours. We both woke around 8pm and popped into town for a few beers, where we met up with the group that Andy had been trekking with earlier. I spent the majority of the night trying to chat up an Irish girl, whilst Andy tried to pull a Norwegian girl. We finally left at 2am and caught a taxi back to our hostel, alone.

The next day we again boarded the Magic Bus and continued our journey North. There were only about ten people aboard, including Ollie who I had met previously. Andy had only a couple of days left in New Zealand before flying home and so he was continuing through to Auckland, whilst I disembarked in Rotorua.

Rotorua is another region of fascinating geothermal activity where the seething power of inner earth comes to the surface in spectacular fashion. It is a Natural Spa, and many homes and business have been quick to exploit the natural phenomena by tapping into the geothermal waters to provide heating or to create therapeutic spa and massage therapy businesses, which abound here.

Ollie and I checked into Hot Rocks Backpackers Hostel, which had a swimming pool and three spa pools, all naturally heated and fed from below ground. As per usual, I immediately set off to see my new surroundings, wandering around the town and along the lakefront. From the moment that I arrived, I knew there was something quite different about the place. There was a rotten egg smell of sulphur wafting through the air and sneaky threads of steam issuing from cracks in the earth in parks, pathways, lawns and streets, and even from the edge of the lake.

On my way back to the hostel I came across the Kuirau Reserve which was similar to Craters of the moon in Taupo, with more craters, bubbling mud pools, steam, and spouting geysers. It was a weird and wonderful environment of geothermal activity almost everywhere you look.

Rotorua is the heartland of New Zealand Maori culture, and although most of the Maori population live in the urban areas, there are about thirty-five marae (meeting grounds) in the Rotorua district. That evening Ollie and I visited Tamaki Maori Village for a traditional hangi feast. The tourist attraction is the winner of New Zealand's Supreme Tourism Award and four times winner of the national heritage and cultural tourism awards. I boarded a coach full of tourists with a crazy Maori driver who called himself 'Dennis The Menace'. As we travelled to the village, Dennis lead us back to pre-European times with stories, history and protocols in preparation for the ceremonies to follow.

Each of the five coaches attending the feast were to be treated as an individual tribe and had therefore to elect a chief from our number, whose role was to accept a peace offering from the welcoming tribe. We arrived at the village, set deep in the forest, where we were greeted by a traditional welcome ceremony; the sound of ancient Maori instruments and singing, followed by the arrival of a warrior who offered a peace challenge through a series of dance steps and cries. Once the peace offering was accepted by our elected chiefs, the warrior led us into the village.

The village itself was obviously a mock up of an original village but was very authentic, with crackling open fires, wooden buildings and elaborate carvings, in which the Maoris were performing and demonstrating various traditional activities. We were then invited into the meeting house called the Wharenui, where the group made welcoming speeches before performing traditional stories, songs and dances, finishing with the famous haka war-dance, complete with rolling eyes and bobbing tongues, which apparently signifies that they find their enemies skin appealing and they want to eat it; fortunately this practise has now died out. Throughout the performance, the Maoris were all smiling and laughing; they all obviously enjoyed sharing their culture with us foreigners.

After the show we were led to the food house called a Wharekai, where a traditional hangi banquet had been prepared. Hangi is the Maori method of cooking food on a bed of hot rocks in a pit dug in the ground. The food is placed in baskets on the rocks and covered with moist leaves and earth, and left to steam cook for three to four hours, before being dug up and served. The meal was fabulous, comprising of various vegetables and meat dishes including lamb, chicken and fish, served buffet style. The only problem was that we only had about an hour to consume it, and I could have easily spent the entire night eating, it was that delicious. Around 10.30pm the Maoris bid us farewell with another song and we returned to our coaches.

It all sounds a little touristy and corny, but the evening had actually been very enjoyable and entertaining, as well as informative. It provided an interesting insight into a culture that almost died out around thirty years ago, but had now been resurrected and was being re-embraced by the Maori people, mainly due to cultural groups like this. The Maori people had crossed the Pacific Ocean from Polynesia over a thousand years earlier in large canoes, carrying livestock and crop plants. They are obviously a progressive people, and this may help explain why they have integrated with the European settlers much better than the Australian aboriginal people have.

The following day I headed to Te Whakarewarewa Thermal Reserve and Cultural Centre, a one and a half hour walk out of town. It was similar to the other reserves I had visited but much larger. The highlight was the Pohutu Geyser, which spurted a constant stream of boiling water and steam about three-metres into the air. Dazzling silica terraces around the base display a kaleidoscope of colour. I stood watching for a couple of minutes when suddenly the geyser erupted spectacularly into the air to a height of about thirty-metres.

Elsewhere in the park was a birdhouse housing the nocturnal kiwi-bird, an odd looking little fat bird with a long beak, no tail and feathers which resemble thick hair. There was also a mock village and a craft centre with a traditional Maori carving school, where all of the carvings around the site were made.

The next leg of my trip took me to the town of Mount Maunganui, in the company of Ollie and a few new faces; Carol from Brazil who I'd met at the Maori cultural night, two Canadian girls named Shannon and Becky who were travelling separately, Brendan from Northampton, Susan from Kent and Terry from Leamington. We arrived at 5pm and we all checked into The Pacific Coast Hostel, to find free pizza, coffee and cakes waiting for us. The hostel was full to brim, including a coach load of Czech old age pensioners. I ended up in a tiny, cramped eight-bed dorm with the other lads from the bus.

A group of us headed out that night for a few beers; I sat chatting with Becky, a very pretty blue-eyed blonde girl; we were getting on really well and I got the impression that she was definitely interested. Brendan put a little dampner on the night, he appeared very bitter and twisted toward women; I presumed he'd had a bad experience. Shannon then moved seats and sat on my other side, and I began to get the feeling that she too was interested in me.

Come closing time, Becky said she was tired and wanted to head to bed, Brendan wanted food, and Shannon and I were up for a bit of clubbing, so we caught a taxi to the nearby larger town of Tauranga. We danced the night away until around 3am; on returning to the hostel, we spent the night together on the sofa under Shannons quilt. On a couple of occasions throughout the night, we were disturbed by the Czech pensioners walking through the lounge to the toilet. Around 6am, we were forced to return to our respective dorms as the pensioners began to get up for breakfast. Why do old people always wake so early?

Around 9am I was rudely awoken by the hostel owner, asking me if I was checking out today; the fact that I had already paid for two-nights obviously didn't occur to him. Unable to get back to sleep, I stumbled out of bed and walked to the shower room in my boxers, almost giving a few of the pensioners a heart attack. After showering, still feeling annoyed at being so rudely awoken, I visited reception and told the owner that I had changed my mind and would indeed be now checking out today. He told me that as the 10am checkout time had now passed, he didn't have to give me my deposit back. I informed him that I was actually checked out early not late, as I was booked in for two days, and so he did have to refund my deposit. He begrudgingly paid up.

Becky came over and asked if I'd had a good night; I presumed that she was unaware of the events. She was also booked in for two-nights and when I told her I was moving on, she looked genuinely disappointed and I hoped that I would run into her again. The Magic Bus arrived at 11.30am and I boarded along with Shannon and everyone from yesterday, except for Becky. We continued north through the small towns of Waihi and Paeroa, before stopping at Thames, the gateway to the Coromandel Peninsula.

By 4.30pm we had arrived in Auckland, which occupies a glorious position on a thin stretch of the North Island, surrounded by the Pacific Ocean on just about every side. It is New Zealand's largest city, with 1.2million people, over one quarter of the countries total population, and is perhaps the most vibrant, bustling and multicultural city in New Zealand as well as the centre of commerce and industry.

Shannon and I checked into a dorm room together in Base Backpackers Hostel, and then we took a stroll through downtown and around Viaduct Harbour, which is the focal point of this most nautical of cities. Viaduct Harbour is a trendy area with lively street cafes, restaurants and bars, with exceptional views of the nearby waterfront, and the yachts moored in the harbour. Auckland has more boats per capita than anywhere else in the world, and is the current residence of the America's Cup; its nickname 'the city of sails' is very apt. We popped into the restored and refurbished landmark ferry building, built in the 1900's and now housing a trendy restaurant and bar, outside of which on the harbour-side proudly sits the winning America's Cup yacht.

We returned to the hostel and spent a very pleasurable half hour in the private, open-air, roof top spa-pool, which provides a great sensation with the contrast of the hot bubbling water against your body and the cold night air around your face. The city views weren't bad from here either. Afterwards we returned to our dorm for an early night!

The following day we caught a bus to Mount Roskill district where we spent the afternoon and evening with Shannon's friend Janet, who now lived here with her Kiwi husband Kim. Shannon had arranged to spend the next week with Janet and they invited me to stay also, but I declined and returned to my hostel on the last bus; Shannon and Janet had not seen each other for some time and I didn't want to come between them.

The next day I changed hostels to The Fat Camel and booked into a private room for my remaining few days in New Zealand. The cost was double that of a dorm bed, but I felt that it would help me rest and recharge my batteries in preparation for my next destination of South America. It was bliss having my own room and a real bed not a bunk, and with no comings and goings throughout the night, I was able to sleep much better.

During my final few days here the weather was generally miserable, grey and wet, which probably clouded my opinion of the city as Auckland is a real outdoor city, and a water lover's paradise, with some of the best beaches, swimming, diving, fishing, sailing, windsurfing and water-sports in the country. I had hoped to spend some time on some of its many beaches, and do a little sailing, but due to weather I never did make it.

Instead I did a little sightseeing, although Auckland is not the prettiest city and is not overly endowed with architectural gems. Auckland Town Hall is one exception, built in the early 20th century in an Italian-style. Albert Park, close to downtown, is a large open expanse of grass and landscaped gardens, with a Victorian bandstand, statues and seating areas, which provides a welcome respite from the city. I also caught the ferry across the harbour to the seaside resort of Devonport, but only stayed for an hour, as there was little of interest there.

Auckland's most recognisable landmark, looming over downtown, is the impressive Sky Tower built in 1997. At 328metres, it is the tallest structure in the southern hemisphere, with a lift that can shoot you up to the observation deck and revolving restaurant in forty seconds. But the panoramic views across the city were nothing special; Auckland is not the most beautiful of cities. Typical of New Zealand, it also offers the opportunity for daredevil types to climb into a harness and throw themselves off.

The cities other striking landmark is the Harbour Bridge, a four-lane highway built in 1959, spanning 1.5km across the Waitemata Harbour connecting the city to the North shore. Owing to the rapid expansion of suburbs on the North Shore and increasing traffic levels, it was necessary to increase the capacity of the bridge. Only ten years after construction, two-lane box girder sections were added to each side, doubling the number of lanes from four to eight. These sections were designed and manufactured by Japanese engineers, which led to the nickname 'The Nippon clip-on'.

My evenings were generally spent in the downtown bars, with a small group of people that I'd met at Base and The Fat Camel hostels. The coolest of which, quite literally, is called 'Minus Five' on Princes Wharf in the Viaduct. It is a bar completely produced from ice; the walls, seats, sculptures and even the glasses you drink out of. The entrance fee of around £8 gets you a complimentary cocktail, but punters are limited to a half-hour visit before they are sent outside to defrost. It is a totally unique experience.

Whilst here I also celebrated my thirty-eighth birthday over a three-day period. The day after my birthday my friends from home, Matt and Ann arrived. They too were travelling around the world in the opposite direction to me. They gave me a belated birthday present of a foul smelling cheap aftershave called Stetson, which was apparently a free gift with a bottle of booze in the airport duty free shop. It was the only card and present I had received for my birthday so I didn't mind at all. We spent one evening together in the local bars and we ran into another familiar face, Steve who I had spent so much time with on the South Island.

On my penultimate day I sorted out my backpack, culling certain items that I would not need in South America; throwing away some and posting home a parcel containing others. I brought a few bits and pieces; second hand books, contact lenses, a spare camera battery and a spare photo memory card.

And so my brief five-week visit of New Zealand was at an end.

I spent my final day attending to a few last minute chores, and around 2pm I caught a shuttle bus to the airport in readiness for my flight to Santiago-de-Chile.

I had thoroughly enjoyed my time in New Zealand, which is one of the most beautiful, friendly and diverse countries that I have visited, with unique attractions and geography; hot stuff indeed!

PART 3

SOUTH AMERICA

17

Back to School
(Chile)

17/09/04 to 06/10/04

I boarded the Lan-Chile plane bound for Santiago-de-Chile and found that I was sitting next to an elderly nun; my thoughts turned straight to the Airplane movie and I was quite relived to find that she didn't have a guitar. I had wandered about the standard of the Lan-Chile service but I needn't have worried; the plane was modern and clean, the staff polite, friendly and impeccably presented, and the in-flight entertainment was excellent and much better than on both B.A. and Qantas. All seats had their own mini TV screens offering a choice off entertainment channels and video games. I watched a movie and then played a couple of video games, before eventually getting my head down for the night.

I awoke the next morning to find the nun playing violent video games, which I found rather amusing; her hands tightly gripping the handset and her thumbs dancing across the buttons. Every so often she would mutter something in Spanish; I'd like to think that she was cursing, "Die you bastard" or something similar, but she was probably just asking the lord for a little divine intervention to help her to the next level!

I was excited at the prospect of travelling in South America, yet at the same time I was apprehensive, and dare I say a little scared of what lay ahead. On my travels I had met many other backpackers who had visited 'The New World', and without exception all had nothing but praise for the continent and its people. However, I had also heard many stories of travellers being robbed, mugged, stabbed and shot by desperate locals.

I had of course taken some precautions against being the victim of an unshaven bandit with a bushy handlebar moustache, "Hey gringo, gimme your monie yu durty pig" I imagined him saying. I had sent home all my jewellery and for the first time on this trip I wore my money-belt concealing my passport, flight tickets and cash, tied around my waist and tucked inside my trousers. I had also purchased a spare wallet to hand over in the seemingly likely event of being robbed, which I padded out with an out of date credit card, a couple of dollar bills and several worthless notes from Asia.

We touched down in Santiago at 1:30pm, and although we had departed at 5:25pm yesterday and had been travelling for 12-hours, we had actually landed on the same day, Friday 17 September. In theory, we had arrived in Santiago before we had left Auckland, due to the fact that we had of course crossed the 180th parallel (International Date Line) and so we had effectively gone back in time.

I passed through Chilean customs and immigration without too much difficulty, other than having two New Zealand apples confiscated from my bag. I was met on the other side of the arrival doors by a throng of taxi drivers looking for business. An official looking guy in a blazer and carrying a walkie-talkie came to my aid and showed me to an ATM and then to the bus, which would take me to the Barrio-Brasil district where I intended to stay. I thanked him for his help with a 500-Peso tip.

As the bus made its way through the city suburbs, my first impressions were favourable; the city appeared orderly and prosperous, with a European look and feel, the roads were excellent, the people dressed in Western attire, many of the women looked quite sophisticated, and I didn't see anyone who looked remotely like a bandito, which pleased me greatly.

We drove past three circuses and dozens of football pitches, many with either games being played on them or with kids having a kick about, and there seemed to be an overly excessive number of people flying kites. Standing along the roadside at each intersection were groups of street performers, jugglers and uni-cyclists, performing for tips from the drivers of the waiting cars. Santiago seemed an amazing and crazy place, however I later discovered that this was not the norm, but that today was the start of a public holiday in Chile to celebrate its independence from Spain.

The bus dropped me in the Barrio-Brasil district, just a few blocks to La Casa Roja (red house) Hostel, where I had pre-booked a weeks accomodation. The hostel was converted from a 19th century colonial style mansion and was being restored by its owners, an Australian and Chilean couple. It was a grand building containing many original features and courtyard style patio gardens.

I entered the lounge where a lone guy sat watching TV. He looked up and said enthusiastically "hello mate, how you doin?"

"Fine" I replied.

"It's me, John, John from Nah-Trang, remember?" I'd met John in Vietnam back in March and we'd spent a few drunken nights in each others company. He looked much different now and so I hadn't recognised him initially; his hair was longer now and tied in a ponytail, and he looked a little more dishevelled and hippy-ish.

I spent my first evening sitting in one of the hostel courtyards with most of the other guests, gaining some useful information on places to go and things to see, and drinking local beer at 45-pence per litre bottle. Around 9pm there was a mad rush for the 'eat as much as you can' BBQ. I stayed up drinking, eating and chatting until about 3am, before finally retiring to my dorm bed.

The following day was Independence Day and I headed to the main thorough-fare, strangely named 'Avenue O'Higgins The Liberator', after the illegitimate son of an Irishman, who had previously served the colonial Spaniards as Viceroy of Peru, before becoming the second in command of the independence forces, 'the Army of the Andes', and ultimately the supreme director of the new Chilean republic.

The streets were lined with bunting, as if to keep the crowds back, but there were hardly any crowds around. There was however hundreds of police and soldiers, all armed, lining the road. A procession of stately looking vehicles then passed, all with flags flying and with a police motorbike escort. Five minutes after the main cavalcade, a smaller cavalcade approached but with a lager police escort. A man waved at the crowds from an open top limousine and the crowds waved back. I approached a plain-clothed security guard dressed in a black suit and wearing an earpiece, "Buenos dias senor, El Presidenta?" I asked, pointing toward the car. He looked at me with a bemused expression and simply replied "Si".

The next day was Armed Forces Day and again the streets were lined with patriotic, flag-waving Chileans, cheering row upon row of marching soldiers, military brass bands and cavalry on horseback, all dressed in full regalia, some with rifles in arm, others with swords drawn. I walked towards the city and came across Cerro Santa Lucia, a hill park with a church and fortifications on its summit. At the base is the ornate Terraza Neptuno, with fountains, a statue of Neptune, curving staircases and stone balconies. I lingered here for a while and watched the military procession, before retracing my footsteps back to the hostel.

On Monday I woke early in readiness for my first day at school, having pre-booked a one-week crash Spanish language course at a local language school. Three other hostel guests had also booked onto the same course, and so we travelled there together on the fantastic metro system, which was clean, cheap and very efficient.

Mike from London and Fiona and Alex from Hull were all younger than me and were all fairly recently out of university, and so they found the learning process a little easier than I, although I had the slight advantage of a little Spanish gleaned from an evening course I had taken before commencing this trip.

The initial four-hour lesson was intense and quite hard going; we were instructed to only speak in Spanish whilst in class, which was not at all easy. We all had similar aspirations from the course; to obtain basic language skills to enable us to get by whilst travelling. However the course seemed more geared to grammar, which left us all rather frustrated as we didn't necessarily want or need to be able to write an essay in Spanish, just communicate in it.

Our first class ended at 1pm and we walked back to the hostel to find Manchester United playing Liverpool live on TV. I sat down to watch and fell asleep on the sofa, obviously still not recovered from the jet lag. I awoke later to see a familiar smiling face sitting opposite me. Steve who I'd travelled with in New

Zealand had arrived here this very day.

That evening Steve and I, and Ian from Wales headed to the Barrio-Bellavista district, a lively neighbourhood with narrow streets lined with cafes and bars. We entered a bar and I tried out my newly acquired Spanish, "Tres cerveza por favour". The waitress replied and not exactly understanding her fully, I nodded and said "Si". She returned five minutes later carrying three pitchers of beer containing about three pints in each. I obviously still had much to learn.

The Spanish lessons became easier as the week progressed and we managed to pick up many of the basic phrases that we would need, although I wasn't quite up to having a full blown conversations just yet. After each lesson I would spend my afternoons exploring the city and visiting the sights.

I was very impressed with Santiago; there were many magnificent and grand buildings, tree lined boulevards, parks, statues, shops, bars and cafes. It was a blend of modern skyscrapers and Spanish colonial architecture, which complemented each other favourably. Founded in 1541 by Spaniard Pedro-de-Valdivia, Santiago is not only the capital of Chile but also its largest city, with a population in excess of 5-million. Many multi-national companies have their regional headquarters here, as Chile is probably the most stable country in South America, both politically and economically. The one blight on the city was the excessive smog, which hung over the city.

The main hive of activity and the historic centre was the Plaza de Armas, the centre of the original planned city set up on a standardised grid pattern, which the Spaniards imposed on all their American territories. The plaza was frequented by artists, shoe shine boys, buskers, political speakers and the like, and is flanked by several imposing colonial buildings, whilst the southern and eastern sides are lined with busy shopping arcades and small fast food outlets which served the most delicious hot-dogs with all the trimmings, called 'completos'.

Close by was Cerro San Cristobel, a large hill park with gardens, monuments and a zoo, which towers 869m over the city. I caught the funicular railway to the summit, where a thirty-six metre high statue of the Virgin Mary stands, enjoying unobstructed views over the city toward the snow-capped Andes Mountains.

My Spanish lessons appeared to be paying off; one evening Steve, Ian and I came upon a local pizza parlour with a sign in the window, which read, "Martes de barato, dos pour uno." I was able to translate to the others, "cheap Tuesdays, two for one." On another occasion I visited the local launderette and deposited my laundry for a service wash, while I popped to a nearby Internet café to catch up on my e-mails. When I returned later, I got a mother-like bollocking from the wash-lady, and I was just able to ascertain that I had mixed the colours and my white t-shirt was now pink!

After an exhausting week back at school, our final day ended with a field trip to the Museum of Fine Arts followed by a visit to the Mercado Centre, a fish and vegetable market with small restaurants inside selling fresh produce from the market. The centre itself is a Victorian cast-iron framed building, which was constructed in London and shipped to Santiago. We had lunch in one of the restaurants, however the food was overpriced and not that great. A trio of two guys on guitar and a large female singer with castanets serenaded us as we ate, for a tip of course.

On my final night in Santiago, I had a few beers at the weekly hostel BBQ, during which I met a guy named Bobby from Devon, who like me was flying to Easter Island tomorrow. As were on the same flight, we agreed to share a taxi to the airport. Later on my classmates and I headed out on the town, joined by Paul and Jo from Birmingham. We generally had a good night drinking in some of the local bars, however the night turned slightly sour when we were turned away from a bar; apparently there was a 'no gringos' policy. Almost immediately afterwards we had a slight altercation with a group of local students brandishing hockey sticks, and so we returned to the safety of the hostel.

By 7am the next morning Bobby and I had checked out of the hostel and were on our way to the airport in a taxi. Bobby had a surfboard with him for some ridiculous reason, and so it took a bit of effort to fit it in the car. Once at the airport we checked in then grabbed some breakfast, and before long we were boarding the plane for a 6-hour flight across the Pacific Ocean to Easter Island.

We landed around 1pm, disembarked onto the runway, and

walked to the small terminal to collect our luggage. A group of girls dressed in traditional Polynesian grass skirts stood on the side of the runway to greet us, which I thought was very nice. Waiting at the airport entrance were a number of local hoteliers and so we were able to fix ourselves up with some cheap guesthouse accommodation in the islands main town of Hango Roa. Our host then drove us to her home, the Apina Tupuna Residential, where we shared a twin room.

Bobby was on an around the world surfing tour. Although from Devon, he tried to speak with a Californian accent, which didn't quite fit with his West Country dialect, and annoyingly he constantly referred to me as dude. Despite these slight drawbacks, he was good company and quite a nice bloke.

He had come to Easter Island simply to surf, unaware of the significance of this tiny volcanic island, a tiny pinprick in the great Pacific, formed where the lava and ash from three separate submarine volcanoes of different ages coalesced in a single triangular land mass of just 117 sq km. This is the world's most isolated bit of land, standing 3,700km from Chile, 4,050km from Tahiti and 1,900km from its nearest inhabited neighbour, Pitcairn. The natives call their island Rapa Nui or Te Pito o Te Henua, 'the navel of the earth'.

The inhabitants are Polynesian and first inhabited the island around 400AD. There presence here is as much a mystery to historians as are the carved stone statues that dot the island. The islanders developed a sophisticated culture dedicated to the construction of altars and the carving of stone statues and monuments of their Gods and ancestors, called Moai, comprising the torso and head of men, usually around ten metres high, often built on enormous stone platforms and burial chambers called ahu.

The island is said to be a microcosm of mankind. The success of the people in cultivating crops led to an increase in population. As they became more successful, the growing number of people eventually began to threaten the resource base, and with no natural water sources on the island, they could not grow sufficient quantities of crops. Simultaneously they also became obsessed with carving and erecting giant stone statues, so much so that they eventually logged almost every tree on the island in order to transport them to their erection sites. The depletion of the natural resources, especially timber, eventually led the tribal warfare, which led to the destruction of many of the monuments, a rapid decline in the population and ultimately the collapse of the civilisation. The culture was all but killed off following the arrival of Peruvian slavers in 1862, who abducted around a thousand of the islanders, including the king.

Today less than 4,000 people inhabit the tiny island, about a third of those from the mainland. In 1995 it was declared a Unesco World Heritage Site, as it is effectively one huge outdoor museum containing a myriad of archaeological artefacts, the most visible of which are the stone moai statues which number over a thousand. Warring islanders toppled these immense sculptures from their ahu platforms, but over recent years many have been restored and re-erected. For years, researchers have puzzled over how the islanders managed to transport these sculptures from the quarry to their coastal resting places; one unfinished moai measures a massive twenty-one metres, and weighs around three hundred tons.

We spent our first day getting to know the town, after which we took a walk along the coast for our first close-up look at the moai statues for which this island is famous. Within one kilometre of the town there are numerous animal-like ancient stone statues and carvings, and several giant restored moai, standing five to ten metres tall, all very similar and yet all very different.

The next day we set off on an 18km round trip walk to the extinct volcano called Rano-Kau. Passing the small Hanga Piko harbour along the way, with its lone moai, we followed the rugged coastline, steadily climbing up to the rim of the volcano crater. The trek took around three-hours, and was hard going in the punishing intense sun, but it was well worth it for the sight that awaited. We stood speechless on the 1.6km diameter circular crater rim, its south and west sides rising over 400-meters straight out of the sea. Deep inside the crater was a reed-covered lake, which gave the impression of standing on the edge of a huge, cooking pot.

On the western side of the rim was the ancient village of Orango, with fifty-three restored stone houses constructed in neat rows on terraces, each house built partly below ground in the shape of upturned canoe.

Lying four kilometres off the coast were the small islands of Nui, Iti and Kao Kao. These islands are significant because of their role in the islands 'Birdman Cult'. Traditionally an annual ceremony would be held at Orango, including fertility dances, reciting prayers, making offerings and even human sacrifice. The climax of the ceremony was the competition to become the tribal birdman, by being the first to find the egg of the sooty tern bird, which bred on these small offshore islands. Each contestant would descend a four hundred metre cliff face and swim out to the islands. He who found the first egg would be crowned 'Birdman' for the ensuing year, providing great status in the community, and no doubt the pick of the hottest chick in the tribe!

The next day three new guests arrived; Isabella from South Africa and Russ and Emma from England. After breakfast Bobby went surfing and I walked into town to check out the cost of hiring a car to explore the rest of the island. On my return I sat on the rocks watching Bobby riding the waves, or should I say trying to. I had assumed that as he was travelling the world surfing, that he was an expert, but he appeared to be having difficulty even standing up on his board, let alone surfing. Eventually he gave up and paddled back to the beach.

Later, Emma, Russ, Bobby and I walked the short two kilometre distance around the coast to Tahai where three restored temples and a plinth with five moai stand. We sat on the hillside and watched the sun set behind the idols; a spectacular sight as the sky turned pink, orange and finally red. We walked back into town and ate dinner together. After dinner we walked back through the town towards our accommodation, stopping of at the towns only supermarket to buy a few bottles of beers, which we drank whilst sitting on the rocks looking out over the ocean.

The next morning Bobby and I set off to explore the rest of the island in our rented jeep. We stopped briefly to see Huri A Urenga, a solitary moai with four hands, before continuing along a tarmac road travelling inland until we reached a rough, bumpy and dusty dirt track leading to the highest point of the island, Terevaka Volcano at 510m. We stopped again at another site, Ahu Akivi with seven giant moai statues facing the sea (all others face inland).

The track then began to climb up the volcano, becoming

gradually worse with large ruts and potholes, steep climbs and slippery mud, which made grip difficult. Close to the summit we reached a dauntingly steep section of track. Bobby stopped the jeep at the base, reversed about twenty metres to give us a good run up, and floored the accelerator. Unfortunately it was enough and half way up the slope we became stuck in a deep rut. Bobby tried to reverse a little to enable us to proceed forward, but we simply slid backwards out of control on the slippery clay-type surface until by accident, thankfully we became lodged in another rut.

With a sheer drop on one side of the track and large boulders on the other, we were both worried and scared, and as there were no other vehicles anywhere to be seen, we could not afford to wait for help. It was obvious that we could not get up the hill, so I took the wheel and attempted to nudge us slowly back down the slope by keeping the right wheels wedged in the rut, whilst Booby stood behind the jeep directing me. The jeep had very little grip and on a couple of occasions we slid out of control. Eventually though, and to much relief, I managed to steer us safely back down to good ground.

We parked the jeep at the side of the road and continued up the volcano on foot. From the summit we could view the entire island, and its true nature became evident, with volcanic cones of various shapes and sizes dotted all over. There wasn't another person in sight, cloud drifted around us, wild horses grazed on the hillside, and it was completely silent. We sat on the grassy hilltop for about half an hour taking in the views before returning to the jeep and continuing our exploration.

We then drove to the opposite (north) side of the island and parked at Anakena, the islands best beach, guarded by seven moai, and a separate plinth with a single Moai, in front of which a herd of wild horses rolled in the sand and grazed in the dunes. The beach was good and relatively deserted and the turquoise sea, sheltered by the headland, was calm. We both swam for a while before retreating to the shade of the palm trees to eat our pre-packed lunch of bread, cheese and crisps, after which we lazed on the beach for a while.

By mid-afternoon we were back in the jeep driving onwards along the barren north coast, before turning inland and driving toward the south coast under the shadow of Poike Volcano. The first site we reached on the South coast was Ahu Tongariki, the largest shrine on the island with fifteen moai. Unfortunately there were several tour busses already there, so we drove onwards to Rano Raraku, a volcanic cone, which was used as a quarry from which most of the stone Moai were carved.

The quarry still contains around four-hundred moai at various stages of the carving process, many standing upright, some lying on the ground and some still in the rock face. We spent a couple of hours exploring the quarry and marvelling at these expressionless stone giants. It is amazing to think that the islanders devoted their entire lives to creating these huge statues, and in such vast quantities that they logged almost every tree on the island to transport them. One can only assume that the moai still at the quarry had been abandoned because there was no way left to transport them once the trees had been exhausted.

Afterwards we returned to Ahu Tongariki, now completely deserted of other tourists. It was spectacular, fifteen moai standing in a line like soldiers on parade, each one different in height, shape and features. Around 6pm we finally headed back, driving along the south coast, arriving at our accommodation at around 7pm. By 8pm we were showered and changed and we were walking into town for dinner. When we arrived Emma, Russ and Isobella were all there and we joined them for dinner. Afterwards we all returned to our accommodation with some red wine, which we drank on the terrace.

We woke early at 6am the next morning in order to return to Ahu Tongariki for sunrise, and make the most of our twenty-four hour hire jeep. Isabella joined us for a lift to the quarry, promising to buy us a both a beer later. We photographed the statues in front of the red sky as the sun rose, alone except for a few grazing horses. We then returned to the quarry for one last look and to collect Isabella, after which we returned the jeep and headed back to bed for a couple of hours.

Peugot Cars were on the island for the South American launch of their latest model, and earlier in the day we had noticed marquees being erected and lighting and sound equipment being set up. That evening the five set off to try and gatecrash their party.

Just as we arrived at the site, the skies darkened, the wind picked up, the rain began to pour, and an upside down cone shaped black cloud appeared on the horizon, moving menacingly toward us.

We ran for cover in the only shelter nearby, a public toilet, watching from the door as the wind grew stronger and the rain became torrential. The marquees looked as though they were about to blow away and the chef and waiting staff were frantically trying to hold then down. Suddenly there was a small explosion and a bright flash as the lighting and sound equipment blew up, causing the roadies to run for cover and join us, as did several of the catering staff. Then, almost as quickly as the storm had arrived, it had gone.

We hung around for a while, hoping to be offered some food and booze, but to no avail, and so we walked back to town for dinner in our favourite restaurant. Back at the accommodation later, we sat on the terrace chatting and drinking wine. Isabella was a little tipsy and her tongue ran away with her a little. She told us how she constantly managed to blag freebies; crying at bus terminals to get a free ride, getting into concerts free by pretending to have lost her ticket, or pretending to have been robbed so as to get someone to buy her meals and drinks. None of us particularly liked her and this did nothing to help.

Over breakfast the next day, Russ, Emma, Bobby and I discussed Isabella's confessions. Emma was furious, as earlier the previous evening Isabella had given her a sob story and asked if she could pay for her dinner, which Emma duly did. Isabella then appeared and joined us at the table, apparently oblivious to the upset and ill feeling she had caused. She like me was flying back to Santiago this day, and she smiled at me and said "Could you help me Lee, I've run out of money and as were both leaving today, I wandered if I could share your airport taxi?"

"Of course you can Isabella, we'll split the fare" I replied.

"But I haven't got any money left, I hoped you'd allow me to share".

"How much money have you got exactly?" She opened her purse revealing about 200-Pesos.

"I suppose that will have to do," I said. I knew that she probably had more hidden away somewhere, but I accepted this.

Bobby and I never did get the beer we were promised!

Rapa Nui is one of the most amazing places in the world, however it is not really on the backpacker circuit because it is so remote and therefore so expensive to get to, with return flights from Santiago starting from £500. Luckily for me I was able to fly here at no extra charge on my 'around the world' ticket, and I felt so lucky to have been able to see this amazing place.

On my return to Santiago I purchased a bus ticket to the resort town La Serena for the following day and returned to La Casa Roja Hostel for a further night. Back at the hostel, most of the people that I had met previously appeared to have moved on, but I soon got chatting to my new dorm mates, Jamie from Cork and sisters Kim and Amanda from Melbourne. It was Jamie's last night of travelling and so we decided to hit the town together. We found a lively bar full of locals sitting and chatting, in which British eighties music was strangely being played. We stayed until around 2am and fortunately on this occasion, we had no trouble with the locals.

I checked out the next day and took the metro train to the bus terminal, which was very busy with dozens of buses coming and going every few minutes, and hundreds of people wandering in and out.

My bus was very luxurious; the huge seats were like armchairs that reclined to an almost horizontal position, legroom was aplenty, there were several TV's with individual speaker sockets in each armrest, a toilet, and we were even served a hot meal of beef and mashed potato. It was more like an aeroplane and I was very impressed, especially as my ticket only cost £6.

The 500km journey North to La Serena was pleasant, following the mighty snow capped peaks of the Andes to the east and the Pacific Ocean to the west. We arrived in La Serena around 6:30pm; I was pleased to see a lady waiting for the bus holding a card for Marias Casa, a guesthouse recommended to me by a several people. The lady was actually Maria herself, she gave me a photocopied map and pointed me in the direction of her home.

My private room was fairly basic but comfortable, with twin beds, wooden floor and terracotta coloured walls, and there was a pleasent garden and courtyard area outside too. Five other guests were sitting around a table in the courtyard chatting. "Hello, Buenos dias" I said. They smiled back and nodded and then continued their conversation, obviously not wanting to include me in their group.

Another guest, an Israeli guy named Avi was sitting inside the house, so I introduced myself. "Where are you heading?" he asked. "San Pedro, then through the desert and into Bolivia, and then onto Peru".

"You should not go to Bolivia, you should go straight to Peru", he said in a matter of fact way.

"Thanks for the advice, but I quite fancy seeing Bolivia".

"You should get the bus to Arica, and cross the border there into Peru. It's much nicer and the journey is quicker".

"I'm sure it is nice, but I'm a big boy and I can make my own decisions thank you".

I didn't particularly like him, and so I excused myself.

"Where are you going?" he asked.

"Just for a quick look around the town".

"I'll show you around".

"Great" I replied. We walked around the compact town, which was pleasant enough but Avi's 'I know best' attitude was annoying me, so I said that I was tired and we returned to the hostel, where I escaped to the safety of my room. He was worse than my dad!

I was pleased to find that two new guests, Michel and Heidi from Germany had arrived the next day; they were much more pleasant than the others and so I spent a little time in their company. Over the next couple of days I generally relaxed and explored the city a little, Chiles' second oldest. It was pleasant enough, compact and pretty, although there wasn't a great deal to see or do.

I visited the post office and sent a parcel home containing two carved wooden moai figures that I had purchased on Easter Island, and I visited an Internet café and uploaded all my South America photos taken to date. I also spent a little time in the shopping mall, where I was delighted to find that at the local KFC, the meals come with an option of coke or beer, which I thought was a marvellous idea.

On leaving La Serena, I took the overnight bus to San Pedro de Atacama, 1200km to the north. The bus was similar to the previous one that I had caught, I took my seat and hoped that there would be no one next to me so I could spread out, but I was to be disappointed. The widest man that I had seen in Chile boarded the bus and sat next to me, taking up half of my seat as well as his own. As we departed, everyone settled down for a long night. The bus made a few stops over the next couple of hours with several passengers coming and going, including my large neighbour who was replaced by a young woman who didn't speak at all. After the penultimate stop in Copiapo around midnight, half of the passengers got off leaving the rest of us with double seats each on which to spread out. As we drove northwards through the night, I finally managed to get a few hours sleep.

I awoke around 7am the next morning with bright sunlight piercing the gaps in the curtains. I looked out of the window to see that we were driving through a barren and dusty, lunar-like landscape, with the Andes Mountains climbing high on the horizon. For as far as the eye could see there was nothing but desert. By mid-morning we had reached Chile's second city, Antofagasta on the Pacific coast, where we stopped briefly before turning inland on the final leg of our journey to Calama, and finally onto our destination of San Pedro de Atacama. We eventually arrived at 2pm after a gruelling seventeen-hour journey.

San Pedro was an odd little town sitting in the middle of the Atacama Desert, one of the driest places on earth. The town looked as though it should be in the Middle East, containing narrow dirt roads lined with white washed buildings, all with flat roofs, and odd goats and dogs scavenged in the litter. The heat was blistering and the air thin. I immediately felt lazy; the conditions drained every bit of energy.

I checked into a shoe-box size single room at the Eden Hotel, recommended to me by Michel and Heidi. It had a laid-back feel with a central courtyard containing hammocks, benches, chairs and tables. I showered and changed clothes and then set off for a look around the town. There was very little to the town, a main square with trees providing much needed shelter from the sun and several narrow streets radiating off it, with various cafes, bars, souvenir shops and hotels. The town seemed to exist for tourism only. I sat in the main square watching life go by, a group of four young boys played football using two brick walls as goals; we may have been on the other side of the world, but for a brief moment it reminded me of home!

A power cut that evening made getting ready difficult but the staff were on hand with lit candles for the guests; this was obviously a regular occurrence. I got ready by candlelight and headed to an open-air restaurant where I'd arranged to meet up with an American guy named Radcliffe that I'd met on the bus. En-route I almost got soaked when a woman opened her door and threw out a bucket of water, just missing me! Radcliffe was waiting inside the restaurant with his friend Blake. We had dinner and a couple of bottles of wine, before doing a little tour of San Pedros drinking spots. We eventually called it a night around 1am.

The next day I booked a three-day jeep tour across the desert and into Bolivia, leaving tomorrow morning. I spent the rest of the day relaxing in one of Eden's hammocks, under the shelter of a tree. I ate dinner alone in the same restaurant as the previous evening, ordering the menu special of chicken with either chips, rice, salad or eggs, or so I thought. When my meal arrived it actually contained all of the above, and all for just £3. Suffice to say even I couldn't finish my meal. By 9pm I was tucked up in bed in readiness for a big day tomorrow.

By 8am the next morning I was standing in the office of Cordillera Travel, meeting my fellow travellers who would be accompanying me on the three-day tour through the Atacama Desert to Bolivia; Martin from Switzerland, David from Australia, Monty from Canada and Crystal and Andrew from Kansas. We boarded an old and battered mini-bus and set off toward the Bolivian border, about an hour away.

18

Staying Alive
(Bolivia)

16/10/04 to 25/10/04

Within an hour of leaving San Pedro we had reached the Bolivian border post at Portezuelo del Cajon, standing under the towering Volcan Licancabur at 5,930m. We were quite literally in the middle of nowhere, and had it not been for the sign posts welcoming visitors to Bolivia and Chile respectively, and the stone shacks standing beside the dusty track, we would not have known that we were leaving one country and entering another.

We ate breakfast of bread, jam and coffee at the roadside before transferring to a jeep to continue the rest of our journey. We drove into the vast, desolate wilderness of the Atacama Desert, a baron landscape of rolling hills of multi-coloured sand; yellow, orange, red, grey and black, speckled with lakes, salt flats, and geysers, and crowned by 6,000-metre high volcanoes. The Atacama is said to be the driest desert in the world; in some parts, no precipitation has ever been recorded.

We passed by Lake Verde, a beautiful aquamarine colour with flamingos bathing in its centre and we then stopped at some thermal geysers and pools with steam bellowing and hissing out of the ground. This would be our only chance to bath for the next couple of days and so we all stripped off and soaked in the hot water for about half an hour.

Continuing on, we climbed higher and higher into the Andes, reaching a mind-blowing altitude of 5,300m, higher than the Alps and the highest I had ever been, yet all around us were towering conical shaped snow-capped peaks. Our driver passed a bag of cocoa leaves (from the same plant that produces cocaine) around the jeep for us to chew; it apparently helps against altitude sickness and the locals swear by it. Just walking a few feet at this altitude left us out of breath and in need of a rest, and we were all becoming increasingly lethargic. Andrew in particular was experiencing difficulty and had begun to slowly turn white.

Around midday we arrived at our overnight accommodation, a simple wooden structure divided into several basic bedrooms. We ate sandwiches for lunch, washed down with coca-tea. Afterwards we drove to the nearby Lake Colorado, red in colour with swirls of brilliant white running through it, an amazing and very weird sight, which looked like it belonged to another world. On its banks were herds of llama grazing, and in the lake a huge flock of flamingo.

We returned to the accommodation around 5pm, where we chilled out for a while, played cards and generally got to know one another a little better over a few cocoa leaves. They didn't give much of a buzz, but they certainly helped me deal with the altitude. Another jeep arrived, and a group emerged from it carrying one of their number, who was delirious with altitude sickness.

As the sun faded, the temperature dropped rapidly and we all put on extra layers to keep warm; the desert temperature often fall to minus 20° at night. With nothing else to do, by 9pm we were all wrapped up in bed.

In the main our group had bonded well. Martin was around 25, very easy going with a good sense of humour, and we immediately hit it off. Andrew and Crystal were in their early 20's, they were pleasant and good company, but unusually for Americans, they were rather quite.

David and Monty were travelling together, having met through an advert on the Internet for travelling companions. They were an odd pair, David was only 19, and this was his first time away from home, however like lost most Aussies he was a real know it all, who really knew nothing. Monty was a 22-year old medical student, Canadian with Asian parents. He was a nice guy, but paranoid about his personal safety. He had neck pouches, bum bags, or as the Americans would say, 'fanny-packs', money belts galore and even his padlocks had padlocks!

The two of them were not getting along too well, mainly due to David's annoying habits; he always had to have the last word, he would continually contradict us all, and he would argue or disagree with each of us over subjects he knew absolutely nothing about. For this reason the rest of us were also having difficulty getting along with him.

We rose at 6am after a cold, uncomfortable and sleepless night. By 8am we were back on the road, continuing through the desert, passing by three salt-water lakes with more flocks of flamingo. We stopped at the third lake for lunch, in the shadow of the active Ollague Volcano with smoke emitting from its summit. We then continued through a landscape of seemingly endless salt flats, perfectly flat and shimmering white, and then we crossed a railway line, running into the horizon without so much as a single bend.

After a long and tiring drive, we reached The Salt Hotel around 5pm, our second overnight accommodation. As its name suggests, the hotel is constructed of blocks of salt; the walls, floors, tables, chairs, and even the bed bases. It was the most bizarre structure yet surprisingly comfortable and perfectly adequate for our simple needs. We played cards for a while and then ate a good dinner of soup followed by chicken, chips, vegetables and rice.

Afterwards the locals put on a traditional music and dance show with typical Andean instruments such as quenas, panpipes and charangos, small banjo-like instruments, the bodies of which are made from armadillo shells. After the show, we all took our first hot shower for a couple of days and by 9pm we were all tucked up in bed.

The final leg of this bizarre journey took us across the 'Salar de Uyuni', the world's largest salt flat, which at 1,200 sq km is around the size of Switzerland; a fact that Martin found hard to comprehend. This is the remnant of a giant prehistoric salt lake and is a perfectly flat, blinding white desert of salt, salt and more salt, stretching for as far as the eye could see. Several teams of workers were shovelling salt into pyramid shaped piles and then loading them onto waiting trucks. Along the horizon in all directions were grey mountains soaring high in to the sky.

We drove across the salar for about one hour until we reached a small island covered in huge cacti, where we stopped briefly for lunch, and by 1pm we had arrived at our final destination, the town of Uyuni. We said our farewells to Martin and our driver, who were both to return to Chile. The remaining five of us purchased tickets for the overnight bus to the capital, La Paz.

After 3-days in the wilderness, we had all been looking forward to reaching Uyuni and what we thought would be some form of civilisation, however the town was very basic with few amenities. I did fortunately manage to locate an international telephone so I was able I phoned home and wish my mom a happy birthday for tomorrow.

With seven hours to pass before our bus departed, we spent the afternoon sitting in the main square watching the locals go about their business, before heading to a local bar where we ate dinner, sank a couple of beers and played cards.

The locals were perhaps the most un-westernised people that I had ever seen. On their heads the women wear bowler hats, which are worn at a jaunty angle and always appear to be too small. The British brought the bowler hat to Bolivia when they were building the railway and somehow it became part of the everyday dress of Andean women. They also wear many layers of petticoats covered by a colourful dress, and over their shoulders they sling a multicoloured striped blanket in which they carry their groceries or their babies, or both!

From the outside our bus looked fairly modern and better than I'd expected, but once we boarded I found that the exterior only masked the reality. Monty, David and I sat on the back seat, and Andrew and Crystal sat one row in front of us. All of our seats were broken, uncomfortable and dirty, but that was to be the least of our worries.

The 300km journey to Oruro turned out to be a real nightmare, and could rival anything that I had experienced previously, including India. We departed at 8pm to a soundtrack of Andean panpipe music blaring out of the radio. We bounced along a bumpy dirt track, the bus windows did not shut and before too long we were choking on a cloud of dust. Meanwhile an elderly lady sitting next to David placed a reed basket under her skirt and proceeded to pee where she sat. We finally arrived in Oruro at 4am, 8 hours after departure, all feeling very dirty and very tired. It was by no means the longest journey of my trip but it certainly felt like it!

Within half an hour we had boarded a second bus bound for La Paz. Fortunately this was cleaner and much more comfortable than the previous, however I was sat next to a young mother and her baby, and I ended up sharing my seat with the infant. Despite this the journey was relatively good and the roads were better, so I was able to catch a couple of hours sleep.

At 4,000m La Paz is the highest city in the world and occupies a spectacular location in the base of a bowl-shaped canyon, and over the centuries it has grown and spread up the canyon walls. We arrived in the capital at 7am and headed to a city centre hotel, which we had picked out from one of our guidebooks. David and Monty shared one room, Andrew and Crystal another, and I a third.

I immediately headed out to explore my new surroundings and get my bearings. La Paz was very different to Santiago, with narrow, steep, cobbled streets, busy with locals going about their daily business. Hawkers and vendors lined the streets selling handy-crafts, food, electrical goods, books, clothing and just about anything and everything imaginable. The locals wear colourful ponchos and bowler hats, and chew cocoa leafs; this was exactly as I had imagined South America would be and I immediately like it very much!

After my brief spell in the desert I was in desperate need of a shave and so I popped into one of the many barbershops, emerging about half an hour later with a cleanly shaven face and head. The barber told me that there was a world cup qualification football game taking place today between Bolivia and neighbours Peru. Back at the hotel later I informed the others of the game, and although not really into football, they decided to accompany me.

We headed into the centre of the city, passing the imposing Church de San Francisco, built in 1549 and standing in an open plaza with lots of street vendors again active. We ate lunch in a restaurant overlooking the main square, before catching a taxi to the national stadium.

We walked the final couple of hundred metres to the stadium hoping to purchase tickets on the black market. We had no difficulty finding sellers and we purchased five tickets for just £3 each. There was a good atmosphere outside the stadium, a real family occasion. Inside was much the same too. We took our seats behind the goal and had a fun afternoon watching Bolivia defeat their neighbour Peru 1-0, sparking mass hysteria and much flag waving, chanting and horn-hooting in the street afterwards.

On the evening I went out to dinner with David and Monty whilst Andrew and Crystal went to the cinema, at least that's what they told us. Andrew later told me that he did not want to spend any more time with David. Monty, David and I walked around for ages looking for a restaurant that we could all agree on; David was a fussy eater and Monty was on a very tight budget. By the time we eventually found a restaurant that was to everyone's liking, we were completely soaked from the first rainfall that I had seen since Easter Island.

Over the next couple of days I continued to explore the city. One morning we saw a young girl dressed in carnival type clothing, and so we followed her hoping that she would lead us to see a local fiesta. She walked down a side street and disappeared through a door. We followed through the door into a courtyard. We were each charged 2-Pesos (15p) to enter the courtyard, inside of which were amassed hundreds of people packed around the perimeter, watching groups of children, performing traditional dance routines. I assumed that the spectators were mostly the families of those performing; we were the only foreigners.

The children were aged from around five up to about sixteen. Each group represented a different school in the area and were all dressed in elaborate, colourful and very detailed costumes; some of the more intricate included men on bulls and Spanish soldiers. At the end of each routine another group would appear wearing different costumes, and they would perform a different dance routine. We stayed for a couple of hours and I really enjoyed watching the children perform, they obviously took great pride in their tradition.

Afterwards we walked to an area of the city known as Mecardo Negro (black market), which was basically a huge market stretching for about eight blocks and selling everything from socks to TV's. We then came upon Plaza de Murillo, the city's main square containing various monuments and flanked by imposing buildings including the Cathedral, the National Congress and the bullet riddled Presidential Palace, a reminder of Bolivia's turbulent and unstable past.

Close to our hotel was the 'witches market', which sold such items as magic potions, herbs, llama foetuses, dead stuffed animals and cocoa leaves. I purchased a couple of Inca statues and then walked to the main post office to send them home.

I had seen a couple of travel agents offices advertising trips to the Amazon jungle, which interested me greatly. I mentioned this to Monty and David and they too were keen, so we visited a travel agent and after a little negotiating, we booked a five-day trip. But before leaving for the jungle, we still had to complete a cycle ride down 'the world's most dangerous road', so called because it claims the lives of over one hundred people each year.

This was to be one of the most frightening and traumatic experience of my life. My first mistake had been to allow Monty and David to book the trip; they were both on a tight budget and so they had visited all of the tour agents in La Paz, eventually booking the cheapest deal they could find. Not a good idea when your mountain-biking down the road of death!

Around 8am a mini-bus arrived to pick us up from the travel agents office. Inside were three guides and three other passengers, two German girls and a French guy. We drove out of La Paz, rising up the side of the canyon in which the city sits. The views looking down into the city were stunning.

Eventually we reached a car park from where we were to start of our downhill journey. We were each given over-trousers, a jacket, gloves and a helmet, and of course our bikes. Before commencing, we tried out the Chinese made mountain-bikes on the car park. None of us were particularly comfortable with the bikes, adjustments were made to suit individual requirements, and around 10am we set off on a seventy kilometre downhill ride, which would take us from an altitude of 4,700-meters in the Andes, to 1,200-meters in the tropical lowlands.

One guide rode at the front and another at the rear, whilst the mini-bus followed behind carrying spare parts and tools. The first section of the road was comfortable and easy-going, the sealed road was in reasonably good condition and wide enough for two vehicles to pass easily, and it was all downhill. Initially it was exhilarating, as we whizzed down the snaking road, overtaking slower moving cars, buses and trucks, and the scenery all around was stunning.

We then reached an eight kilometre stretch of uphill road and I discovered that I couldn't get my low gears, making uphill biking almost impossible. To make matters worse my chain came off and I had to push my bike up the final uphill stretch. As we descended we made a couple of rest stops, to take on water and food, and to take photos, and around noon we made a lunch stop on a stretch of road on which a waterfall cascaded down from a height of about one hundred metres, under which we took a brief natural shower to cool off.

The second half of the journey was much different; the road changed from tarmac to dirt, making grip much more difficult and throwing up blinding dust clouds each time vehicles passed by. There were tight hair-pin bends every few minutes, and the road got steeper and narrower, so much so that at times there wasn't room on the road for a bike and a truck to pass; I would jump off and make myself as flush as possible with the mountain wall. But worst of all was the fact that we were riding downhill on the side of a steep drop, plunging hundreds, if not thousands of metres into the valley below. The exhilaration had been replaced by utter fear!

We were all having problems with our bikes, mainly chains coming off and gears not working, and so we were forced to make several stops for on the spot repairs. It was just a matter of time before the first accident occurred; Monty, who did not look at all comfortable on a bike, lost control on the gravel and came skidding off. I was riding just behind him and with nowhere to go, I was forced to swerve to miss him, bringing me crashing off too; luckily there were no cars or trucks behind us. We each escaped with a few cuts and bruises; although Monty made such a fuss that you would have thought his leg was falling off. I remounted and continued, leaving Monty behind applying band-aids to his knees. Other than David, we all continued to have problems with our bikes; my chain came off a total of four times, which did nothing for my confidence.

We then reached a hairpin bend on which a truck had broken down, leaving no room for vehicles to pass in either direction. There were several vehicles backed up in both directions and our mini-bus had to join the queue of traffic, whilst we squeezed passed and continued on. Not long afterwards my gear mechanism literally fell off my bike, causing me to loose balance and come clattering off again. With our mini-bus stuck in the traffic-jam, it was impossible to repair my bike and so one of the guides switched with me; he would continue on my gear-less bike.

The brakes on my new bike were very stiff and it took all my strength to squeeze them on full. For the remaining hour of the journey, I stayed towards the rear of the pack going as slowly as I could. Finally at 3pm we reached a small town outside Coroico, which signalled the end of our journey. We were all relieved and delighted to have made it in one piece. For my efforts I had cut both knees and had numerous bruises to my right arm and thigh, and my braking hand was black and blue; however I just happy to be still alive after the most frightening and traumatic experience of my life.

Whilst we waited for our mini-bus, we sat in a restaurant and had a meal and a few beers to celebrate surviving 'the road of death'. The mini bus arrived around an hour later and we were soon on our way back up the mountain to La Paz. Our driver appeared to be in rather a hurry, hurtling around blind bends and driving precariously close to the edge of the road. As we climbed higher up the mountain, we were soon driving through cloud making visibility very poor, and if that wasn't bad enough, nightfall began to fall and before long it was pitch black. This was just as scary as biking down! The tension was lifted briefly when the Bee Gees song 'Staying Alive' came blaring out of the radio. We finally arrived in La Paz around 7pm, by which time I had a throbbing headache, probably caused by the quick rise in altitude. I showered and went straight to bed.

I woke headache free the next morning. Monty, David and I checked out of the hotel and caught a taxi to the military airport, from where we took a one-hour long flight to Rurrenabaque in the

Amazon basin on a small, propeller driven, military aeroplane. The flight was uncomfortable as we bounced around the sky, causing the girl sitting opposite me to be violently sick. However the amazing scenery made it worthwhile, for me at least. Flying over the Andes rapidly gives way to jungle-covered mountains and a huge blanket of green stretching endlessly to the horizon, the canopy broken only by the vein-like muddy brown network of rivers snaking through it.

We then sighted a small clearing in the forest; the sheer novelty of landing on a grass airstrip surrounded by exciting looking jungle gives you that wonderful Indiana Jones feeling, as though an adventure is just about to begin. After landing we taxied up to the terminal building, which consisted of one room for both arrivals and departures. Our bags were thrown off the plane onto the back of a pick up truck, which was driven to the airport gates for us to collect.

It was quite an adjustment dropping from the chilly temperatures of La Paz to the Amazon Basin's intense humidity and forty-degree heat, and was not helped by the strange sensation of being coated in a self-perpetuating layer of sticky sweat, which in turn is constantly covered in a fine layer of dust.

A representative from the travel agent was waiting at the gate to collect and transport us to their office in town to await our boat, which was to transport us into the jungle, forty kilometres down the Rio Beni, a tributary of the mighty Amazon.

The staff had no idea what time our boat would arrive and so we had a frustratingly long wait. I took a little walk around the lively town; its narrow dusty streets lined with palm-roofed huts and raised wooden walkways. Considering its size, around 5,000 inhabitants, it was a hive of activity; numerous travellers wandered the streets, locals were busy buying or selling goods from the roadside, and shirtless children merrily played in the dust, chased by the packs of loyal dogs. It reminded me very much of South East Asia.

The surroundings were a reminder that this is jungle territory where many things are forced to take a back seat to nature; mountains loom in the background just waiting to be photographed, and at the end of the main street the Rio Beni drifts swiftly by carrying a constant supply of driftwood.

If you are looking for a jungle experience, Rurrenabaque is a good place to start. The town's tourism is rooted firmly in the tours it offers to the surrounding jungle and the nearby grassy wetlands area known as the pampas, both of which are encompassed within the Madidi National Park.

Stretching from the Andes to the Amazonian Basin, and covering almost 19,000 square kilometres, the park has an unsurpassable level of biodiversity. The Park is scored by multiple rivers and is thought to shelter eleven percent of all the bird species in the world, totalling some 1,200 species. The park also supports numerous insect, reptile, primate and mammal species such as the spectacled bear, the tapir and the jaguar, and is home to a human population of around 1,700.

After a wait of around four-hours, our motorised canoe finally arrived. We loaded our baggage and supplies, and then awkwardly clambered aboard to sit in single file. We finally set off up stream at about 6pm, with our driver at the rear and our guide Antonio at the front. The Beni is a fast flowing muddy brown river about two-hundred metres wide, banked by endless jungle potentially crammed with deadly snakes, spiders and jaguars. Occasionally we would swerve to avoid trees floating downstream like twigs, but as we laid back to watch the jungle and river pass by and birds circle above the canopy with the engine softly putting in the background, all was well.

As we continued night began to draw in and before long the darkness had wrapped around us. Within an hour of setting off it was pitch black, and we found ourselves riding down the river with Antonio pointing a torch into the dark to light our way.

Suddenly there was a crashing sound, the boat came to a sudden halt and we were all thrown from our seats; we had run aground. The driver ordered us into the river to push the canoe free. We all jumped in, all that is except for Monty who was worried that his cut knees would become infected. As we moved the boat free, I suddenly stepped from knee-deep water to chest-deep; I clung desperately to the canoe and with help from my friends, I wrenched myself back in to safety.

Sitting in total silence through fear, we continued up the river;

the only noise was the hum of the engine and the strange and weird sounds of the jungle that had earlier sounded intriguing, but now sounded threatening and dangerous. Above the jungle canopy, lightning flashes provided a free light show in the far distance, but we were in no mood to enjoy the spectacle.

Over the next couple of hours we ran aground another half a dozen times, and each time we were ordered into the river to push the boat free. I was soaked through and for a second day running I was worried for my life. I began to wander what might happen if we were to sink; even if I were able to swim past the alligators and piranha to the bank, what would be waiting there?

The longest four-hours of my life ended when we eventually reached our camp around 10pm. Our cook Candy had dinner waiting for us and by 11pm I was in the bunkhouse, crashed out on my bed under a mosquito net. For the second time in two days I was relieved to be still alive, and although not religious, I wandered if someone upstairs was looking out for me!

I awoke at first light, the jungle was alive with sound but this morning it felt much different to last night. I headed out for a first look of the campsite, which consisted of six permanent tents, wooden framed with canvas covers, including a kitchen and dining tents, and four sleeping tents, each of which contained ten simple wooden beds with mosquito nets.

Over the course of the next two days, Antonio led us on numerous treks through the jungle. Our first step into this strange world was filled with excitement, anticipation and hope. But the moment that we left the sanctuary of camp and stepped into the damp, dark and dense world, the sound of the river was lost below the deafening hum of the insects and we became instantly lost and absent of all sense of direction. All around was a wall of trees of all sizes, competing vertically for sunlight; parasitic mosses and fungi clung to the trees whilst vines hung from their branches and wrapped around their trunks as if trying to choke the life from them.

As we followed the machete-cleared path, ducking, twisting and occasionally tripping as we went, I became aware that the ground was alive. Millions of ants, termites and other weird and wonderful insects busily scurrying across the layer of rotting leaves, branches and fruit, which litter the forest floor.

We would trudge for hours on end through the jungle with not so much as a glimpse of anything bigger than a moth. Our spirits would occasionally be lifted by the sightings of footprints, or the sound of a monkey or toucan high in the treetops, but throughout our stay we saw little wildlife except for a few birds.

I was a little disappointed at not seeing any animals, but the jungle itself was still a fascinating place, and Antonio did his best to make our stay pleasurable and informative. During our various treks he would point out various interesting plants and their uses, such as the bush that produces a glue-like substance, and the tree with hollow branches containing cool fresh drinking water. He also pointed out various poisonous plants to avoid, and conversely medicinal ones used by the native Indians, such as the tree which when cut, oozed a reddish sticky substance, used as a local anaesthetic by temporarily numbing the body part when rubbed on it, and a leaf from another plant which tasted like mint.

Whilst on one of our treks, Monty screamed out after brushing against a huge caterpillar, claiming that he had been stung and had lost all feeling in his leg. I knew it wasn't serious when I saw Antonio laughing, but Monty was convinced that he was about to die. To calm and reassure him, Antonio killed the caterpillar with his knife and squeezed out its innards with the flat of the blade. He then rubbed the smelly, gooey substance onto Monty's leg, "This will kill the poison and stop the pain" Antonio said, with a wry smile on his face. Miraculously, within a couple of minutes Monty had regained all feeling in his leg and we were able to continue. I too got stung, on the neck by a small, colourful spider, but unlike my hypochondriac friend, I suffered no adverse reactions.

I was less fortunate though on another occasion when we reached a wide stream, above which a rope had been hung from the trees to form a swing with a loop tied in the end to act as a foot hold. Monty and David successfully made it across, but come my turn my foot got stuck in the loop and so I swung hopelessly back and forth a couple of times, before eventually coming to a stop in the middle of the stream. Suffice to say that I got very wet and muddy, much to the delight of the others.

Whilst trekking on our second day, Antonio collected various items from the forest, and back at camp later he showed us how the

Indians use them to make jewellery. There was the nut that when opened revealed a hard black spherical seed, which when polished took on the appearance of a shiny black pearl. He also showed us how to make a ring from a nut case, by cutting a cross section out of the nut and then hollowing out its centre and buffing up the exterior until it came up in a shiny mahogany effect. We all had a go and made our own necklace and ring. It was like being back in primary school!

With no electricity, there was little to do in the evenings other than eat, talk and read, and so most evenings we were tucked up beneath our mosquito nets by 9pm. On our second night Antonio took us on a torchlight trek. Again there was a lot of noise but very little to see. Our adrenaline levels shot up when we heard scuffled noise and a scream in the darkness, but it turned out to be just a small hairy wild pig. I'm not sure who got the biggest fright, the pig or us?

After an interesting couple of days, we returned to Rurrenabaque in the canoe; a far more pleasurable journey than our previous experience. Our travel agent Vivien had arranged overnight accommodation in a hotel, the three of us sharing one room. Whilst chatting to Vivien, just being polite and friendly, I mentioned that we would be in the Mosquito Bar around 8pm if she wanted to join us. She took this comment as an offer of a date, much to the amusement of the others. We duly spent the evening in the Mosquito Bar drinking cocktails, but Vivien never did show up.

The next morning the three of us returned to the travel agents office, from where we were due to catch a jeep to the Pampas region for a few days. The Pampas is an area of grasslands, marsh and swamp fed by several rivers, and is home to a wide variety of plant, bird, fish and insect life, and so I was looking forward to finally seeing some wildlife.

Once inside the office, Vivien told me off for standing her up last night. "But I was in the Mosquito Bar all night" I pleaded.

"You did not come to the office to pick me up" she replied. I apologised and explained that I had misunderstood, and to make up for my mistake, I would take her out when I got back from the Pampas. This placated her, but once again Monty and David found this highly amusing.

At 10am we boarded a jeep along with three other adventurers, Belgium couple Kristof and Kim, and Robin from Germany. We drove for around two-hours along a bumpy, dusty dirt track to the town of Santa Rosa, on the banks of the Yacuma River. We had lunch in a small restaurant, which gave us the opportunity to get to know one another. Kristof and Kim were a nice couple but generally kept themselves to themselves. Robin was initially quite shy, but before long he came out of his shell and was great company and good fun.

After a wait of about an hour our guide arrived to collect us in a motorised canoe. We loaded our things aboard and set off. Within a few minutes we had seen more wildlife than during our entire time in the jungle. The abundance of animals is so great that our initial enthusiastic squeals of "caiman!" "turtle!" "capybara!" soon subside into near nonchalance about the number of creatures we were cruising past.

Hundreds of alligators and caiman basked in the sun on the banks, occasionally scuttling into the river. Whole families of capybara, the world's largest rodent, which looks like a cross between a pig and a beaver, wallow in the shadows. Dozens of turtles sit in rows on fallen tree trunks. Literally hundreds of species of birds, including long-legged, stork-like birds squawk from nests high in the treetops, and various types of monkey scamper through the trees.

We stopped by a large tree and our guide Sabino cut up a banana and threw the pieces onto the riverbank. Within a few minutes hoards of small, yellow coloured Capuchin monkeys emerged from the tree and massed on the bank, excited at the prospect of a free meal. Some even ran along the side of our boat trying to steal fruit from our supplies.

We arrived at our camp around 6pm. It was similar to our jungle camp, but slightly better and cleaner, being built of timber on stilts above the ground. Again we had a barracks-style dorm with basic beds and mosquito nets, albeit with a few holes. We dropped our bags on our bunks and returned to the canoe to head to another camp further down river for dinner. Four other travellers, Swiss friends Ursula and Karen, Swede Magnus and American Kelly, were already tucking into their dinner when we arrived. It was their final night in the pampas and they told us of some of the delights that awaited us over the next couple of days.

After dinner we returned to the canoe for a night safari, a slightly unnerving journey with pairs of yellow eyes appearing and disappearing, and indiscriminate squawks and splashes, whilst the volume on the wildlife around us appeared to have been turned up by several decibels. Sabino caught a baby alligator by hand, brought it on board and told us a little about the regions leading predator, before releasing it back into the river.

Sabino woke us at 5am the next day, we climbed into the canoe and headed down the river, stopping at a clearing with a path which led into the Pampas, from where we watched the sunrise. We then set off in search of Anacondas, walking through head-high grass and marshland. There was a lot of waiting around in the blazing sun while Sabino poked and prodded the swamp for lurking snakes. Eventually with the aid of a forked stick, he managed to snare a three-metre anaconda. We all posed for photos with it wrapped around our necks, before releasing it back into the undergrowth; but not before it had shit all over Monty.

We returned to camp for lunch, an afternoon siesta and a shower. The camp had no electricity and no running water, however there was a hand pump, which extracted water from forty-metres below ground. We each pumped the water into a bucket and poured it over our heads to cool down and get cleaned up. Afterwards we crashed out in hammocks slung between the trees.

Around 3pm Sabino got us out of our hammocks and back into the canoe. We headed off down the river in search of the fabled Amazonian pink dolphin. In wasn't long before we found them swimming in a wide stretch of river. We all dived in and swam after them, but the dolphins kept their distance, and in the murky, brown water, we were only able to see them when they surfaced.

Suddenly I felt a nip on my leg, then another and another. "Piranha!" I screamed. We all swam back to the canoe in a state of panic, and clambered aboard to safety. I inspected my legs expecting to find chunks missing, but there wasn't so much as a scratch to be seen. Sabino could not control his laughter; it transpired that sardines and not piranha had actually bitten us.

This particular stretch of river was a favourable spot for them, hence the presence of the dolphins, which feed on them.

We continued down the river and stopped beneath some overhanging trees for a spot of piranha fishing. Sabino cut up some meat to use as bait, and we were each given a line with a hook tied on the end. The method was simple, throw the line into the river, wait for a bite and then yank quickly. Between us we caught about a dozen red-bellied piranha, their little jaws snapping, rows of teeth as sharp as razor blades.

On our way back to the camp, Sabino spotted a large young stork-like bird looking helpless on the riverbank. He told us it was a baby that had probably fallen from its nest, and that it would die if left alone. He took a couple of the fish that we had caught and fed them to the bird on the end of a pointed broken off branch. He then caught the bird and carried it back to the canoe. Although young, it stood about one-metre high and had a large pointed beak, which looked as though it could do a lot of damage. We returned to camp with the bird, which Sabino locked in a storeroom for the night. Our cook then prepared our piranha dinner, which was surprisingly good, although not that filling.

We were all awoken around 6am by loud roars and screams from the jungle. We immediately got up and Sabino led us off in search of the culprit, the howler monkey, watching them in the treetops from a safe distance. We returned to camp for breakfast and then set off again in the canoe for more wildlife viewing, during which we saw an alligator being eaten alive by piranha, ferociously snapping at an open wound on its tail. Sabino said that the alligator had probably been injured in a fight with another alligator, and that the wound was probably preventing it from being able to swim.

We returned to camp around noon to eat lunch and then pack our belongings. We travelled back down the river, stopping once more to swim near the dolphins. By 3pm we were back in Santa Rosa, where a jeep was waiting to drive us back to Rurrenabaque. Once again we spent the night in the Mosquito Bar, and like the gentleman that I am, I kept my promise and treated Vivien to a night-out.

The following morning I was awoken around 11am by the

sound of torrential rain, gusting wind and crashing noises. My curtains were fluttering like mad and rain was pouring in. I peered out of my window to see a tropical storm causing havoc; rain was bouncing off the road and running like a river down the main street, whilst trees were bending almost horizontal in the wind. My room was located at the front of the building on the top (third) floor, facing the storm and within minutes there was a centimetre of water on the floor. Fortunately the hotel staff came to my rescue and moved me to another, more sheltered room at the rear of the building.

I spent the morning lying in bed counting my mosquito bites, which I had managed to collect on just about every part of my body, and I really do mean every part. By midday the rain and wind had died down enough to venture out.

The rest of the group were all due to depart this morning, Robin was heading to the jungle, whilst the other four were booked on the 9am flight back to La Paz. I had decided to spend another day in Rurrenabaque as I had grown tired of David and couldn't bear to spend any more time around him.

I walked into a restaurant to find Monty, David, Kristof and Kim all sitting around a table, their flight had been cancelled due to the weather and they weren't sure when they would be leaving. I just hoped that the weather would improve sufficiently for them to leave later, for my sake as well as theirs.

Walking down the main street, I ran into an eccentric, slightly crazed, and bearded American selling a selection of homemade cakes from his motorised three-wheel bicycle. Each purchase was delivered with a leaflet warning of the coming of the beast, which he claimed was the European Union. Demented maybe, but he did make exceedingly good cakes.

The weather was not better the next day and although I was booked on the 6pm flight to La Paz, I didn't know whether or not the flight would be cancelled. I popped into a restaurant for lunch and bumped into Ursula, Karen, Magnus and Kelly, who I'd met briefly in the Pampas; they too were hoping to be on the 6pm flight. We spent the day together playing cards to pass the time.

Eventually our flight was confirmed and we were driven to the airstrip. After about a twenty-minute wait a small plane appeared overhead and landed in front of us. In total twelve people boarded the Cessna, and although there was no air hostess, food or complimentary drinks, the pilot did kindly offer us oxygen masks for the trip back to higher, thinner-aired climes.

By 7:15pm we had landed at La Paz. There was a general strike in the city and so no buses were running. Realising the opportunity, the taxi drivers doubled their fares, and with no other choice, I took an expensive taxi-ride to my hotel, which took around an hour as the streets were grid locked. Protest marches and demonstrations are a very regular occurrence in Bolivia, and during my short time in La Paz I witnessed several; fortunately all peaceful.

Ursula, Karen, Magnus and Kelly were staying in the same hotel and the next evening we met up together with Robin, who had just returned from the jungle. We played cards for a while and were joined by two English girls and later by four Aussie guys. Before long we were in the mother of all drinking games; between us we polished off four bottles of rum in two-hours.

Feeling in somewhat of a party mood, we then headed out to sample the nightlife of La Paz. On the recommendation of a taxi driver, we found ourselves in Mongos Bar, a club frequented by both locals and gringos. The heavy drinking continued, and at midnight we toasted Magnus's 22nd birthday. Kelly was a young, tall and good looking American guy, the type that girls always go for, and tonight was no exception. Ursula, Karen and the two English girls were all competing, quite aggressively, for is attention. As soon as one moved from his side, another leapt in. It was funny to watch, if a little frustrating for the rest of us.

Robin and I got chatting to two gorgeous Bolivian girls, Claudia and Maria. At first I thought they were working girls, as they were dressed in short, black, revealing dresses, unlike the other local girls in the bar, however they claimed to be travel agents. We spent the night dancing and chatting with them, before leaving together around 4am.

The next evening Robin and I met up with the girls again. They took us to a restaurant called Dumbos, located on the main street, Prado, a long straight road lined with the best shops and restaurants in La Paz, and an disproportionate number of ice-cream parlours.

Each time I had been to Prado, the pavements had been full of courting couples and whole families, mom, dad and kids, all strolling hand in hand, eating ice cream, laughing and generally enjoying a saunter. After dinner the girls took us to their favourite nightclub called Ram-Jams, where we again partied the night away, until the early hours.

I had thoroughly enjoyed my time in La Paz and I didn't particularly want to leave, but my schedule was tight and so the next day I reluctantly caught a bus to Copacabana, on the banks of the fabled Lake Titicaca. The bus took around an hour to get out of the city, but once in the countryside the scenery was wonderful, and before too long the blue shimmering lake was in sight.

We drove along the shore of the vast lake for at least an hour until we reached the small port of San Pablo de Tiquina. The driver ordered everyone off, and as much as I could understand, I gathered that this was a lunch stop. I went to buy some food and when I returned five minutes later the bus was floating across the lake on a ferry. Luckily for me, a small passenger boat was preparing to depart. I boarded and a couple of minutes later we set off for the opposite bank. Fortunately we arrived a couple of minutes ahead of the bus and I was able to re-board.

We arrived in Copacabana around 3pm and I checked into the Hotel Ambassador, which according to my guidebook was a quiet establishment; perfect for my purposes as I was growing travel weary and needed a few days of peace and quiet to rest my old bones.

At an elevation of 3,820metres, Lake Titicaca is the world's highest navigable lake, and at 230km long and 97km wide, it is South America's largest. It straddles the Bolivia-Peru border, with snow capped Andes peaks reflected in its brilliant blue waters. To the ancient Incas it was sacred, according to legend the sun was born here, and their first Inca emperor rose from the lakes Isla de Sol. The lake is dotted with storybook isles and whole villages that float on reed beds.

I dropped off my bags and set off to explore the town, which may share the same name with the famous Brazilian beach resort, but it was clearly obvious that Barry Manilow had not been talking about this particular Copacabana. It had none of the glitz and glamour of Rio, but instead offered small town charm. Copacabana is landlocked Bolivia's main beach resort, its two kilometre long narrow beach is festooned with hawker stands and cafes, and a plethora of rental pleasure boats.

The Moorish cathedral, built between 1605 and 1820 on the site of an Inca temple, dominated the centre of the small quaint town. Outside of it stood a small, badly made, miracle-performing statue of the Virgin of Copacabana. In 1583 a native sculptor created an image of the Virgin for the local cathedral. From day one the statue performed miracles as if they were going out of fashion. She has broken droughts, cured illnesses, saved drowning fishermen and her fame has spread throughout the Americas (Rio's famous beach is named after her). Here, the Virgin Mary is not only the mother of Christ, but also the Admiral of the Bolivian navy, and following her coronation in 1925, the Queen of the Bolivian Republic.

These days the Virgin also conducts car blessings, a truly weird ceremony that takes place every Saturday morning; my timing couldn't have been better. Dozens of cars, buses and trucks were lined up, all washed and dried, then sprinkled with confetti and adorned with strings of fresh flowers and brightly coloured ribbons. I watched as a brown-robed monk emerged from the cathedral with a bucket of holy water in one hand and what looked like a white stick in the other. One by one he blessed each vehicle by dipping his stick into the bucket and sprinkling the radiator three times, but not before he had inspected the engine, checked out the interior and spun the steering wheel; the more casual observer could have mistaken him for a papal RAC inspector. With such a godly blessing, it is no wander that Bolivians do not take out motor insurance!

I spent the night alone in a pleasant bar, returning to my room around 10pm for an early night. However my hope of a few days rest and relaxation were shattered; the hotel was full of kids running through the corridors and screaming, my TV didn't work and my bed mattress sank in the middle.

I was rudely awoken around 7am the next morning by screaming kids. I showered and shaved, ate breakfast, checked out, and went in search of a quieter establishment, which I found in the Hotel Paris. My large room with a huge, comfy bed, a nice bathroom and lake views cost just £2 per night.

I spent the morning looking around the town and checking out tour operators for trips to the Isla de Sol and busses to Puno on the Peruvian side of the lake. After which I spent a lazy day sitting by the lake reading and writing up my journal.

After an early night of wonderful undisturbed sleep, I rose early at 7am ready for a trip to Isla de Sol, the birthplace of the Inca Empire. I walked to the lake and by chance bumped into Kelly, who was also planning a visit to the mystical island. We boarded a boat along with about thirty other tourists and set off around 8am, arriving at Cha'llapampa in the north of the island after a pleasant two-hour journey.

We were led ashore by our Spanish speaking guide who took us first to a very poor museum, before leading us along a coastal path to some Inca ruins including a stone sacrificial table, a labyrinth of Inca walls and the 'Rock Of The Puma', which supposedly looks like a puma, although none of us could quite see it.

We then had the option of either walking approximately ten kilometre to the south of the island, or taking the boat to another island, Isla de la Luna. We chose to walk and were joined by an English girl named Kate and two English guys named Jim and Alan. The walk, along an original Inca path took us up and over several hills, the highest around 4,000m. The sun was blazing down and there was no shade, and at this altitude it was quite a strenuous walk, taking us the best part of four hours.

Isla de Sol was reminiscent of a Greek island, quite baron and ringed with agricultural terraces, although I didn't really see anything growing. We passed a few locals including a couple of kids with llamas, all available to pose for tourist's photographs, for a small fee of course. I bribed one little girl with a bar of chocolate to pose for me.

We re-boarded the boat in the south of the island and by 6pm we were back in Copacabana. At 7:30 we all met up again for dinner in Mankha Uta Restaurant. I ordered the four course set menu of salad, tomato soup, trout in garlic sauce with vegetables and potatoes, followed by banana in chocolate sauce, a bargain at just £1. After dinner we went to Nemos Bar where we sank several beers whilst playing cards. Kate was quite drunk and was keen to continue the night in a karaoke bar. We were the only customers in the bar, but it didn't stop us partying away until we were eventually thrown out at closing time around 2am. I returned to my hotel to find that I was locked out and I had to ring the bell a few times before someone eventually let me in.

The next day I boarded a swish double-decker luxury coach to transport me to my next destination, Peru. I was pleased to see a couple of familiar faces on board, Tim and Claire from Bristol who I kept running into.

I had had a wonderful time in Bolivia and I was sad to be leaving. Bolivia has it all, towering mountains, lush forest, unparalleled natural beauty and a vibrant culture, and it is South America's most indigenous country, with over half the population claiming pure Amerindian blood. However, it is one of the poorest countries in the world, and both politically and socially, trouble bubbles constantly beneath the surface, mainly due to an impotent economy, poverty and unemployment. Yet at no time here did I see any trouble or ever feel threatened. In fact quite the opposite, the people were most friendly and welcoming. As is often the case, those with so little are often the ones who give so much! Without doubt Bolivia is one of the highlights of my adventure.

19

Mysteries of The Inca (Peru)

26/10/04 to 16/11/04

Within half an hour of departing Copacabana the bus arrived at the Peruvian border. We all disembarked and passed through Bolivian immigration, then walked across the border and into the Peruvian equivalent. All formalities were soon completed and we were driving on to Puno, located on the Peruvian side of Lake Titicaca, arriving three-hours later.

Along with my bus ticket I had purchased a boat-tour to the intriguing sounding "Floating Islands of The Uros People". I was led from the bus into the terminal building and put onto a mini bus with about ten other people, including Kelly who had arrived here on another bus. We were then driven to a jetty on the lake from where we boarded a small motorboat.

The Uros people began their floating existence centuries ago in an effort to isolate themselves from their rivals, the Incas and the Collas. The islands are constructed from many layers of floating tortora reeds that grow in the shallow waters of the lake. Each of the islands is home to up to fifteen families. The whole life of the Uros people revolves around the tortora reeds; the buildings on the islands are made from them, as are their boats, and they even eat the lower stalk and root, which is supposed to taste like celery.

Today, about three hundred Uros people still live on the islands, surviving mainly from fishing, and increasingly tourism. The boat arrived at the first of the islands and we leapt ashore, landing on a soft and springy bed-like reed floor (the reeds rot away from the bottom and are replaced at the top). The island contained several reed houses and appeared to have been set aside purely for tourism. They were akin to a floating market, with the Uros selling tacky miniature reed boats and woollen products to the flocks of eager tourists.

We were given an option of travelling by traditional reed boat to the next island, and half a dozen of us took up the option. The strange vessel, about five-metres long, resembled a small Viking ship, its stern and bow being pointed and higher than the deck, and the reeds at the bow had been manipulated to form a animal-like figurehead. Two men standing at the either side of the stern powered the boat, rotating their oars in a rhythmic cycle.

On the second island stood a small schoolhouse, a church and strangely a volleyball court, on which several children were playing. A couple of men were building a boat in one corner, weaving the reeds in and out of one another. I took a photograph of them, for which they demanded payment.

Kelly and I had palled up with two German girls, Katrina and Steffi, and with no accommodation booked, once back in Puno the four of us shared a taxi into town and checked into the same hotel. We went out to dinner together that evening and I had my first taste of Alpaca steak, which was quite rich and lean. Katrina ordered the local delicacy of 'cuy', better known to you and I as guinea pig, thinking it would be served like a small steak. However she got the shock of her life when her plate arrived containing the complete creature, head, limbs and all, eyes staring up, squashed in a star shape as if it had been cooked in a sandwich toaster. She couldn't bring herself to eat the poor little thing, so we all shared our meals with her. And not wanting to let fluffy die in vain, we each sampled a mouthful, which for the record wasn't that great.

Kelly left early the next morning to Cusco, and the German girls were heading to Bolivia, and so I found myself alone. With little to do in Puno, I too decided to move on the next day. A bicycle rickshaw carried me to the bus terminal, from where I caught a bus to Arequipa. The journey was tedious and lengthened by numerous stops during which local hawkers would board, peddling their wares of drinks and snacks, llama coats and jewellery. The drive took us through a barren, desert-like landscape, with towering mountains and volcanoes dominating the horizon.

Six-hours after departure we eventually arrived at Arequipa bus station. I hopped into a taxi and gave the driver the name of my hotel, however he must have been hard of hearing because he took me to a completely different hotel instead; no doubt he was on a commission. I refused to go into his hostel and paid him just 2-Sols, half of the agreed fare.

I trudged off on foot, not really sure where I was, but I had soon walked into the impressive city centre with an abundance of grand colonial buildings, and with the help of a friendly policeman, I located the Hotel Regis and checked in. The hotel was housed in a grand colonial building and my room was located on the second floor, off an external corridor type balcony overlooking the street below. I dropped my bag on the bed and immediately set off to explore before nightfall.

Arequipa was founded in 1540 by Francisco Pizarro's envoy, and in 1541 the King of Spain gave the city the title of Villa Hermosa 'Beautiful City'. It is splendidly located at an altitude of 2,380-metres, and sits in a giant lush valley with high mountains rising up on all sides, and in the shadow of three giant volcanoes, Chachani, at 6,075m is the highest, but it is the perfectly conical Misti at 5,825m that draws the attention, whilst poor little Pichupichu at 5,664m rarely gets a mention.

I traipsed along the quaint, cobblestone streets admiring the colonial architecture of block after stunning block of 16th-century churches, ivory-coloured mansions and other stone buildings, many adorned with intricate carvings and with balconies projecting over the street. The streets, cafes and stores were packed with locals of mixed Spanish and indigenous ancestry, a proud race of mestizos who dress in bold colours.

I reached a road junction and stood staring into a vast, beautiful square, with central gardens and a fountain. I crossed the road into Arequipas main-square called Plaza de Armas, as so many of the main squares in South America seem to be. From a bench by the central fountain, I sat and took in the scene; lush gardens of tropical palms and scarlet geraniums, the huge cathedral spanning an entire block, completed in 1629 with twin bell towers and an ornate stone facade with two volcanoes rising majestically behind. Enclosing the square on three sides stand identical, grand, stone buildings with double storied arches forming open arcade style walkways on two levels, behind which lay shops, bars and restaurants. It had to be one of, if not the most beautiful cities I have ever been to, and is surely one of the best-preserved enclaves of colonial architecture in all of the Americas.

Although Arequipa is Peru's second largest city with a population of around one-million, it has the feel of a small town, with the centre being compact and in spite of the sprawl of new development, and the occasional earthquakes (including a severe one in 2001), Arequipa has managed to retain a distinctly colonial atmosphere. The architecture is easily its most spectacular attraction. The centre is built out of a unique white volcanic rock called sillar, which spewed out of nearby Chachani; hence the city is known as 'the white city'. It was declared a UNESCO world heritage site in 1995 because of its colonial architecture.

I had read and heard little of Arequipa and so by chance I had stumbled on this gem of a city that travellers dream of finding. My main reason to come to Arequipa was to see the magnificent canyons and valleys in the region; this area contains the two deepest canyons in the world at Colca and Cotahuasi, each almost twice the size and depth of the Grand Canyon.

I took dinner in a restaurant on a balcony overlooking the Plaza de Armas, after which I walked around the nearby streets checking out Colca Canyon tour prices, and booked a two-day tour starting tomorrow.

On my way back to the hotel later, I turned into a side street and stumbled on a religious procession; hymns were blasted over loud speakers whilst hundreds, if not thousands of people slowly plodding along the street, most carrying candles, some crying. A banner depicting Christ on the crucifix was carried aloft. The surrounding pavements were packed with onlookers standing shoulder to shoulder, whilst other spectators observed from the safety of their first floor windows. I stood amongst the watching crowd on the pavement, there was lots of pushing and shoving and jostling for position.

For some reason I felt my pocket and realised that my wallet had gone, obviously taken by a pickpocket in the crush. I had withdrawn 160-Sols from the ATM only an hour earlier, however as the cost of living is so cheap in Peru, 160-sols equates to just £26 so I was quite fortunate. Less fortunate however, my wallet also contained my ATM card, which was my main source of withdrawing cash on the road. I found a policeman and reported the theft; and within minutes the tourist police were on the scene to take the details, not that there was much they could do. I then visited an Internet café and cancelled my ATM card online. That done I returned to the hotel around 11pm and went straight to bed.

Around 9am the next morning a mini-bus arrived to pick me up for my two-day tour of the Colca Canyon. On the bus were an English couple, a German couple, four French guys, two Brits named Matt and Andy, and Andrew and Crystal who I'd last seen in La Paz. Over introductions, our driver passed around the customary bag of cocoa leaves. Some of the group foolishly rejected the offer, but Andrew, Crystal and I each took a handful; I immediately popped a couple straight into my mouth, rolled them around into a gooey ball, and wedged them against my gum with my tongue. The rest I slipped into my pocket for later.

It was a long, bumpy five-hour ride to the canyon but fortunately we had a number of stops along the way to break up the journey. Our first stop was the Vicuna Sanctuary, where we were lucky enough to come across a small herd of vicunas fairly close to the highway. They are the smallest of the camelidae family and look like tiny llamas. Throughout the trip we were to spot many more.

We drove into the inhospitable but stunning altiplano desert landscape, bare except for scattered gnarls of cactus, soft green eucalyptus trees or yellow desert flowers. Herds of graceful llamas, alpacas and vicunas grazed below a backdrop of snow-capped mountains, a primeval lunar landscapes of shattered volcanic rock; this area is often referred to as the 'Valley of the Volcanoes'. We stopped at a lookout to view El Misti and again at Mirador El Andes (Andes lookout), 4,910m above sea-level, from where six peaks all around 6,000m high, spread out around us. Just to put things into perspective, the highest point in Europe is Mount Blanc in the Alps at 4,800m.

Even here, in the middle of nowhere, the souvenir sellers were out in full force. An army of women huddled behind a wall of alpaca wool pullovers, socks and hats, waiting hopefully to catch the eye of a potential buyer, and woe betide the tourist who makes eye contact, for they will be badgered relentlessly until they part with a few Sol. Each group was distinguishable from the other by their dress. While Colca men wore nondescript trousers and shirts, the women's clothing was infinitely more elaborate. Richly coloured embroidery adorned their hats and blouses, worn over voluminous skirts.

After the pass we continued the long decent into the valley to the market town of Chivay. The vast majority of the valley was desolate and sparse, but the bottom of the valley, watered by the Colca River, sprang life with beautiful green terraces. Chivay was a showcase of ancient Andean history, with a few Inca ruins and a Spanish colonial chapel built in the mid-1600s. The adobe homes of locals were interspersed with more recent structures made of chalk-white sillar. The townsfolk were dressed in brightly coloured scarves and white hats covered with flowers. According to tradition, the style of hat and placement of flowers indicate the status of the women; widows wore one colour, spinsters another, single women one flower, married two.

We ate lunch in a little restaurant before being shown to our rooms, where we crashed out for an hour or two. We all met up again at 4:30 for a visit to the natural hot springs, a wonderful complex containing hot spring-water pools and chambers fed by the bubbling, boiling brooks which emerge from the mountainsides all around. There was an indoor pool and a larger outdoor pool, both with a water temperature of around thirty-eight degrees. Sitting in the outside pool was wonderful; the contrast between the cold air blowing around your ears and the hot water is fantastic, especially sitting a metre or so from the inlet where the water comes into the pool at around fifty degrees. And the views looking down the deep valley with towering mountains on either side weren't bad either.

Around 7pm we headed to a nearby restaurant for dinner and to watch a traditional music and dance show, along with a cosmopolitan assortment of tourists. A peña all-male band belted out an upbeat set of Andean folk songs, whilst four women dressed in extravagant costumes did their best to coax members of the audience up to dance. Afterwards, me, Andrew and the three English guys headed into the main square where we found an Irish pub to pass a couple of hours. I got the impression that the Peruvian owner had purchased the 'Irish Bar starter kit' containing a map of the emerald isle, several old Guinness posters, a few beer mats, a wooden shamrock and a tin of green paint!

We were woken at 5am the next morning. A light breakfast of bread, jam and cocoa-tea had been set out for us. Three-hours later we arrived at the Colca Canyon, which is over 100km long and 3,400 meters deep. Formed by seismic activity and earthquakes along a fault in the Earth's crust, it measures twice as far from its valley floor to its rim as the Grand Canyon and ranks only behind the neighbouring Cotahuasi Canyon as the world's deepest.

We walked for a little while around the edge of the canyon, its huge cliffs dropping down to the Colca River snaking through its base. Looking over the edge was the largest drop I had ever seen in my life. But what was most impressive was the sweep of colours: the sky was clear and blue, the distant mountains were deep brown covered with pure white snow and the canyon walls were laced with the green patchwork terracing, a legacy of Inca days. Portions of the canyon are still habited, the stepped terraced fields still support agriculture and human life; archaeological records indicate some human habitation in the canyon as far back as 5,000BC.

Around 8:30 we reached Cruz del Conda, a popular tourist stop to view the Andean condors, the worlds biggest bird of flight. These magnificent birds have a wing span of three metres and stand over one metre tall. We stopped at the edge of a cliff, where a large crowd of camera-toting tourists and backpackers from across the globe, including Tim and Claire who I kept running into, was gathered on a rocky outcrop overlooking the canyon rim.

Just as we arrived, a condor made a brief appearance from behind the rocks and then almost immediately disappeared again far below us. Every few minutes a cry would go out and the waiting crowds would jump to their feet, cameras at the ready, but each sighting was a false alarm. We waited for an hour without seeing another Condor. Then, just as we had all but given up hope, a gasp from the crowds signalled the long-awaited arrival. The majestic bird appeared directly in front of us, gracefully soaring on thermal up-draughts rising from the valley floor, zigzagging effortlessly across the canyon. Within a minute or two it had disappeared out of sight, but our brief glimpse of this wonderful creature had been well worth the wait.

No sooner had the Condor disappeared than the herds of tourists all returned en-mass to their buses, to begin their return journeys to Chivay and Arequipa respectively. On our return we visited the Toro Muerto Inca cemetery, where the Inca were buried in a foetal position, built in a ninety-degree steep cliff face. Seeing it, you wonder how the burial party managed.

We returned to Chivay where we stopped for lunch before continuing on touring through the valley, making a final stop at a small village. A local man stood in the dusty main square inviting tourists to have their photo taken with his large pet eagle, for a small fee of course. I paid my 1-Sol (16p) and got a couple of snaps with the giant bird perched on my head. Soon afterward we started the long bumpy drive back to Arequipa.

I spent the next day relaxing and enjoying the delights of Arequipa, hanging around in the Plaza de Armas. I also had a date to keep with the mysterious and beautiful ice-maiden named Juanita. Clutching her alpaca shawl and surrounded by offerings, including silver and gold figurines, she was found by explorers during an expedition up the side of nearby Mount Ampato in 1995. The young girl was apparently sacrificed in an Inca ritual, and now takes pride of place in a glass refrigerator in the museum. Preserved for 500-years by the subfreezing temperatures on the mountainside, the child-mummy was in remarkably good shape, wrapped in a blanket and wearing a bright red headdress. Remarkably, as you look at her tiny face, she appears to smile back.

That evening the streets were full of families out for a stroll. It was Halloween and the Peruvians had taken on the American tradition of trick or treat, with most of the kids dressed up for the occasion. Unfortunately however, not all had fully grasped the concept, and whilst there were a few scary looking Dracula's, ghouls and ghosts, I also saw a Snow White, a Spiderman, a cow, a chicken, numerous cowboys and even a Mini-Mouse. Nevertheless, the kids seemed to be having a great time and I was happy to throw a few Sol into their collection buckets.

The next day I returned to the police station to collect the crime report needed for my insurance claim. The Peruvian system is not as straightforward as it could be; before releasing the report I was told that I needed to pay 3-Sols to the National Bank, who would in-turn provide me with a receipt, which I was then to give to the police in return for my crime report.

Unfortunately the bank was closed, as it was All Saints Day, a national holiday. I returned to the police station and explained that I had not been able to get the receipt because the bank was closed and that I was due to leave the city later today. The officer said that he would need to send a fax to Lima to get permission to release the report and that I would have to pay 10-Sols for the cost of the fax. I handed over the cash and the officer disappeared into a room, returning less than a minute later with my report, which he duly handed over. He certainly hadn't had time to fax the report and so I assumed that my 10-Sols had gone towards the police Christmas party fund.

I was due to depart for Cusco, the sacred city of the Incas, and I was quite excited at the prospect of seeing the undisputed archaeological capital of the Americas, and also meeting up there with my friend Paul, who was flying in from the UK to meet me. Whilst the adventurous traveller would have taken the fifteen-hour overnight bus across the Andes and along a winding, part paved road, I was growing increasingly travel weary and so opted for the much easier half-hour flight. The flight was very pleasent with views over the Andes and Colca Canyon, and the approach to Cusco down the lush sacred valley, surrounded by towering mountains was stunning.

Founded in 1100AD, Cusco is one of the oldest cities in the America's and is steeped in history, tradition and legend. It was the spiritual, political and economical centre of the Inca Empire and sits at an altitude of 3,300m in a valley under the shadow of the Andes mountains.

At its height, the Inca Empire stretched from Colombia in the north down through Ecuador, Peru and Bolivia to central Chile in the south. Although the empire existed from the 12th century, it remained small until the mid-15th century. Over the next one hundred years it expanded massively only to come crashing down through civil war and its conquest by the Spanish.

In 1533 a band of one hundred and twenty Spaniard conquistadors had conquered Cusco with little difficulty, aided considerably by the internal strife and civil war that had ravaged the Inca Empire for the preceding eight years. One side in the civil war had believed that the white men from the coast had come merely to help their cause; they realised that the Spaniards had less honourable intentions only when it was too late!

Accommodation in Cusco was plentiful but expensive, in comparison to elsewhere that is. I trudged from hostel to hostel until I found the Hostel Rojas, a basic but acceptable establishment close to the Plaza de Armas, and at 15-Sol (£2:50) per night, it was most reasonable.

I immediately went for a walk around the city and was instantly impressed. It is beautiful to the eye, a low-rise city (there were no buildings other than the cathedral and church above two stories high) with an abundance of classical stone buildings, red tiled roofs, Inca walls, churches and citadels, and from just about anywhere in the city the views of snow-capped Andean peaks add to its grandeur.

The Plaza de Armas was very agreeable, with central gardens, benches galore and an unusual fountain. Like Arequipa, there were open arched buildings with hotels, shops, cafes and bars enclosing two sides of the plaza, whilst on the other two sides were the city's imposing Baroque cathedral, built in 1559 by the Spanish on the site of an Inca palace, and an equally substantial and ornate church, which looks every bit as impressive as the cathedral.

Cobblestone streets radiate out from the Plaza in all directions, just aching to be discovered. I wandered up one of the streets and by chance bumped into Paul who had flown into Cusco that day. The airline had lost his case and so he had been out underwear shopping, not easy in a country of small people when you weigh over 100kg!

We had lunch and a beer together and agreed to meet later for dinner. I spent the rest of the afternoon trudging up and down the maze of steep streets and alleys, containing hundreds of souvenir shops and rustic restaurants that could take days to investigate on their own. I met Paul for dinner later, followed by a late night drinking session at Paddy O'Something's Irish Bar.

I spent the next morning continuing my exploration of Cusco. Massive Inca stonewalls line the city's central streets and form the foundations of both colonial and modern buildings. The Inca walls are amazing, constructed of huge stone blocks, mostly square or rectangular, which fit so precisely together, and the joints are that tight that no mortar is required. They taper as they rise, being thicker at their base, and slope at an angle of around 18-degrees, apparently making them earthquake proof.

Around 2pm I met up with Paul and we returned to the Irish pub for a huge lunch; he was still without underwear! Afterwards we walked around the city, ending up in the Plaza de Armas, where we were hounded by friendly kids selling chocolate, postcards and woollen finger puppets, or offering to shine our shoes. I made the mistake of buying from one to get rid of them, but that simply compounded the problem and so we were forced to make a hasty retreat.

We walked down Hathrumiyoq, where a 12-sided stone sits in the middle of an ancient Inca wall, which is today part of the foundation for the Archbishops house. Throughout the day I bumped into a number of familiar faces, a girl from my hostel in Santiago, Mike from my Spanish class, and Katrina and Steffi from Puno.

Cusco has a real back-packer scene and a party atmosphere and craves and succeeds in attracting the tourist dollar. It came as a little bit of a surprise to find so many gringos in one place, but it's easy to see why they come. Cusco has all the Peruvian charms that postcard maker's like; its architecture is unique, its people are bona fide and it is within touching distance of one of the world's greatest ruins, Machu Picchu. The problem with modern Cusco, I soon discovered, is that the locals seem to delight and positively thrive in making money from the hordes of gullible gringos that flock here. Everybody wants you to visit their restaurant or bar and will almost frogmarch you in if you show the slightest bit of interest.

Around 5pm I returned to my hostel for an afternoon siesta. I met Paul at 8pm in a bar called Las Perros (The Dogs), which was very laid back, with large comfy sofas and playing a mix of western and local music. We had dinner and a couple of beers, and then went on for a few more in Rosie O'Gradys Irish Bar, where I ran into Katrina and Steffi again.

We then went in search of a more lively establishment, and were almost knocked over by the throng of touts handing out free drinks vouchers to lure you into their bar. We soon realised that it was possible to drink for free in these bars, simply by crossing the square from one bar to the other and collecting free vouchers as we went. We did this until the early hours, when our powers of speech and our ability to stand eventually failed us.

After a rare lie I met Paul at noon for lunch, after which we walked to the plaza to join a group of other worldly tourists for a city tour, which we had booked yesterday. We were put on a mini-bus, which drove around the Plaza stopping every fifty metres or so to pick up other passengers from the various other travel agents offices. Eventually, after about half an hour, the bus was full and we drove around the remainder of the Plaza and stopped at the cathedral, close to where we had started. Why we had simply not been told to all meet outside the cathedral was a mystery!

Our guide led us into the cathedral and began his tour, speaking in both English and Spanish. Paul and I soon got bored with the tour and so we sneaked off to look on our own. The building was magnificent, in the plan shape of a cross, the two arms of which were actually individual chapels. There were several small rooms inside containing hundreds of original paintings, including an unusual depiction of The Last Supper showing Jesus and his disciples dining on roast guinea pig!

After a quick look around the Korikancha Museum, built around the Inca ruins, the tour then left the city and we drove up a steep winding road to the impressive Inca fortress temple called Sacsayhuman, pronounced sexy woman, which the guide found hilarious and so annoyingly kept repeating. Sacsayhuman is a huge hill top Inca ruin with unusual zigzag walls containing huge stone blocks. The fort saw one of the bloodiest battles between the Incas and the Spanish.

After their conquest, the Spaniards tore down many of the

walls and used the stones to build their homes and principal buildings, including the cathedral. After the guide had finished his spiel, we were left with only ten minutes to look around ourselves and to take photos. I wasn't best pleased, especially considering we had spent about an hour in the cathedral, which we could have visited on our own as it is in the city centre. The rain was pouring and the wind howling, which made sightseeing very unpleasurable.

We continued to Qenko, a ceremonial rock and cave with carvings and an altar used for human sacrifice. The next stop was the Tamba Machay, a ceremonial bath with intricate water channels. The guide told us that this water, when splashed on the face gave eternal youth. I think just about everyone on the tour splashed water on their faces, except that is for sceptical old me. I found it hard to believe, given that most Peruvians look over 100 years old!

Paul and I met up with Jackie and Ann for dinner, two English sisters who we had met on the tour, after which we spent the night drinking pisco sour in Las Perros Bar. Pisco sour is a cocktail containing pisco, a regional brandy made of Muscat grapes, lemon, liquid cane sugar and raw egg white. It is a silky-textured drink with a sharp, pungent taste like you've never experienced before, somewhat of an acquired taste, but after a couple they flow down very nicely indeed. Both Chile and Peru claim pisco sour as their national drink.

The next day Paul and I joined another escorted bus tour of the sacred valley of the Incas. Also on board were Matt and Andy who I had met on the Colca Canyon tour. Our first stop was at the town of Pisac, a quaint little town famous for its traditional market that takes up its entire Plaza, where I purchased a couple of gifts.

The bus then drove up a winding mountain road to a car park overlooking the valley below, patch-worked by patterned fields and rimmed by vast terracing. We were led along an original Inca path to a mountain citadel and ruins. On the summit sat the well-preserved walls of the citadel and in the upper sector of the ruins, one of the Incas' most impressive examples of masonry, the main Sun Temple. The temple was an astronomical observatory; one particular stone instrument resembling a sundial actually helped the Incas to determine the arrival of important growing seasons.

Another section housed a ritual-bathing complex, fed by an intricate system of water channels and canals cut out of solid rock.

The Pisac ruins are some of the finest and largest in the entire valley and despite the excellent condition of many of the structures, little is conclusively known about the site's actual purpose. It appears to have been part city, part military complex and part religious temple and ceremonial centre. From a semi-circular terrace and fortified section at the top, the views south and west of the gorge and valley below and agricultural terraces creeping up the mountain slopes are stunning.

We returned to the bus and followed the Vilcanota River through the fertile plains of the Sacred Valley, with mountains ringed with stepped terraces and small villages. Our next stop was at the town of Urubamba where we were served a buffet lunch. After lunch we drove further into the valley to Ollantaytambo, an attractive little town located at the western end of the Sacred Valley. The town has been built on top of original Inca foundations and is the best surviving example of Inca town planning. The town is divided in blocks, which are almost entirely intact. Each block has only one entrance, usually a huge stone doorway, which leads into a central courtyard.

The town is located at the foot of the massive and spectacular Inca fortress ruins and another mountain ceremonial site, with massive stone terracing and steps leading up to it. I escaped the guided tour and climbed the steps to the temple area at the top, leaving Paul behind; he wasn't in the best of shape and didn't fancy the steep climb. Paths at the summit led around the mountain to other defensive ruins. The fortress protected the strategic entrance to the lower Urubamba Valley and from the summit it looked a formidable site. The complex was still under construction at the time of the conquest and was never completed.

After the Inca was defeated at Sacsayhuaman, they retreated to Ollantaytambo, pursued by a Spanish force of seventy cavalry, thirty foot soldiers and a large contingent of natives. From their stronghold, the Inca forces rained down showers of arrows, spears and rocks upon the Spanish, who were forced to make a hasty retreat, and Ollantaytambo became the only place ever to have resisted Spanish attack. However, their victory was short-lived when the Spanish returned with four times their previous force. The Inca retreated to their jungle stronghold in Vilcabamba and Ollantaytambo fell into the hands of the Spanish.

I returned to the bus and said farewell to Paul; he was leaving the tour to stay overnight here before catching the morning train to Machu Picchu. The rest of us continued back towards Cusco making a stop at the small Andean Indian village of Chinchero, located high up on the windswept plains with uninterrupted views across the Sacred Valley, with the Cordillera Vilcabamba and the snow-capped peak of Salkantay dominating the western horizon.

In the main plaza an adobe colonial church, dating from the early seventeenth century, stood upon the foundations of an Inca temple. Under its shadow, hoards of local women had set out their woollen handicrafts in the main plaza to sell to the daily busloads of tourists that stop here.

Over the next couple of days I generally relaxed and saved my energy ahead of my forthcoming trek of the Inca Trail, spending my days shopping for gifts, sitting in the Plaza reading or in one of the numerous bars watching movies. Each afternoon the heavens would open up for a couple of hours; it did not bode well for my forthcoming trek. I bumped into a few familiar faces, Jackie and Ann, Bobby, who I had last seen on Easter Island, and Tim and Claire, who I'd met everywhere since La Paz; the gringo trail was a small place in deed.

Walking through the back streets one morning I came across a Peruvian girl sitting on stone steps in an alley. "Hola" I said with a smile as I passed by.

She smiled back. "Where are you going?" she asked.

"No where special, just walking around".

"Come sit with me". I sat next to her on the steps and we chatted for a while. She was name Elizabeth, she spoke very good English and was very pretty, more Spanish than Indian, with beautiful big brown eyes and a lovely smile. She wore a low-cut sweater, which revealed tantalising glimpses of her buxom cleavage each time she leaned forward. It was nice to sit and chat with her for a while but I didn't expect anything to come of this casual meeting, and so I said goodbye and stood up to leave.

"Where do you go now?" she asked.

"Back to my hotel"

"May I come with you?"

I hadn't expected that and it threw me a little off-guard. I wasn't sure if Elizabeth was a working girl or just very friendly, but either way, I thought what the hell. "Um, yeah, sure, why not" I replied. Back at my hotel, one thing led to another and the inevitable happened. We lay in bed together for ten-minutes or so afterwards, and then realising I had a date to keep with Paul, I got up and dressed.

"Elizabeth, I have to go out, you must go now", I said.

"I want to stay here", she mumbled.

"You can't, you must go now".

"Then I come with you".

"No Elizabeth, please get up, you must go". Elizabeth slowly rose and dressed, continuing to ask me if she could come with me, which I refused. Finally she was fully dressed and I opened the door for her. I expected her to ask for money as she left, but she simply looked at me with her big sad eyes, leaving me feeling a little guilty. I never did see her again and to this day, I still do not know whether she was a working girl or whether she just found me irresistible!

I duly met up with Paul, who had returned from Machu Picchu and we spent one last day together; I was due to commence the Inca Trail trek tomorrow whilst he too was moving, with vague plans to travel into Brazil or Venezuela by riverboat. Paul was not only my friend but also my ex-boss, and part of his coming to meet me was to discuss my future employment, and the possibility of me rejoining his firm. This must have been the most unusual job interview ever.

Travelling alone is great, but travelling with a close friend is fantastic. You can promise to tell one another when you are getting on each others nerves, support one another on bad days, share fabulous experiences with someone from home, and you can have someone to reminisce with on your return; all your other friends soon tire of your endless yarns.

At 5:45 the next morning a bus arrived to collect and transport me, and the rest of the group of fifteen, to the start of the Inca Trail. Having learnt my lesson in Nepal, I took with me my day pack containing just essentials; a towel, a couple of tee-shirts, one change of trousers, one fleece top, a jacket, three sets of socks and pants, toiletries, some food, my mp3 player and my camera.

Our two guides, Marcello and Frank introduced themselves and then ran through the details of the four-day, forty-five kilometre trek, before handing out bags of cocoa-leaves. They then introduced us to our nineteen porters and cook, all local farmers who supplement their meagre income by carrying tourists bags along the trail. We stopped at Urubamba for breakfast, before continuing on past Ollantaytambo to km-82 checkpoint, where our trek was to begin.

At the checkpoint we each had to show our passport and sign in before being issued with a permit. Regulations designed to limit the impact of visitors on the Inca Trail and at Machu Picchu eventually took effect in 2001; everyone must now walk the trail with a licensed agent, you must camp in the designated sites, and perhaps more significantly, the number of visitors allowed on the trail has been reduced from 800 to 500 per day, including porters and guides.

At 10:30 we crossed a rickety suspension bridge and began the trek. Day one was the easiest day, twelve kilometres of gentle walking. Our porters, who were each carrying about 25kg in sacks slung over their shoulders, immediately ran ahead of us, as if it were a race, whilst we followed behind at a more leisurely pace, enjoying the scenery and generally getting to know one another.

Our group consisted of a mixed bag of nationalities and ages. Alan and Karen and Ben and Andrea were both English couples and had come to Peru specifically to do the Inca Trail, as had Phil and Helen, an Aussie couple in their fifty's, and John and Bonnie, an American couple of similar age, and American father and son, Dennis and Paul. Like me, for Nick and Jo, a thirty-something English couple now living in Australia, and Aussie sisters Allison and Rachel, the Inca Trail was another adventure on their backpacking trips.

As were plodded purposefully along, we made regular stops for photos, snacks and just to rest. We passed by the ruins of an Inca hill-fort (Huillca Raccay) perched on the sheer slopes above the mouth of the Cusichaca River. We took a lunch break and were all amazed to find that the porters had set up kitchen and dining tents for us, and had even placed bowls of water, soap and towels for us to wash our hands. We sat around the dining table on foldout chairs and were served an excellent four-course lunch. This really was five star service and not at all what I'd expected.

After lunch we continued on the trail with great views of the Urubamba mountain range and the snow-capped peak of Veronica at 6,860m. We saw our second Inca ruins, the extensive sight of Llactapta, and then followed a river to the small village of Wayllabamba, which was to be our camp for the night.

Arriving at 4pm, we were again astounded to find that the porters had already erected all of our tents and had also prepared hot drinks for us. We spent the early evening playing cards and drinking cocoa-tea, followed by a four-course dinner. By 8:30 everyone was feeling tired and bloated by the huge meal, and so we all retired to our tents. I had a two-man tent to myself, which was pretty roomy, whilst the others, who were all in pairs or couples, had three-man tents. As the rain began to patter against the canvas, I soon fell into a deep sleep.

We were sharing the trail with around a dozen other groups, each containing around fifteen or so trekkers, of all ages, sizes and colours and from every corner of the world. Several trekkers were having difficulty with the altitude and many were simply unfit, but there was a great camaraderie between everyone on the trail. Amazingly, I even met two English guys on a stag do. Throughout, everyone chatted, encouraged and helped each other, and although I didn't know anyone's name, we had all almost become friends, with the exception of four rude French people that is.

We were woken at 5am; I opened my eyes to see a hand extended into my tent grasping a mug of hot tea. Once dressed, I stumbled to the dining tent to find a breakfast feast set out; mixed fruit, pancakes, toast and coffee. By 6:30 we were off, on what was to be the hardest day of the trek, twelve kilometres of almost entirely uphill walking.

We began by following the Llulluchayoe River for about one hour, climbing steadily along a stone Inca path until we reached a small bridge, which took us over the Huayruro River. From here we continued onwards and upwards through steepening woods and increasing spectacular terrain for about three-hours. We stopped for tea at Llulluchayoe at 3,680m. We were all fairly tired and glad of the rest ahead of the most difficult section of the trail, a one and a half hour uphill trek to the appropriately name Dead Women's Pass 'Warmiwanuska', the highest point of our trek at 4,200m.

The sun was shining and everyone was in good spirits as we began to climb. The group had already begun to divide into three groups. At the back were the oldest of our group Phil and Helen, who were finding the going very tough and Ben and Andrew, who although only in their twenty's, were also struggling; they had all the gear but it was obvious that they were not the outdoors type. In the middle group were Dennis and Nick and Jo, who were happy just to take their time, and Alan and Karen who were struggling with the altitude having only recently flown in to Peru. Up front were myself, Paul, Allison and Rachel, and surprisingly John and Bonnie, who although in their 50's were surprisingly fit.

We reached Dead Woman's Pass around 11:30 and as we did so, we were exposed to the full force of the Andean elements. The weather on the other side could not have been more different. From glorious sunshine we stepped into driving wind, torrential rain, hailstones and thunder and lightning. I was soaked through before I could get my waterproofs on. We had all arranged to meet at the pass and continue down the other side together, but in the horrendous conditions I decided to press on alone. The thunder was frighteningly loud as it echoed through the deep valleys and the downhill path, a series of stone stairs, took on the appearance of a mini waterfall.

Through a combination of running, hopping and jumping, I literally bounded down. When I reached the bottom I found a number of small individual campsites being set up for each group. I knew we were due to camp at number twelve site, but I had no idea where it was, and there were no porters waiting to point the way as promised. I wandered around for about fifteen-minutes before I eventually stumbled across our campsite, still in the process of being set up by the porters. They were surprised to see me so early as it was only 12:15. I collapsed into my tent and climbed out of my wet clothes.

I resurfaced an hour later to find that Paul, John and Bonnie had also arrived. The rain had eased off, and we were finally able to take in the beauty of our surroundings. Our campsite was positioned in the bottom of a steep V-shaped valley, rugged snow-capped mountains loomed ahead of us, and as we looked back toward the pass we could see three thundering waterfalls cascading down the mountainside. The rest of the group staggered in over the next couple of hours, Phil and Helen, accompanied by guide Frank arriving last at 3:30; they looked ready to curl up and die.

We hung our wet clothes out to dry anywhere we could, on the tent cords, hanging from the branches of trees or thrown over bushes. A few of us spent the afternoon drinking cocoa-tea and playing cards in the dining tent, and by 8:30pm we were all tucked in our sleeping bags, completely exhausted. Suffice to say, I didn't need any rocking to fall asleep.

We were woken at 6am the next morning, coffee in bed again, and another breakfast feast. My clothes were still soaked and I was reluctant to wear my spare trousers, fearing that if they too got wet then I would have nothing to change into on the night. Instead I wore thermal long johns beneath waterproof over-trousers, much to the amusement of my comrades.

Today was the longest of our trek, covering fifteen kilometres of both up and downhill trekking. We started at 7am, climbing from our campsite for about one hour to the astronomical-related ruins of Runkuracay, overlooking the Pacamayo valley. One hour later we had reached the second pass known as Abra da Runkuracay at 4,000m, and an hour later we arrived at another ruin called Sayacmarca 'Inaccessible Town' by way of a steep stone staircase. These ruins are located on a hilltop and are protected on three sides by sheer cliffs. From here the trail descended into a magnificent cloud forest, full of ferns, mosses, flowers and a few orchids.

Exiting the forest, the trail hugged the mountainside, passing through a damp and rather menacing Inca tunnel carved out of the rock. The trail was almost entirely original Inca with uneven stone paving around one metre wide. It is a remarkable feat of engineering even by modern standards. The immaculately laid, white granite slabs trace the landscape with great ease, leading us often along a precipitous edge above deep valleys, pausing at times to indulge in tremendous views.

We stopped for our usual four-course lunch and a well-deserved break before beginning another climb up the third and final pass at 3,700m, from where several snow-capped peaks came into view. Dropping down from the pass we reached Phuyupatamarca 'Town In The Clouds', the best Inca ruin so far with a series of ritual baths with water still actively running through them.

Leaving the ruin, we descended down a stone staircase of approximately one thousand steps, which was a real strain on the knees. We continued on for about another half an hour until me, John and Bonnie, at the front of the pack, reached another Inca ruin. We were the only people there, which meant that we must have missed a turning somewhere. We could see the campsites in the distance far below, and so we made our way down a series of yet more steep steps in the general direction of the campsite, eventually arriving around 4:30. Although we had taken a wrong route, only Paul, Allison and Rachel had arrived before us.

Our final campsite at Winay Wayna had a bar and toilet block and the only showers on the trail. The girls all we rewarded themselves with a hot shower, whilst the guys all rewarded themselves with a refreshing cold beer, or two. Whilst tucking into our final dinner, another four-course extravaganza, we had a whip-round for our guides, porters and cook, who had all done a magnificent job.

Nick, Paul and I returned to the bar for a few more extortionately priced beers afterwards. The bar was packed with the fellow trekkers that we had been sharing the trail with over the last few days and there was a great atmosphere inside. A Brazilian girl approached and pulled me on to the dance floor to salsa with her, but surprisingly for a Brazilian she couldn't dance, and so after a couple of minutes I flung her in Paul's direction. By the time that we returned to camp, it was silent; everyone else in our group was already tucked up for the night.

We were woken at 4am for our final day. Another huge breakfast awaited us. We were on the trail by five and by six we passed through the checkpoint where our permits were carefully logged in. The last short leg of the trail up a vertical flight of stairs brought us to the final pass at Intipunku, and the 'Sun Gate', one of several entrances to Machu Picchu, the fabled lost city of the Inca. From here we should have witnessed picture-postcard views of Machu Picchu, but unfortunately the entire area was shrouded in thick mist and so we couldn't see more than a few metres ahead. We waited around for half hour for the mist to clear but to no avail, and so we began to slowly descend the steps to Machu Picchu.

Finally the mist began to lift, slowly revealing the whole of Machu Picchu spread out before us. It was a spectacular sight, hundreds of stone buildings sitting on a mountaintop with stone terracing stretching down beneath. Left breathless by the view, we walked silently toward the magnificent ruins.

Marcello and Frank walked us around the site, "I believe Machu Picchu was a temple for pilgrimage' Marcello said, 'or perhaps a summer palace or a place of learning. But the truth is, we just do not know." Hiram Bingham, the American historian who re-discovered the ruins in 1911, imagined it to be a sanctuary for 'virgins of the sun'. And whilst the debate rages on amongst the guides and archaeologists only one thing seem certain, Machu Picchu was and still is a very special location.

"The site was occupied for less than 100 years and we are sure that only a few people came here', Marcello continued, 'It is hard to say, but I believe it was an exclusive place. I think that no more than a few hundred people would have lived here at a time." The very fact that the ignoble Spanish conquistadors never found the site suggests that it may have been a state secret, unknown to the Inca minions. Whatever its origins, the Inca turned the site into a small but extraordinary city. Invisible from below and completely self-contained, surrounded by agricultural terraces sufficient to feed the population, and watered by natural springs.

Approximately two hundred buildings still stand today, minus their original thatched roofs. Carved from granite, these structures are wonders of both architectural and aesthetic genius. Many of the stone building blocks weigh over fifty-tons, and are so precisely sculpted that they fit together perfectly.

One of Machu Picchu's primary functions was that of astronomical observatory. Similar to the one at Pisac, the

Intihuatana stone 'Hitching Post of the Sun' is a column of stone rising from a larger square stone block. It has been shown to be a precise indicator of the date of the two equinoxes and other significant celestial periods. At midday on March 21st and September 21st, the sun stands almost directly above the pillar, creating no shadow at all.

We climbed up the terracing to the watchman's hut positioned high on the slopes. This is the picture post card position that we all know so well, with the entire site spread out below us; an improbably beautiful setting, sitting on a ridge above a precipitous gorge at 2,380 metres surrounded by snow-capped peaks. It is these unique qualities that make this site Peru's number one tourist attraction, receiving eighty-five percent of Peru's half a million annual visitors. It was a magnificent panorama and we all snapped away like crazy.

Around 1pm we left Machu Picchu and caught a bus to the nearby town of Aguas Calientes, where we met up in a restaurant with the rest of our group for our final lunch together. At 4pm we caught the train back to Cusco. The journey was spectacular but painfully slow, leaving me time to sit back and enjoy the scenery of the Sacred Valley, whilst reflecting on the last four-days; it is easy to see why this trek has been canonised by travellers, and I was wishing that I had walked the Inca Trail ten years ago. Who knows, perhaps I will return in ten years hence!

The following day I awoke around 10am to find that my legs were aching and felt like lead. I took my first shower in days, which felt wonderful. I spent the rest of the day relaxing my aching limbs, popping out of the hotel only briefly to deposit some unwanted clothes in to Peru Treks office for their porters. That evening I met up with Nick, Jo, Alan and Karen for dinner and a few beers. We were all shattered and by ten we each headed off to our beds.

The following day I took a taxi to the bus station where I again bumped into Tim and Claire. We were all going to Nazca and so we brought tickets for the same bus and checked our luggage in as you do for a flight. Two busses arrived at the same time, each displaying the destination 'Nazca'. We tried to board the first, only for the driver to point us toward the other bus. We showed our tickets to the second bus driver and he waved us aboard. Just before 5pm the first bus left, and shortly afterwards some other passengers boarded our bus with tickets containing the same seat numbers as ours. We were then told that we were on the wrong bus. Worse still, our bags were on the other bus that had already left. As we departed, I wondered if I would ever see my backpack again.

Around 9pm we arrived at a service station in the middle of nowhere. Sitting across the forecourt was the first bus containing our bags. Tim and I disembarked and approached the other driver and tried to explain the mix-up with our bags. With a mixture of my broken Spanish and sign-language I managed to persuade the driver to let us swap buses and so we were re-united with our backpacks. Content and relieved, I climbed into in my sleeping bag and settled down to watch a violent Japanese film with Spanish subtitles, before turning in for the night.

The bus arrived in Nazca around 6am. We had come to Nazca for one thing and one thing only, to view the mysterious Nazca Lines. We took a taxi into the town on the promise that the driver would provide us with a coffee in his café. The versatile taxi driver, come café owner, come tour guide then showed us details of his 'flight tour', and after a little negotiation, we agreed on a price.

Once at the airport we boarded a six-seater Cessna plane with a Danish couple that I'd met briefly on the Inca trail; they had both been ill with altitude sickness. The plane took off around 8am and flew out across the parched desert towards one of the world's great mysteries, the Nazca Lines; a collection of eight-hundred lines, three-hundred geometric shapes and seventy animal and plant drawings etched into five-hundred square kilometres of arid desert, some time between 1,500 and 2,500 years ago. Some of the more intricate shapes include a ninety metre long monkey, a condor with a one hundred and thirty metre wingspan, a whale, a dog, a spider, a hummingbird, a parrot, a tree, a pair of hands and a waving figure with a large head with looks suspiciously like an astronaut.

So as to give us better views of the figures below, the small plane banked from side to side throughout the half hour flight, so much so that the poor Danish girl was violently sick in to a plastic bag and missed the entire spectacle. I came close to joining her on a couple of occasions, however despite feeling extremely ill, it was a truly fantastic experience.

The Nazca Lines are one of the world's great mysteries; just who created these lines and for what purpose when they can only be seen from the air? There are various theories of course; astronomical calendars, ritual walkways and even UFO landing strips. I guess we will never know the truth, but I'd like to think they were created by an ancient crop-circle prankster!

Our taxi driver dropped us back in town at the bus station, just in time to catch the 9am bus to Ica. On the bus were Ian and Shirley, another couple that I'd met in Cusco. We arrived two hours later, Claire and Tim planned to stay overnight, whilst Ian, Shirley and I were keen to get to Lima today. We took a local bus at 11:30 and duly arrived in Lima around 4pm. We had each decided to stay in different districts of the city and so we said farewell and headed off in separate taxis. I arrived at my chosen hotel, the Espana in the central area, checked in, and collapsed on the bed, exhausted after a long day on the road.

The next day I set off to explore the capital and headed towards the main square, once more called Plaza de Armas. I had received many uncomplimentary reports on Lima from fellow travellers who had described the city as ugly, dirty and dangerous. Certainly on the approach to the city yesterday I could not disagree, but the centre seemed quite pleasant. There were many grand colonial buildings, the streets looked pretty clean and I didn't feel at all threatened, although I did think it a little strange that there was a large police presence on the streets, dressed in riot gear and with a few armoured vehicles in back up.

Nevertheless, I didn't see any trouble and happily wandered around for a while. I strolled down a side street and suddenly chaos broke out and I found myself in the middle of a riot. Protesters brandishing sticks rampaged through the streets, cracking passers by and smashing shop windows. Without hesitation, I turned and ran back toward the main square as shopkeepers hurriedly pulled down their shutters. With seemingly know where to go, I dived under the falling shutter of a pizza parlour, where I sheltered until the police had ruthlessly and efficiently quelled the riot. So all in all it had been a pretty exiting day, and the pizza wasn't bad either!

Within half hour the streets were back to normal and I continued my explorations. Lima, named the 'City of Kings' by the Spanish Conquistadors, was founded in 1535 by Francisco Pizarro, where the River Rimac meets the Pacific Ocean. As the most important Spanish city during the colonial era, it reached a population of about 100,000 inhabitants. Today, it is a bustling city, home to more than six million people. The historic centre is filled with beautiful Spanish colonial buildings and restorations have been carried out in recent years to the beautiful main plazas, ornate facades and wooden balconies. Like most major cities, the centre is full of international shops, as well as local stores, hotels, restaurants, cafes and bars, and despite the riot, I liked it very much.

The following day I returned to the Plaza de Armas to meet Tim and Claire. Once again, the square was ringed off by police, who were only letting tourists or school groups go inside. I entered and sat watching a group of small children, about four-years old, dressed in passing out gowns and mortar-boards, posing for class photos.

The oldest surviving part of the plaza is the impressive bronze fountain, which was erected in 1650. Surrounding the plaza is the exquisite Archbishops Palace, the cathedral where the conquistador Francisco Pizarroís tomb lies, and the Government Palace where uniformed guards stand on duty all day. Beyond its iron gates, a military band began to march and play, and a small crowd of tourists and school children gathered to watch through the railings.

I met up with Tim and Claire and we walked along the pedestrianised main shopping street, stopping in a fast food restaurant for lunch. After lunch, we got up to leave and Claire discovered that her bag had gone from under the table. None of us had even noticed anyone near us. We went to the police station and reported the loss. Claire was not enjoying Lima, only yesterday her camera had been stolen. Maybe people were right about Lima after all!

We all returned to the hotel to checkout, Tim and Claire were due to fly to Ecuador this evening, and I to Argentina. My taxi ride to the airport was a hair-raising experience, the driver was like a man possessed, darting through lanes and cutting up other cars, busses and trucks. I was being thrown all over the back seat and was worried that we wouldn't make it to the airport alive. "Slow down amigo, I want to go to airpuerto not hospital," I said. My driver just nodded, then swerved from the left lane across the road and oncoming traffic to turn right. My relief when we arrived unscathed was immense.

Peru had been everything that I'd hoped for and more, containing some of the world's truly wondrous, magical and mystical sights. In the main the people had been welcoming and friendly, and although I had had the misfortune of being robbed here for the first time on my travels, I had still thoroughly enjoyed this unique country.

20

Siesta, Steak and Soccer (Argentina & Uruguay)

16/11/04 to 30/11/04

I was excited at the prospect of spending a few days in Buenos Airs, a city bridging the gap between Europe and South America, a city that conjures images of pulsating nightlife, sensual passion and excitement. Everything that you would expect from a city that invented tango.

Having managed a few hours sleep on the plane, I felt reasonably fresh as we touched down in Buenos Aires at 6am. I took a shuttle bus into the city centre and a second bus to the Milhouse Hostel in the downtown Congresso area. After checking in I helped myself to a free breakfast and chatted to some of the other guests in the communal lounge. Everyone was very friendly and from top to bottom there was a good vibe. A notice board on the wall listed activities for the day and evening; guided city walks, tango classes, a football game, a movie and karaoke.

Converted to form a huge hostel, the marvellously well-preserved and renovated 1890 colonial house exuded charm. The core of the house is a typical courtyard, full of light and appeal, which runs through the centre of the entire building. Each floor has balconies opening onto it where guests can sit and rest. The ground floor contained the reception, TV room, in-house travel agency, a bar, kitchen, laundry room and communal sitting areas. An elevator and an original marble staircase lead to the upper floors containing the dorms and bedrooms, as well as a sitting room on each floor. My dorm was spotlessly clean and contained six bunks and its own bathroom. This was the best hostel that I had ever stayed in.

On my first afternoon, I joined twenty-six other guests on a guided walking tour of Recoleta, an upmarket district of grand buildings, tree-lined avenues and leafy parks. We started in the weird and wonderful Cementario de la Recoleta, the final resting place of the elite of Buenos Aires Society, including many past presidents, generals and most famously, Eva Peron. The grand, ornate shrines of the rich and famous are like miniature buildings. We lunched in a lovely little restaurant and for the first but not last time, I ordered the famous Argentinean beefsteak, and wasn't disappointed. The tour finished in a modern art museum, which wasn't my cup of tea.

Back in the hostel later, several guys had tickets to see the Argentina play Venezuela in a World Cup qualification football game. I tagged along with them in the hope of picking up a ticket outside. My chances appeared slim as I walked around the stadium without seeing a single tout. I then approached an official gentleman guarding an entrance gate and flashed a twenty dollar bill at him. With a nod of his head he indicated for me to follow him through the gate and into the stadium. He then held out his hand for the money. "Bolletto" (ticket) I said. He bent down and picked up a torn off stub and handed it to me. I figured that as I was already inside the stadium, this would do and so I handed over the cash and ran up the steps and into the arena.

I took a seat high up in the third tier, right on the halfway line. The stadium looked only half full as the game kicked off and right up to half time, crowds of people kept filing in. By the final whistle, I would guess that the stadium was about seventy percent full. The game was pretty entertaining, Argentina winning 3-2, and the atmosphere was good, but not quite as good as I'd expected.

I left ten-minutes before the final whistle to escape the crowds, catching a taxi back to the hostel. When I arrived around midnight, I found the lounge packed with dozens of travellers, chatting, drinking and dancing. I joined them until around 3am, when finally fatigue got the better of me and I headed to bed.

There were two distinct crowds at Milhouse; the party crowd who spent their days in bed and their nights on the town, drinking and dancing until dawn; and the sightseeing crowd, who spent their days exploring the city and their nights tucked up in bed. Only between late afternoon and early evening did the two crowds come briefly together. I and a few other travellers flirted between both crowds, and during my week-long stay here I made many friends and had a wonderful time both exploring this vibrant, cosmopolitan capital and experiencing its wonderful nightlife.

More European than South American in flavour, this energetic and seductive port city has been the gateway to Argentina for centuries. Its heart boasts bustling streets, grand avenues lined with faded architectural glories, tango bars, treasure-filled antique shops, old-time cafes and stylish restaurants. The city has no dominating monument and no natural monolith that serves as its focal point. Instead, Buenos Aires is composed of many small and intimate places. The cities neighbourhoods are small and highly individualized, each with its' own characteristic colours and forms. Portenos, as its people are known, value their European heritage highly; Italian and German names outnumber Spanish, and the lifestyle and architecture are markedly more European than any other in South America.

During those days when I was able to get out of bed, I hung out with a mixed international crowd; Marit from Norway, Anita from Australia, Andy from Germany, Bill from Scotland, Kevin from Australia and Christian from South Africa. We would head by bus to the various city districts and explore, visit the fabulous restaurants, or just stroll around the main shopping area and theatre district, both located within a stones throw of the hostel.

The city centre contains many splendid 19th Century buildings. Some of Argentina's most important historical events took place in The Plaza de Mayo; surrounding it is the Government House, the Metropolitan Cathedral, the Cabildo (town hall) and the Casa Rosade (pink house) from where Eva Peron stood on the balcony and addressed her adoring fans. When I visited there was a peaceful demonstration in process, gay rights I think, closely watched by a sizable police contingent.

Perhaps the most colourful district I visited was La Boca. Here an assortment of brightly painted low houses made of wood and pressed tin burst upon the eyes in a scene that could almost be from Scandinavia; a legacy of the past when the poor Italian immigrants who worked at the docks used left over paint pots from ships to decorate their homes.

Although better known throughout the sporting world as the home of Boca Juniors, one of South America's top football clubs, La Boca is today a popular tourist destination. The main street here is Caminito, which has an artisans and painters fair, open air tango shows, and typical Italian cafes serving pasta and pizza. The area however is still poor and home to a large working class population. Many of the streets off the tourist patch are therefore considered un-safe to visit. We walked around for a while before taking lunch alfresco at a restaurant, where the in-house tango duo provided us with a free show.

A common and strange sight on the streets of Buenos Aires is that of professional dog walkers, often accompanied by as many as a dozen dogs of all shapes and sizes, and it is quite common in the cities parks to see a pack of dogs leashed to a tree or lamp-post whilst their walker snoozes on a nearby bench. Another strange and unusual sight is that of couples practising the tango in parks and open plazas. You just don't see things like that in Birmingham!

Argentina is known as the beef capital of the world, exporting to over 80-countries and consuming more beef per capita than any other nation. Eating out in Buenos Aires is a wonderful event, the restaurants are extremely social and the food excellent and cheap. If you're a carnivore, Argentina is heavenly; the huge, thick steaks served here are so good that I ate one on each and every day I spent here, and two on some days!

One evening our little group visited a 'free fork' restaurant, or as we would call it, 'eat as much as you like'. We arrived to find a queue of locals waiting to be seated, always a good sign. There was a self-service buffet including salads, meats, fish, potatoes, pastas, rice, noodles and various specialist dishes such as sushi. There was also a BBQ where you could select the meat of your choice, which the chef would cook to your specific requirements. We each made a couple of visits to the buffet before selecting steaks from the BBQ, which were the best I had ever tasted. Although stuffed, I was still able to find room for a visit to the cheese board and desert trolley. Several local families in the restaurant were celebrating birthdays and this added to the occasion. With wine included, we all put 20-Pesos into the pot, which left enough over for a very good tip. Probably the best £4 that I think I've ever spent!

Buenos Aires is never more alive than it is at night. Avenues come alive with sophisticated, glitzy and beautiful people on their way to restaurants and theatres, all dressed to impress. Typically they eat around 10pm and stay out until dawn partying.

Matching the mood of the city, Milhouse was a hostel for those that want non-stop fun and excitement. At night the lounge transformed itself into a buzzing bar-like environment before everyone headed out to the restaurants, bars and nightclubs. It is a fantastic party hostel where you feel guilty for sleeping!

On one particular night I hit the town with a gang of medical students from Belfast, five lads and three girls. We found ourselves in a small, dark and plush club frequented by a young local crowd. There were many beautiful girls, but they didn't seem too interested in us gringos, and the local guys were not exactly friendly either. Despite this we drank, danced and partied until closing time around 5am. Four of us then caught a taxi to another club, where we raved-on until around 8am. Travelling home in daylight through the rush hour traffic was a weird experience.

Once back at the hostel we ate breakfast before going to bed. I had barely fallen asleep when I was woken by two Yanks having a loud and meaningless conversation:

Yank one: "Where are you from dude?"

Yank two: "The U.S."

Yank one: "Wow, me too"

Yank two: "No way – cool."

Yank one: "Do you know they dance the tango here?"

Yank two: "No way!"

Yank one: "Way dude, you wanna come to a show with me later?"

Yank two: "Hell yeah man".

Yank one: "And they play soccer too, I just gotta see a pro game here".

Yank two: "Awesome. I play minor league soccer back home, offensive shield".

I put the pillow over my head and tried as best I could to shut out the intellectual words of my roommates.

The Milhouse organised a trip to watch a football game between River Plate and their local rivers Independiante, and Marit, Andy, Anita, Christian and I joined around twenty or so other hostel guests on what turned out to be akin to a school trip. We were taken by bus to the stadium, during which our overprotective guide lectured us on the potential dangers that lie ahead should we stray too far from his side. Not until we reached the entrance gates did he give us our tickets, and once inside the stadium, he immediately collected them back off us for 'safe keeping'. I was just relieved that he didn't make us all hold hands!

Fortunately we made it to our seats unscathed about half an hour before kick-off and sat patiently for the game to begin. At the far side of the stadium the visiting Independiante fans had filled their section and were jumping and singing loudly, whilst many of the River Plate fans were still entering the stadium and were quieter. Just before kick off, with the stadium full but for an empty section behind one goal, we heard the sound of drums and chanting to our right. Suddenly a procession of flag waving, drum playing, singing supporters entered the stadium and made their way along the terrace, as if marching to war, to take up a position in the empty section behind the goal. Their entrance was greeted with almost hysterical fever, rapturous applause, chanting and flag waving by their fellow supporters, and suddenly the atmosphere was electric.

The two teams entered the arena, newspaper like confetti filled the air, flags appeared all around the stadium and the River fans began to sing as one. The game became almost a sideshow to the spectacle of the crowd. Both sets of supporters sang and jumped throughout the entire game, during half time and in the case of River, who incidentally won 3-0, for twenty minutes after the final whistle. Even the Independiante fans, that had seen their team get thrashed, never stopped singing, jumping and supporting until the bitter end. In thirty years of watching football, I had never experienced an atmosphere or such fanatical support like it before.

I learnt from the man sitting next to me that the favourite chant of the River supporters, which they sing whilst bouncing up and down, roughly translates to "Everyone jumps except for the

Englishmen", a reference to the 1986 World Cup when Diego Maradonna scored one of the greatest goals of all time to knock England out of the tournament.

Back in the hostel later I had a little run in with an Aussie girl, who sat uninvited amongst our group and then proceeded to dominate the conversation, talking over other people and butting into conversations. She then ranted about how she hated England and the English.

"Where have you visited in England?" I asked.

"London" she replied.

"Where else?"

"No where, London was bad enough, I didn't want to go anywhere else".

"So what you really mean is you don't like London".

"No. I hate England. The pubs are boring, the beers rubbish, there's no nightlife, the shops are useless and the supermarkets have no choice".

"So you think the nightlife and shops are better in Australia than London?"

"Definitely".

Everyone else sat in silence. I laughed out loud and shook my head. "Now if you had said that the beaches are crap or that it rains too much, I would agree with you, but London has some of the best nightlife and shopping in the world. Don't even try to compare Australia to England on that score" I retorted.

"And you've got no history" she snapped back, to which everyone burst out laughing. Fortunately this had the desired effect; she stood up and stormed off.

I had arranged via e-mail to meet my Swiss friend Martin, who was now living and working in the city; we had met during my journey across the Bolivian salt flats. We met in a bar in San Telmo, a district of charming cobblestone streets lined with colonial mansions, antique shops, atmospheric cafes and bars. It was good to see Martin again and meet his Argentinean girlfriend, and what better way to catch up than over a few beers.

After a fabulous but exhausting week in Buenos Aires, I eventually decided that the time had come to continue my journey. I had loved Buenos Aires and was sad to be leaving; it is a beautiful city with wonderful people, great nightlife and fantastic food, if you are a carnivore. However my wallet was glad to be moving on. Although Argentina is cheap, eating steak twice a day and drinking until the early hours every night had taken its toll; still it had been a great week!

Like me, Marit was also ready to move-on, so we decided to travel together through neighbouring Uruguay and on to Brazil, from where we were both due to fly home from just before Christmas. We checked out and caught a taxi to the ferry terminal where we hoped to catch the 9am ferry across the Rio de la Plata to Uruguay.

We arrived with ten minutes to spare and stood in a queue, which we presumed was for tickets. We reached the front only to be sent to another counter on the opposite side of the hall. With time running out, we ran across the hall to the other counter where a miserable, unhelpful woman informed us that we were too late. Fortunately, a guy at another counter came to our aid; he sorted out our tickets, expedited our luggage check-in and then rushed us through immigration. We made it on board by the skin of our teeth, and within a couple of minutes the ferry was pulling out of Buenos Aires.

Marit slept throughout the crossing, cuddled up with her teddy bear, whilst I caught up with my journal. Marit was a sweet Norwegian girl, 25 going on 15 and very naive, innocent and a tad dippy. Like most Scandinavians, she spoke exceptional English, certainly better than my Norwegian, but occasionally she would say the oddest things such as, "Today I want to be a vegetable", when what she really meant to say was "Today I want to eat vegetarian".

She was great company and had a good sense of humour, but she had one irritating fault – she would get into conversations with locals, nodding knowingly and saying, "Si, si" as they spoke, without actually having a clue of what they were saying, as she didn't speak a word of Spanish. This was often funny, however occasionally these conversations were held with people whom we actually needed information from, like hotel staff and taxi drivers, with disastrous consequences. Nevertheless, she was so nice that you easily forgive this little fault.

We arrived in the port of Colonia at 12noon and immediately walked to the long distance bus terminal where we stowed our bags and booked tickets for the 4.30pm bus to the capital, Montevideo. With a few hours to explore Colonia, we walked into the town centre and set about obtaining some Uruguayan currency. There were about five banks in the town but all of their ATM'S were broken. We then went through a long-winded process to withdraw some cash over the bank counter, which involved completing a lengthy form and handing it over the counter together with our passports and visa cards. We then took a seat and waited whilst the forms were passed between several employees for their approval. Eventually, after almost an hour, we received our cash and we left.

Colonia was the focus of struggle over control of the area between the Spanish, who founded the settlement at Montevideo, and the Portuguese. For years it operated as a contraband port, evading the strictures imposed on trade by the Spanish crown. Located just fifty kilometres east of Buenos Aires across the Rio de la Plata, today it is a resort city, a port, and a common tourist destination for Argentines, but less so for other foreigners.

We walked into the old town, founded by the Portuguese in 1680. A restored drawbridge marks the beginning of the historic district, built in 1745 by the Portuguese as the only entrance of the walled city. The small cobbled windy streets are lined with tall trees and historic buildings, colourful stone houses alternate with small bars, excellent restaurants, art and craft shops and museums, whilst the El Faro lighthouse, constructed in 1857, is the centrepiece of the town. We ate lunch alfresco at a quaint restaurant, outside of which stood two vintage cars, their interiors replaced with dining tables.

After a pleasant few hours, we departed Colonia on the 4:30 bus bound for Montevideo, where we arrived a couple of hours later. Aboard the bus we had met a guy named Rich from Carlisle, and the three of us shared a taxi from the bus terminal to the Hotel Arapey, where Marit and I had arranged to meet our friend Christian, who we had met in Buenos Aires.

Around 9pm the four of us went out for dinner, joined by an American guy named Dave who we'd met in the hotel elevator.

Uruguay shares many characteristics with its Argentine neighbour, including its dining options, and once more we found ourselves in another 'eat as much as you can' buffet restaurant.

The conversation revolved around getting to know each other and about our various trips. Rich was just beginning a four-week break, whilst Dave, who I nicknamed the 'Quiet American' on account of his non-stop talking, had left the U.S. for the first time in his life and had come to South America to help kick a drug habit. I'm no expert, but I'd have thought that the last place to go to kick a drug addiction would be South America!

Dave was extremely honest and openly told us of his drug addictions and his failed relationships. The upshot was that he had lost everything as a result of a heroin addiction, which he had now kicked. He had sold up and left his home in Florida to travel and try to write a novel. He was certainly no backpacker; in fact he was travelling with five suitcases. We left the restaurant around midnight and walked to a nearby bar where a local band was playing their brand of local rock. We sat drinking and chatting until around 4am.

I woke around 12noon the next day. There was a note on the bedside table from Marit saying that she had gone to the bank. I seemed to remember her hitting me over the head with her teddy bear sometime during the early hours. Christian and I waited in the hotel lobby for Marit to return, during which time Bill, who we'd also met in Buenos Aires, turned up and checked in. Rich had moved on this morning to the beach resort of Cabo Polonia, where we were heading to next, and there was no sign of the Quiet American. By 1pm Marit had still not returned and so Christian, Bill and I headed towards the old city, leaving a note for Marit at reception.

With a population of around 1.3 million, I was immediately struck by the contrast between the hectic pace of life of the Argentine capital and the relaxed atmosphere of Montevideo. Founded in 1726 as a fortress city on the northern shore of the River Plate, it was in a strong trade position and, following a turbulent and often-violent early history, its growth was rapid. The nineteenth century saw mass immigration from Europe resulting in a vibrant mix of architectural styles and cultures, giving the city a cosmopolitan atmosphere that persists to this day. It was a nice enough city, a blend of colonial Spanish, Italian and Art Deco styles, safe and laid back, friendly and welcoming.

We visited the Mercado de Puerto (Port Market), a steel-framed Victorian building originally built by the British as a railway station, but never used as such. Enclosed within are numerous 'Parrillas', traditional stalls that prepare all kinds of meat over a charcoal or wood fire. Marit arrived in time to join us for lunch, and once more I devoured a fabulous slab of steak.

Afterwards we explored the capital a little more. An archway at the west end of Plaza de la Independencia, a part of the old city wall, marks the entrance to the old town, with its narrow streets and 18th century buildings. In its heart lies the cities most interesting buildings – the Plaza Constitición, the cathedral, the Stock Exchange and the Customs House. Pleasant, but not exactly the most beautiful, interesting or inspiring city that I had ever visited.

Uruguayans share many cultural characteristics with their Argentine neighbours, including a near compulsive affection for mate, the traditional gaucho tea-like drink. Almost every Uruguayan you see carries a thermos of hot water, a gourd and a bombilla. The gourd is traditionally a wooden decorated vessel and a bombilla is a silver straw like device for drinking the mate. Mate is most definitely an acquired taste, a cross between green tea and coffee, with hints of tobacco and oak.

After seeing just about everything that Montevideo had to offer, Marit and I checked out of the hotel the next morning and caught a bus to La Paloma, a beach resort on the Atlantic coast approx 220km to the east, whilst Christian was heading back to Buenos Aires and Bill had decided to hang around for a little longer.

The bus departed at 12noon, Marit slept through the entire journey whilst I read a little and watched the countryside pass by; lush, patchwork fields in which flocks of sheep and herds of cattle grazed, no doubt before they end up in a barbecue platter. It reminded me oddly of England, perhaps a little flatter. The odd palm tree provided a reminder that we were still in South America.

We arrived at the La Paloma bus terminal around 4:30pm and

we walked to a hotel in the centre recommended in our guidebook, only to find it closed. As it seemed were the majority of hotels and restaurants; summer season had not yet started and the place was dead. Marit offered to search for another hotel while I guarded the bags. She returned around fifteen-minutes later, accompanied by Dave, the Quiet American. I had hoped for a peaceful few days at the beach but it looked as though I could forget that idea, there would be no quiet time with Dave around!

"Guys, you've gotta come stay in my hotel," Dave said.

"We've already got somewhere else lined up," I lied.

"Marit said you were looking for somewhere".

"Well, kind of. I wanna try a place in my guidebook, on the sea-front".

"OK, if its no good then come back you hear".

"Yeah, will do Dave".

Fortunately the Hotel La Tuna turned out to be perfect, and we took a room on the first floor with a balcony overlooking the ocean. We spent the late afternoon resting up in the room. I read a little whilst Marit played with her new toy which she brought in Montevideo, a child's kaleidoscope, the kind that you put to your eye like a telescope and twist around to reveal patterns of coloured glass. This kept her occupied for hours like a small child. Strange people the Norwegians!

We headed into town around eight for dinner, but we could only find one restaurant open, and so we took a table and ordered from the brief menu. We were halfway through our pizza when Dave walked in. He joined us and spent the evening telling us how, spurred on by our travel stories, he had decided to send his suitcases and most of the contents home, buy a backpack and go on a worldwide tour of his own!

After just one day we decided to leave La Paloma and head further along the coast to Cabo Polonia, where Rich had headed to a couple of days earlier. On route to the bus terminal we passed Dave's hotel. He too was checking out, and so he decided to tag along with us, helplessly trying to keep up whilst carrying five suitcases. Once at the terminal we discovered that the next bus to Cabo wasn't due for another couple of hours, however a taxi driver outside the terminal offered to take us for what we believed to be the bargain price of 50-Pesos (£1).

The taxi-fare turned out to be 500-Pesos not 50. We were dropped at the main highway ten kilometres short of Cabo, which was cut off from civilisation by sand-dunes and a wood of the tall pine trees, part of a national park; the only way there being by horse or four-wheel vehicle along a sand track. Waiting at the start of the track were a couple of truck-like vehicles. We climbed onto the open-back of one of them and set off, my knuckles turning white from gripping the bars as we bounced along the snaking, bumpy path across the dunes.

Eventually we reached the isolated Atlantic coast, turning north we drove along the beach until the small the ramshackle fishing village of Cabo Polonia came into view, built around a lighthouse built on a headland. I had never seen anything quite like it before; the scattering of rustic huts and rickety shacks built haphazardly along the beach and on the dunes serve as shelter for the local fishing community. There was no permanent town, no main square, no roads, no cars, no telephones, Internet and not even electricity.

The view alone merited the long bus ride and off-road odyssey to Cabo Polonia; immense rolling sand dunes, a long curved beach, sea-lions lounging on rocky boulders as if also on vacation, and beyond all this the immense glistening ocean and relentless surf.

There were only the two hotels. Marit and I took a room in The Hosteria La Perla, a twelve-room wooden inn facing the ocean, with a veranda containing sun-loungers, hammocks, tables and chairs. It seemed the perfect spot to relax and rest up for a couple of days. Dave took a room in the other hotel, which at least guaranteed us some peace and quiet.

We enquired with the owner if there was another English man staying at the hotel and she confirmed that there was an English man who spoke with a Spanish dictionary. It sounded like Rich and indeed it was. On the evening, the four of us ate dinner together; grilled white fish served in cream sauce, and cold beer on the veranda of our hotel, just yards from the crashing waves. We were joined by a Argentine couple named Gonzalo and Mirancol, who were in Cabo for their friends wedding tomorrow on the beach, which they kindly invited us to.

The next evening around 11pm the four of us set off on foot in search of the wedding party, with just one torch and the moonlight to guide us. As we trudged down the vast beach, suddenly the silence was shattered by a loud scream; Dave had trod on a sharp shell leaving him limping badly. As we pressed on, Dave managed to walk into a bog and trip over on a couple of occasions, each mishap greeted with roars of laughter from the rest of us.

After about an hour we had seen no sign of the wedding party, and as far as we could ascertain, the beach was deserted for as far as the eye could see; there was no lights and no music. Reluctantly we gave up our search and turned back. It was 3am by the time we had reached the hotel, by which time poor Dave was covered in mud and hobbling badly!

Over the next few days we relaxed, read, played cards, ate, drank, walked along the beach, swam in the ocean and watched the local sea-lion colony. They seemed oblivious to the presence of people and so I was able to sit just a few metres from them and watch and photograph them basking in the sun, fighting and playing. Here time doesn't seem to matter, the only thing to do is relax and rest!

One morning Marits' habit of getting into a conversation that she didn't understand struck again. The waitress brought our complimentary breakfast to our table. "What food is this?" Marit asked. I'm not sure if the waitress understood Marit, but she answered in a long Spanish sentence. Marit listened intently, nodding knowingly, "Si, si" she said. The waitress smiled back at her, and then picked up our meals and carried them back into the kitchen. I looked at Marit and shook my head. "Marit, if you don't understand, please don't say si," I pleaded. The waitress returned with our breakfast a few minutes later, covered in chocolate and cream!

During our brief stay here our little group grew to five when a girl named Lisa joined us. Oddly she claimed to be Swiss, although from her accent it was obvious she was English. Dave in particular took a shine to her and spent his days and nights following her around like a lost puppy.

One afternoon we challenged a group of local guys to a game of beach-football. To my and their surprise, we scored the first goal, then a second, third and forth. This despite the fact that our team contained a useless forty-two year-old American and two girls, whilst their team consisted of five fit teenage lads. Luckily for us these lads had never heard of teamwork, and refused to pass the ball to each other. At 4-0 down, the Uruguayans became quite aggressive and the tackles came hard and fast, as is typical of Uruguayan footballers when loosing. I finished the game limping with a throbbing big toe, and for the record, we lost 6 – 5.

After just three days I had begun to tire of my surroundings. Cabo was nice, relaxed and peaceful, but maybe it was a little too peaceful for my liking. We were the only foreigners here, and as the summer season had not yet began, there were very few Uruguayans here either. Both hotels were empty other than for us, the only bar here had no customers, and there was just one shop, with a minimal selection of products. I was even growing bored of the hotel menu; it seemed that I had eaten every dish on the menu at least a couple of times.

We befriended a group of four Uruguayan medical students who were renting a wooden beach shack in Cabo for a week's holiday. We spent a couple of evenings with them, drinking wine and teaching them card games. After a few too many vino's one evening, the conversation turned to the plight of South America, and in particular the Uruguayan economy, which had collapsed a few years ago.

Their families were of European descent and so they considered themselves to be European and not South American, as many Uruguayans and Argentines do. They blamed Europe, more specifically European farming subsidies for ruining their exports and thus their economy. They spoke passionately about how they believed Europe had turned its back on them and how they felt betrayed. They seemed to think that Europe owed them after their nation had supplied beef to Europe after WWII. I felt sorry for them and we did our best to sympathise, but what could we say?

Uruguay's future may yet lie in tourism, yet the nation appears slow to react to it, unlike many of their neighbours who have been quick to embrace and exploit the tourist dollar. Very few tourists currently visit Uruguay, mainly because they know nothing about it as the country does little to promote itself. Little wonder then that so many tourists omit Uruguay from their itineraries.

To break the boredom, Rich, Marit and I arranged for a fishing trip on one of the local boats, or at least that's what we believed we'd arranged. The fishing boat turned out to be a large rowing boat with an outboard motor, as opposed to one of the larger commercial fishing-boats that we expected. And our all-day fishing trip turned out to be nothing more than an hour cruise to a rock a couple of miles offshore where a colony of sea lions lived.

Once more the language barrier had been a problem. The Spanish language spoken in Uruguay and Argentina was somewhat different to that spoken in Chile, Bolivia and Peru. Not only do they speak very quickly here, they also change the end of many words; it must be like a Spaniard learning to speak English in Oxford, and then trying to talk to a Geordie. Suddenly my Spanish seemed useless; it was very frustrating.

I was beginning to feel trapped in Cabo; it was so isolated that it was not easy to escape. No one at the hotel seemed to have any idea of the days and times that the busses ran along the main highway toward the Brazilian border, or if they did they weren't telling. Consequently It felt like a place that you could never leave, like being trapped in "The Twilight Zone".

With each day that passed, Dave grew on me more and more, and he helped to keep me laughing and entertained with some of his weird observations and comments. One morning we were all lounging on the veranda when Dave appeared carrying his personal CD player, earphones in, head nodding violently to the beat of the music. "Hi guys, any of you like Russian Surf Music?" he asked. We all collapsed in fits of laughter, much to his surprise. I never did find out what Russian Surf Music sounded like.

Eventually my chance to escape arrived when I met a driver of one of the trucks that ferry visitors back and forth across the dunes. He informed me that a bus left for the Brazilian border tomorrow morning from the nearby town of Castillo, and so I arranged for him to take me there first thing tomorrow.

The next morning I boarded the truck together with Dave and Lisa, who were also keen to escape Cabo and join me in Brazil. Rich was due to return to Buenos Aires to catch his flight home and Marit wanted to stay here and relax for another few days.

By 11am we were in the town of Castillo, from where we duly caught the bus to the border town of Chuy, three-hours away. Chuy was a strange town with a real 'wild-west' frontier town feel. The central reservation in the dual carriageway running through the town was quite literally the border between the two countries. By 4pm we were on another bus, stopping briefly at the border to conclude passport formalities, during which I noticed that Lisa had an English, not Swiss passport. Strange that she should pretend to be a different nationality!

21

Sun, Surf and Samba (Brazil)

01/12/04 to 23/12/04

And so I entered Brazil, the eighteenth and final country of my journey. By 8pm we were in the town of Pelotas, which was not our chosen destination, but the nearest town en-route. From Pelotas we took another bus bound for Porto Alegre, arriving exhausted and hungry at 11:30pm. Fortunately there was an overnight bus due to depart at 11:55 bound for the city of Florianopolis, our ultimate destination; we boarded and settled down for a long night.

My brief introduction to Brazil was favourable, the roads were good, the busses luxurious and the countryside lush and scenic. But the most notable thing was the girls; they were simply stunning!

We finally arrived in Florionapolis at 7am after a gruelling twenty-two hour journey. The city stands part on the mainland and part on the island of Santa Catarina, linked by the Hercilio Luz Bridge, the longest suspension bridge in Brazil.

Outside the terminal a taxi-driver approached us, "Halo my friends, you look for accommodation where?" he asked.

"Barra de Lagoa" I replied.

"Maybe you like to rent a cabana? Very cheap".

"Maybe".

"I take you there in my taxi, if you like then OK, if you no like, then you pay taxi-fare".

It sounded like a reasonable proposition so we jumped in the taxi and set off. Once in Barra de Lagoa, our driver gave us a quick tour of the town and then took us to his cabana. It contained a dining kitchen, a bathroom and two bedrooms, one with a double bed and the second with a pair of bunk beds and one single bed. It was close to the town centre and the beach, and at just 20-Real (£4) each per night, it was not only cheap but also perfect for our needs.

After sorting out sleeping arrangements, we headed out to explore our new surroundings. Barra da Lagoa is a picturesque little town encompassed by a gorgeous stretch of beach known as Praia Mocambique. A narrow river inlet that runs up to a small bay divides the town, making half of the town accessible only by boat or via a footbridge that spans the river.

But whilst very quaint, Barra da Lagoa was a busy and happening place, with a full and modern infrastructure, including phone and Internet connections, and numerous restaurants and bars. The white sand beach was long, clean and not too crowded; the local girls sunbathed in skimpy bikinis, and the men posed in tight Speedos. A few guys were playing a friendly game of beach footie and the water teemed with surfers. It was everything that I'd pictured Brazil to be.

We returned to the Cabana around 5pm for a siesta in readiness for our first night out in Brazil. We went to dinner at 8pm, only to find that we were the only people in the restaurant. Like Argentina, dinner doesn't really start until 9pm and nightlife at around 11pm. Unfortunately, the local bars were very also quiet and somewhat of a let down, and so we caught a bus to the larger town of Lagoa, about 5km away. We cruised the bars drinking freshly made capirinhas, the national drink made from sugarcane rum, crushed limes, ice and sugar.

We then headed to a nightclub called Latitude 27-Degrees. Brazilian clubs have an ingenious system whereby customers can enter and drink without once putting their hand in their pocket. Instead, each time you order a drink you hand over your personal drink-card given to you on entry, and the bartender records your drink. On exit your drinks bill is calculated and added to the entrance fee, 20-Real (£4) for men and free for women. Wonderful you may think, but the system has its drawbacks. It is difficult to keep tabs on what your spending, as I was to later discover to my cost, and god help you if you loose your card, for you will be handed a bill which will leave you thinking that you've paid for everyone's night out!

At first the club was good, the DJs playing a wide selection of music from hip-hop, to techno, and of course samba. There were dozens of gorgeous girls; many vibrantly dancing while others sat chatting and sipping capirinhas. Then suddenly the entire mood of the club changed when a live rock band began to play. By about 2am I had had enough and so had Dave. Lisa was chatting with some other travellers and wanted to stay so we bid her farewell and left.

We climbed into a taxi outside, "Nightclub, mucho girls" I said to the driver.

"Si senor, Florionapolis" he replied, and we drove off toward the city. The ride took ages and when we eventually arrived the fare was a whopping 50-Real (£10). I think the taxi driver had simply chosen the most distant club in order to boost the fare.

Like the previous club, we were each given a drinks-card to pay on exit. We entered the club to find that it was actually a hostess club; obviously the taxi-driver had taken my instructions a little too literally. We sat at a table and ordered a couple of drinks and decided to make the most of it. Before too long a girl approached and sat next to Dave, shortly followed by two more who sat either side of me; all three were young, beautiful and scantily dressed. As the night progressed we drank a few cocktails and brought our new 'friends' a few too.

The club closed at 4am and as we attempted to leave we received the shock of our lives when we were handed a bill of about 800-Real (£160). I didn't have anywhere near that kind of money on me, but luckily Dave had his credit card and so we avoided a possible 'beating' by the doormen. We stood outside in shocked silence and I looked at Dave and said, "Just think how expensive the girls would have been".

Dave laughed, "Lets go," he replied.

We jumped in a taxi and began the long journey home. The driver woke me on arrival in Barra; I directed him to our cabana, paid the fare and woke up Dave who was fast asleep, slumped across the backseat. We stumbled up the path of our cabana, getting in at 5am, totally pissed and skint.

We woke around 11am the next morning to find the rain pouring down. With no chance of getting down to the beach, we spent the morning in the laundry and then caught the bus into Lagoa to withdraw some cash and check e-mails. Marit had sent word asking where we were staying.

After the previous evening we were all in need of a quiet night. The three of us ate dinner together, after which we returned to the apartment and chilled out. Dave was complaining that his eye was sore, so Lisa accompanied him to the hospital. They returned a couple of hours later, Dave sporting a huge white eye-patch.

We popped out to a local bar to cheer up Dave. The locals were all friendly, especially the owner named Sabrina. The Brazilians have some odd drinking habits, literally helping themselves to other people's beer. If you leave a bottle sitting on a table or the bar counter, then they will pour themselves a glass from it. When I first realised that the guy sitting next to me was drinking from my bottle I almost punched him, but I decided not to make a fuss; he was considerably bigger than me. However, they all take it in turns buying bottles and expect and accept that others will help themselves also; a little like an unofficial round. By the end of the night it all works itself out and by the time we left the bar, I'd had as much of the other peoples beer as they'd had of mine.

I received an e-mail from Marit the next day saying she was on her way and expected to be here around 3pm. I was pleased; Dave was good company for the most part but had a habit of wandering off on his own, whilst Lisa took herself far too seriously and had no sense of humour, so wasn't the best of company.

I spent the next day on the beach, relaxing, reading and admiring the eye-candy. The sun was so hot that every half-hour or so I would wade into the ocean to cool off. Marit never arrived, I assumed that she'd underestimated the length of the bus journey and had stopped off for the night somewhere en-route.

We spent the evening on the beach, where a party was scheduled at one of the bars. We arrived to find dozens of teenage boys outside, as if it were a school disco, and inside were as many girls of a similar age. I sat on the beach chatting with a local girl called Maria, "The girls can enter the bar for free, but boys must pay" she explained. "So the girls go inside to dance while the boys drink on the beach as they have no money".

"But they are only children" I said.

"Yes, soon they will begin to drift home and later adults will come to party until the morning". The kids did indeed drift home, but only a few adults turned up, a mixture of locals and travellers, and the party never really got going. A drunken local couple entertained us for most of the night, attempting to dance on the beach.

Dave and Lisa caught a taxi into Lagoa town, only for Dave to return on his own about an hour later. I stayed chatting to Maria on the beach for most of the night and thought that my luck was in; that is until her boyfriend arrived. By 3am both Dave and I were tucked up in bed.

At 8am the next morning my sleep was rudely broken by Marit jumping up and down on me shouting, "Mr Lee, Mr Lee, wake up!" It turned out that she'd been travelling for forty-eight hours and had been stuck on the bus for about ten of those in a traffic jam following a crash. I was pleased to see her again. The four of us ate breakfast together and then crossed the river via the footbridge. On the opposite bank numerous trails lead to fishermen's houses and bungalows that are strung out along a flower-covered hillside. We walked along one trail, which led to a small deserted beach, where we spent the day lazing.

Dave, Marit and I spent the evening together; we had no idea where Lisa was. We dined in an excellent little seafood restaurant recommended by Sabrina, sharing one very large meal of fish, rice, potatoes and salad. Afterwards we returned to Sabrina's bar and spent the night drinking beer and caprianis and chatting to the friendly locals, although we weren't too sure what exactly was being said as they had very little English, and we even less Portuguese.

We left around 11pm to catch the bus to Lagoa town but by midnight it still hadn't arrived. Along with about twenty other travellers, we crammed into three taxis; there were six people in ours, me and Marit in the front seat and four in the back. We drove to a samba party in a two-storey, wooden shack style bar. We were the only foreigners there and although the locals weren't hostile towards us, they weren't exactly friendly either. I didn't feel particularly comfortable there and so after about an hour, Marit, Dave and I left to go to a more run of the mill establishment.

Marit, Dave and I left the next day to continue our journeys, whilst Lisa decided to stay on; she never said but we assumed that she'd hooked up with a guy. Leaving the apartment at noon, we caught two local busses, the first to Lagoa and the second to Florionapolis. From there we purchased tickets for the 4pm bus to Foz de Iguazu on the Brazil – Argentina border.

We had hoped for a luxury bus with fully reclining bed-seats, however we were to be disappointed; the bus was very basic and smelt of urine. On a plus note at least we each had a double-seat to ourselves to spread out. Around 10pm the bus fell silent and everyone bedded down for the night.

Foz stands at the confluence of the Iguazú and Paraná rivers, close to where a geological fault on the Paraná riverbed has created a stunning series of waterfalls. Called Foz do Iguaçu in Brazilian, and Cataratas del Iguazú in Spanish, the falls lie on the Argentina – Brazil border and are a UNESCO World Natural Heritage Site. Taller than Niagara Falls and four times the width, Iguazu Falls one of the top destinations in South America with nearly two-million annual visitors.

We arrived in Foz at 7am after a fifteen-hour journey. Inside the bus terminal was a desk for the local YHA, which looked surprisingly good and so we took a taxi directly there. We checked in for two-nights, which would give us time to see the falls from both the Brazilian and Argentine sides. The YHA had fantastic facilities and was more like a resort than a hostel, with a swimming pool, football pitch, outdoor bar and pleasant lawned gardens.

After a quick shower and change of clothes, we set off to see this wondrous spectacle. As we walked along the highway toward the park, an old, beat up car pulled up alongside us, "Iguazu?" the driver asked, pointing down the road.

"Si" we replied in unison. He signalled with his hand for us to climb in and he duly dropped us outside the park entrance a couple of kilometres down the road.

We heard the roar of the falls long before we set sight on them. However despite what we had read, none of us were prepared for what we saw; the view of an eighty-metre high wall of white water strung out along the rim of a crescent-shaped cliff about four kilometres long. A series of some two-hundred and seventy-five individual cascades and waterfalls separated by rocky, densely wooded islets, with clouds of mist and spray rising high into the sky above them creating a dazzling display of rainbows. Little wander that on seeing them Eleanor Roosevelt said, "Poor Niagara".

We followed a trail along the river stopping at various viewpoints to take photographs. The Falls, which would be memorable in any setting, are made all the more beautiful by their lush surroundings. They are part of a singular practically virgin jungle ecosystem, 55,000 hectares of pristine subtropical rainforest protected by Argentine and Brazilian National Parks on either side of the cascades.

The luxuriant forests are filled with over 2,000 plant species, 400 birds, and a variety of mammals, reptiles and insects. Brilliantly feathered parrots and macaws squawk in the foliage of bamboo, palms, and delicate tree ferns, colourful butterflies flit between exotic blooms of wild orchids, begonias, and bromeliads, and lizard's scamper in the undergrowth.

The trail eventually led to the most impressive of the falls, the spectacular Garganta del Diablo 'Devil's Throat', where fourteen falls drop eighty-metres with such force that there is a permanent thirty-metre fog of spray overhead. A boardwalk extended across the river stopping approximately one-hundred metres short of the falls. I stripped down to my shorts and strode along the platform, the noise from the gushing water was ear-splitting, and within seconds I was soaked from head to toe from the spray. The sheer power of the falls was awesome.

We then continued up a series of stairs to a viewing platform looking down on the falls. We ate lunch here at a fast food outlet and then took the free bus back toward the park entrance. Dave and I took a guided tour through a section of jungle, followed by a boat-ride up to and under the falls, and for second time we were soaked through, but it was worth it.

Along with about fifteen other guests, Dave, Marit and I boarded the hostel shuttle-bus at 8am the next morning, bound for the Argentine side of the falls. We passed through Brazil immigration and then stopped in the centre of a bridge spanning the Iguazu River, literally on the border between the two countries. Our crazy Argentine driver then produced a Boca Juniors (Argentine football club) flag, which he draped across the bus dashboard. We continued through Argentine immigration and by 10am we were inside the Argentine side of the national park.

The Argentine side contains seventy percent of the falls and gives a closer view and experience. It is so vast that a free train runs through the park linking various walking trails and viewing platforms. From the main entrance we took the train to Cataratas Station, from where both the Lower and Upper Walking Circuits begin.

We started by following the Lower Circuit, which contains many stairs and so required a lot of physical effort. The trail took us through sections of jungle and across streams; we stopped to catch our breath at several viewing-balconies, all with marvellous, jar-dropping bottom-up views of the falls.

We followed the Lower Circuit all the way down to the river, where we took free shuttle-boat over to San Martin Island, a small rocky island encircled by the river and falls. We climbed a very steep and uneven stone staircase and walked along a jungle-trail to a viewing-balcony for a close-up, ear-splitting and very wet view of San Martin falls.

We retraced our footsteps and caught the return shuttle-boat back to the mainland and made our way back along the trails to a refreshment area where we made a brief lunch stop in one of the fast-food outlets. Dave headed off to make an urgent telephone call and Marit and I made our way to the Upper Circuit, a half-hour walk along a trail extending deep into the jungle, fortunately with no more stairs. All of a sudden we ran into breathtaking side-on views of the falls. The different observation points along this trail allowed us to get lots of intimate views of the falls from above.

For Marit time had beaten her, we kissed goodbye and she headed off to catch her bus; she was leaving to head to the Brazilian Pantanal region for a few days. I continued alone, catching the park train to its furthest point, Garganta del Diablo Station. From the station I followed the trail through the forest and along a

1,200m long series of catwalks extending between the numerous islets of the wide upper Iguazu River, which gives the impression that you are crossing several different rivers.

The walk took about half an hour, all the time the thundering roar of 'The Devils Throat' grew louder and louder. The final stretch led to a large viewing platform, positioned right over the point where the river takes its grandest leap, plunging off the edge of the plateau, like an ocean pouring into an abyss. I spent about one-hour here taking in the awesome spectacle and sheer power, whilst getting completely soaked from the spray and almost deafened from the noise.

Iguazu was simply an amazing sight, the grandeur of the falls, the tremendous amount and power of water thundering down, the sub-tropical location and just the sheer beauty was the most wonderful natural spectacle that I have ever seen, a true once-in-a-lifetime experience. Iguazu is said to be the most spectacular waterfalls on earth and I wouldn't disagree for one second.

At 7pm our bus returned to pick us up. The driver still had his flag proudly displayed in the front window, and as we drove through the streets he enthusiastically waved it at passers by and other vehicles whilst hooting the horn. Everyone we passed waved back as if they knew him. I presumed he was a well-known local 'character'.

Downstream from the falls where the Parana and Iguazu rivers meet, so do the borders of Argentina, Brazil and Paraguay. Each country has created a landmark in their national colours on their border. We drove to a viewpoint where you can see all three. At the viewpoint car park, three young girls boarded the bus, kissed the driver, and proceeded to walk down the aisle selling cakes. I got the impression this was a regular occurrence.

The following day Dave and I checked out and took the 2:40pm bus to Rio de Janeiro. Opposite me sat a woman and two kids, all scoffing chocolate and sweets, and guzzling fizzy drinks. It wasn't long before one of the kids threw up, and for the next hour or so we were treated to the sounds of a child calling to God with his head buried in a plastic bag. To pass the time, I read a little and tried to watch a couple of movies being shown. At 10pm the driver turned out the lights and everyone settled down for the night.

I woke at first light around 6am, just as we were entering the suburbs of Sao Paolo, South America's largest city. Sao Paolo is Brazils' commercial and industrial powerhouse, with little of interest for tourists, and so I had decided not to stop here. Most of my fellow passengers disembarked, to be replaced by as many other travellers.

Eventually the bus arrived in Rio at 3.30, twenty-six hours after leaving Foz. From the bus terminal we took a taxi to the Ipanema district. As we drove through the suburbs, the beauty of the city immediately struck me; the exuberant cultural capital of Brazil is dramatically tucked between the rainforest clad mountains and the ocean, and is endowed with a natural beauty that ranges from the beaches to the mountain peaks.

Rio de Janeiro is one of those unique cities, in a small league of famed cities of the world. Mention Rio and immediately the name evokes images of sultry street parades, the Sugarloaf Mountain, Christ The Redeemer statue, two of the world's most famous beaches at Ipanema and Copacabana and the 'itsy-bitsy, teeny-weeny' bikinis.

However it is also a city of kaleidoscopic contrasts; modern skyscrapers stand cheek-to-jowl next to colonial-style Portuguese houses, whilst over a third of the population live in shantytowns called favelas, which cling to its hillsides like a blanket of rubble. It is a never-ending story made up of one-hundred and fifty districts each characterised by unique features. With eight million inhabitants, it is one of the most densely populated places on earth, built on a series of hills; its highways burrow through mountainside tunnels, opening up new and unfamiliar vistas.

With just two weeks of my year-long trip remaining, my plan was to make the most of Rio and treat the next fortnight like a holiday; spending my nights partying away and my days relaxing on the beach, topping up my tan and generally taking things easy, or should I say easier!

We checked into the Vermont Hotel in the suburb of Ipanema, and after a much needed shower and change of clothes, we headed out. Immortalised in a popular song, 'The girl from Ipanema', this part of Rio offers not only its legendary beach, but is Rio's wealthiest area with bustling nightlife, quality restaurants, numerous excellent hotels and sophisticated shopping boutiques, many of which are guarded by private armed security guards, making it also one of the safest areas in the city.

The skies were overcast and there was rain in the air, so the streets were a little quiet. We walked along the esplanade admiring the wonderful but deserted beach, and then we strolled through the chic streets. We grabbed a bite to eat and then feeling shattered from our epic bus journey, we returned to the hotel for a siesta ahead of our first night out in Rio.

We commenced our night in the nearby district of Leblon, which disappointingly was a little too quiet for our liking. We then headed to Lapa on the opposite side of city. We arrived to find a street party in full swing beneath and around the arches of the viaduct that runs through the area. Musicians spontaneously played samba, street vendors sold booze and hundreds of people danced in the rain, seemingly without a care in the world.

Standing on a mountain-top 710m high above the city, seemingly suspended in the darkness that surrounds it, the floodlit statue of Christ the Redeemer could be seen from everywhere; a reassuring sight, arms outstretched in welcome, or as if preparing to dive into the cities streets to rescue a poor soul from the jars of death.

Dave kept disappearing, which concerned me as Rio is not the safest city, and this was far from its safest district. Rio is a city with a definite dangerous side. Violence, street crime, drug abuse and police corruption are widespread. Many of Rio's people live in poverty, and these people are often so desperate that they will stop at nothing, including murder, to part a wealthy looking tourist from their wallet, watch or jewellery. I had heard of many stories of travellers being robbed here, including one girl who was mugged at knife-point on Copacabana Esplanade whilst out jogging; obviously she wasn't jogging quickly enough. I was slightly paranoid about being robbed here and consequently throughout my stay, I kept all of my valuables in the hotel's safety deposit box and carried just the bare necessities on my person. Rio was the only place that I visited throughout my journey where I did not wear my watch or carry my pocket camera or wallet with me everywhere I went.

There were many dodgy looking characters hanging around and we gringos stood out like a sore thumb, so it was vitally important that we stay together and watch each others back. Dave didn't seem to realise the danger, I asked him not to wander off and to stick close by, but he wandered off again. On his return I told him that I wasn't going to hang around these streets alone and I jumped in a taxi and returned to Ipanema. Dave chose to stay in Lapa.

I woke the next morning to see Dave lying safely in his bed across the room; over breakfast he apologised. We took a taxi to possibly the world's most legendary beach Copacabana, occupying four kilometres of sand framed by hills. This famous Rio beach neighbourhood was just a small fishing village until a new highway changed the face of it sometime in the 1900's. The Copacabana Palace Hotel first opened its doors in 1923 and the area mushroomed with Neoclassical and Art Nouveau skyscrapers, penthouses and apartments.

Whilst the glamorous Palace Hotel is still the place to be seen, today Copacabana has a reputation for sleaze and danger, especially off the main strip. Again it was a gloomy, grey day and the white sand beach was empty, its kiosks and cafes deserted. It began to rain again, the drizzle turned to torrential rain and so we returned to hotel.

Rio was a beach city, and in the rain there was nothing to do; we spent the afternoon lying on our beds watching TV. The rain eased off later and I spent the late afternoon walking up and down the streets of Ipanema searching for Harmonia Hostel, recommended by several travellers that I had met. The Vermont Hotel was fine but it wasn't great for meeting people, in fact we hadn't met any other travellers there whatsoever. Eventually I found Harmonia, tucked away off the main street in a private avenue containing about a dozen private homes, of which three were hostels. There were lots of travellers around and it seemed like a nice, friendly place, so I booked a bed for tomorrow.

On our third day the sun finally came out and suddenly Rio was transformed into a bubbling, energetic and joyful place full of glamorous, beautiful, smiling young things. Suddenly it was the most beautiful city on earth. Dave and I checked into the Swedish owned Harmonia Hostel. I took a dorm bed whilst he took a private room, however I think I got the best deal; the male dorm was full and so I had to sleep in the girls dorm with three gorgeous blonde Swedes, Jenny, Anna and Julia. There were a friendly group of international travellers there and I immediately felt more at home.

Making the most of the sunshine, I spent the afternoon on Ipanema beach, joined by Dave, even though he didn't like the sun. I lay on my towel soaking up the rays, whist Dave sat in his jeans and t-shirt, in a rented deckchair under the shade of a parasol. Within half an hour hyperactive Dave was bored and so he headed off.

Rio de Janeiro is mainly known for its beaches, and even though there are many other attractions in the city, the beaches are a highlight for any visitor. Fortunately they not only draw foreigners, but are also popular with the Cariocas, as the inhabitants of this city are called. They are much more than just a place to get a suntan or a dive into the ocean. In Rio, the beaches are social gathering places, people come here to chat, play sports, listen to music, hunt for a partner, surf the rolling waves of the Atlantic, or just to relax. It is this fact, together with the spectacular backdrop, that make the beaches in Rio such a unique destination.

The beach was packed with tanned bodies of various ages, shapes and sizes, though mostly young and fit. I had never seen so many beautiful people in one place at one time, mostly squeezed into the skimpiest of thongs, known locally as dental floss, for the obvious reason. And that was just the men!

One of the exciting attractions of the city are the tremendous girls. Without exception beach loving, they sometimes seem to be exhibitionist, and they eagerly show off their curvaceous bodies, squeezed into the tiniest of bikinis. Nearly all girls wear them, and it seems that the motto is, 'less is more'. Of course, they need to be brightly coloured, if only for the fact that they might otherwise go unnoticed. The girls of Rio de Janeiro's beaches are sensual, exotic and sparkling, they are the jewels on the crown of this fabulous city.

Me, Dave and a young American named Tyler booked a taxi to take us to Rio's most famous landmark, the statue of Christ the

Redeemer standing majestically on top of Corcovado (hunchback) Mountain 710m above the city. We drove up the winding mountain road to a car park just short of the summit, from where we continued on foot up a series of staircases until we arrived at the foot of the statue. Hundreds of other eager tourists and come to pay homage, and there was much jostling amongst the crowd for the best photogenic position.

The statue itself is wonderful, standing thirty-metres high and weighing over 1,000 metric tons, arms outstretched as if greeting his flock. It was first planned to be completed in 1922 as part of Brazil's centenary independence celebrations, but wasn't finished until 1931. From its feet there are jaw dropping three-hundred and sixty degree views; the whole of Rio and Guanabara Bay laid out before you. To the north the Contro district and the enormous bowl shaped Maracana football stadium. To the east the majestic Sugar Loaf Mountain and the suburbs of Flamengo, Botafogo and Copacabana with its long golden beach and the glistening blue ocean beyond. To the west the lush, green, forest clad mountains, and to the south the lagoon, jockey club and the districts of Ipanema and Leblon. There can be no better view in the world.

On our return, we passed by the edge of a Favela clinging to the hillside. It took me a few minutes to ascertain that these were indeed peoples' houses, as they resembled uncompleted building sites, abandoned or neglected. It was only the washing draped outside the crude orange bricks that indicated any sign of habitation, and the waif like children playing in the rubble.

The favelas of Rio first appeared in the 19th century when thousands of Brazilians flocked to the city from rural areas looking for work. Today the favelas are functioning communities, often run by drug-lords. They have a dangerous reputation, and violence abounds, and many are no go areas, even for the police.

That evening Dave and I headed out on the town with Tyler and two Swedes, Freddy and Martin, to one of Rio's top nightspots. Unfortunately we arrived to find it shut down. We found another bar close by where we ate dinner and sank a few capirinhas. We then took two taxis to another bar, Martin, Freddy and I in the first, Dave and Tyler followed in the second, but for reasons only known to them they never arrived.

Whilst sitting drinking beer at our table, someone suddenly lunged at me from behind, scaring me half to death. It was Marit; she had arrived in Rio a few hours early from the Pantanol and was with an English couple, Gary and Liz. Martin and Freddy left soon afterwards and I stayed with Marit and her friends. At the end of the night I returned with them to their hostel. The three of them were sharing one room, Gary and Liz in a double bed, Marit in a single. Just as the lights went off there was a knock on the door. Gary opened the door; outside, the hostel security guard stood holding the register. He asked my name, obviously realising that I wasn't a paying guest. I offered to pay for a night's accommodation and when that didn't work I tried bribery, but to no avail, and I was unceremoniously thrown onto the street.

Walking alone through the streets of Rio in the early hours of the morning is an unnerving and dare I say frightening experience, especially when you have to pass the park. Deserted other than for a few stray seedy characters hanging menacingly around dark doorways, I walked as quickly as I could without actually running, looking continually over my shoulder as I went. I managed to attract the attention of a couple of youths who followed me briefly, but they stopped when fortunately a police car drove past.

The next morning I took a stroll along the esplanade to clear my hangover and admire the eye-candy in the process. The beaches of Rio attract different crowds at different times of the day. Then again, different areas of the beaches attract different people. Walking from Leblon to Ipanema, to Arpoador and then on to Copacabana, this becomes clear. Leblon and Ipanema attract the rich set, while Copacabana is the most popular beach. The gay crowd favour a stretch of Ipanema beach, whilst a section of Copacabana is a well-known hangout for prostitutes.

The esplanades are paved in wavy black-and-white mosaic patterns and were full of locals jogging, rollerblading, cycling, working out, preening, and posing. Along its full length, vendors set up stalls offering colourful t-shirts, Brazilian football shirts, sarongs, sunglasses and skimpy bikinis.

Both Ipanema and Copacabana beaches have white sand and are festooned with kiosks offering food, drinks, deckchairs and parasols. There were plenty of beach football and volleyball games going on; at Copacabana there is even a beach volleyball arena. All along the beaches you see locals juggling footballs with skills that would put many a Premiership player to shame. Ipanema and Copacabana are everything you've heard and much, much more.

Via the wonder of e-mail I had arranged to meet up with Alex and Fiona from my Spanish class, who by chance were also in Rio, and I had left a message for Marit to meet me also. I ran into Dave later, he too had bumped into Marit and she had asked him to tell me that she would meet me at Harmonia. I waited until 8 but she never arrived and so I headed out to meet Alex and Fiona.

We went in a popular churrascaria (barbeque) restaurant, where on entry we were each given a disk, red on one side, green on the other. When you wanted meat you simply turned your disk green side up and numerous waiters would appear at your table, each with a different cut of meat which they would carve onto your plate, as much and as often as you liked. It was marvellous and we spent about three-hours swapping yarns of our respective journeys, whilst devouring piles of lamb, chicken and beef and an assortment of vegetables, salad and other delights from the self-service buffet table. At 11 we called it a night as Alex and Fiona were flying home to England tomorrow.

The next evening I joined a group of lads from the hostel for a night out on the town. We headed to club called Nuth in Barra (pronounced Ba-ha) district. Outside, a large well dressed crowd congregated, many being turned away. Two girls were handing out invites. Dave approached them and after a little grovelling, managed to obtain five passes. On entry we were each given a credit card like piece of plastic for obtaining drinks; a more sophisticated version of the drinks-card.

Rio's jet set were gathered inside, little rich kids, all very snobby and generally unfriendly. Dave made straight for the dance-floor, bouncing around like a teenager as per usual. Over the course of the night we all got split up and I ended up alone with an annoying Londoner named Des, who was so drunk that he could hardly stand up. Throughout the evening he would wrap his arm around me and although I'd only met him the day before he would say, "Lee, you're my best mate". Worse still, he constantly criticised and slagged off the others. Eventually I managed to loose him, and I headed home alone at about 4am.

A German guy name Alex arrived at Harmonia the next day. He was keen to see the sights and as I still hadn't seen Sugar Loaf, I offered to accompany him. Pão de Açúcar, named Sugar Loaf because of its resemblance to the loaves of sugar used by the Portuguese colonists, is one of several granite rocks jutting into the Rio sky. What makes Sugar Loaf special is that it is situated right on the shore and is an integral part of the city skyline, as familiar a sight as Big Ben, The Eifel Tower or The Sydney Opera House.

The summit can be reached by a two-stage cable car ride. The first bubble-shaped cable car carried us up 168-metres to the Morro da Urca, where there is a restaurant, amphitheatre, heliport and spectacular views of the Yacht Club and Botafogo Bay.

The second stage conveyed us the rest of the way to the summit. There was surreal feeling when you're standing 396-metres above the city of being in the midst of a scene you've seen on screen and paper so many times before. Rio de Janeiro laid out at your feet in all her glory, a sweeping view of the city's twenty-three, white-sand beaches including Copacabana, Ipanema, Flamengo, Leblon and Botafogo, and standing high up on the distant green hills, Christ The Redeemer. We just couldn't stop taking photos. However within minutes of reaching the summit a thick blanket of mist had descended around us and the view vanished. We hung around for a while waiting for the mist to lift but to no avail, however many other tourists continued to pose for photos in front of the now invisible vista, as if there were no mist at all.

I spent my penultimate night in Copacabana with Dave and fellow hostel guest Tony. We walked along esplanade stopping in several bars, all of which were a little sleazy, full of voluptuous young girls and dirty old men. The streets weren't much better, lined with touts trying to drag passers by into their bars and clubs and prostitutes hung around the corners looking for business.

For research purposes you understand, we found ourselves in one such establishment called Barberellas, a high-class pick-up bar with stunningly beautiful girls. We had a couple of beers and chatted to a few of the girls, but it was very expensive so after indulging our curiosity we moved on.

We ended up in another bar where we chatted to three beautiful girls. We all left together at the end of the night and as we waited for a taxi, I thought we'd struck lucky. That was until my girl announced that she needed the toilet; she duly squatted in the gutter and began peeing in front of everyone, including passers by. If that wasn't bad enough, when she'd finished she strode up to me as bold as brass and said, "You give me fifty-dollar and take me home and fuck!" I gave her 10-Real for a taxi home and sent her packing.

I couldn't visit Brazil without seeing a football game and when the opportunity arose to visit the legendary Maracana stadium to watch a league-game between local Rio rivals Fluminense and Palmeiras, I just had to go. The huge stadium was eighty percent empty, and although the fans did their best to create an atmosphere by banging drums and waving flags, the experience turned out to be a big disappointment, and the game was pretty dismal too.

I would stick my neck out and declare that Rio de Janeiro, the original sexy city, must be the most beautiful city in the world. It's not often you find a place where soaring mountains run down to white sand beaches, rainforest and high rise buildings live side by side, and a thirty-metre high statue of Christ surveys it all with open arms.

Rio can be described a lot of ways; flashy, trashy, vibrant, infectious, hedonistic and beautiful. One thing for certain, it definitely isn't boring. It appears to exude an ambiance that just makes people happy and friendly, but then again how can one not be when staying in such a great location. And for the record, I never did get robbed there!

After almost a year away, my great adventure was finally at an end. It was a strange feeling knowing that I would soon be back at home after so long away. I was sad that my adventure was over, but at the same time I was totally shattered after a year of living from a backpack on the road, and I was also excited at the prospect of returning home to my family and friends at Christmas.

My penultimate flight to Madrid departed on time. Dinner followed by several beers helped me sleep through the flight. From Madrid I boarded my interconnecting flight to London to find that I had a free upgrade to Business-Class, for the first and only time on the twentieth and last flight of my journey; a pity that it should be on the shortest flight of my trip, but I wasn't complaining.

"Good afternoon passengers and welcome aboard British Airways flight BA457 from Madrid to London, our flying time will be......"

I looked at the guy sitting next to me and smiled, "Hi, Lee" I said introducing myself.

"Hello, John", he replied.

"Going home for Christmas?"

"Yes, and you?"

"Yes"

"Would you like a drink sir?" the stewardess asked.

"Beer please" I replied.

"And you sir?"

"Beer please," John replied.

A smile came onto my face as I sipped my beer and contemplated my wondrous adventure circumnavigating the globe.

Afterword

Arriving home was a real shock to the system and somewhat of an anti-climax. Although it was good to catch up with my family and friends after so long away, the initial excitement soon disappeared and within a week it's as if you've never been away. And leaving the sunshine and tropical climes of Brazil to return to England in December is not recommended.

My friend and boss Paul helped ease me back into normal life. On my return a new car and mobile phone were waiting for me, which was nice.

Christmas came and went and before I knew it I was back at work. Nothing can quite prepare you for work after a year-long break; I can not begin to tell you how difficult I found getting back into the daily routine of waking at seven and shaving, etc. But the worst was not being able to take an afternoon siesta!

Life seemed to have stood still whilst I'd been away. The same old faces sat in the same chairs in the same corner in the same pub telling the same stories. Nothing had really changed.

Within a few months of being back behind a desk my waist-line had begun to expand rapidly and before long I was unable to fit into any of my favourite travelling t-shirts; in fact the only clothes that now fit are my shoes!

The biggest effect of my year away on me was to restore my faith in people, and make me realise just how lucky we Brits are. I had met many people in many countries who would give anything for the freedom, education, health and wealth we enjoy in Britain, and so I now get very annoyed when I see or hear people complaining over petty things.

I also now fully realise the beauty of Britain, and I have come to appreciate it much more. Since returning I have noticed so many things that I had never really noticed before, such as the wonderful sunrise and sunsets. And I have also come to realise just how understanding and tolerant we Brits are compared to many of the nationalities that I met around the world.

My year-long adventure has only wetted my appetite to travel and see more of this wonderful world and continue Globe-Trekking.